Japan's Contested War Memories

Japan's Contested War Memories explores the ways in which World War II has been remembered and commemorated in Japan, with a particular focus on the period from 1972 (the return of Okinawa to Japan) to the 60th anniversary commemorations in 2005. Analysing the variety of ways in which the Japanese people narrate, contest and interpret the past, the book seeks to define and challenge the 'orthodoxy' in the English-language media which is critical of 'the Japanese' or 'Japan' for the way in which they have 'inadequately addressed the past'. Instead, Seaton argues that the ideological 'memory rifts' in interpretations of history and contestation over the government's handling of war responsibility issues have ensured that war history in Japan remains a subject more divisive and widely argued over than in any of the other major World War II combatant nations.

By drawing on extensive analysis of the Japanese media, *Japan's Contested War Memories* applies the latest international war memory and media studies theory to provide a significant and engaging study that will appeal to scholars and students of Japanese history, politics, cultural studies, society and memory theory.

Philip A. Seaton is an Associate Professor in the Graduate School of Media and Communication, Hokkaido University, Japan. His webpage, which contains links to many online resources and an online appendix, is www.philipseaton.net.

Routledge Contemporary Japan Series

A Japanese Company in Crisis
Ideology, strategy, and narrative
Fiona Graham

Japan's Foreign Aid
Old continuities and new directions
Edited by David Arase

Japanese Apologies for World War II
A rhetorical study
Jane W. Yamazaki

Linguistic Stereotyping and Minority Groups in Japan
Nanette Gottlieb

Shinkansen
From bullet train to symbol of modern Japan
Christopher P. Hood

Small Firms and Innovation Policy in Japan
Edited by Cornelia Storz

Cities, Autonomy and Decentralization in Japan
Edited by Carola Hein and Philippe Pelletier

The Changing Japanese Family
Edited by Marcus Rebick and Ayumi Takenaka

Adoption in Japan
Comparing policies for children in need
Peter Hayes and Toshie Habu

The Ethics of Aesthetics in Japanese Cinema and Literature
Polygraphic desire
Nina Cornyetz

Institutional and Technological Change in Japan's Economy
Past and present
Edited by Janet Hunter and Cornelia Storz

Political Reform in Japan
Leadership looming large
Alisa Gaunder

Civil Society and the Internet in Japan
Isa Ducke

Japan's Contested War Memories
The 'memory rifts' in historical consciousness of World War II
Philip A. Seaton

Japanese Love Hotels
A cultural history
Sarah Chaplin

Population Decline and Ageing in Japan
The social consequences
Florian Coulmas

Japan's Contested War Memories

The 'memory rifts' in historical consciousness of World War II

Philip A. Seaton

Routledge
Taylor & Francis Group

LONDON AND NEW YORK

First published 2007
by Routledge
2 Park Square, Milton Park, Abingdon, Oxon, OX14 4RN

Simultaneously published in the USA and Canada by Routledge
270 Madison Ave, New York NY 10016

Routledge is an imprint of the Taylor & Francis Group, an informa business

Transferred to Digital Printing 2010

Typeset in Baskerville by
Florence Production Ltd, Stoodleigh, Devon

British Library Cataloguing in Publication Data
A catalogue record for this book is available from the British Library

Library of Congress Cataloging in Publication Data
A catalogue record for this book has been requested

ISBN10: 0–415–39915–7 (hbk)
ISBN10: 0–415–48780–3 (pbk)
ISBN10: 0–203–96374–1 (ebk)

ISBN13: 978–0–415–39915–9 (hbk)
ISBN13: 978–0–415–48780–1 (pbk)
ISBN13: 978–0–203–96374–6 (ebk)

Contents

Illustrations

Figures

Tables

Acknowledgements

I have incurred numerous debts in the course of writing this book. In Dr Alistair Thomson of Sussex University I could not have asked for a better mentor to guide and inspire me through the years of doctoral research which form the basis of the book. A scholarship from the Japanese Ministry of Education enabled me to undertake fieldwork at the University of Tokyo under Professor Takahashi Tetsuya, whose guidance regarding Japanese-language materials was invaluable.

I have received great encouragement from many people. First and foremost, this book simply would not have been possible without the love and patience of all my family and friends. As the research developed, Professors Tony McCaffery, Neki Akira and Koike Kiyoyuki provided invaluable practical and moral support at critical junctures. Colleagues at Nagaoka University of Technology and Hokkaido University have been unfailingly supportive, as have all the staff at the dozens of libraries and museums where I have carried out the research. I owe special thanks to Bill Underwood and Rachele Stucker for their invaluable comments on earlier drafts of the book. Stephanie Rogers and Helen Baker at Routledge have been unfailingly supportive editors. And last but not least, this book would not be what it is without the hundreds of Japanese people, many of whose names I never knew, who have taken the trouble to explain to me their views about the war and suggest useful materials.

Needless to say I have done everything I can to ensure the accuracy of the information contained in this book. Any mistakes remain my sole responsibility.

Notes on text

This book has been written using minimal endnotes. I have avoided illustrations because relevant visual images are now widely available on the Internet and can be accessed via an online appendix, www.philipseaton.net/jcwm.html.

Japanese names have been kept in the Japanese order, family name followed by given name. Macrons in romanized words indicate long vowel sounds, but are omitted on words commonly spelt without macrons in English, for example Tokyo. Because there are not always agreed best translations for Japanese words, I have tended to use Japanese terms alongside translations to preserve the nuance of the key Japanese terminology.

Abbreviations and glossary

APM	Aichi Peace Museum
BO	Box Office
CC	Critics' Choice (critical rankings of films)
Chūkiren	Chinese Returnees Association (a group of ex-soldiers who have confessed to atrocities in China)
'comfort women'	The 200,000 women, mainly Koreans, who worked as prostitutes for the Japanese military. Many were tricked or coerced into what is now usually termed sexual slavery
Diet	the Japanese Parliament
ERLPC	Exhibition and Reference Library for Peace and Consolation.
ETV	Educational Television (name of some documentaries on NHK-Educational)
GHQ	General Headquarters (during the occupation)
Heisei	the era of Emperor Akihito's reign (1989–present)
HMH	Historical Museum of Hokkaido
HPMM	Hiroshima Peace Memorial Museum
JET	Japan Exchange and Teaching Programme
JHS	junior high school (ages 13–15)
Jiyūshugi	'Liberalism', the ideology of Fujioka Nobukatsu and the Tsukurukai (see below)
Kinema	Abbreviation of Kinema junpō, a cinema magazine
KMWP	Kyoto Museum for World Peace
KPM	Kawasaki Peace Museum
LDP	Liberal Democratic Party
MOFA	Ministry of Foreign Affairs
nenpyō	chronology
NAWBFP	National Association of the War Bereaved Families for Peace
NGO	non-governmental organization
NHK	Nippon Hōsō Kyōkai, Japan's public broadcaster (the 'Japanese BBC')
NMJH	National Museum of Japanese History
NPO	non-profit organization
ODA	Overseas Development Aid

OMMPM	Oka Masaharu Memorial Peace Museum
OPPMM	Okinawa Prefectural Peace Memorial Museum
PCC	Pia Cinema Club
PKO Bill	Peacekeeping Operations Bill
PMKP	Peace Museum for Kamikaze Pilots
POW	Prisoners of War
PTSD	post-traumatic stress disorder
SCAP	Supreme Command for the Allied Powers
SDF	Self Defense Forces (contemporary Japanese military)
sengo	postwar
shinbun	newspaper
Shōwa	the era of Emperor Hirohito's reign (1926–89)
SHS	senior high school (ages 16–18)
TBS	Tokyo Broadcasting Service, one of the commercial television stations, linked to the *Mainichi* newspaper
Tsukurukai	Japanese Society for History Textbook Reform, the nationalist group at the centre of the 2001 textbook crisis
Unit 731	Japan's biological and chemical warfare unit
VAWW-Net Japan	Violence Against Women in War – Network Japan, a feminist group active on the 'comfort women' issue
WBA	War Bereaved Association (Izokukai)
WGIP	War Guilt Information Program
WMD	weapons of mass destruction

Introduction

The first time that I had a conversation about World War II in Asia and the Pacific,[1] 1937–45 (hereafter 'the Asia-Pacific War' or 'the war'), with a Japanese person was in August 1994, about a month after I arrived in Japan for the first time. Like many young Westerners, my introduction to life in Japan came via English teaching. I was at the beginning of what would be two years of teaching in a Japanese junior high school. The students were practising marching, which forms the basis of the Olympics-style opening and closing ceremonies of the school sports day. I was watching them with one of my Japanese colleagues. As the students marched past the podium where the headmaster was standing, they turned their heads towards him and did a straight-arm salute. Images of Nazi Germany filled my mind.

'Do students practise marching in England?' my colleague asked. I thought I was being diplomatic when I answered the only time people practise marching is in the army. My colleague got flustered and told me that Japan was a peaceful nation now and that the students practise marching to develop teamwork. It was a short, sharp lesson in how sensitive the war is in Japan. Not wanting to make waves at this early stage in my new job, I changed the topic.

This book has been twelve years in the making since that first seed was planted in my mind. In the intervening years I have lived predominantly in Japan. I have always been interested in history, particularly World War II history. As a young boy I watched many war films such as *The Dam Busters* and *Where Eagles Dare*, and as a history undergraduate I specialized in twentieth-century history. While living in Japan, I took the chance to read more about the war in the Pacific, and the war naturally came up as a topic of conversation with Japanese friends: one told me how her grandfather had been in the army; a man in his eighties gave a talk in one of my adult English classes about his experiences as an army doctor; I heard stories of surviving air raids and repatriation from colonial Korea at the end of the war; and a man who had been training to be a kamikaze pilot when the war ended told me how he considered his entire life since 15 August 1945 to be a bonus.

These stories deepened my interest but simultaneously challenged every preconception I had about the war. When I first arrived in Japan my views were probably typical of most British people: I was critical of Japanese war conduct, particularly the treatment of British POWs, and my impressions had come largely from watching *The Bridge on the River Kwai.* But I was beginning to see other aspects of the Japanese war experience. Furthermore, I was beginning to realize how comfortable it was to remember my own grandfathers' war service (one had flown with RAF Bomber Command and the other was a member of RAF ground crew in Palestine) free from questions of war crimes, guilt and responsibility.

Eventually, Japanese war memories metamorphosed from being an interest to the subject of a formal academic investigation. However, from the beginning I felt there should be two guiding principles. First, I felt the need to focus on the factors that were central to my own 'memories' of World War II, such as films, higher education, museums and the personal experiences of relatives and friends. In time this developed into the media and cultural studies approach throughout this book. Second, given that conversations with Japanese people had challenged my preconceptions, I felt the study should be based primarily on materials in which Japanese people told their side of the story. My objective became encapsulated in the following mission statement: to conduct a comprehensive study of what the Japanese say to each other in Japanese about the Asia-Pacific War.

The 'orthodox' interpretation of Japanese war memories

As I started reading more about Japanese war memories, I noticed that much of the literature and reportage in the international media focused on history education at Japanese schools, diplomatic spats in East Asia, official government statements, acts of commemoration, and inflammatory comments by right-wing politicians and academics. I also discovered many references to the 'ignorance', 'amnesia' and 'denial' of ordinary Japanese people. This broadly critical view has been duplicated in numerous conversations about my research over the years. I have been told many times that the Japanese do not know or learn much about the war, or that they deny they committed any atrocities.

These statements were not consistent with what Japanese acquaintances were telling me: their views, like mine, seemed to be rooted in personal and family experience, the media and popular culture more than in what politicians or textbooks said. Nonetheless, the prevalence of these critical interpretations of Japanese war memories has led me to call it 'the orthodox interpretation of Japanese war memories in English-speaking Allied countries', hereafter 'the orthodoxy'.[2]

In a nutshell, the orthodoxy is critical of Japan through the following pattern of argument:

1   Japan was an aggressor nation and committed numerous atrocities during the Asia-Pacific War, therefore Japan has heavy war responsibility;

2   the Japanese government has not properly addressed these war responsi-
     bility issues;
3   Japanese people, like their government, fail to adequately acknowledge
     Japanese aggression; and
4   as a result, 'Japan' needs to do more to address the past. In practical terms,
     the litmus test for Japanese people 'adequately' remembering the war will
     be their government saying and doing the 'right' things.

The orthodoxy has two main types, although most texts freely mix the two
in varying proportions. The first is political and in war memory parlance is a
'state-centred approach'. Analysis centres on the official narrative of the
Japanese government. Government statements, official apologies, the
compensation policy, comments by politicians in the ruling LDP (Liberal
Democratic Party) elite, and the contents of government-approved textbooks
are the core topics of investigation. The official narrative becomes the
representative way in which Japanese people look back on the Asia-Pacific
War. If references are made to war discourses within Japanese society, then
the focus is on Japanese nationalists, who justify Japanese war aims and
deny or downplay Japanese atrocities. Progressives, who criticize both
Japan's aggressive war and contemporary official responses to war
responsibility, are portrayed as unrepresentative, outnumbered and atypical
voices of conscience.

The second type is what may be called a 'culturally determinist' approach.
It is anthropological or sociological and focuses on the ways in which
supposedly Japanese characteristics – such as conformity or an unwillingness to challenge authority – make Japanese people reluctant to challenge
the inadequate stance of the government and the wider collective memory.
Japan is presented as a relatively homogeneous nation in which the conformist
nature of Japan's group society makes it difficult for Japanese people to hold
conflicting views.

This orthodoxy is flawed in three critical aspects. First, it shifts uncomfortably between issues of war responsibility (the ongoing legal, moral and
political implications of war conduct) and war memories (the ways in which
people look back on the past from the standpoint of the present). The two
are inextricably entwined but distinct. For example, the Japanese government may refuse to pay compensation (a responsibility issue) but this does
not necessarily say anything about what any given Japanese person
thinks/remembers about the war (the memory issue). Conversely, how
Japanese people feel about the compensation issue is probably based on
their memories of the war. Memory and responsibility need to be clearly
distinguished, and there needs to be an adequate theoretical link between
the two.

Second, the orthodoxy contains a fundamental assumption that there is a
'correct' way for Japanese people to interpret war history. That 'correct' way
is for the Japanese to acknowledge guilt for the actions of the Japanese military

and assume an apologetic stance. However, Japanese people may have good reasons for remembering other aspects of the war more, such as an air raid or the death of a brother. Furthermore, while we may argue against those whose views we disagree with or even impose personal or political sanctions (such as diplomatic pressure), ultimately war memories are a matter of individual conscience. Polemics about what the Japanese 'should' say ultimately focus on what the writer believes the Japanese 'do not say', or the writer's own views of World War II. Either way, polemics detract from the task of explaining the nature of Japanese war memories.

Third, the concentration on the state and/or cultural level does not provide an explanation for how, why or how much diversity exists within Japan. It assumes or promotes the idea that there is a typically 'Japanese' way of looking back at the war, or that there is a dominant cultural narrative in Japan. The core conclusion in this book is that contestations over war history have prevented the emergence of a dominant narrative. There is no single typically 'Japanese' way of looking back on the war, although there are a variety of identifiable competing cultural narratives which will be described throughout the book.

In order to explain diversity within Japanese war memories, analysis must take place at levels other than the state and/or culture. This requires a focus on Japanese cultural representations of war in the media and popular culture as well as official representations. There are a number of scholars – including John Dower (1999; 2002), Caroline Rose (1998; 2005), Laura Hein and Mark Selden (2000), James Orr (2001) and Beatrice Trefalt (2003) – who have illustrated the complexity of Japanese war memories. But the dominance of the orthodoxy (and the critical polemic that usually accompanies it) in the media, certain sections of the academy and popular culture indicates the resilience of the orthodoxy in the face of contradictory evidence provided by these leading scholars.

Despite its flaws, the orthodoxy has become dominant for various reasons. First, the orthodoxy is simple. It is a soundbite understanding of Japanese war memories and can be summed up in one phrase: 'Japan has not adequately addressed the past.' The research is relatively easy to undertake because it focuses on the easily identifiable official stance. There is little need to analyse public debates, although most orthodox texts do mention token progressive 'voices of conscience' and contrast them with nationalist intellectuals who make a living out of denying Japan guilt. Progressives are frequently portrayed as 'the exception that proves the rule' about the general Japanese 'inability' to face the past. Their inclusion adds to the critical tone through the implication that 'if progressives can face the past, others should be able to as well'.

Second, translation issues determine access to Japanese views and, for the most part, it is the government's view that appears in translation in the international press. For non-Japanese, it is a massive linguistic undertaking to deconstruct Japanese public discourses in the original Japanese. Consequently, a state-centred approach is the default position for those without the inclination or the Japanese-language ability to analyse public debates.

Third, the nature of the international media means that Japanese war memories become newsworthy at times of dispute and controversy. In the international media, 'controversial' invariably means 'nationalistic' – for example, when Japanese politicians make nationalistic statements – so the balance of coverage is about Japanese nationalism. The resulting *image* of Japanese war memories is that they are predominantly nationalistic.

Fourth, travel guides indicate the places travellers to Japan are most likely to visit, and the six sites listed in one popular guidebook, published by Lonely Planet (2003), exemplify how war-related tourism can foster critical views:

1 Yasukuni Shrine: the controversial 'war shrine' in Tokyo where 2.46 million military dead are commemorated and its nationalistic museum (Yūshūkan) that defends Japan's wars and eulogizes its fallen soldiers (156);

2 Hiroshima: the A-Bomb Dome, Peace Memorial Museum and Peace Memorial Park that commemorate the world's first nuclear attack (451–4);

3 Tachiarai Peace Memorial Museum: a small museum 'that even locals don't know about' which commemorates the kamikaze and victims of American air raids (651);

4 Nagasaki: the Hypocentre Park, Nagasaki Atomic Bomb Museum and other sites related to the second bomb dropped on Japan (659–62);

5 Chiran: the Kamikaze Peace Museum, the main commemorative site to the 'special attacks corps' (690); and

6 Okinawa: various war sites commemorating the Battle for Okinawa (April–June 1945) in which over 200,000 Japanese died. The sites include the Underground Naval Headquarters, the Okinawa Peace Memorial Museum and the museum to the Himeyuri nursing corps (720–1).

The sites divide into two categories: sites glorifying or commemorating the military (Yasukuni, Chiran and Tachiarai), and sites commemorating Japanese victimhood (Hiroshima, Nagasaki, Tachiarai and Okinawa). These epitomize the orthodoxy: Japanese people defend their actions or deal with the past through 'victim mentality'. Notably missing are any sites indicating Japanese contrition, even though they do exist (such as the progressive municipal 'peace museums' in Osaka, Kawasaki and other cities).

Fifth, disputing the 'Japan has not adequately addressed the past' conclusion is risky because it will probably be interpreted as apologia for Japanese war actions, or as a statement that Japanese compensation and apologies have been sufficient. These are stands that few outside Japan are prepared to take given the ongoing demands of many victims (such as ex-POWs and forced labourers) for acknowledgement of and compensation for their suffering at the hands of the Japanese. By contrast, the argument that Japanese war guilt is perpetuated in a collective failure to acknowledge that guilt is comfortable and beneficial. It is comfortable because criticizing Japanese perpetrators and identifying with their victims allows researchers to claim the moral high ground. It is beneficial because occupying the moral high ground bestows moral authority and political power. To say to Japan that it had sufficiently addressed the past would be to relinquish a major moral/political/diplomatic trump card: the war issue. A cynic could conclude that Japan will never be deemed to have adequately addressed the past because such a conclusion would sacrifice a significant source of political leverage vis-à-vis Japan.

Finally, interpretations of Japanese war memories always exist in the context of one's own war memories and national/cultural narratives. In the English-speaking Allied nations there are dominant narratives of a 'good war' against the evils of fascism. Japanese memories incompatible with these Allied memories must be resisted. For example, Japanese memories of victimhood, particularly of the A-bombs, are uncomfortable for the Allies because the standard rationales for indiscriminate bombing of civilian targets were to end the war, stop Japanese aggression and save lives. Validating Japanese narratives of victimhood undermines these justifications, casts the Allies as perpetrators and subverts the 'good war' narrative. Japanese 'victim mentality', therefore, must be criticized for not being contrition, even though it is unrealistic to expect *hibakusha* (A-bomb victims) to prioritize collective memories of Japanese atrocities (that they may have had no personal involvement in) over their personal experiences of the A-bombs. And the nationalistic narrative that Japan helped liberate Asian nations from Western imperialism has to be resisted at all costs: it subverts the 'good war' narrative by making Western colonialism, not Japanese militarism, the primary evil of the 1930s and 1940s.

Consequently, the only Japanese narrative compatible with the Allied 'good war' narrative is contrition for Japanese war guilt. All other narratives have to be criticized as inadequate. Given the strength of the 'good war' narratives in Allied nations, it is hardly surprising that criticism of Japanese narratives that threaten to subvert the 'good war' narrative have become orthodox.

In summary, these criticisms of the orthodoxy fit within three theoretical frameworks. First, within war memory theory the orthodoxy can be criticized for being a state-centred approach with excessive focus on the government: it portrays the official stance as representative of people's views and fails to represent or explain the complexity and diversity of war memories within Japan. Second, in media and cultural theory the orthodoxy can be criticized for bias and stereotyping because it assigns undue attention to those who defend Japan's wars and marginalizes those who do acknowledge the aggression of the Japanese military. And third, in terms of Edward Said's orientalism thesis, the orthodoxy[3] can be criticized for being not so much an investigation of Japanese views but a tool in the power relations between Japan and the English-speaking world. The orthodoxy's primary result (one might even argue function) is to maintain the moral and political superiority of the

West over the Orient, of the Allies over Japan, in war memories as well as in war actions.

'Memory rifts': reframing the discussion of Japanese war memories

This book takes a different approach. Its basic thesis is that Japanese war memories remain contested. Using a mixture of memory, just war, media and cultural theory, it seeks to deconstruct and analyse the variety of interpretations of war history in contemporary Japan. A by-product of the argument that Japanese memories remain contested is a critique of the orthodoxy regarding Japanese war memories, particularly in the English-language media (see Appendix). These critiques do not dispute the voluminous evidence of Japanese aggression and atrocities during World War II, and neither are they intended to undermine the efforts of victims' groups still seeking justice. As I will argue more fully in Chapter 3, I believe the orthodoxy hinders more than it helps the search for justice. Instead, the critiques highlight three major issues: first, the extent to which Japanese war memories have hereto been largely dismissed as 'inadequate' rather than analysed for the insights they can provide into the processes of remembering war; second, how Japanese memories have been represented in largely stereotypical, frequently inaccurate and politically self-serving terms; and third, the extent to which attitudes and government policies in the former Allied nations have contributed to Japan's struggles to come to terms with its past.

However, the primary focus of the book is war discourses in contemporary Japan. The basic thesis is as follows. Even though sixty years have passed since Japan's surrender, the war maintains a powerful grip on the modern Japanese psyche. Japanese commentators have repeatedly announced the end of the 'postwar', only for a new revelation or controversy to bring all the painful memories and recriminations over the past to the surface again. Given that Japan has not fought in any war since 1945, the experience of the Asia-Pacific War remains the primary lens through which war is viewed. Modern wars from Vietnam to the 2003 Iraq War have frequently been discussed in Japan with explicit or implicit reference to the Asia-Pacific War.

In Japan, the war has not yet been consigned to 'history'. Even beyond the sixtieth anniversary of Japan's defeat, the war remains in living memory for many in the nation that leads the world in longevity. For the postwar generations, the war remains a 'current affairs' issue. The ways that Japanese people interact with their Asian neighbours, attitudes towards conflicts in other parts of the globe, nuclear issues, and attitudes concerning the core symbols of Japanese nationhood – the flag, emperor, national anthem, constitution and Japan's wider global role – are all inextricably linked to memories and interpretations of Japan's wartime past. The war has not been forgotten. Quite the opposite, the Japanese seem unable to let it go.

I will also make the case that theories of war memory, media and cultural studies rather than anthropological theories of Japanese society offer the clearest explanations for the nature of and processes within Japanese war memories. The Japanese are not an 'exceptional' race who possess a different set of war memory rules from the rest of humanity. While there are, of course, Japanese idiosyncrasies and particular characteristics stemming from Japanese culture and the Japanese experience, overall the pattern of memories in Japan is not unique.

Consequently, it is necessary to escape from the restrictive frameworks of state-centred analysis (Japanese war memories are represented by the position of the Japanese government) and *nihonjinron* ('theories of the Japanese', in which Japanese war memories can be explained by supposedly 'typical' Japanese characteristics). These paradigms have become deeply ingrained in Western analysis of Japan, but it is necessary to have a fresh epistemological start. To help achieve this, I am introducing the notion of 'memory rifts' and a 'Japanese war memories as seismic activity' metaphor to reframe the discussion about Japanese war memories.

George Lakoff and Mark Johnson (1980) have described how our thinking is subconsciously pushed in a particular direction by metaphors. We think of 'business as war' in the 'strategies' to 'capture' market share, or we think of 'relationships as buildings' based on firm 'foundations' and in need of 'upkeep'. The common forms of discourse and language usage that exist in our own cultures greatly affect the way that we conceptualize and interpret the world around us.

The metaphor that underpins this book is a 'Japanese war memories as seismic activity' metaphor. There are few symbols of Japan as immediately recognizable as the bullet train hurtling past a snow-capped Mt Fuji. Mt Fuji's perfect volcanic cone is a spectacular testament to the seismic processes that formed, and continue to form, the Japanese archipelago. Japan lies on the Pacific 'Rim of Fire' and frequently experiences major earthquakes and volcanic eruptions. The ongoing seismic activity around and beneath the Japanese archipelago has impacted deeply on Japanese history and culture, which makes it a suitably 'Japanese' metaphor.

Seismic activity is caused by geological rifts below the earth's surface. At the same time a rift is a 'split' or an 'argument', as in 'a rift in the family'. Consequently, the term 'memory rifts' symbolizes the divisions deep beneath the surface that shape the landscape of Japanese war memories. There are ideological fault lines within Japanese society. In particular, there is a rift between, on the one hand, liberal Japanese ('progressives', *shinpoha*), who see apology and atonement for the past as the best way to restore self-respect and international trust; and on the other hand conservatives, who see a positive version of history and commemoration of the sacrifice of the war generation as the best way to achieve national pride. For the most part, when the war is out of the public gaze, these two ideological groups clash in academic journals and other cultural forms, causing great friction but few recognizable tremors on the surface. But when the pent-up friction cannot be contained, such as when the contents of school history textbooks are being reviewed, it is released in massive social and political jolts that can dominate the national agenda.

Then there are the eruptions of controversies. Whether it is a Japanese politician making a nationalistic comment or former victims of Japanese imperialism arriving in Tokyo on a usually fruitless mission to gain some compensation for their sufferings, these controversies can erupt without warning. The fallout can be devastating, or completely change the political landscape within a matter of days.

Japan's seismic heritage does not only have negative effects. One of the most popular leisure activities among Japanese people is soaking away the stresses and strains of life in an *onsen*, a natural hot-spring bath. Naturally occurring hot mineral waters are continually bubbling up to the surface all over Japan. In a similar manner, discussion of the war continues quietly across Japan on a day-to-day basis. It also provides a form of leisure for some and a source of income for others. Hot-spring owners – like publishers, film-makers and war museum managers – are in the business of attracting customers. The levels of cultural production in Japan indicate that war memories and commemoration are a multi-billion yen industry. War history and seismic activity are not only about tragedy and suffering: they are about business and recreation, too.

Finally, Japan's seismic heritage and war history tend to evoke similar emotions in people. Wars and natural disasters frequently become defining moments in people's lives. They produce powerful stories of grief, tragedy, heroism, comradeship, fear, common purpose, overcoming adversity, loss, and even joy or exhilaration. After such life-changing experiences, people frequently reflect on feelings of powerlessness in the face of forces too big for them to control, or feel that no other experience could ever produce an equal intensity and sense of being alive.

In sum, the 'Japanese war memories as seismic activity' metaphor highlights Japanese war memories and commemoration as extremely complex phenomena. But above all, the seismic metaphor draws attention to the memory rifts deep beneath the surface of Japanese society. The key to understanding Japanese war memories is not assessing what Japanese people 'know' or 'do not know', but identifying the conceptual frames they use to evaluate war-related issues when they come across them in their daily lives. This book attempts to explain how and why competing conceptual frames concerning war history have emerged in Japan and how these memory rifts continue to affect the lives of people today.

1 Historical consciousness in contemporary Japan

Theoretical approaches to the study of war memory

In recent times, the field of memory studies has developed dramatically due to growing awareness that 'history' is highly dependent on the social, political and technological environments within which the past is remembered. In their survey of contemporary war memory theory, Ashplant *et al.* have identified two principal paradigms within which war memory and commemoration are studied. The first is a political paradigm where memory is 'a practice bound up with rituals of national identification, and a key element in the symbolic repertoire available to the nation-state for binding its citizens into a collective national identity'. The second is a psychological paradigm where 'war memory and commemoration is held to be significant primarily for psychological reasons, as an expression of mourning, being a human response to the death and suffering that war engenders on a vast scale' (Ashplant *et al.* 2000: 7).

Ashplant *et al.* also identify three principal theoretical approaches: the state-centred approach, the social agency approach and the popular memory approach.

The state-centred approach focuses on the political paradigm. It is a 'top-down' approach which privileges the official narrative, told through state commemoration, national institutions (such as museums and the education system) and government statements. The strengths of the state-centred approach are twofold: it focuses on the single most wide-reaching and influential narrative in any given society; and it is relatively simple to identify and analyse the narrative because it has already been distilled into an easily digestible form for the purpose of domestic dissemination. However, such simplicity is also the weakness of state-centred approaches. Ashplant *et al.* cite the under-conceptualization of the 'complicated relation between the various different agencies and arenas that are in play', 'over-play[ing] the unity of social elites' and 'weak[ness] on the ground of individual subjectivity' as the primary problems (ibid.: 10–11). These are some of the weaknesses identified in the state-centred 'orthodox' approach to Japanese war memories outlined in the Introduction.

Central to the social agency approach, developed by Jay Winter and Emmanuel Sivan, is the psychological paradigm. The social agency approach focuses particularly on mourning: the healing, reconciliation and coming to terms with the loss of loved ones, which is a process that may never reach a conclusion (Winter and Sivan 1999: 32). In the social agency approach, agency is 'the product of individuals and groups who come together, not at the behest of the state or any of its subsidiary organizations, but because they have to speak out' (ibid.: 9). The focus is not on the state, but rather on the range of activities of groups and individuals within civil society. Winter and Sivan place their approach at the 'midpoint' between two 'extreme and unacceptable' positions: one which treats all personal memories and narratives to be an inevitable result of membership of a social group, and one in which memories and narratives are uniquely individual and unaffected by cultural or other narratives (ibid.: 10).

Ashplant *et al.* have criticized the social agency approach because 'in practice, it pushes [the state] out of the frame of consideration' (Ashplant *et al.* 2000: 9). Mourning cannot be separated from the state because mourning is so often channelled through acts of state commemoration, such as Veterans' Days. As Ashplant *et al.* argue:

> The politics of war memory and commemoration *always* has to engage with mourning and with attempts to make good the psychological and physical damage of war; and wherever people undertake the tasks of mourning and reparation, a politics is *always* at work.
>
> (ibid.: 9)

Ashplant *et al.* also criticize the social agency approach along the same lines that they criticized the state-centred approach: for the under-conceptualization of the 'complicated relation between the various different agencies and arenas that are in play', 'over-play[ing] the unity of social elites' and 'weak[ness] on the ground of individual subjectivity'. However, whereas the weakness of the state-centred approach in these regards resulted because the internal dynamics of the society are largely ignored in favour of the official narrative, the weakness of the social agency approach stems from the underdevelopment of the explanations for the political power, or lack of it, of any given group of social agents and their narratives. As such, the social agency approach is weak in explaining how agents' narratives relate to and become incorporated within a wider cultural memory.

The third approach is the popular memory approach of the Popular Memory Group, which was subsequently developed by Alistair Thomson.

> [T]he study of 'popular memory' is concerned with *two* sets of relations. It is concerned with the relation between dominant memory and oppositional forms across the whole public (including academic) field. It is also concerned with the relation between these public discourses in their

contemporary state of play and the more privatized sense of the past which is generated within a lived culture.

(Popular Memory Group 1998: 78)

The popular memory approach focuses on how private memories are affected by the various public narratives within a society. It is used primarily by oral historians and those basing their studies on life history narratives of people who have experienced war. The approach has revealed many important aspects of war memories, such as how similar experiences during war can manifest themselves in divergent political activities after the conflict (Ashplant *et al.* 2000: 14).

Ashplant *et al.* recognize that all three approaches (state-centred, social agency and popular memory) have made important contributions to the understanding of war memory. Consequently, they argue for:

a theory able to integrate insights from each of these approaches, so as to identify the transactions and negotiations that occur between the various agencies involved in producing war memories: those of the state, civil society, 'private' social groups and individuals.

(ibid. xii)

The challenge is how to synthesize the strengths of the three approaches into an 'integrated theory' of war memory applicable to the Japanese case.

Towards an 'integrated approach'

Historical memory is the way in which historical events are looked back upon from the standpoint of the present. At the heart of the concept of memory is the past–present relationship. This past–present relationship exists on both a collective and an individual level. The term 'memory' highlights that 'looking back on the events of the past' may say as much about the present priorities and politics of the individual or society as it does about the past.

Within war memory, there is an important distinction between people with and without personal experiences of war. Unlike members of the war generation who base their war memories on recollections of personal experiences, members of the postwar generations can only possess what the Popular Memory Group calls a 'privatized sense of the past' (1998: 78). This is a personal interpretation of the war based on learning, whether in formal education or less formal activities such as private conversations or watching television. People who experienced the war also have a privatized sense of the past, although it requires a slightly different definition: it is a combination of memories of personal experience and subsequent learning about the war. The memories and narratives of people both with and without personal experience of war come within the scope of a study of war memories. Consequently, a study of Japanese war memories is not limited to the testimony of the war generation. It is also about the way in which postwar generations in Japan look back on events that occurred before they were born.

War discourses start from the expression of thoughts on war. An individual does not necessarily have to have experienced the war to express a personal/individual narrative: the public expression of memories or the individual's privatized sense of the past. The distinction between a narrative and memories is important. Memories of personal experience that are still clear in the mind may be excluded, altered or added to in the recounting of a personal narrative: to express the memories may be too painful, there may be fears of repercussions for telling the truth (if one confesses to a war crime, for example), or a story may be embellished to make it more appealing to the listener.

Both personal memories and narratives evolve over time. Memories may fade or become confused as subsequent narratives instil doubt over the accuracy or even validity of one's memories. As Alistair Thomson argues, memories undergo a process of 'composure':

> 'Composure' is an aptly ambiguous term to describe the process of memory making. In one sense we compose or construct memories using the public languages and meanings of our culture. In another sense we compose memories that help us to feel relatively comfortable with our lives and identities, that give us a feeling of composure.
>
> (Thomson 1994: 8)

Memories are worked through over time in the (not necessarily successful) process of trying to compose 'a past we can live with' (ibid.: 9). Consequently, just as memories are liable to change over time due to composure, narratives based on memories are also liable to change.

Personal narratives can also vary according to the 'particular publics' within which and to whom the narratives are expressed. Contexts or audiences affect the content, tone and wording of narratives. For example, a veteran may tell a very different story of his personal experiences to his comrades at a veterans' reunion compared to the story he tells his grandchildren.

Memories and narratives exist not only on an individual level, but also on a collective level. 'The process of transmission of war memory from the direct experience of survivors to the "cultural memory" of their successors' (Ashplant *et al.* 2000: 43) embodies two entangled processes: the transition from individual memories to collective memory; and the transition from the memories of the war generation to the cultural memory of the postwar generations.

The first process in the creation of cultural memory is the transition from the individual to the collective. Following a personal experience of war, many factors influence decisions by individuals as to whether they articulate their memories in public. If these personal narratives are heard and resonate with the memories of other individuals, shared memories emerge among groups –

for example, veterans in the same platoon. Individuals and groups may then seek to gain a wider audience and recognition for their personal and shared memories through expressing their personal and sectional narratives in public, either politically or through cultural forms (such as literature or museums).

If they reach the public arena, individual and sectional narratives compete with other narratives. The relative prominence and power of narratives within cultural memory may have little to do with the numbers of people who had those experiences. It may have more to do with the perceived importance of the experiences or events, and the political or cultural power of those who present the events. For example, the memories of 'the few', the pilots of Fighter Command during the Battle of Britain, have a central role in British cultural memory of World War II; however, memories of members of the merchant marine fleet, while numerically vastly superior, permeate British public consciousness much less.

The power of narratives depends largely on access to those who wield political and cultural power. Veterans' groups typically have significant access to the corridors of political power as part of an unwritten 'contract' between themselves and the government that asked them to fight and risk death for their country. Meanwhile, other groups may benefit from prominent cultural links: for example, the Home Guard in Britain has gained high prominence in British cultural memory because of the popularity of the comedy series *Dad's Army* on British television. The example of *Dad's Army* also illustrates that narratives often become prominent not so much through the efforts of the people whose narratives are being told, but through the efforts of people already in positions of political and cultural power (such as politicians, newspaper editors and film-makers) who champion or present a narrative.

The second process in the creation of cultural memory involves the transition from the war generation's memories to the postwar generation's cultural memory. This may generate substantial conflict within a society 'as survivors seek to ensure that "their" version of war is not forgotten, whilst successors struggle with the conflict between acting as the "trustees" of survivor memory, and reassessing this legacy and their own relation to it' (Ashplant *et al.* 2000: 43). As the war retreats further into the past, postwar generations, who cannot draw on personal experience of the conflict, assume greater responsibility for the narration of the war experience. Ultimately, a point is reached when there are no surviving members of the war generation, and war discourses within a society are conducted entirely by those with only second-hand experiences and knowledge of the war.

Often, the result of these two processes is that a dominant cultural memory emerges. This does not mean narratives compete until only one narrative survives. As Thomson writes:

> My argument is that an official or dominant legend works not by excluding contradictory versions of experience, but by representing them

in ways that fit the legend and flatten out the contradictions, but which are still resonant for a wide variety of people.

(Thomson 1994: 12)

Put in a slightly different way, a truly dominant cultural memory emerges in societies where the contradictions *can* be ironed out. This is usually achieved by weaving a common theme through the majority of the sectional narratives. Among the sectional narratives within British dominant cultural memory of World War II are the Blitz, the Battle of Britain, D-Day, rationing, convoys and 'Dad's Army'. These are divergent narratives but are held together by the 'good war' narrative: the almost universal British belief that the war was a heroic, just and victorious struggle against the evils of Nazism.

However, if a common theme cannot be found or created, the contradictions cannot be ironed out easily. In this situation, multiple cultural narratives exist and a truly dominant cultural memory cannot emerge. War memories become openly confrontational as groups struggle to turn their disparate versions of the past into the dominant cultural memory. War memories become an issue of national division rather than national unity. This is the fundamental reason why Japan's war memories remain contested.

Whereas a dominant cultural memory may or may not emerge, states develop an official narrative, which is the sectional narrative of the contemporary ruling elite. However, this does not necessarily mean that the contemporary ruling elite presents a coherent narrative subscribed to by all members of the ruling elite. The official narrative may be contested among politicians and the bureaucracy just as cultural memory is contested within society at large. Official narratives can also exist on differing levels: national, state/prefectural and municipal. Regional official narratives, presented by local politicians and bureaucracies, may be distinct from the narrative presented by the national government. Local governments may be of a different political colour from the national government, which may give regional official narratives an ideological stance distinct from that of the national narrative. Or a region's particular war experience may form a central part of a local narrative but only a marginal part of the national narrative. The differences in national and local official narratives are particularly evident in museums, which are key sites for the presentation of official narratives.

National and local governments are particularly powerful and active agents within a society and attempt to shape cultural memory though the cultural forms and political apparatus at their disposal, such as commemorative events or the education system. At the same time, official narratives are responsive to narratives within civil society. Official narratives that do not resonate with or appeal to the people become a source of political opposition to national and local governments. Consequently, official narratives must balance attempts to shape cultural memory to fit the ruling elite's narrative and responsiveness to cultural memory.

Even in the case of a truly dominant cultural memory or widely accepted official narratives, war memories always remain open to contestation from sectional narratives. In time, sectional narratives may succeed in replacing or changing the nature of the dominant and/or official narratives. Changes in government can lead to wholesale changes in the official narrative, such as when communism fell in eastern Europe. The fact that such changes to the official narrative occur indicates that competing narratives exist even within societies presided over by repressive governments. However, cultural memory cannot change as quickly as an official narrative, which may change in a matter of days. This is another important distinction between the official narrative and the dominant cultural memory.

But cultural memory is not only negotiated at the national level. Societies and the cultural memories they produce do not exist in a vacuum, but as part of an international society of states and cultures. In technologically developed societies, where transportation and communications technology have made information from abroad a part of everyday life, cultural narratives are influenced by narratives from other societies. As with contestations between narratives within a culture, political and cultural power plays a crucial role in the interaction between competing narratives across national boundaries. For example, Hollywood has given the US a powerful cultural form for exporting its culture unrivalled by any other nation's cinematic industry. Similarly, nations may be unable to resist diplomatic or political pressure for the inclusion of others' narratives within their own cultural memory. In Japan's case, political and diplomatic pressure from China and South Korea has given Chinese and Korean narratives a major role in Japanese domestic war debates.

Another powerful external narrative is the hegemonic master-narrative, which changes as a 'consequence of the reordering of global power relations' (Ashplant *et al.* 2000: 60). The World War II frame of Allied–Axis conflict was replaced with the East–West confrontation of the cold war after 1945; and since 1989, there has been a new era of 'globalization and fragmentation' presided over by a single superpower, the US. The year 2001 saw the beginning of another global narrative following the attacks of 11 September: the so-called 'war on terror' or the 'clash of civilizations'. A society places its own narratives within the context of the global political situation, and a hegemonic master-narrative may help to crystallize the parameters of debate within a culture. In Japan's case, war debates essentially centre on whether to accept or oppose the hegemonic master-narrative of Japanese aggression and war guilt in World War II, with progressives accepting the master-narrative, and conservatives and nationalists challenging it.

Cultural memory, therefore, can be influenced by any narrative ranging from the voice of an individual up to hegemonic master-narratives of the global order. But this process of the creation of cultural memory is only half the story. Memory creation is a continual, two-way process of contestation and negotiation. In turn, cultural memory affects the individual and sectional narratives that have informed it.

The analysis of how cultural memory affects personal memories and narratives has been developed particularly within the popular memory approach: '"Private memories", the Group argues, "cannot . . . be readily unscrambled from the effects of dominant historical discourses. It is often these that supply the very terms by which a private history is thought through"' (Popular Memory Group, cited in Ashplant *et al.* 2000: 13). The public–private relationship is central to the popular memory approach, and at the intersection between the private and public the key concept is identity, the way people define themselves and the groups they feel they belong to. Identity is both 'multidimensional' and 'situational' (Cohen 1994: 205; Smith 1991: 14). It is multidimensional because identities can exist on many levels, such as gender, political affiliation, nationality and religion. The unique combination of identities is the source of every person's individuality. And identity is situational because people employ identities appropriate to their situation: political identities inform voting choices, and national or regional identities commonly determine the allegiances of spectators at sporting events.

Two forms of identity have particular but not exclusive significance for war memories. The first is the banner under which people fight and die. This is usually national identity but it can also be religious, political or regional identity. The second form of identity is an individual's role-identity, an identity stemming from personal experience or the role played in society (Smith 1991: 3). Examples of role-identities that profoundly affect war memories are 'veteran', 'history teacher' and 'peace activist'. However, these two forms of identity are not of exclusive significance. Gender plays an important role in war memories. This can be seen either in analysis of the masculinity of soldier heroes, or from the perspective of feminist critiques of war as an example of male violence. The 'comfort women' (*ianfu*)[1] issue, concerning the treatment of 200,000 mainly Korean women, many of whom were tricked or coerced into working in Japan's infamous military brothels, has given gender issues a central role in Japanese war discourses since the 1990s.

Identity mediates transactions in both directions between the public and private, informing choices about how to compose and express memories. Thomson writes:

> Our memories are risky and painful if they do not fit the public myths, so we try to compose our memories to ensure that they will fit with what is publicly acceptable. Just as we seek the affirmation of our personal identities within the particular publics in which we live, we also seek affirmation of our memories. 'Recognition' is a useful term to describe the process of public affirmation of identities and memories.
>
> (Thomson 1994: 11)

Identities play an important role in determining the groups people aspire to belong to, or whose recognition they seek. Consequently, identities affect the ways in which people compose memories and express narratives so that they are publicly acceptable to the groups with which they identify. Or, looking at it from a different direction, people may not even mind if their views offend those with whom they do not identify. Conversely, identities act as a filter for public narratives: the narratives of the groups people belong to (or aspire to belong to) gain particular importance, and people may ignore the narratives of those groups with which they do not identify.

In conclusion, the relationship between the private realm of personal memories and public realm of cultural memory is both dynamic and complex. Personal memories and cultural memory affect each other in an ongoing, two-way process. Personal memories are the raw materials of cultural memory, which always remains open to contestation, 'while personal memories are in part shaped by pre-existing national and local cultural memories' (Ashplant *et al.* 2000: 18).

Judgemental war memory

In war discourses in contemporary Japan, debate more usually concerns 'war responsibility' (*sensō sekinin*)[2] and 'historical consciousness' (*rekishi ninshiki*) than 'war memory'. In Japanese, 'war memory' (*sensō kioku*) usually refers to a narrower meaning: personal memories of the war generation's experiences. As argued in the Introduction, the issue of war responsibility (the ongoing moral, legal and political implications of conduct during wartime) is a separate issue to war memory. However, the term 'historical consciousness' highlights that war responsibility is a critical component of war memories in Japan, and that war history and experiences are thought through in overtly political and ethical terms. Consequently, a theoretical link between war memory and ethical judgements on war is necessary.

The opening sentence of Michael Walzer's *Just and Unjust Wars* is, 'For as long as men and women have talked about war, they have talked about it in terms of right and wrong' (Walzer 1977: 3). 'Right and wrong' may incorporate political or strategic judgements, but the vocabulary routinely used in war discourses indicates that most aspects of war memories are infused with ethical judgements. Individuals, groups and nations become perpetrators (or aggressors), bystanders and victims (judgements on guilt); wars become aggressive wars, wars of self-defence or holy wars (judgements regarding the reasons for fighting); soldiers are brave or cowardly, cruel or humane (judgements on war conduct); people are patriotic for supporting the war and may be called traitors for opposing the struggle (judgements of loyalty and identification); perpetrators deny, acknowledge or justify their crimes (retrospective judgements on actions).

The ethical dimension is an integral part of war discourses. As Walzer states:

> The moral reality of war is divided into two parts. War is always judged twice, first with reference to the reasons states have for fighting, secondly with reference to the means they adopt. . . . Medieval writers made the difference a matter of prepositions, distinguishing *jus ad bellum*, the justice of war, from *jus in bello*, justice in war.
>
> (ibid.: 21)

Concerning *jus ad bellum*, Walzer uses a legalist paradigm to articulate a basic theory of aggression based on six propositions:

> 1. *There exists an international society of independent states. . . . 2. This international society has a law that establishes the rights of its members – above all, the rights of territorial integrity and political sovereignty. . . . 3. Any use of force or imminent threat of force by one state against the political sovereignty or territorial integrity of another constitutes aggression and is a criminal act. . . . 4. Aggression justifies two kinds of violent response: a war of self-defense by the victim and a war of law enforcement by the victim and any other member of international society. . . . 5. Nothing but aggression can justify war. . . . 6. Once the aggressor state has been militarily repulsed, it can also be punished.*
>
> (ibid.: 61–2, italics in original)

However, this theory does not resolve all arguments over whether a war is just or unjust. What constitutes 'imminent threat', 'self-defense' and a 'war of law enforcement', and therefore what constitutes just grounds for initiating war, remains contested.

The second aspect of just war theory concerns the conduct of the war, *jus in bello*. Thomas Nagel has distinguished two approaches to moral responsibility in war. 'Utilitarianism gives primacy to a concern with what will *happen*': it is an approach in which the ends may be used to justify the means. 'Absolutism gives primacy to a concern with what one is *doing*': it is an approach that says there are certain actions which cannot be justified however worthy the ends (Nagel 1974: 4). Nagel offers a 'somewhat qualified defense of absolutism' because absolutist intuitions 'are often the only barrier before the abyss of utilitarian apologetics for large-scale murder' (ibid.: 6). Pure utilitarianism is the inherently dangerous argument that any means are justified by the cause.

Nagel argues that 'Few of us are completely immune to either of these types of moral intuition, though in some people, either naturally or for doctrinal reasons, one type will be dominant and the other suppressed or weak' (ibid.: 4). But when utilitarian (the cause justifies the means) and absolutist (some actions cannot be justified by the cause) principles coexist, the result can be an acute moral dilemma as, individually and collectively, people deliberate what constitutes an acceptable approach to resolving a military conflict, and whether they should be involved in the military conflict at all.

Combining the two concepts of *jus ad bellum* and *jus in bello* provides four basic judgements about a war. However, only three of these are coherent within the context of judging an entire war: first, the war was just and conduct during the war was ethical; second, the war was just but war conduct was unethical; and third, the war was unjust and war conduct was unethical. The fourth combination, an unjust war but ethical war conduct, creates an anomaly and cannot be applied to an entire conflict: if the war was unjust, then any acts of war were simply murder. However, the 'unjust war/just conduct' combination does exist, usually as a judgement of selected individuals who are deemed to have fought ethically, and often bravely too, in a manner inconsistent with their unjust cause. Erwin Rommel, the German general who was untainted by Nazi war crimes, would be one example of an individual who many people believe fought justly, albeit in an unjust cause.[3]

In reality, any individual ethical judgement concerning a war will be highly complex and dependent on a multitude of factors, including people's political priorities and the level of personal involvement in the conflict. However, these three basic positions – unjust war/unjust conduct, just war/unjust conduct, just war/just conduct – are the key 'marker points' in a spectrum of ethical judgements on war. They are the basic positions in relation to which individuals can contextualize their opinions regarding a conflict.

In short, moral judgements are central to people's stances on war. While the thrust of Walzer's and Nagel's arguments concern judgements on present or future conflicts, just war theory can equally be applied retrospectively. Consequently, 'judgemental war memory', the retrospective application of just war theory, can be defined as 'retrospective ethical judgements made using the individual's own value system concerning personal and/or collective war actions in the past'. Actions or events in the past are remembered in ethical terms, as being consistent or inconsistent with an individual's core political and personal beliefs, and it is in the consistency between our values and war memories that we can compose, in Alistair Thomson's phrase, 'a past we can live with' (1994: 9). The concept of judgemental memory is particularly, but not exclusively, relevant in case studies where issues of war responsibility impinge on war memories, such as Japan.

Japanese war memories: a hypothesis

In recent times, contestation over the wording of the Japanese government's official narrative about Japan's actions in the Asia-Pacific War has centred on two key phrases: 'aggressive war' (*shinryaku sensō*) and 'aggressive acts' (*shinryaku kōi*, a euphemism for atrocities). Debate over the term 'aggressive war' relates to *jus ad bellum* and indicates that Japanese opinion is divided concerning the overall justness of the Asia-Pacific War. Debate over the term 'aggressive acts' relates to *jus in bello* and indicates that Japanese people question whether Japanese war conduct was ethical.

By combining the two concepts, we can create a simple model of Japanese war memories. This model (Table. 1.1) presents four key groups: progressives who are critical of both Japan's aggressive war and atrocities; conservatives who deny an aggressive war but acknowledge aggressive acts (broadly, the official line); nationalists denying both an aggressive war and aggressive acts; and the anomalous position of an aggressive war but no aggressive acts (which is typically a way of acknowledging collective responsibility while denying the personal guilt of a relative).

However, the model is too simplistic for a number of reasons. First, the Asia-Pacific War involved multiple conflicts and was also entwined with issues of colonial domination and rule. Four separate aspects of Japanese war and colonial responsibility are judged: the China War, starting with the Manchurian Incident in 1931 which developed into all-out war in 1937; the treatment of Asians colonized prior to 1941, such as the Taiwanese and Koreans; the treatment of Asians in the colonies captured from the Western powers after 1941, such as Indonesia; and the Pacific War against the Western powers, particularly the US. Each of these generates its own retrospective ethical judgement, but in general, many more Japanese are willing to categorize Japanese colonialism or wars against other Asians as aggressive than are prepared to characterize war against the Western colonial powers as aggressive.

Second, victim consciousness (or 'victim mentality', *higaisha ishiki*) is a key issue in Japanese war memories. However, the above model only analyses Japanese actions. A model incorporating judgements of Japanese experiences, and thereby victim consciousness, is necessary.

Third, there are Japanese people who are uninterested and uninformed about the war to the point where they answer 'don't know' on even the most basic opinion poll questions about war issues. Whereas excessive categorization of Japanese people as 'ignorant' should be avoided, a model that includes the 'don't knows and don't cares' is necessary.

In the light of these three criticisms, a more complex hypothesis about the nature of Japanese war memories emerges. Japanese judgemental war memory can be considered as a spectrum of moral reasoning. At one end is the progressive 'unjust war/unjust acts' position, and at the other end is the nationalist 'just war/just acts' position. Within this spectrum there are five primary groups whose characteristics represent the five most important conceptual frames that Japanese people use in looking back on war history. Opinion poll data suggests that since the 1990s, four of these groups have

Table 1.1 Japanese judgemental memory: a basic model

	Aggressive war	*Not aggressive war*
Aggressive acts	Progressives	Conservatives
Not aggressive acts	Anomalous position	Nationalists

been of roughly equal size, about 20–30 per cent each: (1) progressives, (2) what I call the 'progressive-leaning group', (3) the 'don't knows and don't cares', and (4) conservatives. There is a fifth group, nationalists (also called 'revisionists'), but this is a relatively small group at the right wing of the spectrum (perhaps 3–5 per cent).[4]

The first group comprises Japanese progressives, who argue that Japan fought an aggressive war in Asia and committed many 'aggressive acts'. This aggression in Asia brought Japan into conflict with other colonial powers, which cut off supplies of oil and other key natural resources to Japan in response to Japanese aggression in China. The Pacific War was fought to secure the natural resources in South East Asia that would allow continued aggression in China, so the Pacific War is also characterized as aggressive. Progressives use the absolutist reasoning that no cause could have justified Japanese atrocities. They have an internationalist outlook, advocate a human rights agenda, and criticize Japanese official apologies and compensation as inadequate. Progressives are equally critical of war crimes committed by the Allies but judge that overall Japan was more of an aggressor than a victim.

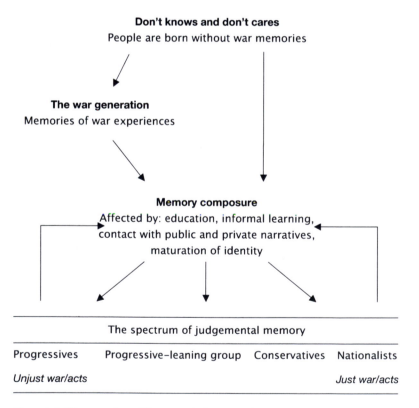

Figure 1.1 The creation of Japanese judgemental memory

Consequently, they argue that claims for Japanese victimhood in the absence of an acknowledgement of Japanese aggression are hypocritical.

The second group, comprising progressive-leaning people, shares the progressives' views that the China War was an aggressive war. But, by saying that the China War or Japanese colonialism were also 'inevitable' results of Japan's geopolitical situation up to the 1930s, and that both Japan and the Western colonial powers share responsibility for the outbreak of the Pacific War, the progressive-leaning group gives a comparatively watered-down version of war responsibility. Nonetheless, the progressive-leaning group, like progressives, supports additional official apologies and compensation to Asia. Japanese atrocities are acknowledged, but there is felt to be a degree of moral equivalence between Japanese actions, such as the massacres in Nanking following the fall of the Chinese capital in 1937, and Allied actions such as the firebombing of Japanese cities.

The progressive-leaning position can also be categorized as the 'both perpetrator and victim' position, with Japanese guilt stemming primarily from its actions against Asians, and Japanese victimhood stemming primarily from American and Soviet actions. However, according to progressive-leaning people, the blame for Japanese victimhood not only lies with the Allies, but also with the recklessness and cruelty of their own military. The progressive-leaning group is broadly anti-war and critical of both the Japanese military and the Allies. This is probably the single largest grouping, the 'most representative' conceptual frame. The progressive-leaning 'Japan was both victim and perpetrator' line has become a common 'compromise position' presented in official sources such as textbooks and museums.

The third group, 'the don't knows and don't cares', is the unavoidable starting point for Japanese people's historical consciousnesses because people are born without any knowledge of war history. Most people will leave this group at some stage in their lives through the gradual accumulation of knowledge via education or the media and through the maturing of political identity. The group comprises predominantly the younger generations. People who remain in the group long term do not see the relevance of war history in their lives in modern, prosperous, peaceful Japan. Most members of this group are not completely 'ignorant', although Japanese television occasionally shows street interviews with young people saying 'We fought against America. When?' Levels of knowledge also range widely from topic to topic, with very few people being unaware of the A-bomb issue, for example, but many more being unaware of the abuses of Allied Prisoners of War (POWs) on the Burma Railroad.

The fourth group, comprising conservatives, occupies the 'just war/unjust conduct' position. However, 'just war' does not summarize the conservative position as well as Carol Gluck's characterization 'if not a just, then perhaps a justifiable war' (Gluck 1993: 83). Using more utilitarian than absolutist reasoning, conservatives focus on defending the Japanese cause rather than actively justifying it. They accept that Japan committed some 'aggressive acts' but say the war, particularly the Pacific War, cannot simply be called an aggressive war. Conservatives make a stronger case than the progressive-leaning grouping that there is moral equivalence between Japanese 'aggressive acts' and Allied actions. They also highlight the bravery and sacrifice of the military in a tragic, losing cause.

Conservatives deflect state responsibility and place responsibility for 'aggressive acts' more at the individual or unit level, or even abstractly on the cruel nature of war. Nonetheless, Japan did pay compensation in the 1950s, 1960s and 1970s, and continues to issue apologies; so, according to conservatives, Japan has addressed its responsibility and the compensation issue is closed (*kaiketsu zumi*). Narratives of victimhood are prominent within the conservative narrative, but victimhood is cast as the result of Allied excesses or the inevitable tragedy of defeat rather than the result of the military's recklessness. This position is closest to the official narrative of Japan's conservative political elite.

The final group, comprising Japanese nationalists, occupies the 'just war/just conduct' position. Using almost pure utilitarian reasoning (Japan's cause justified its actions), nationalists promote an affirmative theory of the Asia-Pacific War and deny any 'aggressive acts', of which 'Nanking massacre denial' is the most infamous. It was the Allies, argue nationalists, who were the aggressors. Japanese war responsibility became an issue only because Japan lost, so compensation and apologies were always unnecessary. Rather than self-pitying victim consciousness, nationalists revere the bravery, patriotism and sacrifice of those who fought foreign aggression. At the right wing extreme are the *uyoku*, the emperor-worshipping nationalists who can be seen driving around cities throughout Japan in trucks blaring out military music. Such groups are xenophobic and regularly intimidate those critical of Japanese war actions. However, despite their high profile, nationalists are a relatively small group at the extreme political right wing.

An alternative way of characterizing these five groups and their respective conceptual frames for viewing war history is the routes to contemporary national pride implicit within the stances. Pride is a constant theme in Japanese war discourses. It not only clarifies the centrality of the past–present relationship within war memories, but indicates the difficulties Japanese people have in incorporating war history into a positive aspect of national identity.

For progressives, pride stems from having the courage to acknowledge past wrongs and squarely face the past. It is also about breaking down narrow-minded and confrontational nationalism through transnational identification, whether through gender, ideological or simply 'we are all human' identities. Progressives regard themselves as humanitarian leaders of moral conscience, and perhaps even as a model for how others struggling with ongoing war responsibility issues (such as Americans over Vietnam) should face up to their pasts.

Progressives are derided as masochistic (*jigyakuteki*) by nationalists and conservatives. For nationalists, pride is based in denying culpability, lauding soldiers' heroism and affirming positive aspects of Japanese militarism, in particular the economic development of Japan's colonies and the liberation of Asian nations from Western colonialism. This, however, is derided as denial, insensitivity towards victims of Japanese militarism, and selectivism with the facts by progressives.

Conservatives do not deny the existence of 'aggressive acts' in the same way as nationalists, so pride for conservatives is based more on issues of the patriotism and 'precious sacrifice' (*tōtoi gisei*) of the war generation. Conservative narratives draw heavily on the literary tradition of *hōganbiiki*, '[w]ith its emphasis on the nobility of sacrifice to a losing cause' and 'aura of sentimentality around tales of futile suffering' (Orr 2001: 11). Pride is based in the purity of spirit and the idealized 'Japaneseness' of the war generation, which is why the whole war cannot be acknowledged as 'aggressive': that would delegitimize the nobility of the war generation and render their deaths meaningless (in Japanese, 'a dog's death', *inuji*, is the term used).

The progressive-leaning group bases its pride in moralistic pacifism. Such pacifism is well-meaning but usually stems from the desire that Japanese suffering will never be repeated. It often skirts around the core ideological issue of Japanese war responsibility, so is viewed as shallow by both those on the ideological left and right: the people who use this form of pacifism are frequently criticized as *heiwa boke*, 'empty-headed peaceniks'.

Finally, the 'don't knows and don't cares' are those people for whom war history plays little, if any, role in their national pride and self-identification.

These five groups – progressives, progressive-leaning, 'don't knows', conservatives and nationalists – are not rigid, discrete or unchanging. They are merely the most broad-based and identifiable positions across the spectrum of Japanese judgemental memory. These five groups could be subdivided further. For example, feminist critiques of soldiers' sexual violence towards 'comfort women' and Marxist critiques of Japanese imperialism, while very different in focus, both come within the 'progressive' category. Then there is the anomalous 'unjust war/just conduct' position, which is a sub-grouping towards the conservative end of the progressive-leaning group.

The broad spectrum of opinion highlights how progressives, who are so frequently marginalized or treated as 'un-Japanese' in the English-language orthodoxy, are no less 'Japanese' than nationalists or conservatives: indeed, if being representative of Japanese public opinion is the benchmark, Japanese nationalists are 'un-Japanese'. Progressive and progressive-leaning views routinely exceed conservative and nationalistic views in opinion polls. Typically, 50 to 60 per cent of people characterize the war as 'aggressive', while anything between 50 and 80 per cent (depending on the precise wording of questions) are either critical of the government's 'inadequate' treatment of war responsibility issues (such as the level of compensation) or are supportive of additional compensation and initiatives acknowledging aggression. Once the 'don't knows' have been removed, conservative or nationalist views ('Japan was more the victim' or 'there was never anything to apologize for') account for the remainder, which is almost always under 30 per cent. Those polls that most clearly identify the level of support for affirmative views of the war also indicate the predominance of more progressive views: for example, only 28 per cent of people said they supported the views of the nationalistic group at the centre of the 2001 textbook crisis, compared to 44 per cent saying they opposed the group (Kondō 2001: 3).

Support for prime ministerial worship at Yasukuni Shrine, on the other hand, tends to be more evenly balanced. In 2001, 40 per cent opposed and 50 per cent supported Prime Minister Koizumi's worship, although the anger at Koizumi's Yasukuni worship across Asia has precipitated a reversal: two polls in July 2006 indicated 53 to 54 per cent opposed continued Yasukuni Shrine worship (www.bbc.co.uk 24 July 2006). Support for Yasukuni Shrine worship has been widely interpreted as nationalistic support for the worship of war criminals, but support for official Yasukuni worship does not necessarily equate to nationalism. Many of Japan's war dead are remembered and mourned by their families as patriots who served and died for their country. Support for official *mourning* of the war dead or official recognition of their sense of duty and sacrifice is not equivalent to affirming the aims and conduct of the war (Seaton 2005: 303–4).

However, the problem remains of how victim consciousness fits into the spectrum of Japanese judgemental memory. Victim consciousness, despite its ubiquity, cannot be called a dominant narrative; neither can it be considered the common theme woven through disparate narratives that is necessary to create a truly dominant cultural narrative (in the way that 'the good war' narrative underpins British or American dominant cultural memory). Orr writes:

> In the course of this research, I have encountered many who think of victim consciousness as a conservative tactic to avoid responsibility. This is an unsatisfactory conclusion. First, a victim mindset simply does not fit the style of proud, self-consciously virile conservatives such as Nakasone Yasuhiro. And second, the focus on war victimhood seems more characteristic of the liberal view of war as evil . . . *I will show that victim consciousness has been used by groups from across the political spectrum and has led to conscientious civic activism and, as well, to avoidance of responsibility.*
>
> (Orr 2001: 13, emphasis added)

Victim consciousness can be used in diverse ways because categorizing somebody as a victim and identifying those responsible are themselves ethical judgements. Herman and Chomsky's notion of 'worthy and unworthy victims'

(1994: 37–86) clarifies that victim consciousness, particularly for those who did not personally experience the suffering, is an issue of *identification*. Worthy victims are those we identify with or are encouraged to identify with through sympathetic treatment in public representations of their sufferings; unworthy victims are those with whom we feel little identification, or even those who 'deserve' their fates at the hands of those with whom we identify. Identification can evoke powerful emotions and lead people to suspend or bend their normal ethical judgements about war. Victim status can even be given to war criminals. For example, a Japanese soldier who bayoneted Chinese prisoners for killing practice could be represented as a victim – if he was identified with sympathetically as an ordinary man drafted into an abusive military system that forced him to follow illegal orders and to commit acts that he would never otherwise have committed, leaving him psychologically damaged.

Even if there is universal agreement concerning a group's victim status, such as *hibakusha* (A-bomb victims) in Japan, there remains scope to debate who bore responsibility for their suffering: the Japanese military for waging an unwinnable war, the emperor for not insisting on surrender earlier, the Americans for dropping the bomb, the inherent atrocity of war. The Hiroshima narrative remains contested unless it is completely decontextualized from any background explanation as to why the bomb was dropped. Such decontextualization frequently occurs (particularly in television coverage of the Hiroshima commemorations), but this only creates the *appearance* of national unity through victim consciousness. When the background to the A-bombs must be referred to, confrontation re-emerges.

Consequently, general statements such as 'the Japanese suffer from victim mentality' miss the true significance of victim consciousness in Japan. As long as judgements about responsibility remain open to debate, victim consciousness cannot act as a truly unifying factor in the context of war memories: the discussion inevitably returns to judgements concerning Japanese actions. Consequently, it may be more appropriate to use the plurals – victim consciousnesses and victim mentalities – given how identification and ideology render invalid any notion that victim consciousness is a unified phenomenon.

The significance of victim consciousness in Japan is twofold. First, victim consciousness allows people to identify with those who have been deemed to occupy the moral high ground through their victimhood (because guilt, and therefore the moral low ground, lies with the perpetrator 'other'). Within public discourses about the war in Japan, which so frequently deal with issues of guilt and responsibility, a chance to identify with people on the moral high ground offers comparatively high levels of comfort in the ongoing processes of memory composure. What is considered the moral high ground is dependent on the ethical belief systems and conceptual frames that are also used to judge Japanese actions, so the nature of victim consciousness always depends on the nature of judgemental memory.

Second, if discussions about who the perpetrator 'other' might be are left sufficiently vague, victim consciousness (particularly concerning the A-bombs) is the one mode of discourse that allows a modicum of national unity about war history. Discussion of the 'passive victims' of Hiroshima is less risky and provokes far less acrimonious confrontation than discussion of the conduct of the 'active agents' in the Japanese military.

Consequently, the place of victim consciousness within the 'Japanese war memories as seismic activity' metaphor can now be clarified. Victim consciousness is like the earth's crust. It is the superficial level of Japanese war memories that is most visible, and with which both Japanese and non-Japanese ordinarily have most contact. It covers over the memory rifts and for much of the time preserves an appearance of calm and national unity in Japanese remembering. But the real forces that shape the landscape of Japanese memories are deeper down. When progressives assert that the war in China was an atrocity-soaked war of aggression, and nationalists declare the war to be justified and atrocities such as Nanking 'fabrications', there is no room for compromise. The superficial crust of victim consciousness offers no protection against the upheavals caused when the friction between powerful oppositional forces below the surface (the 'ideological tectonic plates') becomes too great.

In short, while the superficial unity offered by victim consciousness may be the most visible aspect of Japanese war memories, the core issue is the memory rifts in judgemental memory. What I have called 'judgemental memory' is, in my understanding and usage, virtually indistinguishable from what the Japanese term 'historical consciousness' (*rekishi ninshiki*). I have only employed the term 'judgemental memory' thus far because it is a more literal statement of the phenomenon and more obviously derived from the terminology of the just war theory that underpins it.

A media/cultural studies approach

The Popular Memory Group argued that 'in the capitalist West [which can include Japan in this context], the intersections of formal political debates and the public media are probably the crucial site' in the negotiation of cultural memory (1998: 77). In order to study how Japan's contested war memories are played out within the public field of representations, a media/cultural studies approach is necessary.

Cultural studies has been called 'higher education's most upwardly mobile discipline' (du Gay *et al.* 1997: 1). 'Culture' is a word with various meanings and connotations. It can mean '"the best that has been thought and said" in a society', a reference to what might also be called 'high culture' or 'art' (such as philosophy and painting); it can also refer to 'mass culture', the popular entertainments that 'ordinary people' take part in during their everyday lives; then there is a more 'anthropological' definition in which 'culture' refers to the shared 'way of life' in a community; finally, there is a more sociological definition in which culture refers to 'shared values' (Hall 1997: 2). However, within cultural studies, 'culture' refers mainly to meanings and practices:

shared, taken-for-granted knowledge is an essential element in what we call 'culture'. Our heads are full of knowledge, ideas and images about society, how it works and what it means. Belonging to a culture provides us with access to such shared frameworks or 'maps' of meaning which we use to place and understand things, to 'make sense' of the world, to formulate ideas and to communicate or exchange ideas and meanings about it.

(du Gay 1997: 8–10)

The hypothesis concerning Japanese judgemental memory presented above, therefore, already exhibits the key aspect of a cultural studies approach: it focuses on the principal 'shared frameworks or "maps" of meaning' that Japanese people use to interpret war history.

More practically speaking, a cultural studies approach also provides a methodology for the analysis of war-related cultural forms in the key locus of public discourse: the media. The media, in this instance, does not distinguish between the 'mass media' and the 'academy', but refers to any cultural form that *mediates* war-related discourse within the public sphere, from an academic journal to a web page, or a television drama to a museum. In order to study an object culturally, 'one should at least explore how it is represented, what social identities are associated with it, how it is produced and consumed, and what mechanisms regulate its distribution and use' (ibid.: 3). In short, there is a 'circuit of culture' connecting five key concepts:

1   *representation*: how war is depicted across the range of cultural production from books to museums to television;
2   *regulation*: the constraints on representations of war, either official (such as textbook screening or film classification) or unofficial (such as 'self-censorship');
3   *identity*: how war history engages the various aspects of people's multi-layered and situational identities, and how identities inform people's choices about interaction with the public field of representations;
4   *consumption*: the consumption of war-related forms, either in an economic sense (buying a book, visiting a museum) or in terms of message con-sumption (accepting or rejecting the intended message); and
5   *production*: the economic and political conditions that affect the viability of particular representations in different cultural forms.

Such a survey of public media texts cannot be considered an exhaustive survey of private memories, but nevertheless, examination of the public field of representations clarifies the public narratives and modes of discourse that provide the language and conceptual frames within which private memories are thought through.

Another methodological issue concerns what texts should be analysed. The approach I have chosen is content analysis, 'the non-selective monitoring

. . . of the total [media] output for a specified period. It is not concerned with questions of quality, of response or of interpretation, but confines itself to the large scale, objective survey of manifest content' (Fiske and Hartley 1978: 8). I have followed this approach particularly in the surveys of newspapers (Chapter 4), television (Chapter 5), magazine articles (Chapter 6) and cinema (Chapter 7). Content analysis is not without its flaws. The volume of war-related representations may be 'abnormally high' in the chosen period (particularly an issue in the television survey), categories (such as 'war-related materials') may be chosen by researchers 'to serve their own purposes', and materials may be counted 'according to their subjective perspectives' (Williams 2003: 158). Nevertheless, content analysis with clearly defined parameters constitutes a more methodological and systematic approach than the arbitrary selection of supposedly 'representative' texts.

Once content has been established, the power and reach of texts can be established through their levels of consumption, in viewing figures, sales or numbers of visitors to a museum. Such analysis often reveals that the iconic texts favoured in international analysis of Japanese war memories are not necessarily those that have the greatest impact within Japanese society: a work of literature may be read by a fraction of the number of people who see a documentary, for example.

However, such issues of reach and economic consumption are distinct from message consumption. Here the key concept of identity provides more overlap with the integrated approach to war memory theory outlined above. My definition of identity as both multilayered and situational indicates a broadly postmodern approach, and in the context of Japanese war memories I tend towards the 'less contemptuous view' of the audience of John Fiske that 'audiences can actively construct meanings from media images. They can make their own messages and resist the intentions of the producers or authors of media messages and as a result can resist the media' (Williams 2003: 64–5). This is because the absence of a dominant narrative and plurality of interpretations of war history in Japan mean that competing ideological branches of the media supply the counterarguments to each others' claims. I assume that people tend towards economic consumption of media texts that affirm and nourish their pre-existing historical consciousnesses, so when they encounter oppositional texts they are aware of the possible rebuttals. But identities are fluid and may always be revised: 'conversions' to a competing ideological camp are essential in accounting for shifts in public opinion over time.

At the same time, the ability of people to be critical media observers should not be over-idealized. As the existence of the 'don't knows and don't cares' group within Japanese war memories illustrates, it cannot be assumed that all people are knowledgeable or that they engage equally with public narratives. It is helpful to categorize the nature and level of interaction between Japanese individuals and the public field of representations in terms of the activity and passivity of individuals as 'avoiders', 'consumers' and 'producers' of war-related cultural forms. *Passive avoiders* are apathetic and display little interest in any cultural forms representing war history. *Active avoiders*, by contrast, probably have reasonably high knowledge or even personal experience of the war, but avoid the war issue to protect relationships or personal reputation, or even as a form of denial. *Passive consumers* readily consume war-related information if it reaches them as part of their daily lives (such as in a television news bulletin) but do not seek it out in the way that *active consumers* do. Active consumers categorize war history as an interest and are relatively knowledgeable. *Passive producers* are those people who volunteer testimony or considered opinions when prompted or pressed, while *active producers* are involved in some level of activism, take the initiative in raising the war issue or produce war-related cultural forms for public consumption.

These varying levels of engagement with war discourses may vary over time within an individual: for example, people may have phases of active consumption of war-related texts before tiring and choosing to avoid them. In general, however, individuals' profiles are determined by how far they progress towards the 'active' and 'producer' positions. Furthermore, these categorizations highlight that 'the media' and 'society' are not separate entities but that every media text within a society has been written, produced, edited, translated or sold by individuals or groups within that society. Just like cultural and individual memories, the media has its own two-way relationship with civil society: the media is a product of the society, but at the same time it plays a role in shaping the society.

Overall, a cultural studies approach is not a precise science. Even when hard data is available, it must be treated with some scepticism. For example, viewing figures may not accurately measure the impact of a television documentary: the television could have been merely 'on in the background' in many homes or the programme's message widely rejected. Neither is methodology uncontested within cultural studies. I have chosen to focus on content analysis because my main aims are to define the 'mental maps' within Japanese war memories, to illustrate how these mental maps operate within contemporary Japanese society, and to convey the sense of how a public field of representations composed of millions of war-related texts relates in diverse ways to millions of individual lives. This approach is not without methodological difficulties, but nevertheless a cultural studies approach is essential for creating as accurate a picture as possible of the public war discourses that provide the cultural context in which private memories are thought through.

The war representations business: a hypothesis

The term 'information business' is often used within media and cultural studies to highlight that the media is not an altruistic provider of information for the public good but a competitive business. Some cultural forms – particularly newspapers, television and cinema – involve such prohibitively expensive production and distribution costs that the market is limited to a handful of huge corporations and some smaller-scale subsidiaries or independents. In Japan, five media conglomerates (Fuji–Sankei, Asahi, Yomiuri–Nippon TV, Mainichi–TBS, and Nikkei–TV Tokyo) dominate television and the national press, and have extensive interests in other media businesses such as publishing. NHK, Japan's public broadcaster (often called 'the Japanese BBC'), is the other major corporation in television and radio. Two major film studios (Tōei and Tōhō) dominate cinema, although independent cinema also flourishes in Japan. Other cultural forms, such as books and digital multimedia, can be produced and disseminated by much smaller corporations. Nevertheless, publishing is also dominated by huge corporations, including Kōdansha, Shōgakukan, Iwanami, Bunshun and Shūeisha. Overall, there are thousands of media businesses of varying size that rely on radically different levels of revenue to make the media texts they produce profitable.

The behaviour of media corporations has typically been discussed within the context of two basic models: the hegemonic and pluralist models. The hegemonic model derives from Marxist theory, which 'encourages us to see the media as a means to promote a certain set of views and ideas – the ideology of the bourgeoisie – and to exclude or deride alternative or oppositional views or ideas' (Williams 2003: 37–8). The term 'hegemony' is particularly associated with the neo-Marxist Gramsci, who

> used 'hegemony' to refer to the *process* by which general consent is actively sought for the interpretations of the ruling class. Dominant ideology becomes invisible because it is translated into 'common sense', appearing as the natural, unpolitical state of things accepted by each and everyone.
>
> (van Zoonen 1994: 24)

In short, the hegemonic model treats media corporations as part of, subservient to or sharing the same priorities as the political elite. A variant of the hegemonic model is the 'propaganda model' of Herman and Chomsky (1994), which highlights the acquiescence of the American media in supporting the agendas of power elites, particularly in relation to foreign policy.

The Japanese media has typically been analysed and criticized in terms of the hegemonic model. In particular, the Japanese media is represented as subservient to political elites through the effects on reporting of press clubs (groups of reporters attached to government ministries and large corporations), which, it has been argued, lead to self-censorship, a lack of democracy within the Japanese press, and homogeneity in media stances (for example, Gamble and Watanabe 2004: 348–53; de Lange 1998: 193–5; van Wolferen 1990: 96–7). Such views have become predominant within Western representations of the Japanese media since the late 1980s (Pharr 1996: 23). However, they tend to be infused with assumptions about a mythical and idealized Western 'free press' model that the Japanese media fails to emulate, even though critiques of Western media – such as the Glasgow University Media Group's critiques of the British 'lobby system' (1985: 1–12) or Herman and Chomsky's 'propaganda model' – present remarkably similar arguments. Furthermore, as I have argued elsewhere (Seaton 2006b), the arguments about the homogenizing effects of press clubs are not always consistent with content analysis of Japanese media.

Nevertheless, the hegemonic model interpretation of the Japanese media sits comfortably within the orthodox, state-centred approach to war memories: the media toes the government line, therefore public discourse mirrors the government's views, therefore state-centred analysis of Japanese war memories is valid. However, given the hypothesis of this book, Japan's contested war memories, it stands to reason that division in media opinion must also exist. This suggests that the Japanese media conforms more to the 'pluralist model'. 'Pluralism conceives of the media as reflecting the diversity of their audiences. Viewers, readers and listeners are regarded not as passive dupes of the media but as agents who can exercise influence over them' (Williams 2003: 50). Corporations driven by the profit motive allow the production of cultural forms that reflect the diversity of opinion because there is profit to be made by providing what the market demands or out of ideological desires to challenge the status quo. The media plays the role of a platform or mediator for popular views, and it can act as a watchdog to those in power because criticism of elites may be good business.

Whereas both models provide insights into the nature of the media, they both suffer from weaknesses. The hegemonic model tends to focus on media conglomerates and to marginalize the roles of alternative sources of information, particularly scholarly or independent media and the Internet, which are sites of often radical challenges to those in power. By contrast, the pluralist model is weaker at explaining the roles of power relations, patronage and financial considerations within media production, particularly in the high-cost media of cinema, television and the press. In short, media theory resembles war memory theory in that there are a number of approaches but none on its own can be considered comprehensive. So, just as an integrated theory of war memory was necessary, so too is an integrated theory of the media.

The key concept of the *profitability threshold*, the level of consumption required to ensure that a media text makes a profit (also measurable in non-financial terms, such as prestige) for the organization that produced it, allows the insights from both the hegemonic and pluralist models to be incorporated in a hybrid view of the media. The more expensive it is to produce a given media text and the higher its profitability threshold, the more likely it is to be produced by a media conglomerate, to represent or reflect the views of the political elite, or to maximize the receptive target audience in an attempt to maximize consumption levels. In this situation, the hegemonic model is more likely to apply. Conversely, the cheaper the production costs and the lower the profitability threshold, the more easily the media text can be produced by a smaller corporation or be aimed at a specific niche in the marketplace. In this situation the pluralistic model is more likely to apply.

To assess the implications of the profitability threshold for war-related representations, it is necessary to return to the hypothesis of Japanese judgemental memory outlined earlier in this chapter. The broadest mainstream is a narrative of Japanese victimhood (preferably with 'innocent' victims) that avoids explicit reference to Japanese war responsibility. This representation can transcend the judgemental memory spectrum and resonate equally with conservatives and progressives alike. It is no coincidence that Japan's most visited war museum (Hiroshima), the most popular television drama depicting the war (*Oshin* 1982, see Harvey 1995), the highest-grossing war film at the cinema (*The Burmese Harp*, 1985) and many other successful novels, films and books focus firmly on Japanese victimhood: their message maximizes the receptive market for a war-related representation. This also explains the prominence of narratives of victimhood on Japanese television (see Chapter 5). Of all the cultural forms, television has the highest profitability threshold: 10 per cent viewing figures (approximately ten million adults) is the threshold above which the price of advertising time rises steeply. NHK faces a different set of circumstances from commercial broadcasters. It is required by law to be politically neutral, but this still inclines NHK towards depictions of Japanese victimhood: Japanese victimhood is the most politically 'neutral' in the context of the domestic Japanese audience.

After victimhood, the next most resonant representation is one that mixes Japanese suffering with critical representations of the military (particularly the army) or of aggressive war. This will resonate with around 50–70 per cent of the population, the progressive and progressive-leaning groups. This form of representation is particularly common in television documentaries (where the profitability threshold is lower than for dramas) and those official cultural forms in which Japanese war responsibility needs to be addressed: museums and textbooks.

When more ideological progressive and conservative positions are represented in the media, the potential receptive audience drops to under 30 per cent. Newspapers' profitability thresholds neatly coincide with this size of potential market: Japan's five national dailies have circulations of between two and ten million. As will be outlined in Chapter 4, they have stances that closely mirror the five main groups: progressive, progressive-leaning, 'don't knows and don't cares', conservative and nationalist. War cinema can also operate profitably at this level, but as will be discussed in Chapter 7, the narrative conventions of cinema give conservative films a distinct advantage over progressive films in what is essentially an entertainment format.

Finally, the prominent but small minority of nationalists makes this the smallest potential market for media texts, although many nationalistic texts benefit from the controversy they cause to register large sales. Nationalists have developed a significant niche within the markets for publications (books, manga and magazines) where the profitability threshold is typically 2,000–10,000 sales for a hardback or paperback, and over 30,000 for a cheap paperback (*bunko* or *shinsho*) or magazine. There is also a nationalist grip on straight-to-video/DVD documentaries, many of which are eulogies to the military or aimed at the military enthusiast market. In general, books, magazines and academic journals are the cultural forms in which the greatest diversity of war-related topics and opinions can be found. The profitability threshold is lowest (allowing the targeting of very specific markets) and authors typically have far more individual control over their work than if they worked for a television station, newspaper or film studio.

However, the size of the potential audience receptive to a media text's message and its relation to the profitability threshold is by no means a sure guide to the success of a media text. The artistic or scholarly qualities of the text, promotion, distribution and the inexplicable x-factor that makes some texts hits and others failures all have a role to play. Exceptions to the hypothesis also include occasions when celebrity, sensationalism or controversy attract disproportionate publicity. Nevertheless, such exceptions aside, the hypothesis provides rationales for this book's broader conclusions: nationalists disseminate their message primarily through books, magazines and videos; progressives use publishing and television documentaries; conservatives do well in publishing and cinema; publicly funded museums and textbooks tend to present a progressive-leaning 'Japan was both victim and perpetrator' line; private museums present specific ideologies or powerful vested interests; Japanese victimhood predominates in all cultural forms but particularly in war-related television dramas, which have the highest profitability threshold of any media text (viewing figures of 10 per cent is a basic benchmark for success); and the market for national newspapers is such that the stances of the national press accurately mirror the spectrum of judgemental memory.

Conclusions

Drawing on war memory theory, just war theory and media/cultural studies theory, I have presented a complex hypothesis about the nature of Japan's contested war memories and public war discourses. The marked differences between the five main conceptual frames for viewing war history (progressive, progressive-leaning, 'don't knows and don't cares', conservative and nationalist) clarify why Japan has not been able to find a dominant cultural memory for World War II. In other words, there is no unifying conceptual frame that allows war history to be comfortably incorporated into contemporary Japanese national identity. As such, Japanese war discourses bear little resemblance to Allied war discourses, such as in the UK and US, where the moral narrative of the 'good war against the evil of fascism' has allowed strong dominant narratives of World War II to emerge. Such broad-based consensus is elusive in Japan. Instead, Japanese war debates bear a close resemblance to the current liberal vs conservative confrontation in the US, or the moral debates on issues in the West, including abortion, fox hunting and capital punishment. Rather than war history being an issue of national unity against an external other, it has become an issue of national division along the lines of moral intuition and ideology.

This contested cultural memory has been presided over by a stable conservative ruling elite since 1955, with only a brief interlude in 1993–96 when the Liberal Democratic Party (LDP) did not control the premiership. Conservatives have maintained a grip on the official war narrative of the Japanese government, while progressives have wielded political power mainly through bringing foreign diplomatic pressure to bear on the Japanese government, or through public expression in the cultural forms at their disposal.

As such, Japanese war memories are stalemated: there is an ongoing clash between, on the one hand, a *politically powerful conservative lobby* whose war stance in recent times (since the 1970s) has been a minority opinion but which has maintained control over the official narrative and policy, and, on the other hand, a *politically weak progressive lobby* which has had the support of a small majority of public opinion but has failed to turn that support into the political power necessary to change the official narrative. Highly active and committed progressive and conservative or nationalist ideologists, who share virtually no common ground, fight vociferously in the media to persuade the masses that their views are right. The masses may lean one way or the other according to the issue, time and circumstances, but the entrenched agendas on both sides barely budge. The origins of this situation date back to Japan's defeat in 1945, and an overview of how this state of affairs has evolved over the 'long postwar' (Gluck 1991) is the subject of the next chapter.

2　The 'long postwar'

> Private memories cannot, in concrete studies, be readily unscrambled from the effects of dominant historical discourses. It is often these that supply the very terms by which a private history is thought through.
>
> (Popular Memory Group 1998: 78)

As the Popular Memory Group has argued, private memories and public war narratives are inextricably linked. The concept of the public–private relationship can also be reworked and applied to discussion of how war narratives have related to wider non-war narratives within postwar Japanese society. In other words: 'War memories and cultural narratives of war cannot be readily unscrambled from the effects of wider cultural, historical and political discourses. It is often these that supply the terms by which war history is thought through.'

War memories co-exist with and relate to all narratives within a society, from politics to religion, and popular culture to sport. War narratives also compete with those narratives for attention and prominence within public discourses. War memories are not simply a case of remembering and/or forgetting, or of knowledge and/or ignorance. There is an issue of *prioritization*, on both collective (cultural) and individual levels, in relation to all the other narratives and activities that have made up Japanese people's daily lives in the postwar. For example, a Japanese person may have been interested in war issues until pollution from a local factory became of more immediate and personal relevance; or the need to care full-time for an ageing relative may have reawakened interest in the war through listening to the relative's reminiscences about the war years. With so many 'worthy' social, political and environmental issues that people 'should' be thinking about, war memories cannot (perhaps 'should not') always be of top priority in people's daily lives. War memories assume different levels of importance depending on the individual, time, place and circumstances.

This chapter contextualizes Japanese war memories within the 'long postwar'. 'Since a government paper on the economy first declared in 1956 that "the postwar is over," the end of Japan's *sengo* (postwar) has been reported many times, all to great exaggeration and little avail' (Gluck 1991: 73). The 'long postwar' can be divided into four key phases:

1   *Occupation*, 1945–52, when the administration of Japan (and therefore control of public war narratives of the government and media) was in the hands of the victors.
2   *Japan's return to the international community*, 1952–72, when Japan regained political autonomy, restored diplomatic ties with its neighbours and achieved its current territorial boundaries with the return of Okinawa in 1972.
3   *Up to the end of the Shōwa era and '1955 System'*, 1972–93, when there was a growing focus on Japanese aggression in Asia (precipitated mainly by comparisons with the Vietnam War and the restoration of relations with China), Emperor Hirohito's death (1989) revitalized the debate concerning the emperor's war responsibility, and the first non-LDP government since 1955 was established in 1993.
4   *Japan's contested war memories in the Heisei era*, 1993–2005, when the passing of the war generation and concern over the 'weathering' *(fūka)* of memories have taken place against the backdrop of economic and social uncertainty in the post-bubble economy and the search for Japan's global role as the world's number two economy.

Occupation, 1945–52

Noon on 15 August 1945 has become the symbolic moment when the war ended. The Potsdam Declaration demanding 'unconditional surrender' had been accepted on 14 August, Allied bombing continued until the afternoon of 15 August, the Soviets' occupation of Japan's Northern Territories continued into early September, and the surrender was officially signed on 2 September; but nevertheless, Emperor Hirohito's exhortation in a radio broadcast for his people to 'endure the unendurable and bear the unbearable' has become the mythical beginning of the postwar (Satō 2005: 74–88).

When the war ended, Japan was exhausted and in ruins. Of the 3.1 million Japanese who had died, 800,000 were civilians (International Society for Educational Information 1994: 353). On the home front, years of rationing had left people hungry, air raids had reduced most cities to ashes, and few families had been untouched by bereavement. Three million Japanese civilians in Japan's colonial territories faced repatriation, loss of their possessions and vengeance at the hands of bitter, liberated colonial subjects (Orr 2001: 156). The remnants of Japan's military had been decimated by suicide attacks, disease and battle deaths. Hundreds of thousands of troops surrendered to the Allies, and over 600,000 soldiers and civilians caught up in the Soviet advance in Manchuria were led off for years of internment in Siberian labour camps.

Within this context of desperation lay the seeds of Japan's much maligned 'victim mentality'. Japanese people have been widely criticized for portraying themselves as victims of a war in which the Japanese military had inflicted upwards of 20 million deaths – over six times the level of Japanese casualties. However, numerically speaking, the people who had been in a position to perpetrate the crimes of the Japanese military constituted a relatively small proportion of the population. At the end of the war, there were 5.47 million Japanese in uniform, of whom 2.94 million were in the home islands, Korea and Taiwan (Igarashi *et al.* 1999: 450). Adding all military dead (2.3 million) and wounded, approximately 8 to 9 million Japanese had seen active service. Apart from the military and the 3 million civilians who lived overseas, the remainder of Japan's population of 75 million saw the war from the home front. Many had wholeheartedly supported the war effort, and some (such as overseers of slave labourers) bore personal responsibility for war crimes; but for the vast majority of people, their personal experiences came to be defined predominantly in terms of bereavement, hunger, air raids and defeat.

However, to portray the years immediately after the war as a period of undiluted self-pity would be misleading. According to Irmela Hijiya-Kirschnereit, 'On the whole, the early postwar years were tinged by a strong progressive current, which also reflected the fact that Japanese intellectuals had regained contacts with the international scene' (Hijiya-Kirschnereit 1991: 103). Freed from wartime censorship, the occupation era saw a 'hunger for words in print' (Dower 1999: 180). Despite the shortage of paper, hundreds of new magazines were launched and provided a platform for intellectuals of all persuasions to contemplate defeat and Japan's future. In this atmosphere Iwanami Publishing Co.'s monthly magazine *Sekai* was born in 1946 (ibid.: 180–7). To this day, *Sekai* remains a key publisher of essays critical of Japanese war conduct and responsibility by progressive scholars.

Furthermore, as the censors of public discourse and with their War Guilt Information Program (WGIP), the occupying Allies disseminated their version of the war. The Japanese military had attempted to cover up many of its crimes by burning incriminating documents immediately after the surrender, but with the high publicity given to the International Military Tribunal for the Far East (Tokyo War Crimes Trials) and the confessions of some of the returning soldiers, knowledge of Japanese atrocities became widespread after the war.

Shocked by these revelations, many Japanese were openly critical of the military immediately following defeat. Returning soldiers were often treated as 'pariahs in their native land'. '[M]any ex-servicemen found themselves regarded not just as men who had failed disastrously to accomplish their mission, but also as individuals who had, it was assumed, participated in unspeakable acts' (ibid.: 60). In many cases this reaction contained an element of denial or could be argued to be duplicitous. '[D]enouncing the nation's war acts while maintaining a discrete silence on personal involvement' was the 'safe course' immediately after the war (Orr 2001: 23); and the feelings of superiority towards the rest of Asia that underpinned Japanese imperialism remained widespread after the war (Yoshida 1995: 52–3).

Overall, the prevailing mood was of defeat and despair, and even guilt for war crimes could be turned around into victim mentality. There was a substantial process of 'Remembering the Criminals, Forgetting Their Crimes' (Dower 1999: 508–21), or recasting the perpetrators of Japan's war crimes as victims. In *Testaments of the Century* (1953), a collection of the last words of executed war criminals, many cast themselves as victims who 'ha[d] lacked any real control over the events in which they participated' (ibid.: 518). Furthermore, some families waited up to ten years for their relatives to return from Siberia during which time their internment metamorphosed from punishment to victimization. And for those coming to terms with what their relatives had done, revelations of atrocities committed by loved ones did not change the fact that they were loved ones. Being the close relative of a perpetrator can itself be a form of victimhood.

SCAP (Supreme Command for the Allied Powers) played a central role in the formation of Japanese war memories during the occupation. Some policy decisions have had long-term ramifications.

First, there was the decision not to try the emperor for his role in the war. By absolving the emperor of war responsibility, those who had acted in his name were also absolved. But someone had to take the blame and so the military was deemed to have acted against the will of the emperor and the people. SCAP went to extraordinary lengths to ensure their designs for a democratic Japan with Hirohito as its constitutional monarch were not upset. These even included telling the defendants at the Tokyo War Crimes Trials what they could and could not say in their testimony, and coaching Tōjō Hideki on how to recant his testimony when he strayed from the agreed line (Dower 1999: 325).

The result was that two closely linked interpretations of war responsibility had emerged as the Tokyo War Crimes Trials drew to a close: the '*damasareta*' (we were tricked) and '*shidōsha sekininkan*' (leaders' responsibility view) (Yoshida 1995: 29–32, 54). In these views, Japanese people were not only victims of the horrors of war but had been victims of their own leadership, and the emperor had been powerless to curb the military. With the full complicity of SCAP, this was being taught to schoolchildren by 1947. A textbook for junior high school students about the new constitution stated:

> During this war, the emperor had a very difficult job [*gokurō wo nasaimashita*]. Under the old constitution, because the people who helped the emperor in the affairs of the state were not chosen by all the Japanese people, their views were different to the will of the people [*kokumin no kangae to hanarete*] and this situation eventually led to war.
>
> (Ministry of Education 1947: 28)

In other words, the Japanese people, and by implication the emperor as well, were innocent because they never wanted the war in the first place. Orr concludes:

> The ideology of Japanese victimhood evolved from the idea that the people had been innocent of the nation's various transgressions during the war. As most Japanese scholars argue, belief in this innocence was encouraged by the assignment of responsibility to the militarists – either individually, as in the Tokyo Trials, or generically as in textbooks and other reeducation media. . . . By disassociating the emperor from the wartime state, SCAP effectively created a history that united him with his people as passive agents in the face of an aggressive and manipulative state (and unintentionally made both its victim).
>
> (2001: 32–4)

Another crucial policy decision emerged as the cold war situation developed in Asia. With communists the new enemy, particularly in China, the scene was set for the 'reverse course', the U-turn from Japan as Pacific War enemy to cold war ally. Prosecuting militarists and purging them from public office became less important than purging communists. The 1949 'red purges' signalled the rehabilitation or 'depurging' of wartime politicians and bureaucrats, many of whom later returned to prominent positions in public life (Dower 1999: 432–8, 525). The purging of the political left, the most consistently critical voice regarding Japanese imperialism, was a setback to popular acknowledgement of Japanese actions. Ultimately, cold war realpolitik made pursuing the issue of Japanese war responsibility counterproductive for the victors: 'as the cold war intensified and the occupiers came to identify newly communist China as the arch-enemy, it became an integral part of American policy itself to discourage recollection of Japan's atrocities' (ibid.: 508).

A further significant policy decision was designating *Taiheiyō sensō*, 'Pacific War', the acceptable name for the conflict instead of the term used during the war, *Daitōa sensō*, 'Greater East Asian War'. This helped focus attention on the war in the Pacific since 1941 (namely, Japanese defeat and suffering at the hands of the Americans) rather than the war in China since 1937 (namely, Asian suffering at the hands of the Japanese). As Carol Gluck has argued, the Asian war came to be seen as the 'prologue to the main tragedy', the Pacific War from 1941 (Gluck 1993: 83).

In summary, the occupation of Japan, while remarkably humane given the years of vicious war that had preceded it, was a period when the opportunity for Japanese people to reflect on what their military had done was overtaken by cold war politics. Victim mentality had become firmly established, but while the widespread focus on the suffering of the Japanese can be argued to have contained an element of psychological denial regarding the military's atrocities, total defeat had created Japanese suffering on a large scale, too.

The sense of victimhood was enhanced by the interpretation of war responsibility promoted by the occupiers. Yet, even during the occupation, the contentious issue of to what extent Japanese people could view themselves as victims and to what extent they should view themselves as directly or indirectly responsible for Japanese aggression had begun to emerge.

Japan's return to the international community, 1952–72

The second phase of memory began in 1952 with the withdrawal of the occupation forces and the return of sovereignty to Japan. By this time, the cold war was raging most fiercely in neighbouring Korea, Japan's former colony. It was a cruel irony that while Japan avoided German-style partition into east and west camps, the Korean peninsula, having just gained its independence, was torn apart by cold war politics. In addition, Japan benefited greatly from Korea's tragedy because the *tokuju keiki*, the Korean War boom, kick-started Japan's postwar economic recovery as the Japanese economy mobilized to provide war *matériel* for the US-led UN forces.

The occupation formally ended on 28 April 1952. General Headquarters (GHQ) was disbanded and Japan regained its sovereignty under the government of Yoshida Shigeru. In effect, the occupiers left the government of Japan in the hands of the very elite that had fought the war. Yoshida had been an ambassador in London before the war, was a committed imperialist who displayed 'contempt for Asia', and had believed Japan should follow the British imperial model (Wakamiya 1999: 59–70). His pro-Anglo-American views made him an ideal cold war partner for the occupiers, but not the ideal choice for encouraging national reflection on the past. Indeed, Yoshida's government organized a national memorial service for the war-dead on 2 May, just four days after the end of the occupation. As one of the newly autonomous government's first actions, this was deeply symbolic. It raises the question of the extent to which the wartime/postwar elite was largely unrepentant and had been biding its time during the occupation, waiting for the opportunity to return to 'business as usual'.

Another reason to pose this question occurred later in 1952. Emperor Hirohito had renounced his divinity on 1 January 1946 and was recasting his image as an 'emperor of the people' during a series of tours around Japan (the last being to Hokkaido in 1954, Ruoff 2001: 204–11). On 16 October, he worshipped at Yasukuni Shrine, the spiritual home of Japanese militarism. Imperial worship at Yasukuni Shrine was a regular feature of newsreels in the final stages of the war (ibid.: 40). Hirohito had worshipped again on 20 November 1945 before SCAP's policy towards Yasukuni Shrine became clear in the Shintō Directive of 15 December 1945, whose purpose was

> to relieve the Japanese people from any compulsion to believe in or practice any religion sponsored by the state, to free them from the duty

of financially supporting such a religion, to prevent any future use of Shintō for nationalistic or militaristic ends, and to assist them in realizing the ideal of democracy.

(Hardacre 1989: 136)

SCAP had considered abolishing Yasukuni Shrine altogether and there was even support for the idea among ordinary Japanese, but abolishing religious sites sat uncomfortably with the 'freedom of religion' planned for the constitution. SCAP eventually opted for stripping Shintō shrines of government patronage (Yasukuni Shrine became an autonomous religious organization on 3 April 1951) and the constitutional separation of religion and state. In this context, Hirohito's worship so soon after Yasukuni Shrine had been stripped of government patronage and so soon after the end of the occupation (as well as the six subsequent times he worshipped between 1954 and 1975, all of which the Imperial Household Agency have claimed were 'private' visits) was also significant (Rekishi kyōikusha kyōgikai 2002: 56–68). Both the governmental and imperial commemorative acts in 1952 indicate the significant pre- to postwar continuity, not only in personnel but in attitudes, within the ruling elite.

The 1950s saw the stabilization of Japanese politics under the dominance of the conservative LDP and Japan's commitment to the American camp in the cold war. The LDP was formed in 1955 through the merger of the Liberal and Democratic parties and the '1955 system' endured until 1993. The LDP's long dominance of Japanese politics has been based on its management of Japan's economic recovery, its skilful sharing of the profits and benefits from pork-barrel politics among key voter groups (particularly in rural areas over-represented in the Diet, Japanese parliament), its fund-raising capabilities through ties to big business, and the inability of smaller opposition parties to mount a united front and thereby present a realistic alternative in a voting system that has heavily favoured large parties. Within the cold war environment, the LDP also received significant support from the US. Consequently, while war issues have rarely been major voting issues (although the Izokukai, War Bereaved Association (WBA), lobbies on issues such as war pensions and Yasukuni Shrine commemoration and has strong ties to the LDP – Tanaka *et al.* 1995: 194–205), conservatives have maintained a grip on the official narrative.

Many members of the wartime ruling elite re-emerged within the political establishment after the occupation purges. In 1957, Kishi Nobosuke, a vice-minister for munitions in the war cabinet (who therefore bore direct responsibility for slave labourers shipped to Japan), was elected prime minister, allegedly with the aid of CIA funds (Weiner 1994). Kishi's transformation from class A war criminal suspect released from prison in 1948 to trusted ally given the privilege of making the ceremonial first pitch at a Yankees, game in 1957 was remarkable. It indicated how deeply Japanese war responsibility issues became buried in cold war politics. The US's payback came in 1960 when the US–Japan Security Treaty reconfirmed Japan's full membership of the Western camp. Kishi railroaded the treaty through the Diet despite enormous popular protest (Smith 1997: 25–8).

Whereas the relationship with the US remained central to Japanese diplomatic strategy, the 1950s and 1960s were also a period of re-establishing diplomatic ties with neighbouring countries, signing treaties and paying reparations. Japan joined the United Nations in 1956, and between the 1951 San Francisco Treaty and 1972 restoration of bilateral relations with China, Japan concluded treaties and paid reparations to most of the countries it had fought or occupied (Utsumi 2002: 96–103; Tanaka 1994: 51). Only peace treaties with Russia and North Korea remain elusive. In Russia's case this is because of the unresolved Northern Territories issue,[1] although the 1956 Joint Statement pledged to work towards a resolution. In North Korea's case, high-level contacts had barely existed before Prime Minister Koizumi's historic visit to Pyongyang in 2002, but in the wake of the ongoing nuclear weapons issue and unresolved abductions issue,[2] a peace treaty is not on the cards at the time of writing.

On the domestic front, Japanese cultural representations of the war were now free from the constraints of the occupiers' censorship. Some artists had even delayed projects to avoid censorship, such as Imai Tadashi, whose film about the student nursing corps in Okinawa, *Monument to the Himeyuri* (*Himeyuri no tō*, 1953) became Tōei Studio's most commercially successful film to date (Hirano 1996: 107). Television was still in its infancy: NHK started television broadcasting in 1953 but it was not until after the wedding of Crown Prince Akihito in 1959 and the Tokyo Olympics in 1964 that most people owned televisions. The 1950s was the age of cinema, and 'antiwar films' (*hansen eiga*) dominated for the first ten years after the war (Hamada 1995: 227). The antiwar films of the early 1950s usually had little serious self-criticism of Japanese aggression and focused more on Japanese victimhood. This changed with *The Human Condition* (*Ningen no jōken*, 1959–61, three parts), based on a Gomikawa Junpei novel which broke 'new ground with its grim descriptions of Japanese atrocities perpetrated on Asians and on fellow Japanese' (Orr 2001: 107).

By contrast, the period from the mid-1950s saw the production of many conservative films. In 1953, *Eagles of the Pacific* (*Taiheiyō no washi*) signalled the start of the 'nostalgia films' boom (Yomota 2000: 140). The 'nostalgia films' eulogized the military (particularly the air force and navy) and had a counterpart in publishing in the first 'war memoir boom', *senkimono būmu*. According to Yoshida Yutaka, thirty-six war memoirs were published in 1945–49, but 215 were published in 1950–56 with a peak of sixty in 1956 (Yoshida 1995: 85). Yoshida attributes the war memoir boom to an attempt to regain pride in response to the inferiority complex many Japanese people felt vis-à-vis the US. Most of the memoirs were of the heroic exploits of the navy and pilots rather than the atrocities committed by the army and gave the 'impression' of the 'rehabilitation of nationalism' (ibid.: 86). The war memoir boom also crossed over into the world of manga (comics) in the late 1950s (Natsume 1997: 30–44).

However, not all the memoirs were conservative, including the most famous memoirs of the day, *Kike wadatsumi no koe* (*Listen to the Voices from the Sea*), the memoirs of university students drafted to fight after 1943. The memoirs were edited by professors at Tokyo University and sold a quarter of a million copies between 1949 and the second edition in 1959 (Nihon senbotsu gakusei kinenkai 1995: 308). A 1950 screen version was seen by ten million people (Hosaka 2002: 56). The memoirs were antiwar and idealized the young intellectuals plucked from their studies only to die in Japan's desperate last stands as the war ended. However, conservatives and some relatives of the student-soldiers charge that the memoirs were selectively edited to suit the Marxist ideology of the editors, particularly through the editing-out of pro-military sentiments (ibid.: 44).

The second postwar phase of memory, therefore, is characterized by a swing to the right in the domestic political environment and popular representations of the war. This did not mean that progressives had disappeared or been silenced. Progressive films such as *Ningen no jōken* (1959–61), literature (for example, *Umi to dokuyaku*, *The Sea and Poison* (Endō 1958), about vivisection, see Chapter 7) and ongoing critiques of the war by progressive intellectuals such as Maruyama Masao proliferated within cultural life. Marxist histories also sold well and '[i]t was in 1956 that the prominent intellectual Tsurumi Shunsuke introduced the term "fifteen-year war" in order to draw attention to Japan's aggression against China over the period from 1931 to 1945' (Trefalt 2003: 70). The conservative vs progressive ideological rifts within Japanese memories of the war were already evident in the 1950s, although conservatives seemed to be gaining the upper hand as the cold war deepened.

The conservatives' upper hand was perhaps most visible in education, where the now stable and rehabilitated conservative ruling elite increased its control over the contents of school textbooks. Textbooks during the occupation had famously had their nationalistic parts inked out, but once the occupiers had departed, moves to expunge more progressive statements increased. In 1955 and 1956, there was the first of the three major 'textbook offensives' (the others being in the early 1980s and late 1990s – Rose 2006: 131) by conservatives against 'slanted' (and in the 1990s 'masochistic') textbooks. Textbooks became noticeably more conservative in this period, which Orr calls 'The Apologist Interlude: 1957–Early 1970s' (Orr 2001: 89–97). In this environment, Ienaga Saburō started his famous court battles for the right to include accounts of Japanese atrocities in Japanese textbooks (Ienaga 2001; Nozaki and Inokuchi 2000; Hicks 1997; Buruma 1995).

The high-point of nationalist historiography in this second phase of memory came in the 1960s, when Hayashi Fusao's *Affirmation of the Greater East Asian War* (serialized in *Chūō kōron* between September 1963 and June 1965) became the first major academic defence of Japan's wars. Hayashi viewed the war as the culmination of Japan's 100-year war to rid Asia of Western colonialism, a war that had started in 1845 when the US first demanded that Japan open up to trade and Russia started encroaching into Sakhalin (Fujioka 1997: 74).

But while some battled over the interpretation of war history, for others the war was still continuing. Whereas millions of Japanese had been repatriated in the first years of the occupation, others took much longer to get home. The process of repatriation has continued throughout the postwar: many *zanryū koji*, war orphans left in China, returned in the 1980s and 1990s, and one war-displaced man even returned in 2006 (www.japantimes.co.jp 3 July 2006). But in the 1950s, the main issues were the return of internees from Siberia, army stragglers (who managed to evade capture for years after the war) and the recovery of remains. Whereas the stragglers frequently became curiosities as people stuck in a time warp of outdated, militaristic ideals (Trefalt 2003: Chapters 3–5), the Siberian internees had been detained without trial and endured forced labour in freezing conditions: their stories were easily incorporated into victim consciousness. The last ship carrying Siberian internees returned to Japan on 26 December 1956. Of the 609,448 internees, 61,855 had died in captivity (Horie 2001: 31, 61).

Nuclear issues also became a focal point for narratives of victimhood. Japanese people have felt they can take a stand on nuclear testing as citizens of the only country to experience atomic attack. In March 1954, the 'Lucky Dragon incident', when a Japanese fishing boat became contaminated with radiation after an American nuclear test, fired anti-nuclear activism. Godzilla, an icon of Japanese cinema, was a product of this anti-nuclear environment and exemplifies how war-related issues could be represented on a metaphorical as well as literal level; or, in Igarashi Yoshikuni's phrase, there was an 'absent presence of the country's war memories' (Igarashi 2000: 3). Godzilla was a monster from the deep awoken by a nuclear test and the first Godzilla film was released in November 1954, eight months after the 'Lucky Dragon incident' (ibid.: 114–22). Further examples of metaphorical treatment of the war could be found in the work of Tezuka Osamu, the 'god of comics' (Schodt 1996: 233–74). Tezuka experienced the Osaka air raids (Tezuka 1997: 51–65) and his manga in the 1950s (particularly *Kurubeki sekai*, *Next World*, 1951) contained apocalyptic visions of the end of the world that set a trend for other manga artists (Natsume 1997: 12–27).

Initially, anti-nuclear activism was associated with progressivism more than conservatism. It was not until the 1960s that Hiroshima became a nationwide component of war memories. The feeling that Hiroshima had suffered no more than other cities destroyed by bombing, discrimination against *hibakusha* (A-bomb victims) largely based on medical fears of the long-term effects of radiation, and the prominence of leftist and progressive elements in anti-nuclear activism all slowed Hiroshima's path to becoming a national symbol of victimhood. Orr concludes:

> Ibuse [Masuji's novel] *Black Rain* capped the hegemonic cultural construction of Hiroshima in the 1960s. But it was Yasui [Kaoru's]

political domestication of antinuclear pacifism in the 1950s that laid the foundation for Hiroshima to become the premier enduring icon of Japanese war victimhood in the nation's pacifist heritage.

(Orr 2001: 70)

Black Rain's idealized setting in a 'wholesome', traditional, rural environment gave a politically acceptable face to Hiroshima's victimhood for Japanese conservatives (ibid.: 132–3). *Black Rain* allowed Hiroshima to stop being solely the iconography of left wing pacifism and become a national symbol of victimhood. Against the background of increasing numbers of nuclear tests and the intensifying cold war, the Hiroshima Peace Memorial Museum opened in 1955 and the Hiroshima Dome (the ruins of the Hiroshima Prefectural Industry Promotion Hall) became a listed building in 1966 (Fujiwara 2001: 34).

By the mid-1960s, therefore, conservatism and victim mentality were more conspicuous features of Japanese war memories. However, progressivism remained a force and four events in the second decade of the period (1963–72) played key roles in the ultimate establishment of progressive or progressive-leaning views as the majority popular opinion in Japan.

First, on 15 August 1963 the inaugural government-organized National Ceremony for the Commemoration of the War Dead (*zenkoku senbotsusha tsuitōshiki*) was held. This established 15 August as the mythical 'end of the war' and the focal point of official and media commemorations. At this ceremony in 1993, 'both prime minister Hosokawa and Speaker of the House Doi Takako won popular support by explicitly offering condolences not just to the Japanese but, for the first time, to the war's victims in Asia as well' (Wakamiya 1999: 28). Such condolences to Asian victims have since become standard, ensuring a permanent place at the centre of Japanese official commemorations for non-Japanese victims.

The second and third events were the restoration of bilateral ties with South Korea in 1965 and China in 1972. The treaty negotiations included discussions about reparations and ensured a renewed focus on Japanese actions in Asia. Furthermore, Japan had restored bilateral ties with the two most sensitive observers of Japanese historical consciousness. Diplomatic protests from Seoul and Peking about Yasukuni worship, textbook content and nationalistic statements by politicians have become the most internationally recognizable aspect of 'the history issue' (*rekishi mondai*). They ensure continual media attention on how 'Japan', officially and collectively, remembers the past.

Fourth, the return of Okinawa in 1972 by the US established the current geographical boundaries of Japanese war memories. Whereas memories of the Battle for Okinawa had been narrated in various Japanese cultural forms before 1972 (such as films about the Himeyuri nursing corps), strictly speaking, Okinawan narratives had been outside Japanese war memories. In any case, many Okinawans consider their culture and history to be distinct from people in the 'mainland' (*naichi*), and some Okinawan war memories border on treating 'Japan' as the enemy. For example, former Okinawa Governor Ōta Masahide calls the incorporation of the Ryūkyū kingdom into Japan in 1879 an 'annexation' (*heigō*, the same term used for the annexation of Korea) and argues Okinawa was used as a 'pawn' to save 'Japan proper' (Ōta 1996: 48–50). Such sentiments, combined with stories of Okinawans being executed for not using standard Japanese and the horrific group suicides of people indoctrinated into believing they would be treated with savagery by the Americans, have meant that support for the conservative official line in Tokyo is very low in Okinawa (Ishihara 2001: 88). So whereas the return of Okinawa brought another major narrative of victimhood (the over 200,000 mainly civilian victims of the Battle for Okinawa) back into the boundaries of Japanese war memories, it also brought in more narratives about the cruelty of the Japanese military.

In summarizing this second phase, Japanese conservatives, many of whom had played a prominent role in the war, consolidated their grip on domestic political power as the cold war deepened. Through economic growth, postwar treaties, repatriation and the return of Okinawa, by 1972 Japan had almost completed its physical and economic reconstruction and assumed virtually the same geopolitical conditions that exist today. Reconstruction also continued on a psychological level, in the need to refind a sense of national purpose and national pride. Conservative histories – whether in war memoirs, nationalist histories or textbooks – were part of this process. But as Japan's economic recovery proceeded, particularly in the 1960s with the 'income doubling' plans and the consumerism sparked by the affordability of new goods such as televisions and refrigerators, economic growth dominated the national agenda (along with its costs in the form of environmental pollution). Sport and culture also played a part in the restoration of national pride, from the exploits in the ring against American opponents of professional wrestler Rikidōzan (Igarashi 2000: 122–30) to the Tokyo (1964) and Sapporo (1972) Olympics and the 1970 Osaka Expo. But all the while, narratives of victimhood remained prominent and Hiroshima had emerged as the iconic symbol of Japanese suffering in the war.

To the end of the Shōwa era and '1955 system', 1972–93

As Japan entered its third phase of memory, the Vietnam War dominated the international agenda. Anti-American sentiment, stemming largely from popular opposition to the US–Japan Security Treaty, was widespread during the 1960s. Using the pacifist language of both the constitution (Article Nine, the 'renunciation of war' clause) and anti-nuclear and antiwar rhetoric within the Hiroshima narrative, many Japanese were critical of American policy in Vietnam. Japanese criticism of American actions, however, exposed what Yoshida Yutaka calls a 'double standard': pacifist criticism of the Vietnam War co-existed with a largely conservative domestic environment in which Japan's own war actions were not being fully acknowledged (Yoshida 1995: 127–34). Nonetheless, by offering a comparison with Japanese aggression in Asia, the Vietnam War became a catalyst for more Japanese to consider the nature of Japanese war responsibility.

Much of the impetus for rethinking Japanese war actions came from the postwar generations. By 1970, the baby-boom generation of 1947–49 had come of age and people in their twenties became the largest demographic group (Igarashi *et al.* 1999: 579). In 1976, the postwar generation passed the watershed of comprising over 50 per cent of the population. The mid-1970s, therefore, were a turning point: the balance between the war memories of the war generation and the cultural memory of the postwar generations was at its most delicate, and members of the baby-boom generation were young adults capable of questioning their parents' war conduct. However, the negotiation and narration of war memories within the family is fraught with risk, particularly when cultural narratives of war deal with issues of guilt and responsibility. Many parents still found it difficult to discuss the war with their children in the postwar generations (Yoshida 1995: 132).

Nevertheless, the ageing and passing of the war generation coincided with a marked increase in published testimonies about the war. Activists and historians became more proactive in collecting and preserving the memories of the war generation 'before it was too late', while many members of the war generation felt a greater need to tell their own stories as they entered old age and considered their mortality and legacies. The collection of testimony accelerated in the 1970s. This in turn formed the basis of the 'peace museum' boom in the 1980s and 1990s (ibid.: 154–6) as local governments with cash to spend during the peak of Japan's economic prosperity established museums, many of which were dedicated to preserving local memories.

The vast majority of testimony focused on Japanese victimhood (such as air raids and Siberian internment) and there was continued interest in military memoirs as in the 1950s. However, memoirs detailing Japanese atrocities increased too, sometimes semi-fictionalized or in novel form. In the 1970s, two books by Senda Kakō about the 'comfort women' (women recruited or forced to work as prostitutes for the Japanese military) sold half a million copies (Kobayashi *et al*: 1999: 41). Then, Morimura Seiichi's *Akuma no hōshoku* (*The Devil's Gluttony*, 1981) placed the Unit 731 issue in mainstream war debates. 'A powerful work of fiction based on extensive research', it described the human experiments carried out on 3,000 mainly Chinese prisoners. Morimura was already a well-known novelist, but this book caused a sensation and sold 1.5 million copies (Harris 1994: 116, 116ff.).

Into the 1980s, an increasing number of soldiers started confessing their parts in atrocities, such as Azuma Shirō, whose testimony of massacre, rape, decapitation and pillage in China appeared with other soldiers' testimony in the late 1980s (Lewis and Steele 2001: 41–7; Buruma 1995: 129–35).

The Chinese Returnees Association became the key group of soldiers confessing to war crimes. It was formed in 1957 from the 969 soldiers who were interned in Fushun prison in China, underwent 'ideological education' and returned to Japan in 1956. The group's first testimony collection was published soon after their return, but most testimonies appeared after the 1970s, and particularly through the 1980s and 1990s (Chūkiren 2004). The testimonies are typically graphic and harrowing accounts of war crimes (see p. 162, *Rīben kuizu*; Hoshi 2002). They are personal *mea culpas*, but the Chūkiren has also been active in promoting Sino-Japanese reconciliation (Rose 2005: 36–7).

The explosive impact of vivid testimony of Japanese atrocities has made verification of testimony a key battleground in war history debates. Nationalists have counteracted the confessions of Chūkiren members through accusations that the soldiers were brainwashed by the Chinese (for example, Kobayashi 1998: 183–94). Other soldiers who have confessed to atrocities have received death threats (such as Azuma – see Buruma 1995: 134) or been subjected to concerted academic or legal campaigns by conservative historians wishing to discredit the soldier's testimony. One well-known case concerns the memoir *My War Crimes* (1983) by Yoshida Seiji, in which he claimed he had participated in the abduction of Koreans for work as slave labourers and 'comfort women'. In 1996, Yoshida was forced to admit he had fabricated parts of his story (he claimed it was to protect people's identities) after a concerted investigation by conservative historians to discredit him. But his book caused a sensation and continues to be treated as broadly accurate (if 'inconsistent', *chiguhagu*, as Yoshida himself admitted) by supporters of the 'comfort women' (Fujioka 2000: 104–23).

The period also saw an increase in the prominence of Asian victims' testimony – whether in the media, in books translated into Japanese or as plaintiffs seeking justice in the courts. In this context, Honda Katsuichi's *Journey to China* (1972; see also Honda 1999), based on interviews with Chinese witnesses of the 1937 Nanking Massacre, was groundbreaking. It is widely seen as the trigger for the patriotic education movement that led to the 1982 textbook controversy. Since the 1970s, the Nanking debate has been a key ideological and historiographical battleground (see Fogel 2000) and the number of people killed in Nanking has become a litmus test of a Japanese person's historical consciousness. Nationalists ('deniers' such as Watanabe Shōichi and Tanaka Masaaki) argue it was a 'fabrication' with perhaps a few isolated crimes; conservatives (such as Hata Ikuhiko) place the number of those massacred at 13,000–40,000; while progressives (such as Honda Katsuichi and Kasahara Tokushi) argue that 130,000–250,000 were killed. The official Chinese figure is 300,000 (Fujioka 1997: 45).

Testimony of victimhood also captivated the public imagination, particularly the stories of war orphans in the 1980s. Thousands of Japanese children were left behind in China in the confusion at the end of the war. They were raised by Chinese adoptive parents, many of whom treated the children as their own, an extraordinary act of devotion given the Japanese military's actions in China and the risks associated with adopting a 'little Japanese devil'. War orphans started returning from China after bilateral relations were restored, but they started receiving Japanese government help in 1981 and in June 1982 the courts ruled the war orphans could have Japanese citizenship.[3] The heart-wrenching stories of children separated from their biological families and their tearful reunions nearly forty years later were broadcast on national television. People could empathize both with the sufferings of the orphans but also the heartbreak of the Chinese parents whose adoptive children returned to Japan. Both groups could be seen as victims still suffering from the war's legacy. The war orphans' stories fitted comfortably within Japanese narratives of victimhood, but they also increased understanding of Chinese perspectives of the war.

This increased prominence of non-Japanese testimony epitomized a critical feature of the third phase of memory: the internationalization of Japanese war memory and responsibility issues. Whereas contestation over war issues had continued within Japan from the moment the war ended, international scrutiny of Japanese historical consciousness and war responsibility debates was comparatively low. This all changed with the 1982 textbook crisis. Reports that the Ministry of Education had asked a textbook to change its wording from 'invasion' (*shinryaku*) of China to 'advance into' (*shinshutsu*) China caused a media debate and diplomatic crisis, even though it later emerged that no such revision had been made (see Rose 1998; Yayama 1983). This and subsequent textbook crises (1986 and 2001) have become one of the most internationally recognizable aspects of Japan's struggles with war history. However, while the international media typically portrays these crises as diplomatic spats in East Asia (see Seaton 2005), their roots lie in the conservative–progressive struggle to control a critical battleground for the country's collective memory: the education system.

Further international controversy erupted in 1985 when Prime Minister Nakasone worshipped in an 'official capacity' at Yasukuni Shrine on 15 August. This marked the internationalization of the Yasukuni issue after three decades of domestic controversy. Following the occupation, there had been repeated attempts by the WBA and conservative lawmakers to reinstate government patronage of Yasukuni Shrine and to make it the official centre of Japanese war commemorations (Hardacre 1989: 145–9). The cluster of unsuccessful bills introduced to the Japanese parliament in the early 1970s pre-empted a watershed in 1975: the last instance of imperial worship on 21 November 1975 (like the failure of the Diet bills, initially a result of popular opposition, but after 1978 a result of Hirohito's displeasure at the enshrinement of the class A war criminals – www.asahi.com 22 July 2006), and the emergence of the 'private vs official' worship distinction.

During the period 1951–75 there had been only five years when a prime minister had *not* visited Yasukuni Shrine. The visits occurred mainly during the shrine's spring and autumn festivals (Watanabe and Wakamiya 2006: 88–91). But Prime Minister Miki emphasized the 'private' nature of his visit on 15 August 1975 to reduce the fallout from the first ever prime ministerial worship on the war-end anniversary (Onoda and Nakajō 2006: 18–19). Thereafter, 'private' worship on 15 August became standardized: there were visits on 15 August in 1978 (Fukuda), 1980–2 (Suzuki) and 1983–4 (Nakasone). But Yasukuni worship became increasingly controversial after the enshrine-ment of the class A war criminals (on 17 October 1978) became public knowledge in April 1979. Nakasone's attempt to reinstate 'official' worship on a major anniversary at a shrine commemorating those found guilty of crimes against peace and humanity (verdicts officially accepted by Japan in the San Francisco Peace Treaty) took the controversy beyond a critical mass. The domestic and diplomatic storm forced Nakasone to shelve plans to worship the following year. It was not until Prime Minister Hashimoto's worship in 1996 that another prime minister ventured a public visit (although Miyazawa worshipped in secret in 1992 – Watanabe and Wakamiya 2006: 88, 90).

The textbook and Yasukuni crises in the 1980s, therefore, signalled a turning point. As a defeated nation, Japanese historical consciousness and commemoration had seemed of little international consequence. But with Japan as an emerging economic superpower, they became a high priority. Japan's growing economic dominance of Asia rekindled memories of earlier attempts at military domination. It became more important for Asian politicians to secure the 'right official noises about the war' from Japan. This resulted from concerns of new Japanese domination, ongoing resentment at Japanese war conduct, growing feelings that the past was being 'inadequately' addressed in Japan, and on occasions domestic political expediency – 'playing the war card'.

Meanwhile, in Japan internationalization (*kokusaika*, a buzzword of the 1980s) brought increased attention to the war's legacies. Growing interna-tional business and cultural interaction exposed more Japanese to other countries' views of the war. Overseas travel for leisure was not permitted until April 1964. In 1970 less than a million Japanese travelled overseas annually, but by 1990 nearly eleven million Japanese travelled overseas. There was a nearly fivefold increase in international marriages per year in the period 1970–90 (to 25,626 in 1990, mainly with other Asians). Exchange students (again, mainly Asian) studying in Japan rose tenfold between 1981 and 1993 (to 52,405 students). Exchange programmes flourished, such as the Japan Exchange and Teaching programme (JET), which started in 1978 and had placed over 5,000 mainly native English-speaking teachers in Japanese schools by the early 1990s. And increased business and tourism opportunities precipitated a fivefold increase in visitors to Japan, 1970–90, to 3.24 million (Asahi shinbunsha 2002: 37, 231, 252). All these aspects of inter-nationalization have contributed in varying amounts to raising Japanese consciousness of how Japanese people and Japanese war actions are viewed outside Japan.

However, economic growth not only advanced opportunities for acknowledgement of Japanese aggression, but it gave a new self-confidence to conservative narratives. The *nihonjinron* ('theories of the Japanese') boom of the 1970s eulogized the 'uniqueness' and special nature of the Japanese (Hijiya-Kirschnereit 1991: 106–8); and there was another war memoir boom in the 1970s aimed at Japan's 'corporate warriors', the salarymen. The self-sacrifice of the military for their country during the war became an inspirational metaphor for the self-sacrifice of salarymen for their companies (Yoshida 1995: 148–50). Perhaps the most internationally recognizable face of 'confident conservatives' in the third phase was former novelist Ishihara Shintarō (currently Governor of Tokyo). Ishihara's provocative *The Japan That Can Say No* (1989, co-authored with Sony Chairman Morita Akio) called on Japanese to assert themselves more and not to bow to international pressure. Whereas the book dealt primarily with economic issues, Ishihara's stance on the war was equally assertive and nationalistic: he called the Nanking Massacre a 'fabrication' in a 1990 *Playboy* interview (Lie 1993: 58–61).

Overall, while conservatives and nationalists remained strong within cultural life and maintained their grip on the official narrative, they were fighting a rearguard action against growing popular acknowledgement of an 'aggressive war'. It is a recurrent theme within Japanese war memories since the 1970s that nationalists become more outspoken as the tide of opinion seems to be moving towards acknowledgement of an aggressive war.

Coda: from Shōwa to Heisei, 1989–93

On 7 January 1989 Emperor Hirohito passed away. The man in whose name all Japan's military actions were carried out, but who was never held accountable, was no longer Japan's emperor.

The end of the Shōwa era (1926–89) precipitated a deluge of retrospectives. It also reopened the debate about the emperor's war responsibility. Hirohito himself was ambiguous on the subject, or tended to deflect his own responsibility. In 1975, for example, he stated that the dropping of the A-bombs was 'inevitable', which sidestepped the key issue of whether he could have used his imperial authority to end the war earlier. As the emperor's health deteriorated, debate over the his responsibility intensified within the general public. The incident that gained most attention was the assassination attempt on the mayor of Nagasaki, Motojima Hitoshi, by a right-winger on 18 January 1990. Motojima stated on 7 December 1988 (with the emperor only weeks from death) that he believed the emperor '[bore] responsibility for the war' and, in contradiction to the emperor's 1975 comments, the Battle for Okinawa and the attacks on Hiroshima and Nagasaki could have been avoided if the emperor had acted more decisively to end the war (Field 1991: 178–9).

The ongoing debate about Hirohito's war responsibility gave Emperor Akihito's stance on the war great significance. On a visit by South Korean President Roh Tae-woo in 1990, '[t]he emperor's statement acknowledged Japan's responsibility, distinguishing it from earlier imperial statements of regret' (Ruoff 2001: 152). Two years later, on his historic visit to China in September 1992, the first by a reigning emperor, he said:

> 'In the long history of the relationship between our two countries, there was an unfortunate period in which my country inflicted great sufferings on the people of China. I deeply deplore this.' [Kenneth Ruoff adds,] Emperor Akihito is said to have strengthened the final wording of the apology. Symbolic though his constitutional position is, the new emperor nonetheless has committed himself to a campaign to bring an end to the postwar era.
>
> (ibid.: 153)

Emperor Akihito's ascension, therefore, was a watershed. The figurehead of the Japanese people was no longer tainted by questions of personal war responsibility, and most worryingly for the emperorists on the extreme right, was going beyond his obligation to be merely an apolitical constitutional monarch: he had admitted responsibility and apologized for Japan's actions.

Also in 1989 was the fall of the Berlin Wall and the end of the cold war. The political framework that had required the rehabilitation of Japan's anti-communist conservatives during the occupation also collapsed. The end of the cold war coincided with the beginning of the six-year cycle (to 1995) of the fiftieth anniversaries of the major events of World War II (although the fiftieth anniversary of the start of the China War had already taken place). These anniversaries precipitated a scholarly and popular boom in war commemoration. The collapse of the 'East–West' global narrative of the cold war permitted a revisiting of 'Axis–Allied' frame during the fiftieth anniversaries commemoration cycle. This amounted to a reversing of the 'reverse course': Japan reverted from cold war ally to former Pacific War enemy.

Japan's relations with its cold war allies, particularly the US, entered a strained period with specific reference to war issues. At a popular level Japanese–American tensions had risen because of talk of 'Japan as number one' and trade friction during the 1980s, when American auto workers smashed Japanese imports and Michael Creighton's *Rising Sun* became a bestseller and later a hit film. The late 1980s and 1990s also saw the American academy and media become increasingly critical of how the Japanese had addressed the past following the general scholarly reluctance to criticize a cold war ally from the 1950s to 1970s, particularly when the relationship was presided over by scholar–diplomat Edwin Reischauer (Smith 1997: 25, 29). This is apparent not only in the proliferation of 'orthodox' texts (see Appendix), but also in the emergence of groups such as the Global Alliance for Preserving the History of World War II in Asia, whose campaigns also relate to growing global activism concerning human rights.

Japanese–American tension even began to appear in the usually strong relationship between the Japanese and American governments. The American government was stung by the Japanese government's refusal to send troops to the Persian Gulf in 1990–91 to help in the expulsion of Saddam Hussein's army from Kuwait. Despite a contribution of US $17.3 billion, the Japanese response to the Gulf War was heavily criticized in the US and Europe (McGregor 1996: 64–5). Then, later in 1991, as the fiftieth anniversary of Pearl Harbor approached, talk in Japan of an apology for Pearl Harbor foundered when President George Bush bluntly stated that he would not be considering an apology for Hiroshima (Lifton and Mitchell 1995: 222). These incidents illustrated the significance of the cold war in covering over deep official differences concerning war history. The commemoration cycle seemed to be reopening old wounds more than contributing to reconciliation.

The 1991 Gulf War profoundly affected Japanese war discourses, particularly concerning awareness of the media's role in popular views of war. The Gulf War marked a war-reporting revolution: embedded journalists, live pictures from the battlefield, and twenty-four-hour news coverage on satellite television. How the media reported the Gulf War attracted much attention. This in turn filtered into studies of the Asia-Pacific War. War history increasingly came within the boundaries of media and cultural studies: perhaps the best example is the work of University of Tokyo Professor Yoshimi Shunya, who is Japan's leading media and cultural studies scholar, as well as an active participant in war debates.

Activists from across the spectrum of Japanese opinion became more aware that the medium was as important as, if not more important than, the message. In the late 1980s and early 1990s, the most important new medium was the computer, which provided a new wave of cultural forms depicting the Asia-Pacific War: battle games, flight simulators in Pacific War scenarios, interactive media and eventually the Internet. Computer games in particular raise the issue of fantasy representations of the war: the essence of a computer game in a historical scenario is that history can be rewritten according to the game players' skills. Fantasy representations of the war also emerged in the growing market for 'simulation fiction': novels and manga in which Japan wins the war (see Chapter 7).

The media also played a key role in the eruption of the issue that probably more than any other defined the shape of Japanese war discourses in the 1990s: the 'comfort women' issue. Having previously denied responsibility for the sufferings of 'comfort women', the Japanese government was forced into an apology and humiliating policy U-turn when a scoop in the *Asahi* newspaper (11 January 1992) provided documentary evidence that the Japanese military had been 'involved' in the running of 'comfort stations', and thereby the coercive and abusive ways in which women had been recruited by and treated in Japanese military brothels. The second of two investigative reports released on 4 August 1993 confirmed the 'involvement' of the military and Foreign Minister Kōno restated the government's apology in one of the LDP government's last acts before losing power to Hosokawa Morihiro's anti-LDP coalition.

So, in August 1993, with the shocking testimony of sexual violence suffered by the 'comfort women' and the government's apology fresh in people's minds, in a new era with an emperor acknowledging Japan's responsibility, and with the momentous end of the '1955 system', the stage was set for Prime Minister Hosokawa to call the war an 'aggressive war and a mistake' on 10 August 1993. This was the high point of Japanese official acknowledgement in the postwar and an opinion poll found that 50 per cent agreed and 9 per cent basically agreed with Hosokawa's statement (Yoshida 1995: 3). Consequently, phase three can also be called 'Japan's path to official and popular majority acknowledgement of an aggressive war'.

Japan's contested war memories in the Heisei era, 1994–2005

The Heisei era, the reign of Emperor Akihito, began in 1989. Akihito had taken a decisively different line from his father that indicated imperial acknowledgement of Japan's responsibility. With the collapse of the '1955 system' in 1993, it seemed as if the 'long postwar' could finally end. But these thoughts foundered as war issues continued to provoke widespread domestic and international contestation even beyond the sixtieth anniversary of the war's end in 2005.

For progressives, the tenure of Prime Minister Hosokawa was a case of 'so near but yet so far'. After his 'aggressive war' comments on 10 August 1993, Hosokawa was pressured into backtracking by alarmed bureaucrats and politicians in his fragile coalition. In his inaugural speech on 23 August, Hosokawa toned down his 'aggressive war' comments by referring to Japan's 'aggressive behaviour'. There was also no change in the consistent Japanese official position that all compensation claims were settled in postwar treaties (McCormack 1996: 227). Nevertheless, Hosokawa's comments and subsequent apologies during his tenure were well received in Asia.

Hosokawa's anti-LDP coalition collapsed after only eight months. The LDP returned to government on 28 April 1994 as the dominant partner in Prime Minister Hata Tsutomu's coalition government. Hosokawa's 'aggressive war' comments were effectively retracted when Hata used the term 'aggressive acts' (*shinryaku kōi*, the stance that admits atrocities but downplays Japan's state-level responsibility) during parliamentary questions on 20 May 1994 (Yoshida 1995: 5). This retreat from 'aggressive war' to 'aggressive acts' cast renewed international doubt on Japanese reflection on the past. Furthermore, the Hata cabinet had only been in office a few days when Justice Minister Nagano Shigeto called the Nanking Massacre 'a fabrication' (see Chapter 4).

Nagano lost his job, but this and other nationalistic outbursts by politicians in the mid-1990s sent a message about nationalists' determination to prevent politicians like Hosokawa establishing a more progressive official view.

Hata's government lasted a mere two months. He was replaced by Social Democrat Murayama Tomiichi, whose personal views corresponded with Hosokawa's. Murayama led Japan during the fiftieth anniversary commemorations in August 1995, but his hands were tied by the fragility of his coalition, so he issued a personal apology (the Murayama communiqué, *danwa*) to supplement the official line of 'aggressive acts'. The parliament also attempted to formulate a joint statement to mark the fiftieth anniversary of the end of the war in May 1995. However, the statement was vague and evasive, and pleased nobody (see Chapter 4). It had been impossible to formulate a coherent statement that everybody could agree with.

But while the Japanese government's inability to issue a clear apology in 1995 angered many outside Japan, American commemorations of Hiroshima stirred emotions in Japan. In December 1994 a proposed commemorative stamp depicting the mushroom cloud was cancelled after Japanese protests (Dobson 2002: 32–3). Then the Smithsonian Museum's planned *Enola Gay* exhibit illustrating the effects of the bomb on Hiroshima's citizens was heavily criticized by veterans' associations in America. The *Enola Gay* exhibit went ahead, but 'the Japanese victims, and questions about the decision to use the atomic bomb, were nowhere in sight' (Lifton and Mitchell 1995: 296).

However, while Japan's national government struggled to offer a clear apology, local governments in Hiroshima and Nagasaki indicated more willingness to acknowledge Japanese aggression. When the A-bomb museum in Hiroshima was reopened after its renovation in 1994, the new exhibits offered a brief but nonetheless explicit acknowledgement of Japanese aggression and Hiroshima's war role as a military port. After describing how the people of Hiroshima celebrated the fall of Nanking with a lantern parade, the guidebook states:

> In Nanking, however, Chinese were being slaughtered by the Japanese army. Estimates of the number of victims have varied according to time and place from tens of thousands to hundreds of thousands. The Chinese government places the figure at 300,000.
> (Hiroshima Peace Memorial Museum 1999: 15)

Furthermore, Hiraoka Takashi 'was first among Hiroshima mayors to state in 1991 that there was no excuse for Japan inflicting "great suffering and despair on the peoples of Asia and the Pacific" during its reign of "colonial domination and rule"' (Tachibana 1996: 184). Hiraoka repeated his apology to a global audience at the ceremony commemorating the fiftieth anniversary of the Hiroshima attack (*The Times* 7 August 1995).

Overall, the fiftieth anniversary commemorations had exposed the ongoing disagreement about the war both within Japan and on a diplomatic level.

Then, barely six months after the commemorations had finished, Murayama's government fell. It demonstrated that Japan still did not have a party other than the LDP capable of sustaining itself in power, the prerequisite for effecting a fundamental and permanent shift in the official narrative. On 11 January 1996, the LDP regained control of the premiership with the formation of Hashimoto Ryūtarō's cabinet. There were no further opportunities for prime ministers with progressive sympathies to upset the delicate official compromise of 'remorse for aggressive acts' up to the sixtieth anniversary commemorations in 2005.

Nevertheless, Murayama's 1995 private apology did continue to be 'quoted by subsequent LDP cabinets (Hashimoto, Obuchi) as the definitive version of the apology' (Wakamiya 1999: 28–9). But as Gavan McCormack has argued, the *sincerity* of Japanese apologies is the key issue (McCormack 1996: 245). Hashimoto's reiteration of Murayama's private apology sat uncomfortably with his role as an ex-president of the WBA (Izokukai) and his 'private' worship at Yasukuni Shrine on 29 July 1996; and when Hashimoto's private apology (*owabi*) was issued in a letter to former 'comfort women' in 1996 to accompany payments from the Asian Women's Fund (set up in July 1995), the 'private' apology and compensation from a 'private' fund meant that most 'comfort women' felt they were not being offered the *official* apology they sought (Yoshimi 2000: 25). Japan's next prime minister, Obuchi Keizō (1998–2000), was an active supporter of Yasukuni worship and suggested to *Time* magazine that Emperor Hirohito should be nominated as the person of the century (Nelson 2003: 462), although he refrained from worshipping at Yasukuni Shrine during his tenure. Then, in May 2000, Prime Minister Mori Yoshirō's statement that Japan was 'a land of the gods' (*kami no kuni*) nostalgically referred back to the era of State Shintō. Prime Minister Koizumi Junichirō's annual visits to Yasukuni Shrine, 2001–06, merely confirmed the long-standing image that Japan's senior politicians are not issuing sincere apologies.

The government's official narrative and the actions of political leaders, however, are not necessarily representative of popular views on the war. Opinion poll data in the 1990s routinely indicated that Japanese people were critical of their government's handling of war issues. 'A 1994 survey, for example, found that 80 percent of Japanese polled agreed that the government "has not adequately compensated the people of countries Japan invaded or colonized"' (Dower 2002: 241). In public discourses, Japan's war memories were being contested with renewed vigour during the 1990s. This was largely because phase four, particularly between 1996 and 2001, saw a neo-nationalist backlash against the now stable popular majority who had accepted Japan fought a 'war of aggression'.

As in the 1970s when the Nanking Massacre debate precipitated a nationalist revival and a textbook crisis (1982), the tide towards popular and official acknowledgement of an aggressive war and the 'comfort women' issue in the early 1990s provoked a sharp response from nationalists that would culminate in the 2001 textbook crisis. Nationalists' campaigns overlapped considerably with a more general conservative social agenda sparked by malaise about the state of Japanese society: the bursting of the economic bubble, rising unemployment and a stagnant economy; the 1995 'twin shocks' of the Kobe earthquake and the sarin nerve gas attack on the Tokyo subway by the Aum shinrikyō cult; and a sense of social crisis over youth crime, 'classroom breakdown' and 'new' issues such as domestic violence and child abuse. Post-bubble Japan seemed to have lost its way. Conservatives were increasingly nostalgic about the war days and the economic miracle, when there were clear national missions, every citizen had a role to play, and hardships were endured as self-sacrifice for the greater good of the nation.

The most prominent nationalist group, Atarashii rekishi kyōkasho wo tsukurukai, the Japanese Society for History Textbook Reform (hereafter 'Tsukurukai') was formed in 1996. The intellectual father of the movement, Fujioka Nobukatsu, tried to present a 'third way' between what he called the 'Tokyo Trials view of history' (in which Japan was the bad guy) and the 'Asian liberation' view of history (in which Japan was the good guy – see Chapter 6). But the agenda quickly turned nationalistic: to eradicate mentions of the 'comfort women' from the school history curriculum and to replace 'masochistic history' (*jigyakushi*) with 'a history to be proud of'.

The Tsukurukai's campaigns culminated in 2001 when their textbook became one of eight texts approved by the Ministry of Education for use in Japanese junior high schools. The book caused widespread protest both inside and outside of Japan and the campaigns of progressives ensured that the book was only selected for use by a tiny proportion of schools: only 521 pupils, or 0.039 per cent, used the book from 2002 (Tawara 2001: 69). The Tsukurukai only marginally improved the acceptance rate in 2005 (its most notable victory being the textbook's adoption in Suginami ward, Tokyo).

Nevertheless, the Tsukurukai's campaigns succeeded in shifting the balance of content in some other textbooks to the right (ibid.: 66). Furthermore, the debates over patriotic education shifted to the Ministry of Education's ethics curriculum. The ethics textbook *Kokoro no nōto* (*Notebook of the Heart*), distributed for use in all elementary and junior high schools from the spring of 2002, was widely criticized by progressives for attempting to foster nationalism and reintroduce state-written rather than state-screened textbooks (Miyake 2003; Takahashi 2003a: 18–60). It contained topic headings (perhaps 'slogans') such as 'Loving our nation and hoping for its development' in conservative-sounding language: *waga kuni* ('our nation') is common rhetoric in nationalist histories.

Nationalists were also tapping a vein within popular cultural forms, and Aaron Gerow has termed nationalism in the 1990s 'essentially consumerist' (2000: 87). Kobayashi Yoshinori's manga *Sensōron* (1998) sold more than 700,000 copies and his other nationalist writings sold millions more. There was a nationalist revival in cinema with films like *Pride* and *Murudeka 17805* (see Chapter 7). There were progressive films too, although they did not capture nearly the same audience. The most progressive mainstream films were *Three Trips Across the Straits* (*Mitabi no kaikyō*, 1995) and *Asian Blue* (1995), both of which contained uncompromising depictions of the sufferings of Korean forced labourers in Japan (Schilling 1999: 144, 260).

These latter two films coincided with a greater consciousness of the forced labour issue during the 1990s. During the war, approximately 670,000 Koreans and 40,000 Chinese had been transported to Japan to work in construction and mining companies. Around 60,000 Koreans and 7,000 Chinese died in the brutal conditions (Dower 1986: 47). The Hanaoka incident, when labourers rose up against their 'employers' (Buruma 1995: 275–91), is particularly well known. Victims secured an apology from Kajima Corporation in 1990 and an out-of-court settlement in 2000, but this was just one of a number of lawsuits, most of which were unsuccessful (Rose 2005: 69–98; Utsumi 2002: 100–3). Yet such rulings are war responsibility and legal issues that reflect the government's policy. They are not indicative of Japanese war memories or a rejection of the plaintiffs' versions of events. For example, in a lawsuit brought by victims of Unit 731, the plaintiffs' claims for compensation were rejected, although the judges in the Tokyo District Court acknowledged the facts of the case and that the Japanese army had conducted biological warfare (www.bbc.com 27 August 2002).

This Unit 731 ruling coincided with other confirmations of the Japanese army's chemical weapons programme. Ever since the early 1990s, the Chinese government had been pressing the Japanese government to clear up abandoned chemical weapons. Then, in August 2003, the accidental discovery of chemical munitions killed one and sickened over forty in Heilongjiang province and put the issue high on the Sino–Japanese agenda once again (www.japantimes.co.jp 3 September 2003). Soon after, in November, the Environment Ministry published a report indicating that poison gas shells had been abandoned in 138 locations in forty-one of Japan's forty-seven prefectures (www.japantimes.co.jp 29 November 2003). These issues were in the Japanese media alongside the unsuccessful search for Saddam Hussein's alleged weapons of mass destruction (WMD) arsenal in Iraq, and generated significant negative attention for the Japanese military.

In response to issues such as chemical weapons clean-ups, the 'comfort women' and forced labourers, more Japanese lawyers, Non-Profit Organizations (NPOs) and activist groups have assisted Asian plaintiffs seeking justice through the Japanese courts, particularly since the 1990s. This is part of the global increase in awareness of human rights, which provides the basic rationale for those Japanese proactive in opposing their government's stance on apologies and compensation. In particular, feminist activists working on the 'comfort women' issue – such as Matsui Yayori, Suzuki Yūko and Nishino Rumiko – became key figures in war debates. As leading members of VAWW-Net Japan (Violence Against Women in War – Network Japan) they also organized the most significant progressive event of the decade: the Women's International Tribunal on Japanese Military Sexual Slavery. The tribunal was held in Tokyo from 8 to 12 December 2000 and pronounced Emperor Hirohito and the Japanese military guilty of crimes against humanity (Matsui 2003; Kim, P.J. 2001). Furthermore, feminists not directly involved in activism on behalf of former 'comfort women', such as Ueno Chizuko (Japan's leading feminist academic) found the 'comfort women' issue to be too central to Japanese feminism to ignore (see Chapter 6).

In short, the 'comfort women' issue electrified Japanese war responsibility debates and provoked the neo-nationalist backlash that ended in the 2001 textbook crisis. Whereas neo-nationalists gained much media and scholarly attention, progressives maintained the upper hand in war debates and public opinion: according to Sven Saaler, 'since the 1980s the proportion of Japanese subscribing to an affirmative view of the war has been an astonishingly stable 15 to 17%' (Saaler 2005: 163). Furthermore, debate gravitated towards war responsibility issues, which kept the focus on Japanese aggression in Asia. Main issues included whether postwar treaties had adequately addressed Japan's war responsibility, whether the postwar generations should bear any additional financial burden of compensation for the war generation's actions, or whether those victims of the war most deserving and in need of compensation had actually received it. Alongside the debates about 'war responsibility' (*sensō sekinin*), debates about 'postwar responsibility' (*sengo sekinin*) emerged as the postwar generations tackled the complicated legacy of the war generations' actions (for example, Takahashi 1999).

Coda: 2001–05; or prologue, 2001– ?

The summer of 2001 was one of the most intense periods of national debate over war issues in the entire postwar. The textbook crisis coincided with the first of Prime Minister Koizumi's annual Yasukuni Shrine visits (13 August 2001) and soured diplomatic relations in East Asia. Then, the 11 September 2001 terrorist attacks and the start of the so-called 'war on terror' precipitated another shift in the global master-narrative framing Japanese war discourses.

The 'war on terror' precipitated a rerun of processes seen during the occupation red purges and the 'reverse course'. In the Japanese–American partnership there was a new common enemy, (Islamic) terrorism, to replace the common enemy of the cold war, communism. During the occupation, the US rehabilitated the conservative political elite to secure Japan as a cold war ally. The cold war order collapsed in 1989 and there was a revisiting of the Axis–Allied frame during the 1990s. After 9/11 there was a new alliance against terrorism. Those right-wing Japanese politicians who caused most antagonism in the 1990s for their unwillingness to accept the victors' version of Asia-Pacific War history became those with the most stomach to turn Japan into a fully fledged military partner of America in the 'war on terror'.

For hawks in the LDP, the 'war on terror' has provided an environment conducive to their plans to remake Japan into a nation capable of playing a global political and military role. These plans have come a long way since the

1991 Gulf War. In 1992, the first step was taken towards an active overseas military role with the dispatch of peacekeepers to the UN mission in Cambodia; in August 1999, the Japanese flag (*Hi no maru*) and national anthem (*Kimi ga yo*) were made the official flag and anthem despite widespread unease both in Japan and the rest of Asia regarding their imperialist connotations; and the 'war on terror' provided the context for the most important move thus far: the dispatch of Self Defense Forces (SDF) to Iraq in 2003. It was the first overseas deployment of Japanese troops without a UN mandate since 1945. Other aspects are ongoing (in 2006), including moves to revise the constitution – which in practice means the removal of Article Nine (the 'renunciation of war' clause) and the reclassification of the SDF (*jieitai*) as an 'army' (*jieigun*) – and attempts to secure a permanent seat on the UN Security Council.

The most controversial aspect of the conservative project in the new millennium is renewed prime ministerial Yasukuni Shrine worship. Koizumi's annual worship since 2001 has made the Yasukuni issue central to contemporary Japanese war debates. The issue has divided Japan almost down the middle between those in favour of and those opposed to Koizumi's worship. Despite these domestic debates, diplomatic relations in East Asia have plummeted to new lows over the issue. The opportunities for partnership and reconciliation brought by co-hosting the 2002 FIFA World Cup with South Korea and Japan's massive trade links with a resurgent Chinese economy (by 2004, China was second only to the US in importance as a trade partner) have been overtaken by diplomatic rows over history. These disputes were exacerbated by territorial disputes over small uninhabited islands (such as the Dokdo/Takeshima dispute) and disputes with China over gas drilling rights. Anti-Japanese sentiments boiled over in parts of East Asia and were widely broadcast in Japan – such as the August 2004 'booing' incident (when the Japanese football team was heckled during the Asian Cup in Chongqing) and anti-Japanese riots in China in April 2005. When an official Chinese apology for damage caused by rioters to Japanese businesses and consulates was not forthcoming, the spiral of mutual antagonism worsened.

This rising anti-Japanese sentiment in South Korea and China was leapt upon by conservative commentators in Japan. In books, magazines and on television they went on the offensive about South Korea's and China's own 'distorted' views of history, particularly in 'anti-Japanese' textbooks. The anti-Korean tone was significantly offset by the *kanryū* (Korean) boom as Korean television dramas and their stars like Bae Yong-joon enjoyed huge popularity. But nevertheless, the real roots of the problem, the 'history issue' and Koizumi's Yasukuni worship, showed no sign of being resolved. Prime Minister Koizumi stubbornly defended his Yasukuni worship, saying that Yasukuni worship was an internal affair, and continued to worship annually despite growing domestic and international concern.

As the sixtieth anniversary of the end of the war approached, therefore, commemoration of the war had caused the worst diplomatic relations in East Asia for a generation. Elsewhere in the Japanese media, however, the mood was of concern about the 'weathering' (*fūka*) of memories. Realistically, 2005 was the last major anniversary in which significant numbers of the war generation were able to participate in commemorative events. The generational transition from war memories to cultural memory was approaching its final stages: by 2005, people over 65 (who could be expected to have some personal memories of the war years) were under 20 per cent of the population; the average age of A-bomb survivors was 73; and in 2005, for the first time no mother or father of a victim of the war was able to attend the official ceremony on 15 August.

Concern over the 'forgetting' of the war was exacerbated by two incidents at the Hiroshima Peace Park in 2003 and 2005 that seemed to epitomize the perceived 'crisis of remembering'. On 1 August 2003, a student disgruntled at not getting a job set alight and destroyed 140,000 origami cranes left at the Peace Park.[4] And on 26 July 2005, a right-winger tried to chisel off the word 'mistake' from the inscription 'the mistakes of the past will not be repeated' (*ayamachi wa kurikaeshimasen*) on the Cenotaph for the A-Bomb Victims.[5] These acts of vandalism at one of Japan's most 'sacred' sites of commemoration caused much consternation about how the war was being 'forgotten'.

The sixtieth anniversary was marked with many major events and retrospectives (see Chapter 5). But, the anniversary was overshadowed by another event that illustrates the point made at the beginning of the chapter: war memories are an issue of *prioritization* in relation to all other narratives within a society. Koizumi had staked his political reputation on his postal privatization bill, and when the bill was defeated in the Upper House on 8 August 2005 after some LDP members voted against the government, Koizumi called a snap election. The sixtieth anniversary commemorations were largely superseded by discussion of the election in the media. As 15 August 2005 approached, the country was more focused on where Japan was heading and who would lead Japan beyond the sixtieth anniversary rather than the anniversary itself.

Conclusions

This chapter has described some of the transformations within Japanese war memories over the 'long postwar'. From the moment the war ended, the meanings and legacies of Japan's war conduct have been the source of widespread, ongoing debate within Japan. Indeed, the fact that memories remain contested helps to account for the ongoing prominence of war discourses within contemporary Japan.

This chapter has also stressed generational shifts (the transition from war memories to cultural memory) and the technological changes within the public field of representations. The print media (newspapers, books, manga and magazines), the official position (such as government statements and textbooks), radio and cinema have been a permanent presence in the public field of representations in the postwar, although radio and cinema have seen declines in their relative importances with the development of television since the 1950s. Museums proliferated in the 1980s, a decade which also saw the beginning of the computer age, and into the 1990s the explosion in the number of satellite and digital television channels and the spread of the Internet have given public voices to many who were previously excluded from public discourses. More recently, the Internet has made the uncensored (or unedited) expression of views possible to a global audience and constitutes a major development within the field of public representations, although the more 'trustworthy' sources of information – such as NHK, academic scholarship and the quality broadsheets – remain the key sources of war-related information for most Japanese.

But despite the generational transformations, the constants within Japanese war memories over the whole of the postwar have been their contested nature and the inability of the Japanese people to establish a dominant cultural narrative of the conflict. The primary cause of these memory rifts is competing ideological interpretations of Japanese war responsibility, but this chapter has also indicated the significant international context of Japanese memories, which is the topic of the next chapter.

3 'Addressing the past'

'Japan' has been frequently accused of 'failing to address the past'. However, 'addressing the past' (or any of its variants such as 'facing' or 'overcoming' the past[1]) is a somewhat unhelpful concept: it rolls together issues of memory and responsibility, and blurs the distinctions between official, collective and individual narratives. This is particularly evident in many 'orthodox' texts, where arguments concerning Japan's 'official failure to address war responsibility issues' have frequently spilled over into assertions about inadequate Japanese remembering. Furthermore, accusations about Japan's failure to address the past have frequently overlooked both the complicity of the international community in those failings, and the extent to which the agendas and preconceptions of international observers of Japan have obscured those instances in which Japanese people have tried to address the past.

State-centredness: the official narrative and its importance

In July 2005, a Japanese Ministry of Foreign Affairs (MOFA) pamphlet outlined the official Japanese position concerning war history and reparations:

> During a certain period of the past, Japan followed a mistaken national policy and caused tremendous damage and suffering to the people of many countries, particularly to those of Asian nations, through its colonial rule and aggression. Japan squarely faces these facts of history in a spirit of humility. With feelings of deep remorse and heartfelt apology always engraved in mind, Japan, underpinned by its solid democracy, has resolutely and consistently strived for peace by adhering to a strictly defensive security policy, preventing the escalation of international conflict, and dedicating itself to international peace and stability by mobilizing all its available resources. It has adhered to the Three Non-Nuclear Principles. During these 60 years, Japan has never resorted to the use of force. . . . After the end of World War II, Japan renounced all rights, titles and claims to Korea, Taiwan, the Kurile Islands, a portion of Sakhalin, and other territories, and accepted the judgments of the

International Military Tribunal for the Far East (Tokyo Trial), in which 25 Japanese leaders had been convicted of war crimes. Many other Japanese were convicted in other war crimes courts. Japan has dealt with the issues of reparations, property and claims, in accordance with the San Francisco Peace Treaty, the bilateral peace treaties, agreements and instruments. Japan paid reparations to Burma, Indonesia, the Philippines and Vietnam, while others waived them. After the normalization of its relations with the Republic of Korea, China and other countries, Japan extended a substantial amount of economic cooperation. With the parties to these documents, the issues of reparations, property and claims, including the claims by individuals, have been settled legally.

(Ministry of Foreign Affairs 2005)

If this document is taken at face value, Japan has officially accepted war responsibility, continues to issue a clear apology, and has fulfilled all its legal obligations to pay reparations and compensation. Japan has fully addressed the past: case closed.

But books, articles and websites related to Japanese war responsibility issues reveal a palpable anger among a wide variety of groups – from the media and scholars to human rights groups such as Amnesty International – at what they argue to be Japan's failure to address war responsibility issues. Perhaps the strongest challenge was the McDougall report, submitted to the UN Commission on Human Rights. The appendix, 'An analysis of the legal liability of the Government of Japan for "comfort woman stations" established during World War II', concluded:

[T]he Japanese Government remains liable for grave violations of human rights and humanitarian law, violations that amount in their totality to crimes against humanity. . . . [T]he Japanese Government's argument that Japan has already settled all claims from Second World War . . . remains . . . unpersuasive. . . . [A]nything less than full and unqualified acceptance by the Government of Japan of legal liability and the consequences that flow from such liability is wholly inadequate.

(McDougall 1998: Clauses 68–9)

In recent times, the 'comfort women' issue has stirred deep emotions and much anti-Japanese sentiment. The issue illustrates the centrality of the official narrative and policy in perceptions of how Japan has addressed war responsibility issues, and by extension whether 'Japan' has 'addressed the past'. Acknowledgement of Japanese aggression and war crimes by a majority of Japanese people (according to opinion poll data) has been insufficient for promoting the image that 'Japan' has addressed the past: the argument can still be made that even if the people have acknowledged, they have failed in their democratic task to make their political representatives acknowledge, too.

According to Japan's critics, *official* acknowledgement and apologies are necessary. However, when the Japanese government apologized to the 'comfort women' in August 1993, it was welcomed by victims' groups only until it emerged that compensation would be 'unofficial', via the Asian Women's Fund set up in July 1995. From this it can be deduced that an official apology *backed up by official compensation* is the key to satisfying ongoing international demands for Japan to face its war responsibility. But there is a further condition: no other official acts should send a contradictory message about the sincerity of apologies and compensation. Despite issuing a number of apologies, Prime Minister Koizumi's Yasukuni Shrine worship since 2001 has precipitated the frostiest diplomatic relations and greatest public anger in East Asia for a generation. Such conflicting messages cast doubt on the sincerity of any apology, and thereby nullify its effect.

In short, 'apology nullification through nationalist gestures by officials' is the key concept in explaining why 'Japan' is widely perceived to have inadequately addressed the past. This reveals the state-centric nature of the 'orthodoxy', which privileges the actions of officials over public opinion or cultural memory.

This state-centric orthodoxy means that Japan is trapped in a vicious circle and will probably never be deemed to have adequately addressed the past. Furthermore, the international community has contributed to trapping Japan in this situation. First, Japan's compensation policy is either supported or not challenged by most governments and is therefore unlikely to change. Second, the Japanese–American alliance is integral to the political strength of Japanese conservatives. And third, international observers have frequently marginalized and undermined Japanese progressivism, and by doing so, empowered conservatives within Japanese war debates. These are the topics for the next three sections.

Human rights vs state rights: international backing for Japan's compensation policy

Through the 1950s, 1960s and 1970s, Japan signed peace treaties and paid reparations (or had reparations waived) to almost all of the countries that it had occupied or invaded. Most of these treaties contained clauses saying that the compensation issue had been finally resolved by those treaties, and this remains the Japanese official position. If Japanese compensation has been 'inadequate', therefore, to some extent responsibility also lies with the other signatories to the treaties. The 'lenient' levels of compensation (particularly at San Francisco), however, have a historical context. The Versailles Treaty of 1919 demonstrated how excessively punitive postwar treaties can lay the grounds for future conflict. In Japan's case, preventing a resurgence of militarism or a backlash against the harshness of the postwar treaties were key aims. With hindsight, the strategy was successful but possibly taken too far:

in time even a small majority of Japanese public opinion has come to see Japanese compensation as inadequate.

Particularly since the 1980s, victims' groups have come to feel that whatever treaties their governments had signed, their individual sufferings had gone uncompensated. These campaigns were accompanied by growing human rights activism challenging the legal basis of state-level reparations that saw very little, if any, money going to those most directly affected by Japanese aggression. From the 1980s and 1990s, 'comfort women', slave labourers and other victims have made belated attempts for justice in the Japanese courts and to set precedents in international law for individuals to win compensation from foreign governments. The Japanese government has maintained its right to settle reparations at a state level in postwar treaties and turned down all compensation requests. The Japanese compensation issue, therefore, is not simply a case of a nation's inability to address the past. Criticizing Japanese compensation levels also disputes states' rights to negotiate all-encompassing reparations treaties that preclude further lawsuits by individuals; conversely, maintaining the rights of states to conclude such treaties means concluding (as conservatives do in Japan) that Japan has fulfilled its legal obligations, making the 'adequacy' of Japanese compensation academic.

Furthermore, despite the upsurge in lawsuits and anger against Japan, international governments have generally stood by the Japanese government. The US government's support of Japan's compensation policy was explicitly stated by Secretary of State Colin Powell at the fiftieth anniversary of the San Francisco Peace Treaty in 2001 (*Asahi shinbun* 9 September 2001) and plaintiffs seeking justice through the American courts have fared little better than in the Japanese courts (Rose 2005: 80–1). For example, in October 2001 an American judge rejected a compensation case against the Japanese government brought by former 'comfort women'.

> The judge, Henry Kennedy Jr – while acknowledging the suffering of the women – rejected their arguments that Japan was liable in the case. Lawyers for the women, who were seeking to set a legal precedent, filed an immediate appeal. Both the Japanese and US governments had argued for the dismissal of the case. A US Government statement said the American courts lacked jurisdiction because Japan still had sovereign immunity from prosecution.
>
> (www.bbc.co.uk 5 October 2001)

On 6 October 2003, the US Supreme Court put an end to appeals for compensation by former POWs and slave labourers against Japanese corporations. In 1999, a Californian state law had extended the statute of limitations to 2010. This effectively gave victims the right to sue Japanese corporations if the corporations operated in California. The Japanese government, supported by the US government, had opposed the claims. The Supreme Court ruled that federal law overrode state law, so the American national policy of barring claims by US citizens against Japan took priority (*Daily Yomiuri* 8 October 2003).

While American support is proactive, most other governments have taken a 'hands off' approach and avoided involvement in lawsuits brought by their citizens. The British government is unwilling to help British POWs' claims (www.bbc.co.uk 29 April 1998); in 1996 the Indonesian government cited the 1958 treaty, the adverse social effects of massive compensation windfalls to individuals, a preference for compensation that benefits the whole community, and the feelings of the people (there is still much appreciation for Japanese soldiers who fought alongside Indonesians in the war against the Dutch after 1945) as reasons for not helping 'comfort women' plaintiffs (Fujioka 2000: 282–4); and even regarding claims made by Chinese victims of biological warfare, 'The Chinese government has been silent on the issue, not blocking the movement but not helping either. It fears damage to its relations with Japan' (McNaught 2002). In other words, with the key exception of South Korea – which waived the rights of both 'the state and its people' (*kuni oyobi sono kokumin*) to seek additional redress in 1965 (Tanaka 1994: 59) but since August 2005 has started pressing the Japanese government over 'legal responsibility' (namely, compensation) (www.korea.net 27 August 2005) – most governments tacitly accept or openly support the Japanese compensation position.

This situation can be attributed partly to practical concerns. Thousands of war victims all seeking compensation individually would place huge burdens on global legal systems to verify the facts of each case, try them, dispense justice and accommodate any appeals procedures. Understandably, states prefer state-level postwar treaties that settle all claims collectively and finally.

In addition, Japan has become too important a trade partner and aid donor for governments to take a confrontational stance with Tokyo. Japan is the world's largest donor of Overseas Development Aid (ODA) with a 20 per cent share of global ODA, 1994–2003. Since 1954, 60 per cent of Japan's 230 billion dollars in ODA has gone to Asian countries. It is difficult to verify whether Japanese foreign aid to Asia has been tacitly understood to be 'reparations by another name', although the Ministry of Foreign Affairs stressed the 'substantial amount of economic cooperation' beyond reparations in its discussion of the 'Postwar Settlement' (Ministry of Foreign Affairs 2005). If Japanese ODA is considered a form of reparations (although it could be viewed as a carrot to keep the compensation issue closed), it adds a different dimension to arguments about Japanese compensation levels.

Furthermore, states with active militaries (such as the US, UK, Indonesia and China) have much to fear if legal precedents are set for states to be considered liable for conventional war crimes committed by their armed forces in lawsuits brought by individual plaintiffs. So, despite the fact that most people would think victims of Japanese biological warfare are deserving of compensation, world governments can see the benefits for themselves in the Japanese government's resolute position and in defeats for plaintiffs, such as in a 2002 ruling on Unit 731 atrocities when 'The [Tokyo District Court] ruled that under international law, individuals had no right to seek compensation from a state' (www.bbc.co.uk 27 August 2002).

Japan's compensation policy, therefore, is not simply a case of 'Japan's inability to address the past'. The Japanese government adheres rigidly to the wordings of the postwar treaties, is backed or not opposed by most governments (except South Korea), and follows what might be called the 'pragmatic norms' of other states in preferring state-level reparations. Whether the Japanese government is acting sensitively and creating goodwill towards Japan is another issue entirely; and whether such 'pragmatic norms' are 'legal' or 'illegal' is an aspect of law on which highly qualified legal minds around the globe disagree, with politics probably being the main source of disagreement. The net result is that beyond international and domestic public opinion and pressure from human rights activists, there is little concentrated pressure on Japan to change policy. Even a stable progressive Japanese government would be hard pressed to change the compensation policy without the support of principal allies (particularly the US). That seems unlikely, given the wider vested interests involved.

In sum, the compensation issue in Japan is part of a wider global legal battle of 'human rights vs state rights',[2] in which the ability of individuals to sue foreign governments for war crimes is the central issue. The lack of significant state-level pressure on Japan to change policy shows that most governments around the world have recognized their own interests in the Japanese government's resolute 'all claims are settled' policy.

The role of American policy

South Korean and Chinese protests at Japanese historical consciousness have become the most publicized aspect of the 'history problem' in East Asia; but the Japanese conservative political elite, whose views provoke so much of the anger, owes much of its power and survival after the war to American government policy. Apart from the first few years of the occupation and a period of tension in the 1990s, the American government has been less concerned with Japanese acknowledgement of aggression and more concerned with developing a reliable ally in East Asia. As discussed in the previous chapter, the cold war precipitated the rehabilitation of the wartime elite and a policy of covering up Japanese atrocities (such as the amnesties given to Unit 731 researchers in exchange for their data – Harris 1994); and in its support for and covert funding of the LDP, the American government has been an accessory to the Japanese government's official narrative and responses to war responsibility.

In recent times, the two Japanese prime ministers who have enjoyed the most cordial relations with their American presidential counterparts are those who have caused most anger in Asia with their Yasukuni worship. Nakasone Yasuhiro, whose 'official' worship at Yasukuni Shrine in 1985 internationalized the Yasukuni issue, was half of the 'Ron-Yasu' relationship with Ronald Reagan that capped a golden era of leadership harmony (despite trade friction) between Japan and America in the 1980s. The 'Dubya-Jun' relationship between George W. Bush and Koizumi Junichirō has shown similar cordiality (despite a damaging dispute over BSE and beef imports) in the 2000s.

Koizumi's popularity with the Bush administration needs little explanation: Koizumi, like Bush, is a political hawk and sided unambiguously 'with America, not against America' in the so-called 'war on terror' (including sending SDF troops to Iraq). In return, Koizumi received American backing for his wider agenda to return Japan to the fold of military powers, revise the Japanese constitution and to become a permanent member of the UN Security Council. In August 2004, US Secretary of State Colin Powell supported Koizumi's aspirations but stated that Japan must consider revising its pacifist constitution and specifically Article Nine (the 'renunciation of war' clause) if it wants a permanent seat on the UN Security Council (www. bbc.co.uk 13 August 2004). This call for the annulment of the *American-written* constitutional barrier to Japan becoming a military power again is a direct assault on the position of many Japanese progressives who cherish Article Nine.

Furthermore, the American government's reluctance to intervene in the Yasukuni issue tacitly supported Koizumi's worship. Again, this was driven purely by self-interest. Revocation of Article Nine, official Yasukuni worship and permanent Security Council membership for Japan are all part of the same agenda: making Japan into a military power again, a development the US government is promoting. Regular official Yasukuni worship formalizes the commemorative processes by which the 'precious sacrifice' (*tōtoi gisei*, Koizumi's stock phrase) of Japan's *military* war dead is honoured. As Takahashi Tetsuya argues, the commemoration of the fallen from previous wars is necessary to make people willing to lay down their lives for the nation in future wars (Takahashi 2003b: 41). In other words, Yasukuni worship lays the psychological groundwork for future sacrifice, the revocation of Article Nine would make military deployment constitutional, and permanent membership of the UN Security Council would give international legitimacy to Japan's renewed military role.

Consequently, American official policy is to not condemn Yasukuni worship. After Koizumi's fifth worship in October 2005, even when the furious reaction in Asia had become clear, the official 'rebuke' from State Department spokesman Sean McCormack was, 'We would hope that countries in the region could work together to resolve their concerns over history in an amicable way and through dialogue' (www.iht.com 20 October 2005). According to John Tkacik, an analyst at the neo-conservative Heritage Foundation, 'there is a very palpable feeling among a lot of U.S. policy makers that China is basically picking its scabs on the Yasukuni shrine thing – that this doesn't need to be an issue and the Chinese are making it an issue' (ibid.).

Overall, American policy, particularly since 9/11, has been unambiguously helpful to Japanese conservatives. The American government supports the Japanese government on compensation (even concerning claims by US citizens), is in favour of renouncing the pacifist element of Japan's constitution, does not condemn worship at Yasukuni Shrine where all the war criminals executed by the Allies (and officially accepted to be war criminals by Japan under the terms of the San Francisco Treaty) are enshrined, and is actively pushing for the remilitarization of Japan. Some American neo-cons have even suggested that Japan should arm itself with nuclear weapons to confront the North Korean threat, a proposal that horrified many Japanese. Given that all of these are (or would be) viewed as a 'failure to address the past' if pursued unilaterally by the Japanese government, the complicity of Japan's most important ally in that 'failure to address the past' becomes stark.

It is too simplistic to portray the American and Japanese governments always conspiring together. Whatever support the American government has given Japanese conservatives has been driven by realpolitik and self-interest rather than by considerations of Japanese war memories. Whenever the agenda in Japanese–American relations turns to one particular topic, the A-bombs, the divisions remain extremely deep. However, in a paradoxical way, even ongoing American official justifications of the A-bombs have served to help Japanese conservatives.

The uses of atomic weapons against Hiroshima and Nagasaki in August 1945 remain two of the most contentious events of twentieth-century history. Nevertheless, US presidents have never and can never consider an official apology. An apology for using atomic weapons to end the 'good war' would render America's entire nuclear arsenal 'immoral'. Defending the A-bombs is a prerequisite for morally justifying America's ongoing possession of nuclear weapons, so for the American government the bombs were necessary to ensure unconditional surrender and to 'save lives'. Of course, not all Americans subscribe to this official, 'orthodox' line. There is a revisionist view that stresses the role of bureaucratic pressures and the 'message to Stalin' as other considerations in Truman's decision, as well as a compromise view that synthesizes the 'orthodox' and 'revisionist' positions (Bernstein 1996: 40–1).

Nevertheless, any 'orthodox' American justifications of the bombs, whether official or unofficial, are highly provocative for the Japanese. In the postwar, President Truman frequently defended his decision with the phrase 'I'd do it again'. But as Robert Jay Lifton and Greg Mitchell argue:

> Years after the atomic bombings people in Hiroshima were more angered at this kind of statement than by Truman's original decision to drop the bomb. As much as they deplored the weapon and viewed it as criminal, some expressed understanding of how it might be used under the pressure of war; but to speak more or less detachedly of using it again was to dismiss

what victims had been subjected to and reject human lessons of the weapon.

(Lifton and Mitchell 1995: 176ff.)

Official A-bomb justifications and the refusal to issue an apology anger Japanese opinion across the political spectrum, but they also act to jam Japanese official apologies (such as in 1991 – see Chapter 2). More significantly, American refusals to issue an official apology give conservatives and nationalists in Japan a trump card: 'why should we apologize when others do not?' Many people, such as nationalist manga artist Kobayashi Yoshinori, ask simply: 'Why was Nanking a crime but not Hiroshima?' (Kobayashi 1998: 44–5). Progressives have also compared Hiroshima and Nanking, or even Auschwitz and Hiroshima, but face the problem of convincing Japanese people to accept a perceived double standard: Japan must apologize for its war crimes even though the Allies refuse to apologize for what, in Japanese eyes, is their major war crime.

'The orthodoxy' and Japanese war memories

In the English-speaking world, scholars and journalists can have quite different agendas concerning war issues to the policies of their governments. For example, in contrast to the US government's avoidance of any rebuke over Koizumi's Yasukuni Shrine worship in 2005, *The New York Times* blasted it in an editorial as a 'pointless provocation' (*New York Times* 18 October 2005). As Ishizawa Yasuharu has argued, the American media tends to side with the Chinese and South Korean governments on issues such as textbooks and Yasukuni Shrine worship, and while newspaper article content frequently contains a measure of balance, headlines are often critical (Ishizawa 2004: 116–18). This pattern also exists in the British media: Japanese war issues usually make the British media at times of controversy (namely, nationalistic 'apology nullification' by officials), which fixes the image of 'Japan does not address the past' in the media consumer's mind; war issues such as textbook controversies and Yasukuni worship are framed as 'Japan vs China and South Korea', which homogenizes Japanese views and makes the government's position seem representative; and progressive views opposing the conservative officials are marginalized and implicitly treated as 'un-Japanese' (Seaton 2005).

However, while the English-language media is critical of Japan, it frequently fails to point out the complicity of international governments in Japan's 'failure to address the past'. For example, a *Los Angeles Times* report (9 September 2001) about the San Francisco Treaty fiftieth anniversary commemorations in 2001 completely ignored Colin Powell's endorsement of Japan's compensation policy. The headline was 'Japan falls short on war apology' and the article quoted angry former POWs pursuing their claims for apologies and compensation without ever mentioning that the Japanese government had the backing of the US government in opposing their claims.

The critical tone pervades the academy, too. The polemic is usually (but certainly not always) more restrained, but there is a structural bias that encourages negative assessments of how Japan addresses the past: an over-focus on Japanese nationalism. Nationalism, textbooks, the conservative ruling elite and Yasukuni Shrine worship are all important topics and there is much excellent scholarship, but given the balance of opinion in Japan, research into progressive ideology or the reasons why progressive(-leaning) public opinion outweighs conservative–nationalist views is conspicuously limited. Concerning the 2001 textbook crisis, for example, a vast literature has developed concerning the nationalist textbook written by the Tsukurukai and the diplomatic disputes it caused. The progressive campaigns that so vehemently opposed the textbook and ensured its widespread rejection, by contrast, have received far less attention.

In short, the overall tone of English-language representations of Japanese war issues in the media and academy is critical. It is a given that Japan's wars were aggression, the 'comfort women' were victims of orchestrated and large-scale human rights abuses, and that the Japanese government should do more to address war responsibility issues. Such views are not necessarily unwelcome in Japan, given that they concur with many Japanese people's views. The problem comes when foreign commentators are deemed to be hostile or uninformed: the tone quickly shifts to 'rebuttal of Japan-bashing'. Ishizawa, for example, singles out *The New York Times'* Nicholas Kristof (see also Appendix) and describes how editors of *Japangu* (a monthly magazine produced by Japanese residents in New York) compiled a book 'to show how full of mistakes' his reports were (Ishizawa 2004: 121); and Midori Yūko is similarly critical of British journalism in her book *Japan in the UK: stereotyped, misrepresented, misunderstood,* a book that focuses heavily on war issues (Midori 2004). Rather than make Japanese people respond to the impassioned appeals to more fully address the past, therefore, error-prone or seemingly hostile polemic tends to provoke rebuttals based in 'how the west stereotypes and misrepresents Japan'.

Overall, critical state-centric polemic ('the orthodoxy') probably assists nationalists (and conservatives) more than progressives in Japanese domestic war debates. First, by portraying the views of conservatives and nationalists as the more 'representative' of Japanese opinion, the orthodoxy effectively endorses the claims of conservatives and nationalists that they are the 'true Japanese' and represents progressives as 'un- or anti-Japanese'. Second, ideas need exposure for them to become empowered and accepted, so the marginalization of progressives in the orthodoxy weakens progressives by reducing the prominence, 'newsworthiness' and understanding of their views. And third, critical texts, particularly if they are mistake-laden, provide ammunition to nationalists to pursue a favourite form of spoiling tactic: discrediting the whole by discrediting a part. The research in Iris Chang's *The*

Rape of Nanking (1997), for example, has been widely criticized (concerning casualty figures and her portrayal of Japanese culture – Gibney 1999: xii–xiii; see also Appendix) and nationalists delighted in picking it apart and casting it as 'Japan-bashing', even though its powerful evocation of the *nature* of the atrocity in Nanking was correct. Ultimately, progressives had to distance themselves from Chang's book for fear of losing credibility.

The proponents of the English-language orthodoxy, therefore, and Japanese nationalists and conservatives are 'strange bedfellows'. They rely on their mutually antagonistic positions for the headline-grabbing confrontation that helps them to maintain their prominent positions within the international media and their respective public discourse communities. It would be hard to make a case that the English-language orthodoxy has had any decisive effect in empowering conservatives in Japan, but similar processes are visible regarding the similarly critical South Korean and Chinese 'orthodoxies'. Taken together, the broader significance of 'hostile interference' or 'counterproductive criticism' becomes apparent.

These arguments, it should be stressed, are not a call for reduced international scrutiny of the way Japan addresses the past. They are intended to illustrate that the way in which criticism of Japan is made has profound implications for its effectiveness, and why so much international criticism seems to have fallen on deaf ears. Progressives are typically ignored in the criticisms or must distance themselves from hostile, 'stereotypical' representations; conservatives and nationalists, meanwhile, gain prominence, have their ideas rebroadcast to a much wider audience, and have an adversary whose 'anti-Japanese' stance requires continual rebuttal; and across the board there is a feeling that many making the criticisms are displaying not a little hypocrisy or criticizing Japan for reasons of domestic political expediency.

Culturally deterministic approaches

With the perception that Japan has 'inadequately addressed the past' firmly established in English-language discourse, many researchers have sought to explain those failings by using sociological or anthropological arguments about the nature of Japanese society, what may be called a 'culturally deterministic' approach. This approach is based upon a well-established field of cultural analysis. There are countless books, articles and academic papers dedicated to demystifying 'the Japanese'. The penchant for analysing the Japanese is not limited to international observers. The Japanese display a strong appetite for self-analysis: books about Japan are regularly translated into Japanese and an entire genre of self-analytical writing, the *nihonjinron* (theories of the Japanese), has flourished particularly since the 1970s.

Outside of Japan, the *nihonjinron* have earned something of a reputation for being pseudo-scientific musings by nationalistic romanticists who make dubious claims about why the Japanese are unique and special. However, the scepticism concerning such arguments has not stopped similar rhetoric from appearing within the English-language literature. The standard arguments are that Japanese society is relatively homogeneous; it is a 'group society' in which allegiance to family, school and work groups are extremely important; the number of people crowded into a narrow mountainous archipelago and historical necessities of rice production made cooperation and harmony within the group imperative; there is a strong vertical hierarchy in which deference to authority is expected, and in which seniority and the *senpai–kohai* (senior–junior) relationship are valued over competitive meritocracy; and the importance placed on repetition, imitation or rote memorization in education, sports drills and the arts stifle individual creativity and promote conformity.

There is a large element of truth to these familiar generalizations about Japan. However, such cultural characteristics have typically been treated pejoratively and used to justify arguments regarding the inadequacy of Japanese remembering (see Appendix, particularly Paris and Chang/Barker). For example, the group nature of Japanese society, fear of ostracism, conformity and an unwillingness to challenge authority have frequently been cited as reasons why Japanese people are unable or unwilling to debate war history or to acknowledge Japanese war crimes. This is despite ample evidence of contestation in a variety of contexts within Japanese society (Krauss *et al.* 1984).

The fundamental problem with the 'harmonious Japan paradigm' (ibid.: 4) is that it applies Japanese cultural characteristics to the nation, which makes it inherently state- or nation-centric: the group is the nation, ostracism means being 'un-Japanese', and deferring to authority means believing what their political leaders tell them. However, Japanese people's identities do not work exclusively at the national level. When applied at the individual level, there is no contradiction between Japanese cultural characteristics and contestation.

The most important 'group' for a Japanese person is the family (*ie*). Deference to or respect for the elder members of the family place great significance on the war stories of relatives. Stories of family suffering are widespread and 'victim mentality' is a convenient narrative mode because it avoids the potentially painful rifts between family members that can occur if the discussion becomes too focused on issues of war actions and family member responsibility. 'Victim mentality' is more compatible with a 'war causes suffering' or 'war is bad' view, so the prevalence of 'victim mentality' in families and progressive-leaning public opinion in Japanese society does not provide any major contradictions either.

After elder relatives, the next most important authority figures are teachers at school and university. As in many countries, the education profession in Japan attracts many liberals dedicated to the nurture and expansion of young minds. Despite the overwhelming scholarly and media focus on right-wing textbooks and academics in discussions of Japanese history education, teachers, the people who really decide what is taught in the classroom, and their unions have a reputation for being more progressive (see Aspinall 2001: 40, 83). This helps to explain why nationalist historians launch their periodic drives for more patriotic education. Of course, many conservatives and nationalists work in education too, but the point is that deference to authority does not mean deference to politicians or nationalist academics who write controversial textbooks. It means deference primarily to older generations within the family, teachers and other role models such as *senpai* (seniors) or film stars. Japanese people can have war memories at odds with their government's official narrative, but still display characteristic Japanese patterns of deference to role models or authority.

The characteristics of a 'group society' also help to explain why contestation over war memories can be so fierce. Japanese society can be parochial and cliquey with members of groups devoting large amounts of their time to their groups (such as school and university circles who practise and socialize together day after day). War history contains numerous examples of factions and cliques, even within the most disciplined, nationalistic organizations: the imperial army and navy. The actions of these cliques – from violent coups in the 1930s to the army–navy squabbles over starting war with America in 1941 – showed little 'national harmony': on the contrary, they demonstrated how the cliques frequently served their own interests more than those of the nation.

In contemporary Japan, war memory cliques include the numerous activist or media groups who press for the adoption of their views within wider society. Fierce loyalty to groups with different agendas explains why contestation between those groups (nationalist textbook writers vs feminist groups, a liberal magazine vs a conservative magazine) can exist. Ostracism by a competing group is not feared as there is no strong attachment. Criticism of 'the other' can be blunt and there is little taboo against using words such as 'lies', 'brainwashed' and 'masochistic' in Japanese war debates. Personal attacks, smear campaigns and even death threats are also familiar. The important concept of harmony, *wa*, in Japanese society is displayed primarily towards those *within* the group with whom there are important day-to-day relationships. But even this does not prevent the existence of sub-groups, such as the *habatsu* (factions) within the ruling **LDP**, or squabbles and rivalries within groups active on war issues. The Tsukurukai (the nationalist textbook group), for example, experienced great internal upheavals (resignations and reshuffles) in response to the poor uptakes of its textbook in 2001 and 2005 (Tawara 2006). Arguments that 'the group' and 'harmony' within Japanese society prevent war debate is an orientalist myth.

In sum, supposedly 'Japanese characteristics' have been frequently employed as explanations for 'Japan's inability to address the past', but typically these characteristics have been applied to the nation as a whole rather than the individuals who make up that nation. When Japanese people are treated as individuals rather than as 'a homogeneous culture', there is no contradiction between concepts such as 'harmony', 'group society' or 'deference to authority' in Japan and the thesis of Japan's contested war memories.

This is not to say that Japanese culture has no role to play. Religion, for example, obviously infuses rituals of commemoration and mourning, which are central to war memories. Even here, however, the eclectic and pragmatic nature of Japanese religious practices (a person may visit a Shintō shrine to pray for good luck, have a 'Christian' wedding and a Buddhist funeral) indicates why a framework allowing for 'situational religious identities' is important.

Overall, it is my position that Japanese cultural characteristics provide shading and nuance to Japanese war memories, but the underlying processes are better explained by international war memory and media theory. Here, the Yasukuni issue provides a good example. On one level, Yasukuni 'worship' (*sanpai*) is a uniquely Japanese issue about how 'traditional beliefs' and Shintō practices of remembrance of the dead relate to mourning or the separation of religion and state in the Japanese constitution. At a more fundamental level, however, the Yasukuni issue is a universal one: every country commemorates those who have died in the nation's service. If *sanpai* is translated as the universalist and secular 'paying one's respects to the dead' (arguably the better translation given the three instances of 'worship' by Prime Minister Ōhira (see Table. 4.1 on pp. 88–91), who was a practising Christian – Kobayashi 2005: 20), the main issue becomes how the war dead can be commemorated when judgemental memories of their actions are so contested.

International comparisons

There have been numerous debatable comparisons drawn between Japanese war memories and those in other countries, particularly Germany. The most common Germany–Japan comparison in the English-language media concludes that (West/Reunified) Germany has done more to 'address the past' and is therefore a model for Japan (Yamazaki 2006: 115–26; examples include Paris 2000 and McCormack 1996 – see Appendix). This is the position also taken by many Japanese progressives (for example, Awaya *et al.* 1994). Japanese nationalists and conservatives, by contrast, have disputed the appropriateness of Germany–Japan comparisons, either by saying Japan has no war responsibility so such comparisons are meaningless (for example, Takeda 2001: 94–6) or by downplaying the 'model nature' of the way in which Germany has addressed the past (for example, Kisa 2001).

These few examples illustrate that comparison is wide open to manipulation. However, referring to the 1986 *Historikerstreit* (historians' debate) in West Germany, Charles Maier argues that comparisons are unavoidable in the field of historical memory:

> The only way the moral dimension can be addressed is through comparison with similar or less similar situations. The method for assessing responsibility is jurisprudential, that is, by comparison of cases and possible precedents. The historian does not so much tell it as it was as offer analogues to the way it might be now.

> (Maier 1988: 98)

The key question, therefore, is what constitutes a valid comparison. Germany and Japan form an obvious comparison as defeated members of the Axis Alliance. However, this comparison has been developed far more within the Japanese war memory and responsibility literature. Most research from a German perspective has treated the Nazi–Soviet comparison: in the German context, forms of genocide need to be compared, not forms of 'aggressive war', and to compare Germany with Japan risks attracting a 'Holocaust denier' label.

The question of the Holocaust is central to the appropriateness of Germany–Japan comparisons: there is a clear discrepancy between a country that murdered six million people in a state-orchestrated genocide and a country that did not. Furthermore, the three million Soviet POWs estimated to have died in German captivity greatly exceed the around 30,000 Allied prisoners who died in Japanese camps. Otherwise, German and Japanese war conduct bore close similarities: invasion of neighbouring countries, massacre, rape, plunder, forced prostitution,[3] slave labour and human experiments. If a direct comparison must be made, Japanese responsibility is probably most equivalent to German responsibility stemming from its invasion of the Soviet Union, both in nature and the approximate number of deaths they caused – twenty to twenty-five million.

A detailed comparison of responses to war responsibility is beyond the scope of this study of war memories, but Germany and Japan's differing levels of war responsibility, and specifically the Holocaust, complicate all comparisons of compensation, prosecutions of war criminals and apologies. West/Reunified Germany comes out favourably in any *direct* country-to-country comparisons. (West/Reunified) Germany has paid forty times the level of Japanese reparations/compensation (McCormack 1996: 245); it has shown greater willingness to pay individual compensation (rather than Japan's focus on state level reparations) and to keep the compensation issue open (such as through setting up the 'Remembrance, Responsibility, and the Future' fund in August 2000); West Germany had a limited process of trying its own war criminals (such as the 1963–65 Auschwitz trials) whereas Japan did not (Fulbrook 1999: 67–75; Mochida 1994: 7); and (West/Reunified) German leaders have more consistently struck a remorseful tone that convinces the outside world that Germany is addressing the past. If one excludes Holocaust-related compensation, trials and apologies, however, the Germany–Japan discrepancy diminishes greatly: a far smaller differential in compensation; most trials were for Nazi or Holocaust-related crimes rather than aggressive war; and many of the most important symbolic gestures of German remorse, such as Willy Brandt's tearful kneeling contrition at the Warsaw ghetto, cannot be counted.

Alternatively, compare Japan with East Germany (which had a hostile policy towards Israel and only apologized and officially admitted responsibility for the Holocaust in 1990 – Herf 1997: 384–90) and the comparison is probably in Japan's favour, although East Germany's apology when it did come was 'comprehensive and satisfie[d] on many levels the requirements of a good apology' (Yamazaki 2006: 124). There are even cases to be made that Japan has done more to address specific aspects of war responsibility than West/Reunified Germany. For example, Kisa Yoshio argues that the 'comfort women' issue has resulted in much awareness and research about forced prostitution in Asia, but there is a widespread 'taboo' about discussing the women forced into prostitution by Germany (Kisa 2001: 79–88).

Kisa's position ('Germany's unresolved past'), while conservative in Japanese terms, coincides with the received wisdom in the scholarly literature specifically about Germany: the research of Niven (2002), Neumann (2000), Fulbrook (1999), Herf (1997), Maier (1988) and others indicates that addressing the past in the Germanies (East, West and Reunified) is much more complex than the often idealized images created in the orthodox literature about Japan and by many Japanese progressives. The Germany–Japan comparison has frequently been employed to support an agenda concerning Japanese responsibility, and in seeking to present 'Germany' as a model for Japan, many writers have evaluated the German case in selective and perhaps unduly complimentary terms.

If comparing responses to war responsibility has resulted in a tendency to stress the difference between Germany and Japan, then comparisons of German and Japanese memories have revealed many common themes. First, there is ideological confrontation over how to incorporate an inglorious era of national history into a positive contemporary national identity. One common reaction in both countries has been to characterize fascism/ militarism as an aberration caused by a particular set of historical circumstances. The characterization of an 'aberration' limits damage to national pride but is essentially an avoidance strategy. Ultimately, the past still needs to be narrated and judged. Here, ideology takes the prominent role. Charles Maier cites Hans Mommsen's characterization of a 'polarized historical consciousness' in Germany, and describes how during the *historikerstreit* 'two different historiographic agendas were at stake, corresponding to different political mentalities' (Maier 1988: 16). Such ideological battles are a common feature of German and Japanese historiography and are in marked contrast to the high degree of ideological conformity in the 'good war' dominant narratives in the Allied nations.

Second, Germans have displayed patterns of victim mentality similar to the Japanese. One pattern involves people casting themselves as duped or forced into complicity for the crimes of the Nazis or militarists, and thereby as victims of their own governments. A further pattern is the prominence of local narratives of victimhood, often at the expense of national/local narratives of aggression. This is apparent in narratives of air raids or the sufferings in post-defeat Germany and Japan (for Germany, see Neumann 2000: 41–91; for Japan, see below, Chapter 8 in this volume).

Third, patterns of public discourse also illustrate similar phases. Jürgen Habermas has identified four phases of memory in (West) Germany which resemble the phases outlined in Chapter 2, albeit accelerated: to partition

(1945–49), economic and social reconstruction and the period of 'communicative silencing' (1949–63), the period of questioning and reorientation, spearheaded by the protest movements of the 1960s and younger generations (1963–74), and the period of reaction with a polarization of ideological positions (1974–89) (Habermas 1996: 3–8). This is a pattern echoed by James Orr:

> In Germany the themes of German victimhood are commonly thought to have been predominant in public memory in the first postwar decade, then supplanted in the 1960s and 1970s by a reawakening to German victimization of others, only to reemerge in the 1980s. In Japan, the timetable is delayed but similar. The narratives of Japanese war victimhood became more prominent in the second decade after the war, that is, from 1955 to 1965, until the anti-Vietnam War movement initiated a continuing rise in themes of Japanese victimizing others through the decades of the 1970s and 1980s.
>
> (Orr 2001: 11)

Finally, in both Germany and Japan there is moral and political pressure to listen to the voices of victims from other countries and to incorporate those voices into national memory. German and Japanese war discourses have international ramifications and must be negotiated in the scrutiny of international opinion. This has led to moves for international textbooks (for Germany, see Soysal 2000; for Japan, see Kimijima 2000) and regional conferences to try to find common views of war history. These are initiatives that the victors have not needed or attempted.

In short, while comparison is essential and the Germany–Japan comparison is fertile ground for analysis both in terms of responsibility and memory issues, any comparison needs to clearly delineate between issues of responsibility and memory and to rigorously justify the grounds for comparison. The danger of slipping into selective, agenda-driven comparisons is acute.

The Germany–Japan comparison need not be the only comparison made in assessing the moral equivalence of Japanese responsibility or the nature of Japanese war memories. Of particular interest are those conflicts that have formed comparisons within the Japanese media over the 'long postwar'.

One such comparison is the Vietnam War, which was instrumental in raising Japanese consciousness of its aggression in Asia. Like Japan, the US was defeated and public opinion remains deeply divided over the morality of the war; but unlike Japan, the US was never forced to accept any responsibility for the millions of deaths in Vietnam, Cambodia and Laos, or for the ongoing poisonous legacy of Agent Orange, which continues to cause terrible health problems in the region. Remembering soldiers and their actions also exhibits similar patterns: American soldiers, like Japanese soldiers, have tended to be judged either as victims conscripted to fight and die in a losing cause, as heroes fighting in a noble cause, or as the perpetrators of heinous atrocities like My Lai and Nanking. Perhaps the greatest difference is in official remorse: for all the criticism of Japan (even though reparations were paid and numerous apologies have been issued) there has never been an American apology or compensation for Vietnam.

Another comparative framework could be imperialism. This is the framework used by Japanese nationalist Shimizu Keihachirō, who declares that the forty years of Japanese empire, 1905–45, was only one-tenth of the length of the 'white man's' empire-building (Shimizu 1998: 20). Shimizu's agenda is to use comparison to downplay Japanese colonial and war responsibility, and his arguments (not least the span of Japanese imperialism) are extremely debatable. Nevertheless, the imperialism frame does focus attention on Western responsibility for its own colonialism, and whether people in former colonial powers have assumed sufficient responsibility for their own nations' colonialism to assume a 'critical without being hypocritical' stance vis-à-vis Japan. The imperial frame also raises issues of Western complicity in Japanese colonialism: by providing a model; establishing practices adopted by the Japanese empire, such as drug trafficking to finance the military (developed by the British after the Opium Wars and taken up by Japan in China, see Brook and Wakabayashi 2000); provoking/threatening Japan into imperialism through expansion into Asia; or open support for Japanese colonialism in its early stages (such as British diplomatic support within the Anglo-Japanese alliance for the annexation of Korea – see Ku 1985).

Alternatively, 'not repeating the mistakes of the past' could be the measure of how the past has been addressed. Japan's postwar is conspicuous for its lack of belligerence compared to that of countries who suffered so much at the hands of the Japanese: China's subjugation of Tibet, the 1989 Tiananmen Square killings and the millions persecuted during the Cultural Revolution; the actions of '300,000 Korean troops that fought against North Vietnam from 1964 to 1973 as U.S. "mercenaries" allegedly killing thousands of unarmed Vietnamese civilians' (Kim, S.K. 2001: 621), which prompted a presidential statement of regret from Kim Dae-jung in 1998 (www.bbc.co.uk 16 December 1998); the ten million deaths Mark Curtis says UK foreign policy has direct or indirect responsibility for since 1945 through wars, arms sales and support for tyrannical regimes (Curtis 2004); the hundreds of thousands of East Timorese killed by Indonesian forces; or the millions killed in the multitude of conflicts that the US has engineered, supported or fought since 1945.

Finally, since 9/11, the so-called 'war on terror' has provided further comparisons. In the initial aftermath of the 9/11 attacks, the preferred comparison was with 'kamikaze attacks' or a 'new Pearl Harbor'. Many Japanese (particularly nationalists) were angered by the kamikaze comparison: the kamikaze only attacked military targets and were uniformed soldiers, not the stateless terrorists of al Qaeda, they argued. But as a psychologically numbing, epoch-defining event, 9/11 probably has more in common with Hiroshima:

the attacks targeted civilians and came 'out of the blue' (both literally, in terms of a beautiful sunny morning, and metaphorically in the unexpected nature of the attacks); they shocked a nation into intense trauma and mourning; they spawned a quasi-religious narrative of suffering; and the emotional power of the victimhood narrative has allowed many to forget the historical events and reasons that led up to the attacks. The major difference is that while Hiroshima 'ended' a war and has become a rallying cry for peace within Japan, 9/11 marked the start of a war and was employed by the Bush administration to justify its 'war on terror'.

In summary, comparisons are unavoidable but never perfect. However, there is no reason why Germany needs to be the only comparison drawn with Japanese war memories. As these few examples have illustrated, almost any comparison *other* than West/Reunified Germany probably leads to the conclusion that Japan has a process of 'addressing the past' that is highly developed compared to many other countries. Japan, for example, is clearly in a different league from Turkey, where writers can be prosecuted for discussing the Armenian genocide of 1915.

The key conclusion is that the very act of choosing what will be compared with Japan is inherently political and largely dictates the image of how Japan has addressed the past. Orthodox critical representations of how Japan addresses the past, therefore, have much to do with the fact that the Germany–Japan comparison is the most common comparative approach within the fields of Japanese war responsibility and memory.

Conclusions

The state-centred nature of the orthodoxy means that the Japanese government's position is pivotal to assessments of how 'Japan' addresses the past. Critiques of inadequate compensation and insufficiently sincere apologies have regularly slipped into negative conclusions about the nature of Japanese war memories. But the international community has simultaneously contributed to obstructing Japanese attempts to face the past, through international governments' policies in support of (or not opposing) Japanese compensation policy, the active or unintentional support given to Japanese conservatives, and the widespread marginalization of the efforts of progressive Japanese.

Japan's 'failure to address the past' has become a reality constructed by the orthodox discourse norms in English-speaking countries. While there are clearly significant grounds for the criticisms levelled at Japan, the analysis underpinning those criticisms has typically been infused with other agendas, self-interest and some major methodological and analytical flaws (particularly the (mis)use of culturally deterministic arguments and international comparisons). The presence of such flaws indicates why I proposed a seismic metaphor in the introduction to reset the conceptual frame and focus attention on the ideological rifts at the core of Japanese cultural memories of the war. It is time, therefore, to return to the approach outlined in Chapter 1 and analysis of Japanese war memories based firmly within the theoretical frameworks of war memory and cultural studies. The remaining chapters of the book all relate to the issues of the representation and interpretation of war history in Japan, and I start with a discussion of the cultural form that most clearly illustrates the five main conceptual frames employed by Japanese people: the national press.

4 The war as a current affairs issue

The war as front-page news

Japan arguably boasts the leading newspaper (*shinbun*) industry in the world. In 2004, newspaper readership was 644 newspapers per 1,000 adults (in the US and UK, by contrast, the figures were 263 and 332 respectively).[1] Japan's five national broadsheets accounted for 56.5 per cent of all newspaper sales in 2005 and sales of the morning editions were: *Yomiuri shinbun* (10.08 million), *Asahi shinbun* (8.26 million), *Mainichi shinbun* (3.96 million), *Nihon Keizai shinbun* (hereafter *Nikkei*, 3.03 million) and *Sankei shinbun* (2.16 million). With subscriptions the norm and a 93.9 per cent daily delivery rate (in 2004), waking up to a newspaper is a way of life in Japan. In 2001, 74.5 per cent of people said they read a newspaper every day; and in research conducted in 1997, men said they spent an average of 44.7 minutes and women an average of 33.5 minutes a day reading the paper. Newspaper sales, subscriptions and readership have shown a slight downward trend in recent years, mainly because of competition from news online, but nevertheless, all this data points to one conclusion: newspapers have an important role in daily life in Japan.

Given the reach of the Japanese press, newspaper stances on war issues are integral to any discussion of Japanese war memories. Newspapers are one of the best places to observe Japan's contested war memories. In terms of *war stance*, the *Asahi* is progressive and frequently criticizes the government regarding official compensation and apologies; the *Mainichi* is broadly progressive but allows voices from across the judgemental memory spectrum into its pages; the *Yomiuri* is conservative and frequently toes the government line; the *Sankei* is nationalist and often critical of the government from the right wing ('Japan apologizes too much'); and the *Nikkei*, a business paper, has relatively little focus on war issues but is close to the government or progressive-leaning. There is a clear congruence between these stances and the spectrum of judgemental memory outlined in Chapter 1.

The prominence of war-related reporting is also important. As part of my investigations into the reporting of the 'comfort women' issue (Seaton 2006b) I looked at the front pages of every morning edition of the *Yomiuri*, *Mainichi* and *Asahi* in 1992. There were five 'front page war story clusters', when war-related stories (usually but not necessarily the same ones) appeared on the front pages of all three papers at least twice during a one-week period:

11–18 January (eruption of the 'comfort women' issue and a prime ministerial apology); 1–8 July (revised history textbook screening rules and publication of an investigative report into the 'comfort women'); 31 July to 13 August (a double cluster, including a court ruling on the constitutionality of Nakasone's 1985 Yasukuni worship, the cabinet's Yasukuni worship plans, and articles related to the A-bomb and war end anniversaries); and 20–8 October (Emperor Akihito's apology on his historic first visit to China). Such clusters are significant not only because millions of Japanese people wake up to the front pages of newspapers every day, but also because if all three major dailies think the same story is front-page news, it is safe to say that other media are carrying the story prominently, too.

The war also appears on the front pages away from such clusters in isolated scoops, stories or commentary. Then there are stories that cannot be understood without reference to the war: for example, in 1992 there were the Peacekeeping Operations (PKO) Bill passed in June (which cleared the SDF to participate in UN Peacekeeping Operations, a sensitive topic given Japan's militarist past) and Russo-Japanese negotiations concerning the return of four islands northeast of Hokkaido which were occupied by the Soviets after Japan's surrender (the Northern Territories issue). Both stories could easily be considered 'war-related' and accounted for numerous front-page stories in 1992.

There is no reason to think that 1992 was a particularly abnormal year for front-page war stories. In more recent times – particularly 1995 (fiftieth anniversaries), 2001 (textbook and Yasukuni crises) and 2005 (sixtieth anniversaries and the ongoing Yasukuni issue) – front-page reporting probably exceeded the level in 1992. Major anniversaries (either particular dates such as the Pearl Harbor anniversary, or important years such as 1995) are inevitably marked with series of special features on inner pages and front-page articles about commemorative events. These are interspersed with the eruptions of crises and controversies that frequently become diplomatic as well as domestic issues. In short, while there are peaks and troughs in the levels of war interest and war-related reporting, the war is an issue that regularly appears on the front pages of Japanese newspapers.

In order to evaluate the longer-term development of the war as a media event, I used six general historical chronologies (*nenpyō*) of Japan (Kanda and Kobayashi 2005; Sasaki *et al.* 2005; Nakamura 2004; Kawasaki *et al.* 2003; Katō *et al.* 2001; Iwanami henshūbu 2001) to create a database of war-related stories from 1972 to 2005. Not all of the events were front-page issues, but their inclusion in the general chronologies indicates either significant Japanese media attention at the time or dates that with hindsight are considered important, and not only as war-related events. Classifying the media events into categories such as 'official apologies' and 'A-bombs' allowed a broad picture to emerge of the recurrent war-related themes within the Japanese media. This chapter illustrates the press stances concerning these themes in Japan's five national papers.

Prime ministerial apologies vs Yasukuni worship

It is a 'common simplistic view that Japan has "never" apologized' (Yamazaki 2006: x). The table of prime ministerial apologies and Yasukuni worship (Table 4.1) clarifies that many apologies have been issued using a variety of wordings. Indeed, it is a diplomatic ritual for the first major summit between a Japanese premier and his South Korean and Chinese counterparts to clarify the Japanese prime minister's war stance, and thereby set the tone for diplomatic relations during the prime minister's tenure. However, Jane Yamazaki's (2006) rhetorical study of Japanese apologies illustrates that the primary issue is not whether apologies have been issued, but whether the language and process of apology can lead to reconciliation.

Table 4.1 reveals the importance of the prime minister's personal opinions in the diplomatic struggle to ensure that 'Japan' exhibits 'appropriate' historical consciousness. Hosokawa's apologies in 1993–94 were the zenith of Japanese apologies, judging by their reception in neighbouring countries, and his apologies seemed to be taking Japan on a bold new course. Murayama's apologies were accepted politely but not enthusiastically: his personal views were well received but he was not viewed as speaking for his government. After Hashimoto became prime minister, Japanese apologies were on a slippery slope back towards being regarded as inadequate. By 2001, any apologies were lost in the storm over Koizumi's Yasukuni worship and the 2001 textbook crisis.

Hosokawa's apologies, therefore, set a new standard of which subsequent prime ministers have been widely seen to have fallen short. His most famous statement was that the Pacific War was 'an aggressive war and a mistake'. Hosokawa was not the first prime minister to use the term 'aggressive war': Nakasone had used the phrase in September 1986, as had Takeshita Noboru in 1988. However, Nakasone's comments were compromised by his worship at Yasukuni Shrine, and Takeshita's comments sat uncomfortably with his claim that the issue of aggression was one for future generations of historians. Hosokawa's was the first admission of an 'aggressive war' that seemed to stem from genuinely held feelings (*Mainichi shinbun* 11 August 1993b). Hosokawa had never nullified his apologies with other actions, which is why they were treated as sincere and well received across Asia.

Given the significance of Hosokawa's 'aggressive war' remarks in August 1993, the newspapers' editorial evaluations are revealing. The *Asahi* (11 August 1993) praised Hosokawa and welcomed the comments as a positive step forward. The *Mainichi* (11 August 1993a) also called the comments a step forward. They were 'extremely fresh' and could be 'well regarded' in contrast to previous vague statements. These are both progressive(-leaning) endorsements of an official 'aggressive war' stance. However, during his inaugural speech of 23 August, Hosokawa had changed his rhetoric from 'aggressive war' to 'aggressive acts', the more conservative stance that admits atrocities but does not characterize the entire war as aggressive. The *Nikkei* (24 August 1993) commented that this was probably due to bureaucratic pressure and

Table 4.1 Prime ministerial apologies vs Yasukuni worship, 1972–2005

Prime Minister / Date became PM	Major prime ministerial apologies*	Number of visits to Yasukuni Shrine / Notable events
Tanaka Kakuei / 7 July 1972	**25 September 1972**: as part of the restoration of Sino-Japanese relations, expresses remorse for the 'trouble' (*meiwaku*) Japan caused. The comments cause some anger because *meiwaku* is not seen as sufficiently strong.	**FIVE**
Miki Takeo / 9 December 1974		**THREE**. In 1975 Miki becomes the first PM to worship on 15 August. Deliberately 'private' (starting the 'official' vs 'private' worship issue).
Fukuda Takeo / 24 December 1976		**FOUR**
Ōhira Masayoshi / 7 December 1978		**THREE**. Worships despite being a practising Christian.
Suzuki Zenko / 17 July 1980		**NINE**. Worships with the cabinet on 15 August 1980, 1981 and 1982.
Nakasone Yasuhiro / 27 November 1982	**22 August 1984**: in Korea, expresses 'deep remorse' (*fukai hansei*) for the trouble and 'terrible damage' (*sangai*) in the past.	**TEN**. First PM to worship at New Year, 5 January 1984. 15 August 1985: 'Official' worship marks the internationalization of the Yasukuni issue.
Takeshita Noboru / 6 November 1987	**6 March 1989**: in the Diet, says the 'militaristic aggression' (*gunjishugi ni yoru shinryaku*) of our country cannot be denied. **30 March 1989**: expresses deep remorse and 'feelings of regret' (*ikan no i*) for colonial rule to North Korea, the first such statement to the North. The comments are welcomed by Kim Il-sung on 4 April.	**NONE**

Uno Sōsuke 3 June 1989	NONE	
Kaifu Toshiki 10 August 1989	NONE	**28 September 1990**: a cross-party delegation led by Kanemaru Shin signs a joint declaration in North Korea saying Japan should 'apologize' (*shazai*) and compensate for its colonial rule. **3 May 1991**: at the ASEAN summit in Singapore, Kaifu expresses deep remorse for the 'unbearable suffering and sadness' (*taenkai karushimi to kanashimi*) caused by 'our nation's acts'. **10 August 1991**: expresses remorse on a trip to China.
Miyazawa Kiichi 5 November 1991	ONE. A secret visit in 1992.	**17 January 1992**: revelations in the *Asahi* newspaper force an apology (*owabi*) to the 'comfort women' on Miyazawa's trip to Korea.
Hosokawa Morihiro 9 August 1993	NONE	**10 August 1993**: comments it was 'an aggressive war and a mistake' (*shinryaku sensō*). **15 August 1993**: Hosokawa becomes first PM to offer condolences to all Asians on 15 August. Speaker of the House Doi Takako announces the parliament is considering a Diet resolution offering an official apology (*shazai*) for aggression against Asian nations. The remarks are widely welcomed in Asia. **19 August 1993**: Secretary of State Takemura Masayoshi reiterates Hosokawa's aggressive war (*shinryaku sensō*) stance, but maintains that 'all compensation claims are resolved'. **23 August 1993**: Hosokawa tones down his 'aggressive war' comments to 'aggressive acts' (*shinryaku kōi*). **27 September 1993**: Hosokawa speech at the UN, we must not forget remorse for the past. **6 November 1993**: in Korea, Hosokawa lists specific Korean grievances (such as the 'comfort women' issue and Koreans being forced to use Japanese names) and comments that 'as the aggressor' (*kagaisha to shite*) he expresses remorse and a 'deep apology' (*fukai chinsha*). This apology is very well received. **20 March 1994**: while in China, expresses remorse and an 'apology' (*owabi*) as well as a desire to look to the future. Participates in a wreath-laying ceremony to soldiers who fought against the Japanese.

Table 4.1 continued

Prime Minister Date became PM	Major prime ministerial apologies*	Number of visits to Yasukuni Shrine Notable events
Hata Tsutomu 28 April 1994		**NONE**
Murayama Tomiichi 30 June 1994	**24 August 1994**: in Manila, expresses remorse and proposes new initiatives for joint historical research. Meanwhile, in Singapore, Leader of the House Doi lays a wreath at a memorial to Chinese massacred during the Japanese occupation. **3 May 1994**: expresses remorse for the unbearable suffering caused on a trip to China. Li gives a lukewarm approval: 'we agree with your views'. Murayama becomes the first serving PM to visit the Marco Polo Bridge. **15 August 1995**: the Murayama communiqué (*danwa*) supplements the widely criticized parliamentary statement (9 June). This personal 'heartfelt apology' becomes the standard prime ministerial apology, but eight members of the cabinet worship at Yasukuni Shrine. South Korean President Kim Young-sam calls for 'correct views of history' in Japan, which indicates that the apology has not been so well received.	**NONE**
Hashimoto Ryutarō 11 January 1996	**26 January 1996**: in the Diet, Hashimoto states it was aggression, and restates the Murayama communiqué, but scepticism exists because of earlier comments (24 October 1994) when as Minister of Trade and Industry he said he had lingering doubts about whether it could be called a war of aggression. **23 June 1996**: Hashimoto apologizes (*owabi*) to the 'comfort women'. Korea and Japan have been made co-hosts of the 2002 FIFA World Cup, necessitating closer ties. **15 August 1996**: Hashimoto expresses remorse to Asians, but after remembering those who died fighting 'for the security of their nation'. He also praises the precious sacrifice (*tōtoi gisei*) of the war generation. **4 September 1997**:	**ONE** Ex-head of the War Bereaved Association. Worships 'privately' on his birthday, 29 July 1996.

	Apologies	Yasukuni worship
	Hashimoto in China repeats the Murayama communiqué and wants to create a forward-looking relationship. **12 January 1998**: repeats the Murayama communiqué to British POWs via Prime Minister Blair who is in Tokyo.	**NONE**
Obuchi Keizō 30 July 1998	**15 August 1998**: Obuchi repeats the Hashimoto and Murayama position. **8 October 1998**: expresses remorse (*hansei*) to President Kim Dae-jung as part of the Japan–Republic of Korea Joint Declaration. **25 November 1998**: President Jiang Zemin visits Japan. Obuchi issues a verbal apology, but there is wrangling over a written joint declaration which only mentions remorse.	
Mori Yoshirō 5 April 2000		**NONE**
Koizumi Junichirō 26 April 2001	**8 October 2001**: Koizumi expresses remorse and apology (*owabi*) in China, and visits the Marco Polo Bridge and the Anti-Japanese War Museum. Koizumi's apologies are ignored in favour of warnings about textbooks and his recent Yasukuni Shrine worship. **15 October 2001**: Koizumi expresses the same remorse and apology in Korea, as well as a proposal for joint history research. But the response is the same: warnings about textbooks and Yasukuni. **17 September 2002**: the Pyongyang Declaration includes an apology to North Korea, but the apology is lost in the Japanese preoccupation with the abduction issue (Japanese citizens abducted by North Korea, five of whom returned with Koizumi to Japan). **22 April 2005**: apology at an ASEAN summit, but by now relations in Asia have dipped to a new low.	**FIVE** (to October 2005) Triggers a major diplomatic row with his 13 August 2001 worship. Further worship on 21 April 2002, 14 January 2003 and 1 January 2004. 17 October 2005: worships in the same way as a private citizen.

Sources: Six chronologies (Kanda and Kobayashi 2005; Sasaki *et al*. 2005; Nakamura 2004; Kawasaki *et al*. 2003; Iwanami henshūbu 2001; Katō *et al*. 2001; *Asahi shinbun*; Watanabe and Wakamiya (2006: 88-91).

* All the apologies are listed in one or more of the six chronologies.

limited itself to speculation about why Hosokawa's stance had changed. By contrast, the *Yomiuri* (24 August 1993) implicitly disagreed with Hosokawa's original 'aggressive war' comments when it cited the rephrased 'aggressive acts' position of 23 August and commented 'One can say this is the appropriate expression'. The *Sankei* had three critical op-ed articles on 11 August and an editorial on 12 August that criticized Hosokawa's views for a lack of depth. More consensus was necessary before such statements were made, it argued. The *Sankei* (12 August 1993) stopped short of a nationalist defence of Japan's wars and admitted the damage to Asian countries, but it challenged both the view that the war against America was aggressive and Chinese accounts of what happened in Nanking.

Many Japanese apologies have been issued, but 'apology nullification' is also a key concept. At a prime ministerial level this has usually meant worship at Yasukuni Shrine. As outlined in Chapter 2, the Yasukuni issue as a diplomatic issue dates back to 1985 and centres on the worship of the prime minister at the shrine where the class A war criminals are commemorated. The Yasukuni issue is considerably more complex than this from a Japanese perspective. Issues relating to Yasukuni Shrine were one of the single most common topics in the *nenpyō* (chronologies), particularly related to prime ministerial worship, judgements in the courts on the constitutionality of Yasukuni worship, international and domestic support for and protests against the worship, and the requests of some people (Japanese and non-Japanese) that their relatives should not be enshrined at Yasukuni.

The renewal of annual prime ministerial worship since 2001 has made Yasukuni the most prominent war-related media issue of the new millennium. The papers took different stances concerning the first of Prime Minister Koizumi's visits to Yasukuni on 13 August 2001 (Sankei shinbun ronsetsu iinshitsu 2002: 301–14). On 28 July the *Asahi* stated it was against Koizumi's planned worship and argued it would damage international trust of Japan and thereby Japan's national interest; and on 14 August (the day after Koizumi's worship) the *Asahi* criticized Yasukuni Shrine's role in Japanese aggression in Asia. The *Mainichi* also stated on 12 July that Koizumi should not worship; and it raised concerns about the constitutional separation of religion and state, and 'historical consciousness' on 11 May. After Koizumi's worship, the *Mainichi* agonized on 14 August over where Japan's relations with its neighbours could go from there.

The *Yomiuri*, by contrast, supported Koizumi's worship. It stated on 9 August that, having promised to worship on 15 August, Koizumi could not give in to international pressure. The *Yomiuri* also openly criticized China: there had been repeated Yasukuni worship between April 1979 (when the enshrinement of class A war criminals became public knowledge) and 1985 with no major diplomatic repercussions, so why, the *Yomiuri* asked, had China become so vocal now? After Koizumi changed the date of his worship to appease international criticism the *Yomiuri* was more conciliatory: on

14 August it called the concession wise. The *Yomiuri* also called for a new non-religious memorial that would even be appropriate for foreign leaders to visit. The *Yomiuri* was keen to support the prime minister 'paying his respects to the war dead', but Yasukuni 'worship' was not sacred or non-negotiable in the way it is for nationalists.

Finally, the *Sankei* was openly in favour of Yasukuni worship. It is the obligation of leaders to commemorate those who sacrificed their precious lives in the service of their country, it argued on 16 May. In later editorials the *Sankei* indicated its scepticism concerning Japanese war guilt by using the terms 'so-called (*iwayuru*) class A war criminals' or putting 'class A war criminals' in inverted commas. After Koizumi's worship, the *Sankei* implicitly criticized Koizumi for reneging on his promise to worship on 15 August: moving his worship two days forward would do nothing to dampen the international reaction, it argued (ibid.).

These stances are mirrored in press reaction to court cases about the constitutionality of Yasukuni worship. In short, the constitutional issue is that, given the separation of religion and state in Article 20 of the constitution, and the prohibition on the use of public money to support religious activities in Article 89, an acting prime minister cannot perform a religious act in an official capacity or offer a gift to a religious organization from public funds; but as a private individual he can exercise his constitutional right to religious freedom (Hardacre 1989: 144). In practical terms, the distinction between 'official' and 'private' is fuzzy and international criticism shows little interest in making such distinctions. It can be argued, for example, that a prime minister can never act in a 'private' capacity when commemorating the nation's military war dead. Nonetheless, in Japan a 'private' visit is distinguished from an 'official' visit in factors such as the use of personal rather than public money to buy flowers, using private transport rather than an official car to get to the shrine, and whether the prime minister signs his name as 'prime minister' in the worshippers' book. Then there is the issue of what constitutes 'worship'. The traditional Shintō ritual is bowing twice, clapping twice and bowing once again: if these rituals are curtailed, does the worship cease to be 'worship', or is strictly observing religious ritual superfluous when 'paying one's respects to the war dead'?

Following Nakasone's and Koizumi's worship (as well as by other local officials) there have been many lawsuits challenging the constitutionality of the worship.[2] While many have failed to give clear-cut judgements, some, including the judgement of the Fukuoka District Court on 7 April 2004 about Koizumi's 2001 worship, have ruled that Yasukuni Shrine worship by officials has been unconstitutional. The national press had already highlighted the constitutional issue before Koizumi's worship, with the *Asahi* and *Mainichi* raising the constitutional issue as a reason why Koizumi should not worship, and the *Yomiuri* asking why it was fine for cabinet ministers to participate in the traditional New Year worship (*hatsumōde*) at Ise Shrine but unconstitutional for ministers to worship at Yasukuni Shrine (Sankei shinbun ronsetsu iinkai

2002: 301–8). After the verdict, the *Asahi* and *Mainichi* supported the Fukuoka court's judgment and urged Koizumi to reconsider his worship, the *Yomiuri* repeated its Ise Shrine arguments and said the worship should continue, while the *Sankei* dismissed the judgment as distorted (*Da Capo* 16 June 2004).

The fiftieth anniversary statement and politicians' gaffes

Inappropriate statements by Japanese politicians about the war, on both collective and individual levels, are a recurrent theme within Japanese war discourses. On 9 June 1995, the Japanese parliament passed a statement to mark the fiftieth anniversary of the end of the war. It read:

> On the occasion of the fiftieth anniversary of the end of World War II, this house offers its sincere condolences to those who fell in action and victims of wars and similar actions all over the world.
>
> Solemnly reflecting upon many instances of colonial rule and aggressive acts in the modern history of the world, and recognizing that Japan carried out such acts in the past, inflicting pain and suffering upon the people of other countries, especially in Asia, the members of this house express a sense of deep remorse.
>
> We must transcend the differences over historical views of the past war and learn humbly the lessons of history so as to build a peaceful international society. . . .
>
> (cited in Wakamiya 1999: 9)

Japanese press reaction was highly critical. The *Asahi's* editorial (11 June 1995) 'The sullied parliamentary resolution' began with the words 'Shameful. Sad. Unbearable' and criticized the lack of a clear acknowledgement of aggression. The *Mainichi* (11 June 1995) was also critical: 'No way to this shameful behaviour'. It described how 171 out of 511 parliamentarians had failed to vote and criticized politicians for parochial squabbles when the resolution needed to be aimed at appeasing an international audience. The *Nikkei* (10 June 1995) took a similar progressive-leaning line in a front-page article, 'Sullied "peace pledge"', which stated that whatever the internal differences in historical consciousness, the war needed to be seen with Asian eyes. The *Nikkei* called on younger generations to rise to the task.

The *Yomiuri* took a different line. As its endorsement of Hosokawa's toned-down 'aggressive acts' comments in 1993 indicated, the *Yomiuri* would not endorse a reference to an 'aggressive war'. The *Yomiuri* (11 June 1995) focused instead on ' "Fiftieth anniversary parliamentary resolution" mired in politics' and dissected the political machinations that had made a coherent statement impossible. The conclusion was that it could only weaken the Murayama cabinet. The *Sankei* (11 June 1995) had a 'bleak' view and said it had always argued against the resolution because a unified official statement was not possible when there was such diversity of opinion.

Ultimately, the fiftieth anniversary resolution was a major embarrassment: it was a 'collective gaffe' by Japanese parliamentarians and drew widespread international criticism. Domestic press reaction in Japan was no less critical, a point that sits uncomfortably with the charges about the 'subservience' of the Japanese press so often made in English-language discussion of Japanese newspapers. Similar conclusions can be made about what Wakamiya Yoshibumi calls 'gaffes' (Wakamiya 1999: 11–15), but what I prefer to call 'nationalistic outbursts' or 'apology sabotage' by nationalistic politicians. The 'gaffes' of Fujio Masayuki, Okuno Seisuke, Watanabe Michio and others featured prominently in the *nenpyō* and have been discussed elsewhere (ibid.; Chang 1997: 202–5; Yamazaki 2006: 90–9), so discussion here will be limited to three gaffes that illustrate the Japanese press' role.

The international media has often interpreted nationalistic outbursts by politicians as evidence of how 'Japan' fails to address the past. But there is another issue: the Japanese press's role (particularly in the 1990s) in 'outing' such nationalists and igniting the controversy that forces them to retract or resign. For example, in May 1994 newly appointed Justice Minister Nagano Shigeto gave an interview to the *Mainichi*. Normally, such interviews appear quietly on the inside pages, but when Nagano called the Nanking Massacre a 'fabrication' and said that Japan had no 'aggressive intent', it made a bold headline halfway down the front page (*Mainichi shinbun* 4 May 1994). Nagano was forced to resign three days later. The context of Nagano's statement, as with all nationalistic outbursts, is important. Nagano had just taken up his post in the first post-Hosokawa cabinet and his comments can be seen as a backlash against the strides towards a more progressive official narrative in the preceding nine months.

The next outburst also had a context. When Sakurai Shin, Director General of the Environment Agency, stated on 12 August 1994 that Japan did not fight with the intention of waging an aggressive war, and that thanks to Japan Asia could 'throw off the shackles of colonial rule', the comment coincided with Prime Minister Murayama's announcement of 100 billion yen for 'peace, friendship and exchange' projects, code for money to be distributed via non-governmental organizations (NGOs) as compensation to 'comfort women' (*Asahi shinbun* 13 August 1994a, 1994b). Sakurai resigned two days later on 14 August, but he had overshadowed the government's initiative. This illustrates the role of such comments as 'apology nullification', or if deliberate, 'apology sabotage'.

Finally, after a press briefing on 8 November 1995, Director General of the Management and Coordination Agency, Etō Takami, told his press club 'off the record' that he believed Japan also did good things during its colonial rule in Korea. Despite specifically stating his comments were off the record, they made the papers. The 'gaffe' precipitated much discussion of the media's responsibility to keep private comments private, and even though Etō had not denied other negative aspects of colonial rule, the media storm still forced Etō's resignation and a written apology from Prime Minister Murayama to South Korea. This incident in particular indicates that the press is not always subservient to power elites: sometimes, a good scoop is too good to ignore in the media business.

Given the potential consequences, nationalistic politicians take great risks in expressing their personal views. However, nationalistic outbursts are precisely that: the *personal views of officials* and not official policy. Many of the outbursts were at relatively low-key venues (an LDP chapter meeting or daily press conference) but were quickly magnified by the Japanese media into national issues. Whereas these nationalistic outbursts have become well known outside Japan, the role of the Japanese press is usually ignored. The press (particularly its liberal wing) publicized all these stories by reporting the comments prominently (typically on the front page). Once one media organization took up the story, the herd instinct of the media took over. Other domestic and international media organizations jumped on the bandwagon and neighbouring governments responded with diplomatic pressure, which created more news. Eventually, the controversy forced a retraction and/or resignation, but the process started with the Japanese press. The eruption of such media-generated controversies indicates why the argument that press clubs are subservient and prevent criticism of politicians is only half-correct. When the media or press club members *collectively* turn against the officials they cover, they have the power to oust those officials.[3]

The press taboo: criticizing the emperor

Whereas the Japanese press, on occasions, has aggressively scrutinized the comments of politicians, it has been far less critical of the emperor. The broadsheets are typically respectful towards the imperial household: honorific language is always used and the broadsheets do not engage in the scandal-mongering about royalty that exists in some Japanese tabloids and weekly magazines. This respect tones down any critical assessments of the emperor's war role and responsibility. 'Uncritical reporting' has also developed because of the constitutional limits barring the emperor from taking an active political role: the press cannot insist on a clear imperial stance about the war (an inherently political topic) without inciting the emperor to be unconstitutional. Nevertheless, as the symbol of the Japanese people and given debate over Hirohito's war role, the emperor and the war issue have frequently combined to make front-page news, particularly concerning imperial apologies, commemorative activities, protests against the imperial household, and wider discussion within Japanese society of the emperor's war responsibility.

Like Japanese prime ministers, Emperors Hirohito (1926–89) and Akihito (1989–present) have issued a number of statements exhibiting remorse for Japanese war actions, usually to dignitaries during state receptions in Japan and on imperial tours overseas, such as to China in October 1992. Editorial reaction to Akihito's comments on 23 October 1992 while in China ('In the long history of the relationship between our two countries, there was an unfortunate period in which my country inflicted great sufferings on the people of China. I deeply deplore this.') indicates the reticence of the press to be critical. The papers were conspicuously positive and in accord. The *Yomiuri* (24 October 1992) and *Nikkei* (24 October 1992) talked of the imperial statement (*o-kotoba*) that represented the feelings of the people; the *Asahi* (28 October 1992) commented on the more positive image Chinese people could have of the emperor; and the *Mainichi* (24 October 1992) described how the statement could be a starting point for deeper friendship. Even the *Sankei* (28 October 1992), which had objected to the emperor's 'apology tour' from the outset, avoided any direct criticism. The stances of the papers diverged, not concerning the emperor's comments but in the implications for other actors: for example, the *Mainichi* saw the comments as a starting point for other acknowledgement by politicians, while the *Sankei* criticized the Chinese not only for putting the emperor in a position of needing to raise the war issue, but also for the Tiananmen Square incident and its military ambitions.

In most other instances, too, the quality press limits itself to respectful reportage of 'their majesties' activities. The emperor and empress play a role as leaders of national mourning and a picture of them bowing in respect to the war dead at the ceremony in Budōkan Hall, Tokyo, on 15 August is one of the stock media images of the war end commemorations. The emperor and empress travel widely to participate in commemorations. During the fiftieth anniversary of the war's end, they embarked on a mourning tour of Japan on 26 July 1995 by visiting a home for elderly *hibakusha* (A-bomb victims) in Nagasaki; on 28 May 2005, the emperor and empress attended commemorations in Saipan, famous for the suicides of civilians at Banzai Cliff; and on foreign trips abroad, the emperor and empress have laid wreaths to non-Japanese victims, such as in Holland in May 2000.

The participation of the emperor in war commemoration creates its own controversy given the wider international discussion about the emperor's war responsibility. In May 1998, former British POWs famously turned their backs to the emperor in protest at his visit, but there have been protests and criticism directed at the emperor from within Japan, too. While on a trip to the Himeyuri (girls' nursing corps) memorial in Okinawa on 17 July 1975, then Crown Prince Akihito had a Molotov cocktail thrown at him by Okinawan extremists; the emperor's visit to Okinawa on 24 October 1987 was also greeted by protests; and *hibakusha* were highly critical of Hirohito's statement on 31 October 1975 that he was sorry about the A-bombs but they were 'inevitable' (*Asahi shinbun* 1 November 1975). Even around the time of Emperor Hirohito's death he was criticized: Nagasaki Mayor Motojima Hitoshi's comments about the emperor's responsibility in 1988 nearly cost him his life (Field 1991: Chapter 3); in late 1988, Communist Party councillors in a number of regional assemblies asked questions related to the emperor's war responsibility, drawing heavy criticism from conservatives (*Asahi shinbun*

30 September 1988); and Leader of the House Doi Takako said she thought the emperor bore war responsibility in a press conference on 18 January 1989.

However, while the press reports these incidents and the *nenpyō* have included them among the most significant media events within postwar Japanese history, the press has always trodden a fine line between reporting debate and avoiding direct editorial criticism of the highly respected imperial household. The reluctance of the press to criticize the imperial household was epitomized in relation to the issue that arguably more than any other shaped war discourses in the 1990s: the 'comfort women' issue. In December 2000, the Women's International Tribunal on Japanese Military Sexual Slavery declared Emperor Hirohito personally guilty for the human rights abuses suffered by 'comfort women' (Matsui 2003: 264–5). This was a taboo too far for all the papers: even the progressive *Asahi*, which had reported the tribunal prominently, felt unable to report this judgement highly critical of the emperor and referred more obliquely to the emperor's responsibility (Yoshimi 2001: 179).

The 'comfort women', lawsuits and compensation

The 'comfort women' issue was probably the biggest single war-related media issue of the 1990s. It is not necessary to recount the unfolding of the issue in detail here, as it has been extensively documented elsewhere.[4] Of particular interest in relation to discussion of the Japanese press are the press's role in the eruption of the 'comfort women' issue, the newspapers' partisan stances, and editorial positions on compensation.

From the Japanese media's perspective, the 'comfort women' issue erupted in January 1992. On 6 December 1991, a group of Korean plaintiffs – including Kim Hak-sun (the first 'comfort woman' to testify using her real name) – arrived in Japan to press for an apology and compensation from the Japanese government. The government denied it had any responsibility in the absence of documentation demonstrating military 'involvement' in the running of 'comfort stations'. Chuo University Professor Yoshimi Yoshiaki located incriminating documents in the Defence Agency archives and they were published in a front-page scoop in the *Asahi* newspaper (11 January 1992). Two days later, the government was forced to admit the military's involvement, and on 17 January Prime Minister Miyazawa issued an apology while in South Korea. Initially, the media issue was the embarrassing government U-turn more than the sufferings of the 'comfort women', but nevertheless the *Asahi* had turned the 'comfort women' issue into a major current affairs issue. A newspaper had not only challenged government policy, it had changed it.

Within Japan, the issue developed into a sensitive and often acrimonious debate in which the newspapers occupied the main positions in the 1990s. As I have demonstrated elsewhere (Seaton 2006b), the *Asahi* newspaper campaigned for the 'comfort women' through document scoops, numerous letters on its 'letters to the editor' page and supportive op-eds or editorials. It called for compensation to the survivors. The *Mainichi* was broadly progressive and sided with the 'comfort women', particularly by prominently reporting international protests against Japan. It recognized the clauses regarding compensation in the 1965 Korea–Japan treaty but supported alternative measures, such as medical care. The *Yomiuri* initially supported the government's apologies, but over the 1990s gained confidence (as most conservatives did) in challenging the 'comfort women's' claims. The *Yomiuri* supported the government in resisting calls for compensation, but supported the establishment of the Asian Women's Fund. From the outset, the *Sankei* grumbled about how Japan always took responsibility for practices that also existed in other countries and cast doubt on the 'comfort women's' versions by citing the lack of documentary evidence. And while the *Nikkei* had relatively little coverage, it was broadly progressive-leaning on the issue.

These basic stances were evident throughout the 1990s and were reflected in the balance of reporting content as well as explicitly stated stances. Progressive activist groups received significant coverage in the *Asahi* and *Mainichi* but were largely ignored by the *Yomiuri* and *Sankei*, who preferred to focus on the positions of conservative politicians with compatible views. Yoshimi Shunya's analysis of press coverage of the 2000 Women's Tribunal also illustrates this trend, albeit restrained by a general reporting 'reticence' largely due to the tribunal's highly critical verdict concerning the emperor's war responsibility (described above). The *Asahi* and a section of the regional quality dailies (whose various stances on the 'comfort women' issue mirror the spectrum in the national press – Sankei shinbun ronsetsu iinshitsu 2002: 96–102) carried the trial prominently, but the *Yomiuri* 'did not write a single line'; the *Nikkei* only published a small article about the opening of the trial and 'even the *Mainichi*' only wrote about the final judgment in an 'un-eye-catching' (*medatanai*) article (Yoshimi 2001: 176–7).

These stances of the newspapers on compensation and apologies to 'comfort women' are essentially the same for slave labourers, victims of biological warfare and all the other victims seeking redress in the Japanese courts. For example, after a landmark court ruling in the Tokyo District Court that confirmed the existence of Unit 731 and its biological warfare in China, but which turned down the requests for compensation in line with the government's 'all claims resolved' policy, the newspapers gave very different styles of coverage. The *Asahi* (28 August 2002) put the verdict on its front page, including a little fact box about Unit 731 that explained the unit's activities in biological warfare and human experiments. This endorsed the court's acceptance of the unit's war crimes as historical fact. On page 30 (the *shakai*, 'society', pages) there was a further article, plus commentary by Yoshimi Yoshiaki (the progressive scholar responsible for the 'comfort women' documents scoop in 1992) and two former Unit 731 researchers, all of whom had testified in support of the plaintiffs at the trial. An editorial (29 August

2002) confirmed the *Asahi's* unambiguous support for the plaintiffs: one can only face the future by squarely facing the past, it concluded.

The *Mainichi* (28 August 2002), by contrast, put the verdict on the *shakai* pages. However, by explaining how this was the second lawsuit confirming the activities of Unit 731 (the first being the third Ienaga textbook trial judgment in August 1997) the paper endorsed the court's verdict about the historical facts of Unit 731's war crimes; and by ending the article with a subsection about the dissatisfaction of the plaintiffs and including a separate short article about how the verdict had been reported in China, the *Mainichi* indicated sympathy, if not tacit support, for the plaintiffs. The *Nikkei's* coverage (28 August 2002) was virtually the same as the *Mainichi's*, but instead of the plaintiffs' grievances there was an *Asahi*-style fact box about Unit 731's crimes.

However, while the *Yomiuri* (28 August 2002) also placed its article on the *shakai* pages, it was much closer to the Japanese government's position of neither denying nor confirming the existence of Unit 731. By using non-committal language ('biological warfare deemed to have been carried out by Unit 731') and simply stating the position of the plaintiffs vs that of the government, superficially speaking the *Yomiuri* was scrupulously 'neutral'. But effectively, it sided with the government and avoided a clear statement about Unit 731's activities. The *Sankei* (28 August 2002) took the same approach as the *Yomiuri*, but chose to make the rejection of the plaintiff's claims its main headline and devoted even less space. With ample Japanese documentary evidence of Unit 731's crimes (much of it in the unit's published articles or in documents handed over to the US by the unit's researchers in exchange for amnesties), nationalists cannot use the 'no documentary evidence' defence they use in 'comfort women' debates. They simply avoid the issue where possible.

Textbooks

Of all the war-related media issues, textbooks featured most prominently in the *nenpyō*, mainly concerning six issues: the lawsuits brought by progressive scholar Ienaga Saburō in his efforts to put more concrete references to Japanese atrocities in textbooks, efforts by conservative politicians to have more 'patriotic education', Ministry of Education guidelines about textbook content, and the three major crises centring on nationalistic textbooks in 1982, 1986 and 2001.

Japan's textbook crises have all been rooted in conservative efforts to correct 'biased', 'unpatriotic' or 'masochistic' views in Japanese education. This section focuses on the most recent history textbook crisis (2001) and the campaigns of the nationalistic group, Atarashii rekishi kyōkasho wo tsukurukai, the Japanese Society for History Textbook Reform ('Tsukurukai'). The Tsukurukai was formed in 1996 and one of its founding aims was the eradication of the 'comfort women' from school textbooks. After the admission of the 'involvement' of the Japanese military in running 'comfort stations' and the official apologies in 1992–93, the Japanese government could no longer block mentions of the 'comfort women', which appeared in some textbooks from the mid-1990s. But by the late 1990s, conservatives had reworked their position so that 'forced transportation' (*kyōsei renkō*, namely abduction) of 'comfort women' was the issue, not 'involvement', and that Japanese documentary evidence was necessary to prove forced transportation. With a 'lack' of documentary evidence to show abductions by Japanese soldiers (a self-serving position considering the Japanese military had destroyed most of the incriminating documents after the surrender) and with a distrustful rejection of foreign documentary evidence and testimony of abduction by 'comfort women', conservatives and nationalists clung to the idea that 'sexual slavery' was a charge that could not be adequately 'proven'. Many conservatives also argued that it was not appropriate to teach children about military prostitution, or that what happened was common practice at the time (other militaries had brothel systems, and the practice of impoverished families selling daughters into prostitution was widespread). Using these arguments, the Tsukurukai led the conservative–nationalist campaign to get the 'comfort women' removed from textbooks.

The inclusion of the 'comfort women' in textbooks provoked another difference in press opinion. In 1998, Agriculture and Fisheries Minister Nakagawa Shōichi stated that he doubted the 'comfort women' issue could be included in textbooks as a 'historical fact' (Yomiuri shinbun ronsetsu iinkai 2001: 234–40). This statement caused outrage in South Korea, but on 4 August the *Yomiuri* supported Nakagawa, reiterated that 'forced transportation' remained unproven and made critical comments about how 'some sections of the media' (a thinly veiled reference to the *Asahi*) were reporting the issue in a way to encourage Korean protests. By contrast, on 1 August the *Asahi* supported the inclusion of the 'comfort women' in textbooks: it stated there was sufficient documentary and testimonial evidence to prove the 'enforced nature' (*kyōseisei*) of their experiences. Nakagawa's comments, concluded the *Asahi*, were a direct challenge to the apology issued by Foreign Minister Kōno on 4 August 1993.

Despite such controversies, by 2001 the Tsukurukai had produced its textbook, minus any references to the 'comfort women'. The textbook crisis began in earnest on 3 April 2001 when the Tsukurukai's textbook passed the screening process. It was carefully written to present a nationalistic version of war history: for example, the textbook avoided stating that the Nanking Massacre actually occurred by saying 'Japan was judged to have killed' many people after the fall of Nanking at the Tokyo Trials (Atarashii rekishi kyōkasho wo tsukurukai 2001: 295).

Reaction in the Japanese press to the Tsukurukai's textbook spread across a broad spectrum (Sankei shinbun ronsetsu iinshitsu 2002: 285–99). Before the Tsukurukai's textbook had even been approved, on 22 February the *Asahi* condemned it for being 'unbalanced', presenting an affirmative view of the war and ignoring the victims of Japanese aggression; after the textbook's approval, on 9 May it noted calls for revisions from South Korea and said revisions should be made where mistakes were found. The *Mainichi* was also critical. On 4 April it said that it did not think the textbook should have been rejected and promoted the 'freedom to choose', but it could not say the textbook was good given the number of revisions required (137, far more than any other textbook) and the way it barely touched upon instances of Japanese aggression. Nevertheless, on 9 May the *Mainichi* differed from the *Asahi's* position in that it rejected the idea of revising the book further after it had been approved.

The more conservative papers took a supportive tone. On 2 March the *Yomiuri* criticized state-produced textbooks in South Korea and China, and it lauded the freedom of speech and diversity of opinion in Japan on 4 April. While not openly saying it supported all the statements of the Tsukurukai, nonetheless the *Yomiuri* supported the Tsukurukai's right to produce its textbook and for education boards to have the freedom to select it. Finally, the *Sankei* was understandably supportive of the textbook given that the textbook's publisher, Fusōsha, is part of the Sankei media conglomerate. On 23 February it criticized the *Asahi* for trying to influence the screening process by condemning the textbook's authors while the textbook was still under review; and after the approval of the textbook, on 4 April the *Sankei* welcomed a new era of diversity in Japanese education and criticized the large number of 'ideologically-biased, anti-establishment teachers' in the social sciences.

This snapshot of editorial opinion does not capture the intensity of public debate surrounding the textbook: the demonstrations, heated exchanges between television pundits and intense pressure placed on boards of education. In the end, the publicity ensured that the textbook became too controversial and it was almost completely boycotted. Nevertheless, the 2001 textbook crisis confirmed the by now clear spectrum of press views on war-related issues, from the progressive *Asahi* to the nationalistic *Sankei*.

The A-bombs

Competing interpretations of Japanese war responsibility underlie the differences in the stances of the papers in all the media events discussed thus far. In other issues, such as the A-bombs, Japanese responsibility is present mainly at the periphery. In such cases, responsibility has not acted as such a divisive issue and a broader media consensus has emerged. Unsurprisingly, the A-bombs attract significant media attention in Japan. However, media discussion of the A-bombs tends to be in ritualized commemorative reportage (see Chapter 5) rather than concerning headline-grabbing controversies. Nevertheless, the A-bombs have assumed headline status and featured in the *nenpyō* in three contexts away from annual commemorations: legislation concerning the ongoing medical treatment of *hibakusha*, Hiroshima as a centre for pacifist and anti-nuclear activism, and the repercussions of American representations of the A-bombs.

For the first postwar decade, *hibakusha* received little favourable treatment. However, the Hiroshima Atomic-bomb Survivors Hospital was established in 1956 and following the 1957 Survivors Medical Care Law, Japanese *hibakusha* became entitled to special assistance (Hiroshima Peace Memorial Museum 1999: 90–1). Given the iconic nature of *hibakusha* suffering in Japan, subsequent laws relating to their medical treatment have typically made the front pages. The medical treatment of the approximately 20,000 non-Japanese *hibakusha* has been a thornier issue. Non-Japanese *hibakusha*, mainly Koreans brought to Japan as forced labourers (such as in the Mitsubishi shipyards and steelworks in Nagasaki), place a narrative of Japanese war responsibility at the heart of the A-bomb narrative. It was not until the 1970s, when there was increased Japanese consciousness of Japanese aggression, that the plights of Korean *hibakusha* were recognized (Dower 1996: 141). Korean *hibakusha's* campaigns for assistance from Japan started in the late 1960s and have received reasonably prominent coverage – from the 'popping flashbulbs of the press corps' in a hospital ward as a Korean *hibakusha* received his *hibakusha* treatment entitlement card during a staged media event (*Asahi shinbun* 26 July 1974) to the front-page announcement of a new Korean *hibakusha* fund in 1990 (*Asahi shinbun* 17 May 1990).

While the prominence of the A-bombs within Japanese cultural memory is often criticized, not least for the marginalization of non-Japanese victims within the narrative, Hiroshima's significance as the site of the world's first nuclear attack has made it a magnet for global anti-nuclear pacifism. There have been numerous anti-nuclear demonstrations and meetings held in Hiroshima; and visits by the UN General Assembly President (6 August 1977) and the Pope (25 February 1981) as well as the A-bomb Dome's designation as a UNESCO World Heritage Site (6 December 1996) have all attracted Japanese media attention. Actions that seem to breach Hiroshima's and Japan's pacifist ideals also make the front pages, such as revelations that munitions for use in Vietnam were being stored in Hiroshima (*Asahi shinbun* 22 May 1972) or American Ambassador Edwin Reischauer's 1981 admission that nuclear weapons had been on American ships in Japanese ports in contravention of Japan's three non-nuclear principles: not to possess, produce or admit nuclear weapons into Japan (*Asahi shinbun* 18 May 1981).

Finally, the Japanese press has been very sensitive to the ways in which the A-bombs continue to be represented in the US. In 1994 and 1995 two incidents made the front pages: the decision by the US Postal Service to abandon the commemorative 'mushroom cloud' stamp on 8 December 1994, and the denouement of the *Enola Gay* controversy at the Smithsonian Museum in Washington, DC, when the exhibits about Japanese victims and the reasons for using the bomb were finally shelved on 30 January 1995. On these issues, however, the press consensus was clear and there was little need for national debate. All the papers reported how Prime Minister Murayama and the mayors of Hiroshima and Nagasaki welcomed the withdrawal of the stamp and regretted the cancellation of the Smithsonian exhibition, as well as the less diplomatically worded criticisms coming from *hibakusha* groups. The *Yomiuri's* editorial (2 February 1995) about the Smithsonian and the *Asahi's* editorial (10 December 1994) about the stamps were virtually indistinguishable in stance, barring a slightly stronger emphasis in the *Asahi* about the need to understand the feelings of others in Japan's own attempts to face its past (a point the *Yomiuri* also made).

Ultimately, the Hiroshima and Nagasaki attacks are American war responsibility issues. Given that memory rifts in Japan are based on ideological contestation over Japanese war responsibility, the A-bombs are not nearly as divisive an issue as the 'comfort women', for example. Events such as the cancellation of the Smithsonian exhibition make the front pages, but attract relatively little *sustained* attention and do not occupy as much newspaper page space as 'homegrown controversies'. By coincidence, one such 'homegrown controversy' erupted on the same day as the cancellation of the Smithsonian exhibits: a Holocaust denial article in the 30 January 1995 edition of the magazine *Marco Polo*, which claimed that 'there were no Nazi gas chambers' (Gamble and Watanabe 2004: 165–209). This caused uproar in Japan and abroad. It was a golden opportunity for the liberal press to criticize a branch of the conservative media (*Marco Polo* was part of the Bungei Shunjū group, whose publications have frequently criticized the *Asahi*, among others). Rather than focus on the Smithsonian, the *Asahi* (1 February 1995) and *Mainichi* (1 February 1995) both published editorials expressing incredulity at *Marco Polo*. The issue continued until *Marco Polo's* editor resigned two weeks later and the magazine was eventually discontinued.

Returnees

The issue of war orphans (*zanryū koji*) bears a close similarity in patterns of media reporting to the A-bombs: whereas a few landmark events in the process of getting war orphans returned to Japan are mentioned in the *nenpyō* or make the front pages (such as the results of official investigations into the whereabouts of war orphans on 12 March 1975, and when 47 war orphans became the first to return to Japan with state aid on 2 March 1981), these few references belie the intense media interest in the human drama aspect of the issue. The war orphans issue in March 1981 is another good example of how the volume of reporting can differ substantially from paper to paper, an issue first raised in the context of the Unit 731 trial verdict. The monthly bound editions of the Japanese newspapers have article indexes (with the exception of the *Sankei*, which is on microfilm). These indexes divide every article published in the paper that month by topic and type. In March 1981, the four national papers with article indexes had a subsection dedicated to the war orphans, and the number of articles was as follows: *Asahi* (46), *Mainichi* (35), *Nikkei* (12), and *Yomiuri* (30). The *Asahi* had nearly four times the number of articles in the *Nikkei*, and 1.5 times the number in the *Yomiuri*. This indicates not only that the volume of reporting on a particular topic (and thereby the priorities of the papers) can vary quite substantially, but also that topics of Japanese victimhood can be just as prominent, if not even more prominent, within liberal reportage than the more conservative press.

The treatment of the war orphans as innocent victims made their press coverage remarkably homogeneous over the various papers. With few war responsibility issues to insert ideological rifts into the issue (whatever responsibility their parents may have had as colonists in China and Manchuria, nobody could place such responsibility on children in many cases too young in 1945 to even remember that they had been born Japanese), the press gave prominent coverage to the heart-wrenching human dramas without ever needing to become involved in ideological posturing.

The stragglers found in Indonesia and the Philippines as long as twenty-nine years after the war had ended also attracted much media attention (such as the returns of Yokoi Shōichi, Onoda Hirō and Nakamura Teruo). Beatrice Trefalt has illustrated the extensive media interest in the stragglers (for example, 2003: 147–9) and the way in which the media organizations competed with each other for exclusive rights to the soldiers' stories. Here is evidence of the media as a competitive business. The press coverage was at the level of human drama: the personalities and experiences of the protagonists were the main issue rather than the potential lessons concerning historical consciousness. This was less the case with the last straggler, Nakamura Teruo, who was an indigenous Taiwanese and who by his origins placed the issue of imperialism within media coverage of his return. Nevertheless, it is the story of Onoda that continues to attract the most attention to this day. A television biopic of his experiences was broadcast in August 2005, and, despite emigrating to Brazil (partly to escape the media attention – Trefalt 2003: 158), he continues to capitalize on his fame by publishing in the lucrative conservative book market in Japan (for example, Onoda and Nakajō 2006).

Conclusions

Overall, the coverage of war issues in the Japanese press offers little support to the dominant view in the English-language media that the Japanese press is subservient to the ruling elite. The outing of nationalistic politicians by reporting their gaffes, criticism of the government's apology and compensation policies (from both the left and right wings), or the unearthing of evidence that challenges or even changes government policy are all evidence of an active press independent of the government on war issues. Neither is the Japanese press a 'well-tuned, single voice choir' (van Wolferen 1990: 96–7). Nevertheless, there are occasions when the press is blandly homogeneous or sings from the same hymn sheet as the government, particularly during the relaying of routine official pronouncements. There are also issues on which broader national and media consensus exists, such as concerning the sufferings of *hibakusha* and war orphans, or when the press is timid and avoids a clear line, such as concerning the imperial household. Overall, however, the five national dailies have clearly identifiable stances on the war, which are congruent with the broader divisions within Japanese war memories.

The combination of the reach of the press and the prominence of war-related reporting constitutes a strong case for the ongoing importance of war issues as current affairs issues. This chapter has been based on a database of some 350 war-related media events listed in general chronologies of postwar Japan. They are important episodes within postwar history, and not simply as war-related stories. One key reason why the war remains a current affairs issue is its controversial nature. Like other media around the world, debate, confrontation, scandal or controversy place a story on the front pages of Japanese newspapers, particularly when it concerns the government. The prevalence of the war on the front pages, therefore, is emblematic of Japan's contested war memories.

5 August commemorations

Television and war memories

Early August has a distinctive atmosphere in Japan. It is the hottest time of year and television news frequently shows images of commuters wiping sweat from their brows, or of the ravages inflicted on the Japanese archipelago by the typhoon season. There are summer festivals and fireworks displays, and the nation is gripped by the drama of the high-school baseball championship at Kōshien Stadium. The first half of August is also the key period of war remembrance and commemoration in the media. Three major war anniversaries – the dropping of the A-bombs on Hiroshima and Nagasaki and the war's end (6, 9 and 15 August respectively) – coincide with two other events that heighten the media mood of remembrance: the anniversary of Japan's worst air disaster (the crash in Gunma prefecture of JAL flight 123 on 12 August 1985) and the O-bon holidays, when highways become jammed with families returning to their hometowns to be with relatives and to remember their ancestors. The downturn in political and business activity during the summer recess typically creates a dearth of 'news', which is compensated for by many retrospectives, documentaries and special reports about the war. Satō Takumi calls this phenomenon 'August journalism' (Satō 2005: 129).

Nowhere is 'August journalism' clearer than on television, the most influential cultural form in advanced contemporary societies.

> Just as the popular press of the nineteenth century was responsible for the creation of the mass reading public and thence the political public, so TV has become the place where and the means by which, a century later, most people have got to know about most other people, and about publicly important events or issues. . . . Broadcast television not only created the largest 'imagined community' the world has ever seen (the TV audience), but through its various textual forms and genres it functioned as a *teacher* of cultural citizenship over several decades.
>
> (Fiske and Hartley 1978: xv–xvi)

This statement about the power of television is congruent with diverse evidence concerning Japanese television and war memories. In 2000, Japanese people watched an average of about three and a half hours of television per day (rising to four and a quarter hours on Sundays) (NHK hōsō bunka kenkyūjo 2003: 137). This compares to the average amount of time spent reading the newspaper per day of thirty to forty-five minutes. Typically, other cultural forms' influences are only maximized via television: a book's main impact may be to make its author into a television pundit, and cinema's impact is often the extent to which films are watched on television. For example, Japan's highest-grossing war film, *The Burmese Harp*, was seen by 3.87 million people at the cinema, but it got a 13.5 per cent viewing rating (in a population of 124 million) on 12 August 1995 (Fujihara 1996: 62–3).

Television's power also lies in its nature as a cultural form. Television provides a multi-sensory experience, which is frequently more 'impression-making' than a book or newspaper. Visual images of events actually happening at the time are often perceived to be more 'authentic' records of the past than the words of historians writing in later years, and soundtracks (including music) heighten the emotional experience of television.

There is also an issue of trust. A 2002 survey indicated that Japan's public broadcaster, NHK, was rated the most trustworthy of six major institutions in Japan: 79.2 per cent said that 'on balance' they trusted NHK, followed by newspapers (63.2 per cent), the courts (58.3 per cent), commercial television channels (37.4 per cent), the government (28.4 per cent) and publishers (23.3 per cent) (Matsuda 2005: 14–15). NHK was rocked by a number of scandals in 2004 and 2005 (discussed below) that may have altered these figures, but television, particularly NHK, is clearly trusted.

Television, however, is a diverse medium with many programme genres, including news, entertainment, documentaries and dramas. The relative importance of television and its programme genres are indicated by a survey I carried out among Japanese university students. As part of a wider historical consciousness survey, 436 students (primarily first- and second-year undergraduates) were asked how much various branches of the media had influenced their views on the Asia-Pacific War. The students – 220 female (50.5 per cent), 212 male (48.6 per cent) and four unknown (0.9 per cent) – ranked cultural forms using a scale of one (no influence) to five (a large influence). The results are indicated in Figure 5.1.

The most influential form was documentaries, followed closely by museums. Television news and films were third and fourth, while television dramas came in ninth. The most common answers for documentaries, television news, films and television dramas were four (had quite a lot of influence). These results indicate that the heavy media and scholarly focus on textbooks in assessments of historical consciousness among Japanese youth misses a critical point. Television documentaries and news (as well as films, probably seen on television) were more influential for these undergraduates than their school education and textbooks, which came in sixth.

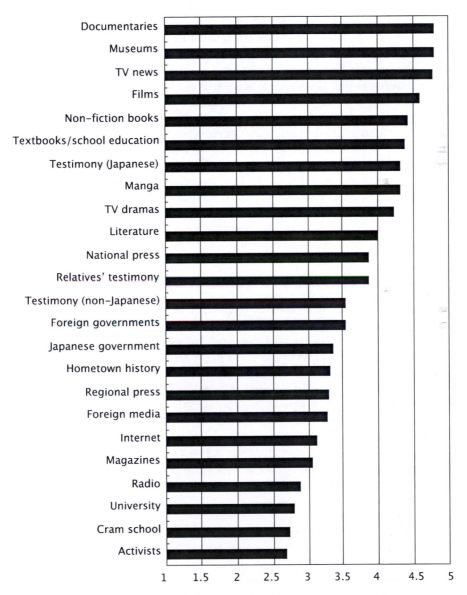

Figure 5.1 The relative importance for historical consciousness of cultural forms on 436 university students: respondents answered on a scale of one to five; the graph shows the average

Given the significance of television, the conspicuous absence of war-related television in most studies of Japanese war memories constitutes a major shortcoming. Television studies pose significant technical and methodological problems for researchers, which probably exacerbate existing prejudices within some academic communities against 'new' and 'lightweight' disciplines such as television studies, or trade publishers' fears that books about television quickly become obsolete (Penn 2003: x). Japan has two public access television archives (the Broadcast Library in Yokohama and NHK Archives in Saitama prefecture[1]), but the range of publicly available materials is limited. Television studies effectively rely on researchers recording their own materials and educated guesswork about when relevant materials will be broadcast. Large-scale studies have only become practical since the arrival of HDD (Hard Disc Drive) videos with digital editing and multi-channel recording capabilities. Consequently, television programme surveys have hitherto been the preserve of researchers working for broadcasting corporations who have the necessary archival access and technical facilities. Nevertheless, the technical difficulties do not change the fact that analysis of war-related television is indispensable in any survey of Japanese war memories.

War-related television: 1991–2005

Japan, like the rest of the developed world, is undergoing a revolution in satellite and digital broadcasting. Now Japanese people can watch hundreds of channels, although terrestrial television attracts the highest viewing figures and is therefore the focus of this chapter (Penn 2003: 2–3). Japan has seven main terrestrial channels, which are listed in Table 5.1 (channel numbers and names are for the Tokyo area). Channels 1 and 3 are NHK channels. NHK, which started television broadcasting in February 1953, is a public broadcaster and receives 96 per cent of its revenues from a licence fee. It has no commercials and is required by law to provide diverse, balanced and politically neutral programming. NHK-General provides a variety of programmes, including news, documentaries, quiz shows and dramas. NHK-Educational shows mainly educational programmes and documentaries. With the exception of some regional programming (such as regional news bulletins), both NHK channels are broadcast nationally. The first commercial television channel started broadcasting in August 1953. The current commercial channel system in the Tokyo area emerged in 1969 (Kojima 1997: 123). Since 1969, the five channels have been part of five media conglomerates (*keiretsu*) made up of a television news network (which broadcasts regionally through dozens of local affiliate stations), one of the five national newspapers, and other media businesses such as publishing (Shimano 2000: 25–45).

War-related television in Japan is heavily concentrated in the period of 'August journalism'. To gain a broad overview of war-related television in this period, I searched the newspaper television listings[2] for the period 4–16 August in the years 1991–2005. All programmes that advertised war-related

Table 5.1 Television channels in the Tokyo area

Channel	Television station	News network	Related newspaper
1	NHK-General	–	–
3	NHK-Educational	–	–
4	Nippon Television	NNN	*Yomiuri*
6	TBS	JNN	*Mainichi*
8	Fuji Television	FNN	*Sankei*
10	TV Asahi	ANN	*Asahi*
12	TV Tokyo	TXN	*Nikkei*

content were categorized by year, date, time, channel, genre and topic. The 876 programmes found cannot be considered an exhaustive list of all the programmes that contained war-related material: the sign language news on NHK-Educational at 8.45 p.m., for example, never advertised its contents but it typically covers the August commemorations. Nevertheless, the database illustrates the basic patterns of war-related programming.

Like other branches of the media, television has peaks and troughs in levels of interest concerning war issues. These cycles operate over the long- and short-term. The peak years were 1995 (fiftieth anniversary), 2001 (Koizumi's Yasukuni worship) and 2005 (sixtieth anniversary) with an average of six to seven programmes per day advertising war-related content. In other years there were two to five programmes per day. Similarly, within any given year there were peaks on the Hiroshima anniversary (an average of 10.5 programmes), a lesser peak on the Nagasaki anniversary (an average of 5.8 programmes), and a gradual rise over 13 and 14 August to a peak on 15 August (an average of 11.5 programmes). Other days had an average of two or three programmes.

The number of war-related programmes by channel illustrates differences in broadcasting policy among the stations. NHK-General was the largest broadcaster of war-related programmes with 42 per cent of the 876 programmes. Of the commercial channels, TV Asahi (19 per cent), Nippon Television (13 per cent) and TBS (12 per cent) had the highest interest, while NHK-Educational, Fuji Television and TV Tokyo had only 5 per cent each. NHK-Educational had few programmes because it does not have scheduled news bulletins and its programmes were mainly documentaries. TV Tokyo, like its related paper the *Nikkei*, focuses on economic stories and had relatively little interest in the war: its war-end anniversary specials typically focused on 'the postwar' and/or economic recovery. But while the three channels linked to the *Asahi*, *Mainichi* and *Yomiuri* newspapers (TV Asahi, TBS and Nippon Television) had levels of war-related coverage broadly compatible with their related newspapers, Fuji Television is conspicuous for its limited output compared to other branches of the Fuji–Sankei group, and in particular the monthly magazine *Seiron*, which publishes numerous war-related articles (see Chapter 6).

The following breakdown of programmes by genre illustrates the variety of formats in war-related programming:

1   ceremonies (5.0 per cent): live broadcasts of the Hiroshima, Nagasaki and war-end anniversary ceremonies;
2   news (38.2 per cent): war-related reports (typically two to six minutes) within a scheduled news bulletin;
3   documentaries (20.5 per cent): a documentary or programme entirely dedicated to a war-related topic;
4   dramas (4.8 per cent): a made-for-television drama;
5   films (3.4 per cent): a made-for-cinema film;
6   'wideshows' and variety programmes (18.7 per cent): war-related reports within an 'infotainment' programme, typically a report followed by comments from a studio panel/audience or as part of a quiz show;
7   talk shows (8.0 per cent): a studio panel discussion or a guest discussing war experiences in a chat show;
8   others (1.3 per cent): programmes that did not fit into the above categories or whose nature was unclear from the TV listings.

NHK tends to be serious and treats the war in news or documentaries, while the commercial television stations prefer 'wideshows' and talk shows. NHK typically produces drama series, while the commercial channels prefer one-off two-hour dramas. TBS was the major producer of war-related dramas and broadcast twice the number of its nearest rival (eleven to Fuji Television's five). The database also indicates how developments in the television industry have changed programming over time. Programmes come and go, programme anchors retire or change jobs, and the number of films shown on television has fallen since the emergence of specialist film channels on satellite television: there were 16 war films broadcast in the 5 years 1991–95, but only 14 films in the subsequent 10 years 1996–2005.

In terms of the timing of war-related television, programmes are spread throughout the day but concentrated in the early morning and evening primetime. On weekday mornings NHK's *Ohayō Nippon* (*Good Morning Japan*) typically runs series of war-related reports during August, as do the 'wideshows' on the commercial channels. On Sunday mornings there are political talk shows when politicians and pundits discuss issues such as prime-ministerial Yasukuni worship. During the daytime, 'wideshows' and chat shows predominate, along with the occasional drama. The early evening (5.00 p.m. to 7.00 p.m.) contains many national and regional news bulletins. This is the best time to watch news of local events and commemorations. During primetime (7.00 p.m. to 11.00 p.m.), NHK-General has had two or three scheduled news bulletins (in 2005 they were *News 7*, *News 9* and *News 10*) in which war-related news can feature prominently. Primetime contains many documentaries on both NHK-General (*NHK Specials*) and on NHK-Educational (ETV documentaries). There are invariably one or more documentaries on the evenings of 6, 9 and 15 August. On the commercial channels during primetime there might be a film or drama, or a report on TV Asahi's *News Station* (*Hōdō Station* since 2004). Fuji Television, Nippon Television and TBS have their evening news programmes in the late-night period after 11.00 p.m., at which time there may also be a documentary on NHK (repeats of *NHK Specials* from previous years are frequently aired in this late-night 'NHK Archives' time) or on Nippon Television (its *Document* programme).

In terms of topic, narratives of victimhood and particularly the A-bombs predominate. Of all the programmes advertised, 37.2 per cent included A-bomb-related content. Other topics typically associated with narratives of Japanese victimhood (including Okinawa, air raids, children's experiences and Siberian internment) accounted for another 12.9 per cent. While some of these programmes may contain references to Japanese war responsibility (such as discussion of Japan's own indiscriminate bombing in China in a programme about air raids), the focus on Japanese victimhood is clear. Direct discussion of Japanese war crimes and responsibility (such as the 'comfort women', war crimes trials or Unit 731) accounted for 5.1 per cent of programmes. Another way to place responsibility issues in a programme was to take the Asian perspective (such as Korean commemorations of their 'liberation day' on 15 August). These accounted for 2.2 per cent.

'Military history' programmes give general overviews of the fighting or focus on members of the Japanese military (11.8 per cent). The stances of these programmes depend on the topic and can range from conservative eulogies of the military to sympathetic treatment of Japanese soldiers as victims to exposés of atrocities. Other categories include 'political issues' (7.9 per cent), such as Yasukuni worship and debates over historical consciousness; 'art and artefacts' (3.5 per cent), in which a war relic tells a story or an art programme features the work of soldier-artists; or '15 August' reports (11.4 per cent) that depict the war-end commemorations or consider Japan's defeat and its implications. The remainder of programmes fell into a 'miscellaneous' category of reports about the war in Europe, profiles of ordinary people and other programmes whose precise content was indiscernible from the television listings.

Finally, the database reveals those programmes that most frequently contain war-related content. NHK's *Good Morning Japan* (NHK-G) and *NHK Specials* (both 69 times) advertised the most war-related content. *News 23* on TBS (47 times) and TV Asahi's *News Station/Hōdō Station* (43 times) led the evening news shows followed by NHK's *News 7* (40 times) and *News 10* (*News 11* to 2000, 32 times). The leading 'wideshows' were Nippon Television's early morning 'wideshow' *Zoom In* (*Zoom in Super* since 2002, 28 times) and TV Asahi's early morning *Yajiuma Wide* (21 times). The leading chat show was *Tetsuko*, hosted by UN Goodwill Ambassador Kuroyanagi Tetsuko, which advertised war-related interviews with a studio guest 27 times.

In sum, war-related television slots easily into the regular routine of Japanese television during the first half of August. There are few major changes in programme scheduling (except on 6 or 15 August, when special commemorative programmes are most common). Japanese people do not have to search out war-related programming: 'August journalism' means that war-related television reaches Japanese people via their regular viewing habits of news and current affairs programmes.

NHK's survey of war-related programming in 1995

The broad conclusions from the television listings survey are supported by an NHK survey of fiftieth anniversary commemorative programming in May (VE-Day) and August (VJ-Day) 1995 in Japan, Germany, the US, UK and South Korea (Kōno *et al.* 1996). This 110-page report (hereafter 'the report') analyses the contents of Japanese television programmes and the impact of war-related television on Japanese war memories.

The report compared how the flagship news programmes on each channel reported the A-bombs. NHK's *News 7* tended to have reports of two to six minutes and had a short report every day between 1 and 15 August except 10, 12, 13 and 14 August. Its stance was largely 'Japan's message as the first *hibaku* nation'. TBS, and particularly *News 23*, tended to have longer A-bomb reports, with five reports of over twenty minutes (7, 8, 9, 10 and 14 August). Presenter Chikushi Tetsuya's long interviews with a number of non-Japanese guests (including Barton Bernstein, Ian Buruma and Richard von Weizsäcker) and focus on the *Enola Gay* exhibit controversy at the Smithsonian highlighted differences in international commemorations of the bombs. In comparison to Chikushi's verbal style, TV Asahi's *News Station* used more visual effects and music in its reports. Nonetheless, *News Station* had a number of reports about the bombs, including a seventy-minute special programme on 15 August. By contrast, *Kyō no dekigoto* (*Today's Events*) on Nippon Television presented by Sakurai Yoshiko (who in recent times has become a conservative pundit) and *News Japan* on Fuji Television had little A-bomb coverage – in total only about six and four minutes respectively for the whole two-week period 1–15 August (ibid.: 36–40). The report concludes: 'Each Japanese TV station had its own characteristic approach toward atom-bomb related news, depending on station policy' (ibid.: 272).

In terms of reporting Japanese atrocities, Japanese war crimes or war responsibility issues were raised 54 times in contrast to the 57 times that Japanese victimhood issues were raised. The main issues were the 'comfort women' (13 times), the POW issue (11 times), Unit 731/human experiments (5 times) and colonial rule of Korea (4 times). Politicians' comments or discussion of 'historical consciousness' accounted for 21 of the 54 items. *News 23* and *News Station* were the most prominent presenters of aggression-related stories. However, only 14 of the 33 television items (42 per cent) about Japanese crimes made 'concrete statements about the facts of Japanese aggression' compared to the 80 per cent of the 59 television items on Japanese victimhood that made 'concrete statements about the facts of

Japanese victimhood' (ibid.: 50–1). As a result, the report concludes that 'Japanese television clearly conveyed the fact that Japan was an aggressor in World War II, but efforts to emphasize that Japan was also a victim were more detailed' (ibid.: 272).

The report also investigated viewing habits. People were asked: 'Around the fiftieth anniversary of the end of the war there were many television programmes about the war. How much did you watch these programmes?' (ibid.: 95). The results are shown in Figure 5.2. While respondents in Germany and the US tended towards the 'not much' and 'not at all' categories, half of Japanese people said that they watched 'some' war programmes. This suggests that Japanese television might have a comparatively significant effect on war memories by international standards.

Furthermore, the report's conclusion that television broadcasting in Japan focuses on victimhood and to a lesser extent aggression is substantiated by the following poll (ibid.). People who had responded that they watched 'some' or 'a lot of' war-related television were asked to choose three statements from a list of ten concerning impressions they had gained from watching war-related television programs. Six of these are indicated in Figure 5.3. Japanese people displayed greater victim consciousness by talking more of the 'terrible nature of war' and the 'suffering of the people', but they also gained the clearest impression of 'armies' inhumane acts' and the 'sufferings of occupied peoples', which confirms that Japanese television showed 'impression-making' programmes of Japanese aggression. Japanese television also ranked last in 'brave fighting scenes', which implies fewer nationalistic, heroic representations of the military.

Finally, people who had responded that they watched 'some' or 'a lot' of war-related programmes were also asked what kinds of programme they watched (ibid.). Respondents could give multiple answers and the Japanese results were as follows: documentaries (74.7 per cent), news (61.7 per cent), films and dramas (42.3 per cent), talk shows (18.7 per cent) and others

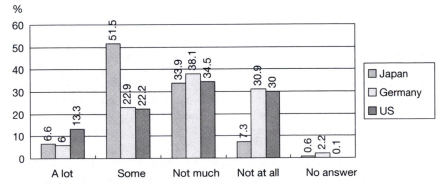

Figure 5.2 How much war-related television did you watch during the war-end commemorations?

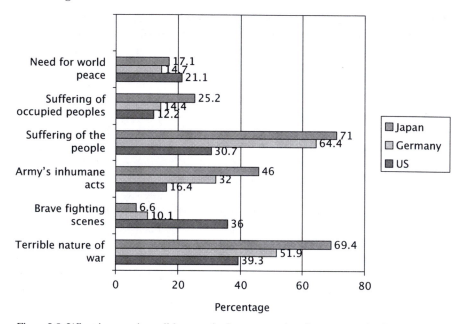

Figure 5.3 What impressions did you gain from war-related programming?

(2.0 per cent). These results are compatible with the results of the historical consciousness questionnaire given to Japanese university students, who ranked their influential programmes in the order documentaries, news, films and dramas (see Fig. 5.1).

In summary, the NHK survey adds to the emerging picture of war-related television: whereas there is a heavy focus on Japanese victimhood, overall Japanese television is more progressive than nationalistic on war issues, and the importance of television for Japanese war memories may be relatively significant even by international standards.

The politics of war-related television

Like the government's stance and the contents of textbooks, the stance of NHK is a key battleground in Japan's contested war memories. NHK, as Japan's public broadcaster, is obliged to be politically neutral. Individual programmes can range from conservative to progressive, but if the totality of NHK's war-related programming is considered, NHK is progressive-leaning. This irritates nationalists, who regularly berate NHK for 'disregarding its obligations' to be 'balanced'.

Since 1989 the flagship documentaries on NHK have been called *NHK Supesharu* (*Special*). They are typically fifty to ninety minutes long and are broadcast in prime time (7.00 p.m. to 11.00 p.m.) on NHK-General, or late at night (particularly repeats). To commemorate fifty years of television broadcasting in 2003, NHK produced a souvenir 'mook' (magazine-book) which listed every *Special* ever made. In the period 1989–2002, 1,554 *Specials* were produced and 84 (5.4 per cent) were about the Asia-Pacific War. Of these 84 *Specials*, 67 were originally broadcast in August, which demonstrates the heavy concentration of war-related programming in the period of 'August journalism' (NHK 2003: 217–25).

The *Specials* exhibit a range of views on the war. Military history programmes are often conservative, such as the two-part special *The Pacific War, A Visual Record* (*Eizō kirokushi, taiheiyō sensō*, NHK-G, 10 and 11 December 1991), which exemplifies a conservative rendering of war history. The story starts in 1941, which marginalizes the China War (whose only significant mention is about Japanese attacks on the Allied supply line to Chiang Kai-shek). Japanese atrocities are not denied but they are barely mentioned: only the Bataan Death March, the Rape of Manila and the Japanese army's victimization of Okinawan civilians are mentioned, but without elaboration. Asians in occupied territories are 'mobilized', but little indication is given of their often harsh treatment. Instead, the documentary focuses on military strategy and the reasons for Japan's defeat at the hands of the US, particularly in naval battles. The documentary utilizes the official newsreels of the time to give Japan's reasons for going to war. No retrospective judgement is made on these pronouncements, which has the effect of endorsing the reasons stated and attaching minimal blame to Japan. Emotional language is reserved for instances of Japanese suffering (the 'tragedy of Imphal' and 'indiscriminate bombing'); and the documentary ends with 15 August 1945, which avoids the issues of war guilt raised at the Tokyo War Crimes Trials.

However, *The Pacific War*'s conservative stance is not mirrored in the majority of other *Specials*. The list of *Specials* in NHK's commemorative 'mook' reveals a progressive slant. A quarter of the 84 *Specials* were about the A-bombs, and others focused on instances of Japanese victimhood. However, Japanese war crimes featured in a way unmatched by conservative defences of Japanese actions: confessions of war criminals in the Chinese Returnees Association (Chūkiren) (15 August 1989), postwar settlements and the Tokyo Trials (14 and 15 August 1992), Korean and Chinese forced labour (1 and 14 August 1993), and Japanese companies' responsibility for slave labour (15 August 1996). Even documentaries that at first glance appear to be 'conservative' can contain progressive arguments. One example is *Ōoka Shōhei's 'Leyte Diary'* (*Shishatachi no koe, Ōoka Shōhei 'Reite senki'*, NHK-G, 14 August 1995). Soldier memoirs are often conservative self-justifications or present the sufferings of Japanese servicemen, but Ōoka (1909–88), a well-known writer and critic in postwar Japan, was candid about how the people of Leyte suffered more than the Japanese. The documentary has interviews with Filipinos detailing instances of Japanese brutality, and about ten minutes detailing incidents of cannibalism among Japanese soldiers. These documentaries (and NHK's 15 August 2005 *Special* discussed below) reveal another pattern in August television journalism: narratives of Japanese victimhood predominate around the A-bomb anniversaries, but the war-end anniversary is when Japanese aggression is treated most.

The overall progressive-leaning stance of NHK is also revealed in the sustained, ferocious criticisms of NHK by nationalists. In his 1983 book *Questions for Biased NHK*, Okada Shinichi attacked the way NHK had covered the 1982 textbook controversy. He accused NHK of 'ignoring the national interest', 'distorting the facts', 'breaking broadcasting law' and of being a 'traitorous broadcaster' (Okada 1983: 4–6). And since 1997, nationalist historian Nakamura Akira has had a monthly column called 'NHK Watching' in the magazine *Seiron*. 'NHK Watching' frequently addresses war-related reporting. For example, Nakamura was incensed that *News 7*'s coverage of the Ceremony of Remembrance for the War Dead on 15 August 1997 had focused on Prime Minister Hashimoto's condolences to the victims of Japanese aggression at the expense of his condolences to Japanese victims. NHK's editing presented Japan as simply an aggressor, argued Nakamura (Nakamura 1997: 184).

The virulence of nationalists' attacks on NHK resembles their attacks on the *Asahi* newspaper, but while nationalists cannot control the stance of a media conglomerate's newspaper, they are licence-fee payers to NHK. Fed up at their money being used to produce programmes antithetical to their views, a number of nationalists even call for the abolition of NHK and have taken advantage of scandals affecting NHK in 2004 and 2005 to promote a boycott of the licence fee.

But it is not only nationalists who criticize NHK. Following the 2000 Women's International War Crimes Tribunal on Japan's Military Sexual Slavery organized by the feminist group VAWW-Net Japan, NHK broadcast a four-part documentary series called *How is War to be Tried?* (*Sensō wo dō sabaku ka*, 29 January–1 February 2001). A number of last-minute revisions were made to the second programme, which focused on the tribunal. These included cutting confessional testimony by Japanese soldiers, the tribunal's judgement that Emperor Hirohito was guilty, and interviews with VAWW-Net leader Matsui Yayori (Yoshimi 2001: 188–9). Conservative historian Hata Ikuhiko was invited to participate in the series, and he expressed his reservations about a 'tribunal' in which none of the defendants were there to defend themselves (for Hata's perspective, see Hata 2006: 138–68).

This precipitated a furious response from VAWW-Net Chairperson Matsui Yayori and Secretary-General Shoji Rutsuko (2001), who sent an open letter to NHK President Ebisawa Katsuji. They claimed that the programme 'presented the Women's International War Crimes Tribunal in such a distorted and biased way that viewers could only have come away full of prejudice and misunderstanding'. They demanded to know why the programme had been changed. But even with the alterations nationalists remained livid. Nakamura blasted the programmes in his May 2001 'NHK Watching' column, and Takeda Tatsuo asked why people should pay the licence fee to such a biased public broadcaster in the April 2001 edition of *Shokun!* (Takeda 2001: 104).

The 'programme revisions' issue had repercussions for years to come. VAWW-Net filed a lawsuit against NHK in July 2001, but the issue became the topic of major media debate on 12 January 2005 when the *Asahi* newspaper alleged that Nakagawa Shōichi and Abe Shinzō (two LDP cabinet ministers well known for their right-wing views) had put pressure on NHK to revise the programme. NHK producer and whistleblower Nagai Satoru stated that the changes were a result of political pressure (Morris-Suzuki 2005; McCormack 2005). Both NHK and the two politicians strenuously denied the *Asahi*'s claims. Conservatives, meanwhile, watched in delight as the two main media organizations they accuse of promoting 'masochistic' historical views (NHK and the *Asahi*) were at loggerheads. The *Asahi* was eventually forced to back down when it admitted the 12 January article contained 'uncertain' information. Akigawa Kōtarō issued a statement of regret, but '[Asahi executives] said the degree of uncertainty was not so severe as to force the paper to correct the January article' (www.japantimes.co.jp 1 October 2005). The suspicion of political interference has never been dispelled and remains the view of VAWW-Net.

NHK suffered a loss of trust because of the 'programme revisions' issue. It coincided with a scandal in July 2004 about misuse of the licence fee by an NHK producer. NHK President Ebisawa resigned in January 2005 and individuals refusing to pay the licence fee increased sharply. Overall, the 'programme revisions' episode demonstrated the thankless task that Japan's public broadcaster has in keeping all sides happy given Japan's contested war memories. It has led to a fear among many progressives and stark warnings from some international observers (Reed 2006; McCormack 2005; Morris-Suzuki 2005) that severe intimidation and pressure by neo-nationalists is making NHK (and other branches of the liberal media and academy) increasingly reluctant to tackle sensitive issues within war history. Despite the pressure, NHK remains progressive-leaning on war issues, and neo-nationalists show little sign of abandoning their 'NHK watching'.

The politics of television programming at the commercial channels follows a different pattern. Unlike NHK, there is no obligation to be politically neutral or even provide 'quality' programmes: war-related programming is subject to the market forces of audience ratings and revenues from advertisers. As explained earlier, the commercial channels are part of media conglomerates, which also contain one of the national newspapers. If a television channel's relationship with its related newspaper was a guide to the stance of the television station, then one would expect Fuji Television (*Sankei*) to be the most nationalistic, and Nippon Television (*Yomiuri*) to be conservative. TBS (*Mainichi*) and TV Asahi (*Asahi*) would be more progressive, while TV Tokyo (*Nippon Keizai*) would have relatively little coverage. This ideological spread is evident to some extent, but war-related programming on the commercial channels tends to be concentrated in the progressive-leaning or slightly conservative mainstream. Television stations have less obvious ideological stances than other branches of the media and tend towards the 'media as a platform for debate' role. The key differences between the channels come in the style and amount of war coverage, or the pundits invited to appear on the station's programmes.

Given its affiliation to the *Sankei* newspaper, one might expect Fuji Television to be nationalistic on war issues. However, Fuji Television has produced some progressive programmes inconsistent with the stance of the *Sankei* newspaper. In 1992, it broadcast a ninety-minute special comparing German and Japanese compensation (*Nichidoku no sengo hoshō, 47-nen tettei hikaku*, Fuji, 8 August 1992). Presenter Aikawa Kinya used the word 'ashamed' (*hazukashii*) when describing how Japan had only paid one-fortieth the level of German compensation. Through frank descriptions of the treatment of Korean forced labourers and comparisons with German official apologies and textbooks, the programme made the case for Japan to do more to address the past.

Nippon Television has also produced progressive documentaries. *Staying Silent, Indonesia's 'Comfort Women'* (*Koe tozasarete, soshite indoneshia no 'ianfutachi'*, Nippon TV, 29 September 1996) took a feminist stance with a young female reporter interviewing former 'comfort women', which provoked an angry denunciation from nationalist manga artist Kobayashi Yoshinori (Kobayashi 1997: 63–74).

Both these documentaries were not only progressive, but one was produced by a television channel linked to a newspaper (*Sankei*) and magazine (*Seiron*) better known for Nanking Massacre denial than calls for compensation, and the other was produced by a channel linked to a newspaper (*Yomiuri*) better known for supporting conservative politicians who resist 'comfort women's' campaigns for justice. A search of the database at the Broadcast Library in Yokohama in 2003 for the most 'conservative sounding' (by title and synopsis) documentary I could find on the two channels turned up *Forgotten Comrades in Arms* (*Wasurerareta senyū*, Nippon TV, 24 August 1992). It had scenes of Indonesian veterans nostalgic for their days fighting alongside the Japanese, but the documentary focused on their claims for military pensions from Japan. It also contained 'comfort women' testimony and discussions of the deaths of 'not a few' of the between two and four million Indonesian 'coolies' drafted by the Japanese. The frank conclusion was that Indonesians cannot easily forget the 'many inhumane acts' that occurred during Japanese rule.

Such progressive arguments on Nippon and Fuji Television contrast with the stances in their related newspapers. How can this be the case? The key reason is viewing figures. As described in Chapter 1, the 'profitability threshold' of television is the highest of any of the cultural forms. Whereas book sales of 30,000, magazine sales of 200,000 and newspaper circulations of two million are basic benchmarks for commercial success, viewing figures of two million (about 2 per cent[3]) are mediocre results for commercial broadcasters, who need figures closer to 10 per cent to increase the prices of their advertising slots. Commercial channels maximize viewing figures by appealing to the broadest possible range of the Japanese public, or in war-related programming, areas of most agreement in Japanese war memories. This means narratives of Japanese victimhood, or if Japanese war responsibility must be raised, a stance that acknowledges 'aggressive acts' or an aggressive war. In most cases, war-related programmes cannot achieve the ratings of a Yomiuri Giants baseball game or one of popular comedian Akashiya Sanma's shows. However, if a war programme is to be shown, chauvinistic nationalism is not the key to maximizing ratings.

A further issue is whether advertisers want to be associated with programmes that take an explicitly nationalistic line. Some companies (such as Mitsubishi in its court battles against slave labourer compensation) have conservative stances in the boardroom and close links to conservative elites (Underwood 2006). But while such views can be kept largely out of the public gaze in court battles, sponsoring nationalistic programming is another matter entirely.

These two factors explain why none of the channels put many nationalistic programmes on television. Nevertheless, conservative and nationalist pundits routinely appear on current affairs programmes and in some cases they are treated favourably. For example, conservative guests like Ishihara Shintarō and Sakurai Yoshiko can present their views unchallenged on Fuji Television's Sunday morning talk show *Hōdō 2001*, although they can expect to be grilled on TV Asahi's *Sunday Project* hosted by Tahara Sōichirō.

Furthermore, conservative documentaries can be broadcast, usually on military history. More usually, however, nationalistic documentaries are straight-to-video productions or restricted to specialist channels on satellite television. The Bunshun group (which publishes the right-wing opinion magazines *Shokun!* and *Bungei Shunjū*) has a video division called Bunshun Nonfiction Video that produces many military histories. A visit to a Japanese video shop reveals rows of such documentaries glorifying the military. This video market exists partly because such documentaries rarely make it onto terrestrial television: they are aimed at too small an audience. However, this does not stop them from being commercially viable when sold on video, where the 'profitability threshold' is so much lower.

Whereas Fuji and Nippon Television's war stances frequently differ from those of their related newspapers, TBS and TV Asahi tend to mirror the progressive stances of their papers, particularly in their flagship evening news programmes. TBS's *News 23* presenter Chikushi Tetsuya and TV Asahi's *News Station* presenter Kume Hiroshi (who presented *News Station* 1985–2004) are well known for their progressive stances. The programme formats of *News 23* and *News Station* (news 'magazines' with lengthy feature reports and the other headlines of the day given in brief) have helped the presenters express their views. By contrast, Fuji and Nippon Televisions' late night bulletins (*News Japan* and *Today's Events*) resemble NHK news: they have reports of more even length, adopt a 'neutral' posture, and include fewer off-the-cuff comments by the presenters.

News Station is of particular significance in discussions of television's impact on war memories. When it was first broadcast in October 1985, a news show in prime time (weekdays, 10 p.m.) was revolutionary. *News Station* was a pioneer in the 'infotainment' genre. Kume had made his name as an entertainment programme presenter and his flamboyant style and simple explanations of news issues won *News Station* a huge following. By the 1990s, other channels had followed suit and introduced late evening news shows: *Today's Events* on Nippon Television, *News 23* on TBS and *News Japan* on Fuji Television (Yomiuri shinbun geinōbu 1994: 604–9). However, *News Station* remained the frontrunner and in 1995 was Japan's most watched news show with viewing figures of 13 per cent, just ahead of NHK's *News 7* (NHK 2003: 248–9).

News Station's stance was clearly progressive-leaning. *News Station's* forty reports in the TV listings survey (1991–2003) included the inevitable reports about Hiroshima and Japanese victimhood, but also reports on the Nanking Nassacre (11 August 1994 and 15 August 2002) and how the Japanese army sold opium in China to fund its war effort (12 August 1996). On three of the 15 August anniversaries (1991, 1995 and 2001) and also on 11 August 1995, *News Station* had special reports from South Korea or 'various Asian countries' to get non-Japanese views on the end of the war.

News Station's stance is confirmed by reading nationalist critiques of anchorman Kume:

> A while back on TV Asahi's *News Station*, it was calculated that if one takes together all the individual compensation claims being made by Chinese people for what they suffered during Japan's aggressive war, it would amount to 20 trillion yen. At that point, host Kume Hiroshi made a comment along the lines of 'Don't you think it would be good to settle for 20 trillion yen'. We can say that Kume's comments were representative of the thinking of not only progressives, but many ordinary people. However, are these people going to say we should pay compensation even if our country goes bust?
>
> (Wakō 2000: 287)

As even nationalists who despised Kume admitted, *News Station's* stance on war issues resonated with many ordinary people. However, after Kume's retirement in 2004, *News Station* was replaced by *Hōdō Station*, which is anchored by another former gameshow host, Furutachi Ichirō. This precipitated a noticeable change in stance: there are fewer war-related reports on less progressive topics, and Furutachi exhibits little of Kume's brazenness to challenge guests or take an ideological stance. Whether this is just Furutachi's style or partly in response to neo-nationalist pressure on the liberal media is unclear.

But the presenter of choice for progressives would be Chikushi Tetsuya of *News 23* on TBS. *News 23* plays to a higher-brow audience and does not attract *News/Hōdō Station's* viewing figures. Chikushi is softly spoken but his sharp views are presented either in off-the-cuff remarks or in his *taji sōron* ('thought for the day') when he delivers a personal statement direct to camera. Within the forty-seven editions of *News 23* advertising war-related content, there were reports about cannibalism (10 August 1992), the 'comfort women' (13 August 1996 and 13 August 1997), chemical weapons in China (14 August 1996), Nanking (11 August 1997), a three-part special about war responsibility (14–16 August 2000) and Unit 731 (16 August 2001). *News 23* also features Yasukuni Shrine issues and particularly the A-bombs, and here too the balance is unambiguously progressive. For this stance, Chikushi and *News 23* are also regularly attacked in nationalist publications (for example, Hata 2006: 112–37; Mizuma 2003).

The sixtieth anniversary as seen on TV

As the sixtieth anniversary of the end of the war approached, television embarked on its ritual cycle of retrospectives and commemorative programmes. Guided by television listings and trailers, I recorded as many programmes as possible with war-related content. The survey covered the seven terrestrial channels plus NHK's two satellite channels (BS-7 and BS-11) in the period 31 July to 21 August and was carried out in Sapporo. I was able to record 174 programmes containing over 86 hours of war-related programming after all unrelated sections of news bulletins, commercials and repeats had been edited out. Cross-referencing these programmes to television ratings (available from Video Research Ltd[4]) illustrates what war-related television was watched by the largest numbers of Japanese people over the sixtieth anniversary. The results are shown in Table 5.2.

Films or dramas, which will be discussed in Chapter 7, featured four times in the top ten ratings. One was *Grave of the Fireflies* (Nippon Television, 5 August 2005). This animated film is an institution of August television with five airings in the period of the television listings survey, 1991–2005. Its poignant story of the struggle for survival of a boy Seita and his young sister Setsuko after the death of their mother in the Kobe air raids has made it an anime classic (Napier 2000: 161–74). So enduring is the resonance of its message of innocent children's suffering in war that nearly two decades after it was made (1988) there are still tours around the key locations. One of these tours and interviews with director Takahata Isao were featured in Nippon Television's morning wideshow *Wake Up!* on 13 August.

Predictably, the A-bombs featured prominently in the television survey. The first of the major anniversaries, Hiroshima (6 August), fell on a Saturday, so the weekday news programmes broadcast their Hiroshima specials on the Friday, 5 August. *Hōdō Station* (16.4 per cent ratings) had an eleven-minute special report featuring Einstein's reflections on his role in the development of atomic weapons and his admission in correspondence to a Japanese philosopher that he considered the bombs to be crimes.

Table 5.2 War-related programming that gained top-ten viewing ratings in its genre, 1–16 August 2005

Date	Time	Channel	Programme	Hours / minutes	Genre	Synopsis	Rating (%)
2 Aug. (Tues.)	21.00– 23.24	Nippon	*Twenty-four Eyes*	2'02"	Drama	A teacher and the war experiences of her pupils.	18.7
3 Aug. (Wed.)	4.30– 8.15	NHK-G	*Good Morning Japan*	0'08"	News	A woman who lost her father in Indonesia. Report in a series of five.	12.9
5 Aug. (Fri.)	18.55– 21.48	TBS	Chikushi Tetsuya Hiroshima Special	2'36"	Documentary	Testimony, computer graphics recreation of the blast, a Manhattan Project scientist meets *hibakusha*.	15.0
5 Aug. (Fri.)	21.03– 22.54	Nippon	*Grave of the Fireflies*	1'29"	Film	Animation film of two children's experiences of air raids.	13.2
5 Aug. (Fri.)	21.54– 23.10	Asahi	*Hōdō Station*	0'11"	News	Einstein's reflections on his role in the creation of nuclear weapons.	16.4
6 Aug. (Sat.)	8.00– 8.35	NHK-G	Hiroshima Ceremony, live	0'35"	Ceremony	Memorial ceremony for the sixtieth anniversary of the Hiroshima A-bomb.	14.2
7 Aug. (Sun.)	8.00– 9.55	Nippon	*Za Sunday*	0'04"	Talk	How the postal privatisation bill will affect Koizumi's Yasukuni worship.	11.8
7 Aug. (Sun.)	8.00– 9.54	TBS	*Sunday Morning*	0'13"	Talk	Nuclear issues: *hibakusha* testimony, should Japan have nuclear weapons, opinion and street polls.	12.0

Date	Time	Channel	Programme	Duration	Genre	Description	Rating
9 Aug. (Tues.)	4.30–8.15	NHK-G	Good Morning Japan *	0'22"	News	Nagasaki commemorations, the dissolution of parliament and the Yasukuni issue, peace education, local news of a play about kamikaze.	13.7
13 Aug.	8.00–9.25	Nippon	Wake Up!	0'10"	Wideshow	Tour of locations and interview with the director of *Grave of the Fireflies*, the Yasukuni issue.	12.3
13 Aug.	21.00–23.09	Fuji	Drama Special: Onoda's Return	1'47"	Drama	Biopic of army straggler Onoda Hirō.	14.3
14 Aug.	8.00–9.54	TBS	Sunday Morning	0'16"	Talk	Review of the week's commemorations, Yasukuni issue, air raids, war and the upcoming elections.	11.5
15 Aug.	4.30–8.15	NHK-G	Good Morning Japan *	0'47"	News	Multiple short reports: including *hibakusha* in Germany, children eat wartime recipes and Siberian internment.	12.8
15 Aug.	9.00–10.30	NHK-E	No Elephants in the Zoo	1'20"	Drama	Animated feature about how zoo elephants were killed.	3.5
15 Aug.	19.30–21.30	NHK-G	Japan and Asia: NHK's war end special	2'00"	Talk	Extensive discussion about Yasukuni, textbooks and war responsibility (part two of three).	12.6
16 Aug.	17.50–18.54	Fuji	Super News *	0'08"	News	Young people's historical consciousness, Hokkaido University students debate textbooks and Nanking.	11.8

* Note: Included local programming in the Hokkaido area.

Meanwhile, on TBS, Chikushi Tetsuya introduced a 156-minute (excluding commercials) special about Hiroshima (15.0 per cent ratings). The programme blurred the boundaries between reportage, polemic and drama. It featured the testimony of a number of *hibakusha* and the effects of the A-bombs on the family of a young actress, Ayase Haruka, who co-presented with Chikushi. Ayase set the emotional tone of the programme. Her *kawai* (cute and innocent) image, which is common among young women on Japanese television, set the stage for Chikushi's authoritative answers to her questions; and on three occasions she was the programme's 'tear-leader', including as she listened to her grandmother's experiences of the A-bomb for the first time.

The main documentary focus of the programme was whether dropping the bombs could have been avoided (it concluded 'yes': there had been missed opportunities on both sides). About one hour was dedicated to a history of the Manhattan Project and the decision to drop the bomb, which featured interviews with Gar Alperowitz, Barton Bernstein and other American scholars who question the 'lives saved' and 'the bombs were necessary to end the war' position. Also featured was a project to produce a computer graphics recreation of the blast based on old maps and witness testimony. This segment doubled as a trailer for TBS's sixtieth anniversary commemorative drama about the Hiroshima attack, in which the entire sequence would be shown. That drama was aired on 29 August to 19.1 per cent ratings.

The programme's climax was a meeting in the Hiroshima Peace Park between Harold Agnew, a Manhattan Project scientist, and two *hibakusha*. TBS had featured this meeting prominently in its trailers for the programme, and segments had appeared in the first twenty minutes. But maintaining viewing figures was clearly in the minds of the producers as the audience was kept waiting until the end for this gripping piece of television theatre. Agnew was the photographer on the *Enola Gay* who took the only existing footage of the actual attack. It was his first visit to Hiroshima and he had been visibly shaken by some of the images of burns he had seen in the Hiroshima museum. By the time of his meeting with the *hibakusha* the next day he had regained composure. The meeting started civilly with all three describing their experiences, but the mood changed when the *hibakusha* asked Agnew whether he felt regret. Agnew answered: 'I don't apologize. We have a saying: Remember Pearl Harbor' and 'If you want to blame someone, blame your military.' One of the *hibakusha* was visibly hurt and dabbed tears from her eyes: 'You just don't understand', she wept.

The meeting ended frostily. Agnew had stressed how terrible war is, how he had lost friends, and that the A-bombs had only done 'more easily' what firebombing had achieved (a point disputed by the *hibakusha*, who have lived with the effects of radiation). But the abiding image was of an old man in denial of the effects of his actions. Chikushi commented on how aggressors (*kagaisha*) often find it hard to truly appreciate the feelings of victims and referred the point back to Japanese war responsibility: a lack of understanding exists in Japan towards Asian feelings, argued Chikushi.

There were forty more minutes of A-bomb-related material later in the evening in *News 23*. which was off the air the following week (a casualty of TBS's coverage of the World Athletics Championships), so the 5 August programmes doubled up as the Nagasaki commemorative programme. Presenting from inside the Nagasaki A-bomb museum Chikushi used his 'thought for the day' to say that whereas Hiroshima could be understood as an attempt to win the war, the necessity of the Nagasaki bomb was far more debatable and it could be thought of as an experiment (and by implication a serious war crime).

The next morning, the ceremony marking the anniversary of the Hiroshima attack was broadcast live, as it is every year, from the Peace Park in Hiroshima. NHK's coverage started at 8.00 a.m. (14.2 per cent ratings). The first ten minutes contained sombre reports about the bomb and scenes from inside a home for *hibakusha*. At 8.15 a.m., there was a call for silence (*mokutō*) and the Peace Bell was struck. A minute of silence was disturbed only by the chirping of cicada, a sound synonymous with Hiroshima in August. Then Hiroshima Mayor Akiba Tadatoshi delivered his peace message. Whereas the message contained no direct references to Japanese aggression (unlike 1995, see Chapter 2), it was fiercely critical of countries in possession of nuclear weapons and called on the Japanese government to do more to help *hibakusha*. 'The mistakes of the past will not be repeated' (*ayamachi wa kurikaeshimasen*), the inscription on the cenotaph that had been defaced just weeks before by a disgruntled nationalist, was repeated twice to end the mayor's message. After Mayor Akiba's speech there were the children's peace declaration and a short speech by Prime Minister Koizumi. NHK's live broadcast finished here at 8.35 a.m.

There was one particular image from the ceremony that was picked up by a number of the evening news programmes. In the middle of the mayor's speech, a close-up shot revealed that Koizumi had his eyes shut and his head slightly to one side. It was a pose that suggested discomfort. The Hiroshima commemoration is the key occasion on which the prime minister loses control of the official war narrative and the Mayor of Hiroshima (whose constituency is the spiritual home of Japan's anti-nuclear pacifism with its generally more progressive view of war history) has a global television audience of millions. Koizumi has forged a strong personal relationship with George W. Bush, so such direct criticism of the US government could have been the cause of his expression. But a clue to more general tensions concerning the Hiroshima ceremony came the next morning on TBS's *Sunday Morning*, the most-watched Sunday morning show. During its thirteen minutes of war-related discussion on 7 August (12.0 per cent ratings), one of the topics was a 2003 *Mainichi* newspaper survey in which 83 out of 480 parliamentarians said Japan should consider developing nuclear weapons. Street interviews featured a number of horrified responses, and Hōsei University Professor Tanaka Yūko argued that the possession of nuclear weapons was a logical extension of the LDP's proposed constitutional reforms to recast the Self Defence Forces (*jieitai*) as an 'army' (*jieigun*). The tensions below the surface at the Hiroshima ceremony, therefore, centre on the clash between the vision of the Hiroshima mayor that Japan should be a pacifist torchbearer and the desires of Japan's more hawkish lawmakers (including Prime Minister Koizumi) to return Japan to the international military fold.

A perennial theme in the media during the sixtieth anniversary was the 'weathering' (*fūka*) of memories. For example, *Good Morning Japan* on 4 August cited an NHK opinion poll indicating that only 38 per cent of Japanese and 74 per cent of Hiroshima residents could name the day the A-bomb was dropped. The presenters then prefaced a report featuring *hibakusha* testimony as helping to prevent the 'weathering' of memories. *Good Morning Japan* was just one of a number of programmes that explicitly expressed this purpose of its war-related programming. It had many short war-related reports in early August. On 3, 9 and 15 August – when it had ratings of 12.9, 13.7 and 12.8 per cent respectively – it broadcast over an hour's worth of different reports on diverse topics, such as a woman who had lost her father in Indonesia, the Nagasaki commemorations, schoolchildren who cooked and ate wartime recipes, and Siberian internment.

However, the media consternation about 'weathering' memories only lasted as long as the war's newsworthiness in relation to other stories. On 6 August, for example, TV Asahi's early evening news (*J Chan*) placed the sixtieth anniversary of the Hiroshima attack after reports about the postal privatization bill (which included an interview with Prime Minister Koizumi in the grounds of the Peace Park where he had just attended the commemorations), a murderer who found victims through suicide Internet sites, seaside and river accidents claiming the lives of holidaymakers, and build-up for the Japanese women's football international against China that evening.

The crucial postal privatization vote, set for 8 August, had already infused war-related television: the day before the vote on *Za Sunday* (Nippon Television, 7 August, 11.8 per cent ratings), there was a short discussion about how the bill would affect Koizumi's plans for Yasukuni Shrine worship. But when the bill was defeated by LDP rebels and Koizumi called a snap general election, the whole tenor of war-related television changed. The upcoming election knocked the war off top billing in political talk shows and news programmes, and an edition of Beat Takeshi's *TV Tackle* (9.00 p.m., 8 August, TV Asahi) that was to have discussed the Yasukuni issue was cancelled so that *Hōdō Station* could be extended to discuss the dissolution of parliament. The war always has to compete with other issues for the attention of the Japanese media and public.

The war end anniversary on 15 August, however, is invariably marked with short reports on the morning shows, live coverage of the Ceremony to Commemorate the War Dead and a major NHK special in the evening. NHK's special in 2005 was a marathon television debate in three parts:

5.30 p.m. to 7.00, 7.30 to 9.30, and 10.30 to midnight. Anti-Japanese feelings, the Yasukuni issue and textbooks were the primary topics discussed by a studio audience of fifty people (about a third of whom were from other Asian countries) and distinguished guests, including Foreign Minister Machimura, conservative pundit Sakurai Yoshiko, a former ambassador to the US, and Korean and Chinese scholars. Given the themes and audience make-up, the programme was guaranteed to place the spotlight on Japanese war responsibility.

The middle segment of the programme achieved viewing figures of 12.6 per cent. It started with a profile of two Chinese who had become active in the anti-Japanese demonstrations in April. One, a student, explained how he had been influenced by his grandparents' stories of maltreatment at the hands of the Japanese and the descriptions of Unit 731's human experiments in his school history books. The other cited the SDF's mission in Iraq as evidence of Japan's growing military ambitions.

The discussion started with the role of 'anti-Japanese education' in the recent protests, with Chinese participants downplaying the 'anti-Japanese' nature of textbooks. But the discussion quickly moved onto the Nanking Massacre. A Japanese woman in the studio audience presented a carefully rehearsed denial of the Nanking Massacre that she had seemed determined to say at the first opportunity. This precipitated fifteen minutes of debate about the 'facts' of the massacre. The next videotaped report was about a Korean singer who had written a pro-Japanese book, but who had been branded a traitor and had had his career destroyed as a result. More recriminations ensued about how unreasonable anti-Japanese sentiment can be before retired ambassador Kuriyama took the conciliatory line: every country needs to look squarely at the dark periods of its history, but victims also need to be open-minded if reconciliation is to be achieved.

The next section about the Yasukuni issue exposed the wide range of interpretations in Japan about how to commemorate the war dead. A woman stated that it was only right for Koizumi to commemorate all those that had died in the war. She was quickly corrected by another woman, who pointed out that Yasukuni only commemorates military dead. The exchange illustrated how historical consciousness can frequently be based on mis-understandings. Then two veterans disagreed: one said he had lost many comrades and it was only natural to commemorate those who had died for their country, while another, who had been an internee in Siberia, adamantly opposed Koizumi's worship. Other people in the audience presented a range of views. A woman said the prime minister should commemorate at a place like the Okinawa memorial, where only people's names and not their nationalities are listed; a man said Yasukuni worship is a sign of peace and that Japan would be more likely to go to war again if Yasukuni worship ended; and in a fax from a viewer, the daughter of a *hibakusha* said 'To the people of Asia: through my family's sufferings I can understand yours. Please accept my apologies.' As the programme drew to a close for the evening news, it was clear that no consensus could be achieved: with Japanese war responsibility issues at the centre of the discussion, Japan's contested war memories had been played out in front of an audience of millions.

Conclusions

After the fiftieth anniversary, NHK's survey of war-related programming concluded that Japanese television clearly showed Japan's role as an aggressor in Asia, although the focus on Japanese victimhood was greater. The television listings survey, 1991–2005, and the sixtieth anniversary commemorations suggest that this conclusion is broadly accurate for the past fifteen years. Producing progressive programmes may have become more difficult since the 'programme revisions' issue, but all the television channels have produced progressive programmes and remain broadly progressive-leaning and anti-war. The NHK debate on 15 August illustrates perhaps the key mechanism that keeps Japanese television broadly progressive-leaning. Under the guise of 'discussing Japan's future in Asia' and media 'objectivity', television programmes play the 'media as a platform for debate' role, introduce war responsibility issues and invite Japanese people with a range of views, and perhaps some Chinese and Koreans, to participate. Conservatives have latitude to express their views, but the programme format presupposes Japanese war responsibility and places conservatives on the defensive.

Pockets of genuinely conservative programming do exist on Japanese television and conservative pundits are ubiquitous, but war-related television across all the channels is conspicuous for being antiwar and concentrated in the progressive-leaning to slightly conservative mainstream. Given the power and reach of television (if the ratings are truly representative of audience levels, then most programmes discussed in this chapter have been seen by between ten and twenty million people), the broadly progressive-leaning nature of Japanese television with its focus on Japanese victimhood and lesser focus on war responsibility helps to explain why Japanese war memories are not nearly as nationalistic as they are frequently made out to be.

6   History and ideology

A statement does not have to be 'factually incorrect' in order to make it biased. The statement 'A-bombs were dropped on Hiroshima and Nagasaki on 6 and 9 August respectively and Japan accepted the Potsdam Declaration on 14 August' is factually correct. However, it points the reader to the conclusion that the bombs were instrumental in ending the war. The following is also factually correct, but implies a more complex explanation of the reasons for Japan's surrender: 'Japan's navy and air force had been almost completely destroyed by the time that the A-bombs were dropped on Hiroshima and Nagasaki and the Soviets declared war on 8 August. Japan accepted the Potsdam Declaration on 14 August.' Even without 'factual inaccuracies', history can appear very differently according to how statements are woven together and prioritized within the argument.

The academic and journalistic ideal is 'objectivity', for interpretation to follow on from evidence that has been collected in a transparent and balanced way. In practice, objectivity is an elusive ideal: the selection and ordering of undisputed facts is itself a matter of subjectivity. Any analysis inevitably uses to some extent ideology, narrative conventions, theoretical frameworks or discourse community norms to frame the issues. Frameworks that survive and proliferate are those that seem to fit the facts best, or are most resonant for the largest number of people. These frames can always be challenged, and for all except the most ideologically rigid, evidence may succeed in altering the frames. But people are often remarkably adept at making the evidence fit their views rather than their views fit the evidence.

The role of ideology is essential for understanding contested war memories in Japan. Contestation concerning 'the facts' does occur, particularly over how many were killed in Nanking. But more usually, contestation is about the interpretation and relevance of particular incidents within war history. Different aspects of war history lend themselves to particular ideologies. An heroic story of a Japanese soldier rescuing a wounded comrade in China, for example, fits much more comfortably into a nationalist rendition of war history than a progressive one, and may be excluded from the latter as a result. Ideology, therefore, works on two particular levels: it provides a framework for how to interpret, accept or reject historical evidence; and it directs people's gazes towards those issues that most affirm the ideology. Much of the discussion thus far has focused on the first type, such as how different newspapers have treated the same topic. This chapter focuses on the second type within war history publishing and school textbooks: which aspects of war history are remembered, by whom and for what purpose; what is considered appropriate historical methodology; and how history can be taught to Japan's youth when that history is so contentious.

Publishing and the selective historical gaze

Japan's publishing industry is huge. It ranked fourth in the world behind the UK, Germany and the US in terms of new titles published in 1996 (Fujitake 2000: 151) and there are thousands of weekly and monthly magazine titles. There is also a vibrant market for cheap paperbacks: in 1999 there were 123 *bunko* series (mainly for novels) and twenty *shinsho* series (for serious non-fiction) (ibid.: 164–5). Reading about the war constitutes only a tiny fraction of total reading and publishing. Publishing's true power is indirect in that a well-received, controversial or best-selling book creates a knock-on effect: it is a researcher's ticket to appearing on television, in magazines and national newspapers, and elicits comment and analysis from other scholars or journalists. Furthermore, browsing in the 'history' and 'new releases' sections of Japanese bookshops reveals that war history is a significant genre within Japanese publishing. According to Munakata Kazuhiro, approximately 14,000 books about the Asia-Pacific War were published in Japan between 1945 and 1994, an average of 280 per year (Munakata 1996: 3). War books would not exist in such numbers if people were not buying them.

In 2000, Japan had around 4,400 publishing companies, of which 32 employed more than 1,000 staff (Fujitake 2000: 179). Whereas the largest companies produce a diverse range of publications by topic, format (books, magazines, comics) and stance, there are many small-scale publishers that specialize in particular fields, including some specialist war book publishers such as Kōjinsha. Publishing companies, particularly the smaller ones, tend to have identifiable stances on the war. This is not a matter of explicitly stated corporate ideology (such as can be found in newspaper editorials) but relates to the kinds of books and authors that are published most frequently. The stances of the larger companies are harder to categorize. Kōdansha, for example, is Japan's largest publisher and issues books from across the judgemental memory spectrum; and whereas Shōgakukan tends to have a conservative slant in its *bunko* (cheap paperback) series and its magazines *Voice* and *Sapio*, its educational manga aimed at children (discussed below) are more progressive-leaning. Table 6.1 shows some of the major publishers of war-related books and the *most common* stances of books within their catalogues.

But perhaps the best place to view the selective ideological gazes of those active in war debate is in the monthly 'opinion magazines' that a number of companies publish. Opinion magazines look more like books than

Table 6.1 Major publishers of war-related books and opinion magazines

Publisher (and webpage)	Orientation	Topics	Opinion magazine (circulation, 2005)
Asahi http://opendoors.asahi.com/index.shtml	Progressive	Compensation issue, books by Honda Katsuichi (Nanking etc.), war crimes, women's war history.	Ronza (19,125)
Bunshun http://www.bunshun.co.jp/	Conservative	Nanking (denial of), pro-Yasukuni worship, critical of China/Korea, military history/memoirs.	Bungei Shunjū (626,750), Shokun! (81,667)
Chūkōsha http://www.chuko.co.jp/	Conservative	Diplomacy, officer diaries, general war histories.	Chūō Kōron (42,333)
Fusōsha http://www.fusosha.co.jp/	Conservative	Affirmative views of the war, books by Tsukurukai members (incl. textbook), Nanking.	Seiron (93,271)
Iwanami http://www.iwanami.co.jp/	Progressive	Main publisher for progressive academics: air raids, Yasukuni, war responsibility/memories.	Sekai (not available)
Kōdansha http://www.kodansha.co.jp/	Neutral	Japan's largest publisher. Books across the spectrum of opinion.	Gendai (93,412)
Kōjinsha http://www.kojinsha.co.jp/	Conservative	Specialist war publisher: soldier memoirs, military history, machines of war.	
Ōtsuki Shoten http://www.otsukishoten.co.jp/	Progressive	Marxist orientation: war crimes, 'comfort women', anti-Yasukuni.	
Sanichi Shobō http://www.san-ichi.co.jp/	Progressive	War crimes, slave labour, Japanese victims.	
Shinchōsha http://www.shinchosha.co.jp/index.html	Neutral	Writers from across the spectrum, major publisher of war literature in cheap paperbacks.	Shinchō 45 (47,050)
Shōgakukan http://www.shogakukan.co.jp/	Conservative	Criticisms of 'masochistic' views, contemporary war-related issues more than war history.	Voice (35,592)
Shūeisha http://www.shueisha.co.jp/index_f.html	Neutral	Large publisher with relatively little war focus. Mixture of progressive and conservative authors.	
Tokuma Shoten http://www.tokuma-jp/index.html	Conservative	Nationalist defences of Japanese actions, pro-Yasukuni, critiques of 'anti-Japanese' views.	

Sources: Orientation based on the predominant topics and authors in the publishers' online catalogues, cheap paperback catalogues and opinion magazines; Opinion Magazine Sales from www.j-magazine.or.jp/FIPP/FIPPj/F/.

'magazines'. They are typically 350–450 pages long and contain around 15–25 essays, each of which is typically ten pages long. Interspersed between the essays are book reviews, advertisements, photograph collections and one- or two-page vignettes. The essays are on a variety of current affairs issues and are written by a combination of staff writers and one-off contributors. Many one-off contributors are academics, for whom the opinion magazines are important places to publish research articles for a general readership. Within a given edition of an opinion magazine there may be a set of three to six essays on a particular theme, particularly when an issue is in the news. Opinion magazines can also serialize up to four or five books at a time. A number of the most significant books within Japanese war debates were first published in instalments in opinion magazines: for example, Yoshida Yutaka's *Nihonjin no sensōkan* (1995), arguably the key study of Japanese war memories in Japanese, was serialized in *Sekai* between September 1994 and May 1995.

I undertook a survey of the war-related content of opinion magazines in the period 1991–2001 (Seaton 2004: 88–92). 'War-related essays' included both essays specifically about a war issue (such as arguing for official Yasukuni worship) and essays that included war history as part of a broader argument (such as historical consciousness issues in an essay about contemporary Korean–Japanese relations). I found just under 1,500 essays in seven magazines (*Sekai, Gendai, Ronza, Shokun!, Bungei Shunjū, Chūō Kōron* and *Seiron*) over the eleven-year period.

The survey reveals many aspects of ideological confrontation in Japan. There were the peaks in war interest evident in other branches of the media in 1991, 1995 and 2001. An overall trend of rising numbers of war-related essays throughout the 1990s reflects growing ideological debate. Much of this debate can be traced to the efforts of neo-nationalists, and in particular the Tsukurukai. There was also a peak in 1997, when the start of the Tsukurukai's activities precipitated a large rise in essays.

The magazines display varying levels of interest in war issues. Those at the progressive and nationalistic poles had a larger focus on war issues. *Sekai* (progressive) and *Shokun!* (nationalistic) averaged around 31 and 23 war-related essays a year respectively, 1991–2001. Essays were spread throughout the year. Other magazines, such as *Bungei Shunjū, Chūō Kōron* and *Gendai*, tended to limit themselves to war-related essays in the period of August journalism, or in response to particular current affairs events. They averaged only between five and nine essays a year. Clearly, the largest publisher of war-related essays was *Seiron*, published by Sankei–Fusōsha. It averaged over 50 essays per year. Following the formation of the Tsukurukai in 1996, *Seiron* became its primary mouthpiece. It covered the Tsukurukai's symposiums in 30-page specials and published numerous essays by its members. This was a case of corporate ideology and business strategy. *Seiron* and its related newspaper (*Sankei*) were publicizing the Tsukurukai's activities in preparation for the publication in 2001 of the Tsukurukai's textbook by Fusōsha.

The link between ideology and the selective historical gaze is demonstrated through the topics of war-related essays. *Sekai* is the leading magazine for progressive intellectuals (*shinpoteki bunkajin*). It does not divulge its sales figures, so 'leading magazine' refers to its reputation. *Sekai* focuses heavily on war and colonial responsibility issues. The phrase 'Japan's aggressive war' is standard in any essay; issues such as compensation feature prominently (such as February 1994); and a collection of ten essays in the July 1997 edition to mark the sixtieth anniversary of the outbreak of the China War was a roll call of Japanese atrocities from Unit 731 to forced labour. There are many essays by Chinese and Korean scholars, and analysis of Asian views or the role of history in contemporary diplomatic relations. Critiques of nationalist theories such as the 'Asian liberation' theory and 'the liberalist view of history' (discussed below) are commonplace, and were particularly so in 1997 after the formation of the Tsukurukai and in 1998 after the publication of Kobayashi Yoshinori's *Sensōron* (for example, December 1998). *Sekai* also has many essays about the A-bombs, but these frequently refer back to war responsibility issues, such as the dialogue (*taiwa*, a transcription of a conversation) between Hiroshima and Nagasaki Mayors Hiraoka and Motojima (1995).

The nationalistic magazine *Shokun!* is also a consistent publisher of war-related essays. Throughout the eleven years of the survey there were only a dozen or so issues in which there was not a single war-related essay. Military history features prominently: between October 1991 and February 1992 Pearl Harbor was discussed extensively, and there were a number of essays criticizing Iris Chang's *The Rape of Nanking* (December 1997 to May 1998 issues). Branches of the liberal media (particularly the *Asahi* newspaper) are attacked, and in the sporadic treatment of the A-bombs and air raids the tone is critical of Allied crimes (Allied bombing is called 'genocide' in the May 1995 issue). The overall tone is chauvinist (*Shokun!*'s readership is 94 per cent male – Yoshimi 1998: 208) and there are very few articles penned by people other than older Japanese men. Feminism is frequently attacked and 'comfort women' testimony rebutted.

Seiron presents a similar ideological line to *Shokun!* and they have comparable sales of 80,000 to 90,000. The main difference is in the sustained campaigns conducted by *Seiron* after 1997. *Seiron* promoted the Tsukurukai (such as its coverage of symposiums in June and October 1997) and instituted two monthly columns that regularly criticize the liberal media on war issues: Nakamura Akira's 'NHK Watching column' (since June 1997) and Inagaki Takeshi's 'Media Watching' column (since July 1996). The large rise in articles in *Seiron* throughout the period (from 25 to 35 a year in the early 1990s, to between 50 and 60 a year in the late 1990s, and over 90 in 1997 and 2001) is emblematic of how the neo-nationalist movement ratcheted up its campaigns through the 1990s.

While *Sekai*, *Shokun!* and *Seiron* are the most prolific publishers of war-related essays, the leading opinion magazine in terms of sales, and by a wide margin, is *Bungei Shunjū*. *Bungei Shunjū* is the journal of the conservative literary establishment and has a readership of over 600,000, although it averages under ten war-related essays a year. The focus is on the Pacific War rather than the China War with espionage, the upper echelons of the military and diplomatic issues accounting for many articles. The 'great and good' of the Japanese establishment are eulogized, either in retrospectives about people such as novelist Shiba Ryōtarō (who Tsukurukai founding member Fujioka Nobukatsu credits for inspiring his own views) or in interviews with members of the political establishment. Other essays are reviews of individual literary and cinematic representations of the war (such as *The Human Condition* in May 1995, or the film *Pride* in August 1998). The tone is less shrill than *Shokun!* or *Seiron*, but the orientation of articles and contributors is predominantly conservative.

The final three opinion magazines in the survey are conspicuous for their relatively limited war focus and/or readership, and for broadly reflecting the stances of the media conglomerates they belong to. *Chūō Kōron* (part of the Yomiuri group) is a highbrow conservative publication in a similar manner to *Bungei Shunjū*, but it has less than one-tenth of the readership (around 40,000). Its English name is *Foreign Affairs* and it treats war history from the diplomatic perspective: it focuses on diplomacy, officer diaries, Germany–Japan comparisons and espionage in its approximately nine essays per year. *Ronza* (part of the Asahi group) is a relatively new magazine (started in 1995). It has low sales figures compared to the other opinion magazines (around 20,000), but a reasonably large focus on war issues (averaging about fourteen essays per year). It is more journalistic than *Sekai* but shares the same progressive stance, with feminism, textbooks, East Asian relations and Japanese war responsibility being key topics. And finally, *Gendai* (published by Kōdansha) is one of the more widely read magazines with a readership of over 90,000, but is conspicuous for having few war-related essays (an average of just over four a year). It also bucked the trend in the other magazines by having many more articles up to 1995 than in the late 1990s. It was as if *Gendai* had decided to lay the war to rest after the fiftieth anniversary, an impression reinforced by the curt rejection of the Tsukurukai's activism in August and September 1997. The articles mixed progressive-style atrocity stories and conservative-style military histories, which indicates an overall 'middle Japan' stance.

The levels of war interest and topics treated in opinion magazines illustrate which aspects of war history feature most prominently within each ideology (see Table. 6.2). Progressives focus on Japanese atrocities and war responsibility issues while Japanese victimhood is related back to Japanese war responsibility; conservatives and nationalists, on the other hand, focus more on heroic actions by the Japanese military and treat Japanese suffering more as the result of Allied crimes. Their levels of interest are markedly higher than in the middle ground. Pet topics also change with developments in war debates. The 'comfort women' issue became the progressive cause célèbre in the 1990s, while critiques of the Tokyo Trials and eulogies to the dissenting judgment of Indian Judge Radhabinod Pal (that found Japan not guilty of aggressive war) have been key themes in nationalist opinion magazines since the mid-1980s, when the enshrinement of the class A war criminals became central to the Yasukuni issue (*Asahi shinbun* 1 May 2006).

Aspects of war history, therefore, divide into three main types: (1) key battlegrounds for the ideological poles (such as Nanking or the 'comfort women', acknowledged or strenuously denied as serious war crimes by progressives and nationalists respectively); (2) stories that are treated broadly across the spectrum (the A-bombs, Siberian internment, the sufferings of soldiers); and (3) stories favoured by a particular ideological camp (kamikaze stories have little to offer a progressive view of history but are rich in themes of sacrifice and patriotism for conservatives; while Unit 731's human experiments confirm the depravity of militarism for progressives but are avoided by nationalists because they do nothing for affirmative versions of the war).

Consuming ideological debate

Browsing in Japanese bookshops reveals much about the consumption of ideological debate. Bookshops, unlike libraries, give good indications of what is selling and therefore, presumably, what people are reading. Whereas the 'war history' section of a large Japanese bookshop contains a wide variety of books in terms of topic and stance, war-related books in the 'new releases' or 'bestseller' sections are more likely to be nationalist. This mirrors the 'opinion magazine' world where nationalist magazines tend to be more prolific publishers of war-related essays and to sell more copies. This can make it seem as if nationalism is more representative of Japanese public opinion. However, the prominence of nationalist publications in bookshops is an indication of what sells rather than wider historical consciousness.

Nationalism as a consumer item has been discussed extensively. For instance, Aaron Gerow has argued that the Tsukurukai's nationalism is 'essentially consumerist', the repackaging of old ideas into an 'attractive and less offensive' format (Gerow 2000: 87). Similarly, Yoshimi Shunya's assessment is that nationalist publications take advantage of unease in modern society and are out of touch with global issues; they are anti-feminist, lacking in any serious analysis and merely consumer items (Yoshimi 1998: 210).

Nationalist books and magazines make appeals to consumers in a number of ways. There is the 'feel-good factor'. Nationalistic publications assuage Japanese guilt and argue there is no reason to feel bad about war history. They flatter readers by inviting them to feel privy to the hidden 'truth' about the war about which the majority of Japan's 'masochistic' population remains oblivious. While often written by researchers with distinguished academic positions, nationalistic publications are aimed at the general public, free of academic jargon and easy to read. Their passionate arguments make strong emotional appeals to readers. And there is always sensationalism ('Nanking a fabrication: stunning new documentary evidence') to draw in the curious or

Table 6.2 War history in war memories: prioritization of aspects of war history within the ideological versions of war history.

	Progressive	Progressive-leaning	Conservative	Nationalist
Bombing: A-bombs and air raids	HIGH: comparisons drawn with other atrocities, e.g. Nanking.	HIGH: suffering of Japanese.	HIGH: suffering of Japanese.	MEDIUM: aversion to self-pitying victim consciousness.
Home Front: social history, civilian memories	MEDIUM: inability of population to resist militarism, civilian hardships.	HIGH: hardships endured by the people.	HIGH: hardships endured by the people, patriotism.	MEDIUM: support and sacrifices made by the population for the war.
Colonialists (orphans, repatriates)	MEDIUM: ambiguous: active participants in colonialism but also victims.	HIGH: victimhood of settlers at the end of the war.	MEDIUM: victimhood of settlers at the end of the war.	LOW: ambiguous – sufferings a by-product of imperial policy.
China War (1937–45)	HIGH: basis of the aggressive war position. Site of many atrocities.	LOW: aggressive war, prelude to the main clash with US.	MEDIUM: some 'aggressive acts', prelude to the main clash with US.	HIGH: aggression and atrocities denied to maintain the just war position.
Pacific War (1941–45)	HIGH: invasion of Southeast Asia, atrocities in occupied territories.	MEDIUM: military history and strategy.	HIGH: military strategy/history and the reasons for Japan's defeat.	HIGH: liberation of Asia from Western colonialism.
Colonization of Korea	HIGH: colonial aggression a prelude to war. Harsh treatment of Koreans.	LOW: vague consciousness compared to the Pacific War.	MEDIUM: colonialism the international norm at the time.	MEDIUM: Japan's positive role in Korean development.

Army	HIGH: atrocities of the army across Asia.	MEDIUM: sufferings of Japanese soldiers in the Pacific War.	HIGH: sufferings and sacrifice of soldiers.	HIGH: heroism of the Japanese army, Asian liberation.
Navy	LOW: supporting role to the army's aggression.	MEDIUM: navy's defeat as a significant factor in Japan's defeat.	HIGH: tragic heroism of the navy, the navy's role in Japan's defeat.	MEDIUM; the navy's heroism and blunders.
Air Force	LOW: Japanese bombing in China.	MEDIUM: tragedy of the kamikaze.	HIGH: heroism and patriotism of fighter aces and the kamikaze.	HIGH: heroism and patriotism of fighter aces and the kamikaze.
'Comfort women'	HIGH: sexual slavery, a large-scale human rights violation.	MEDIUM: sympathy towards 'comfort women' on human rights grounds.	HIGH: a well-intentioned system that contained some abuses.	HIGH: 'comfort women' were well-paid prostitutes.
Nanking Massacre	HIGH: 130,000+ killed, depravity of the Japanese army.	LOW: large-scale massacre, little focus as an uncomfortable topic.	MEDIUM: 15,000–50,000 killed, a massacre, but not as large as Chinese claims.	HIGH: a fabrication – little or no illegal killing.
War crimes trials	MEDIUM: flawed victors' justice, many criminals escaped justice.	MEDIUM: little sympathy for leaders, some for soldiers 'forced' into atrocity.	MEDIUM: a consequence of defeat, verdict grudgingly accepted.	HIGH: kangaroo justice, Judge Pal's dissenting 'not guilty' verdict.
Overall	HIGH: atrocity-soaked war of aggression, but many Allied crimes against Japanese too.	LOW: war brought huge suffering to the peoples of Japan and Asia.	MEDIUM: not simply an 'aggressive war'; Japan given little option but to fight. Some 'aggressive acts'.	HIGH: war of Asian liberation, Japan defending itself against Western aggression.

those progressives who need to know which nationalist claims have to be refuted next.

Given that opinion polls routinely indicate that nationalism is a minority position, the prominence of nationalist publications in bookshop displays suggests that nationalists are a responsive target audience and/or effective at stirring marketable controversy. With a market to be satisfied, publishers and right-wing historians cash in on the profits to be made by glorifying the military and denying Japan did anything wrong. But this is also indicative of the oppositional nature of nationalism to the antiwar mainstream. Both the government's official stance and the majority of the Japanese media (especially television) shun jingoism and nationalists' more controversial arguments (particularly Nanking Massacre denial). Consequently, publishing has become a vital medium for nationalists, both as researchers and consumers: it is the key cultural form in which nationalism can proliferate unrestrained by industry mantras about 'balanced reporting' or 'objectivity' and the need to appeal to the antiwar mainstream.

By contrast, there is not such a vibrant market for progressive publications. Some progressive intellectuals do gain a large following: Takahashi Tetsuya's *Yasukuni mondai* ('The Yasukuni Issue', 2005), for example, quickly sold over 200,000 copies. Generally, however, there is little space for the 'feel-good factor' in documenting Japanese aggression and responsibility. The readability, and therefore 'enjoyment levels', of progressives' books is often diminished further by dense academic language and the meticulous use of evidence. Progressives also face the problem of 'war responsibility fatigue' among a general public that frequently asks how much longer past misdeeds must keep being dragged up.

Instead of reading for 'leisure', people are more likely to read progressives' publications for 'educational' reasons. Nearly half of *Sekai's* readership is involved in education: 28 per cent are students and 15 per cent are educators (Yoshimi 1998: 208). 'Educational reading' of serious academic texts also means that progressives' books target the university library market in terms of price and print runs. Popular texts may then be reissued in a cheap paperback series (such as Iwanami shinsho), which makes them more available for use as a university course text. In university libraries, progressive histories typically have a longer shelf life than populist polemic, whose bookshelf life is only until the next nationalist academic can regurgitate the familiar arguments to more fanfare on the front cover. In publishing, the long-term significance or impact of a book does not necessarily depend on its sales figures: the latest nationalist bestseller piled high in bookshops may actually point most to the fleeting significance of its predecessor.

Ideological confrontation: the liberalist view of history

Not all nationalist books, however, can be viewed simply as consumer products. In particular, the work of Fujioka Nobukatsu and his *jiyūshugi shikan*, the liberalist view of history, is significant as the ideological foundation of the neo-nationalist movement in the 1990s. At the time, Fujioka was a professor of education at the University of Tokyo. He rose to prominence in the 1990s as a founding member of both the *Jiyūshugi shikan kenkyūkai*, Liberalist History Research Group, and the Tsukurukai. Fujioka's form of 'liberalism' (hereafter *jiyūshugi*) is not what would be recognized as 'liberalism' in English. *Jiyūshugi* is perhaps better translated as 'freedomism', the freedom (*jiyū*) to write history without continually apologizing to other nations. Fujioka's mission was simple: to replace 'masochistic history' (*jigyakushi*), in which Japan was presented as the villain, with 'a history to be proud of'.

In *What is the Liberalist View of History?* (1997), Fujioka claimed *jiyūshugi* fell between 'the good guys and bad guys views of history' (ibid.: 11). The 'good guys' (*zendama*) view meant the 'affirmation of the Greater East Asian War view'; the 'bad guys' (*akudama*) view meant either the 'Tokyo Trials view', the victors' judgement of Japanese aggression, or the 'Comintern view', a Marxist critique of Japanese imperialism. Fujioka defined the 'Tokyo Trials view' as:

> The view of history which takes the judgement handed down at the Tokyo War Crimes Trials to be completely true, that says the war Japan fought was an 'aggressive war' in breach of international law, conventions and treaties, and that says that Japan's actions and behaviour were all criminal and wrong.
>
> (ibid.: 39)

Fujioka had two key complaints about the 'Tokyo Trials view': first, it was imposed on Japan by outsiders and Japanese people have been unwilling or unable to challenge it despite its flaws; and second, it had become impossible to challenge victors' history without being labelled a denier or a nationalist.

At the same time, Fujioka also criticized the 'affirmers': nationalists actively justifying Japan's war. He summarized affirmers as employing three principal lines of argument: affirmation by intention, situation and results (ibid.: 109–10). 'Affirmation by intention' was the theory that Japan was fighting a 'holy war' to liberate Asia from Western colonialism. 'Affirmation by situation' centred on a number of arguments, such as that Japan was acting in self-defence, or that clashes between colonial powers were 'inevitable'. Finally, 'affirmation by results' referred to results that were not necessarily key war aims but ultimately made the struggle worthwhile, particularly paving the way for the independence of Asian countries.

In defining his 'third way', Fujioka drew on a number of approaches: he analysed the options open to Japanese leaders at the time, cited the economic benefits Japan brought to its colonies, and presented the '40-year period theory' of modern Japanese history (40 years of positive development, 1868–1905; 40 years of mistakes and aggression, 1905–45; 40 years of peaceful economic growth, 1945–85; and a question mark over where Japan has been going since) (ibid.: 130–76). For Fujioka, *jiyūshugi* had four main characteristics: (1) *Kenzenna nashonarizumu*, 'healthy nationalism': Fujioka wanted to have pride in his nationality but wanted to avoid the negative, anti-foreign connotations that the term 'nationalism' usually implies. (2) *Riarizumu*, 'realism': realism meant making the prosperity of the nation the highest concern of policy-makers. (3) 'Freedom from *ideorogii* (ideology)': Fujioka wanted the freedom for people to have different opinions. And (4) *kanryōshugi hihan*, 'anti-bureaucratism': bureaucratism was when the interests of a section of society overrode the interests of the whole. In Japan's case, militarism was an extreme form of bureaucratism, whereby the military seized power and acted in their sectional interests rather than the national interest (ibid.: 178–80).

On the surface, there was nothing particularly controversial about Fujioka's views, which were conservative but not extremist. However, Fujioka's arguments provoked a furious backlash from progressives. Fujioka's own mission statement was 'to undertake a fundamental re-evaluation of modern history education and to find a way to reform teaching' (ibid.: 30). Within the context of 'a history to be proud of' and criticisms of 'masochistic history', 'reform' and 're-evaluation' of education could only mean one thing: a sanitized version of Japanese history customized to strengthen Japanese pride. Nevertheless, 'we want a national history to be proud of' and 'we should decide ourselves how we view our history' are resonant slogans among conservatives. By distancing itself from the largely discredited and politically explosive topics of Nanking Massacre denial and active justifications of a 'just' or 'holy' war, *jiyūshugi* gained many powerful backers among mainstream conservatives, including within the ruling LDP.

Meanwhile, progressives were busy criticizing every aspect of Fujioka's thesis. For progressives, *jiyūshugi* was dangerous precisely because it made nationalist views seem benign and palatable. Rather than calling it a 'third way', many progressives preferred the term *shūseishugi* ('revisionism') to describe Fujioka's views. *Jiyūshugi* was also targeted by feminists because of the Tsukurukai's stated aim to erase the 'comfort women' from Japanese textbooks and because nationalist defences of the 'comfort station' system were so offensive to many Japanese women (and men) who empathized with the sufferings of 'comfort women'. For example, Ueno Chizuko specifically linked *jiyūshugi* to the type of revisionism that had been seen in West Germany during the 1986 *Historikerstreit* (historians' debate) and called it 'Japanese-version historical revisionism' (Ueno 1998: 147–51). Ueno's critique was framed in terms of the 'comfort women' issue. First, she criticized the Tsukurukai's insistence on documentary 'proof' that women had been abducted. Second, she criticized the way in which the Tsukurukai routinely cast doubt on any oral testimony that challenged their position. Ueno argued for survivor testimony to be treated equally to documentary evidence. Third, Ueno challenged the premise that it is inappropriate to teach schoolchildren about such issues as the 'comfort women'. Finally, she criticized the notion of 'a national history to be proud of' because it becomes a 'game' regarding who is more patriotic: by implication, those who accept the darker sides of Japanese history become 'unpatriotic'.

The ferocity of the criticisms forced Fujioka to respond. In doing so, he slipped towards the affirmative view of the war that he had initially criticized. In various essays published throughout the late 1990s (collected in Fujioka 2000), Fujioka defended the 'comfort station' system; and in his rebuttals of Iris Chang's *The Rape of Nanking* (Higashinakano and Fujioka 1999) he moved towards Nanking Massacre denial. Conservative historian Hata Ikuhiko speculated that their activism was causing members of the liberalist history research group to slip further and further to the right and towards Nanking Massacre denial (Hata 2001: 35–6). So, while Fujioka claimed *jiyūshugi* was offering a 'third way' in the mid-1990s, ultimately progressives' predictions that seeking 'a history to be proud of' would be a slippery slope towards affirmative nationalism were realized.

As can be seen, these ideological clashes between *jiyūshugi* and its progressive critics in the 1990s related heavily to historical methodology and the political purposes of history. The issues of methodology have frequently boiled down to ideology: evidence that supports the researcher's agenda is methodologically sound, evidence that opposes it is suspect. In the context of the 'comfort women' issue, for example, nationalists have insisted on a positivist approach and documentary evidence to illustrate Japanese complicity in the abduction of 'comfort women'. This approach, however, takes advantage of the incomplete documentary evidence (much was deliberately destroyed immediately after the war) and ignores the possibility that documents can be falsified. Nationalists have typically dismissed Asian victims' testimony as unsafe, although this has not stopped ex-soldiers' memoirs from being incorporated into nationalist historiography 'when appropriate': for example, Kobayashi Yoshinori's retelling of Takamura Takehito's memoirs in *Sensōron* (1998: 209–72). Progressives, for their part, have relied more on survivor testimony and international documentary evidence. Nevertheless, methodological debates continue among progressives. Ueno Chizuko, for example, has criticized Yoshimi Yoshiaki (whose discovery of documentary evidence in 1992 triggered the 'comfort women' issue) for his over-reliance on documentary evidence and thereby playing into the hands of nationalists. Yoshimi responded by saying that it was documentary evidence that forced the Japanese government's apology, not testimony (O'Brien 2000: 13–15).

In all instances, however, the selective gaze is evident and there is significant incentive for people to adhere to their ideological lines. Scholars and pundits become prominent in public debate on the back of a distinct, identifiable standpoint that gains them a following and makes them the 'go to' people when the media needs a quote or studio guest. Suddenly, disavowing the research and stance that brought the researcher to prominence is potentially disastrous to a media career. Fujioka Nobukatsu is an example of someone who made a successful 'conversion' (*tenkō*), from Communist Party member to populist nationalist (McCormack 2000: 63–5), although his fame came after his conversion, so there was no public image to remake. In the news media business, however, and particularly on television where the mantra of 'giving both sides a say' rules in studio debates and news reports, becoming a famous pundit means clarity of ideology and a nose for the soundbite in the theatre of public debate.

History at school: textbook content vs history education

The primary aim of Fujioka's *jiyūshugi* was to reform what Japanese children read in their history textbooks. Japanese textbooks are one of the key ideological battlegrounds in Japanese war debates and have spawned vast amounts of media attention and scholarly research. This literature (and particularly reportage in the international media) has tended to focus on textbook controversies: the content of a particularly controversial textbook (2001 and 1986) or advice issued by textbook screeners (1982). However, the key issue in Japanese war memories is what is taught to Japanese children rather than simply what is in their history textbooks. As Peter Cave argues, 'We need to know how textbooks are used, and to what extent teachers go beyond them and encourage pupils to develop a critical approach to the study of history' (Cave 2002: 624).

It is also necessary to consider the purpose of history education at schools. While activists, educators and politicians typically debate the role of history in fostering historical consciousness and national identity – something that is stated explicitly within the Japanese junior high-school curriculum (ibid.: 627) – from the perspective of schoolchildren there is the more practical concern of entrance exams. The format of Japanese exams impacts tremendously on how war history is taught. In both high-school and university entrance exams, the primary mode of testing is multiple choice or short answers. The emphasis is on knowledge and factual recall rather than interpretive and analytical skills. Those taking a university entrance exam in history (which is an optional subject in the national university entrance examination) typically have sixty to ninety minutes to be examined on the entirety of history. The war accounts for a few questions at most, and the longest answer will be a short paragraph in which a formulaic 'model answer' is expected.

This form of testing exists across the curriculum, but especially in a subject such as war history (where questions requiring interpretive answers would be so open to 'subjective marking') the safe course is to test solely candidates' knowledge of agreed facts. This is particularly so given that question papers and model answers are published in the local and/or national press. Consequently, questions that will not appear in a university entrance exam are 'How many were killed in Nanking?' or 'Who was responsible for the outbreak of war between America and Japan?' These are interpretive and/or debated. Questions that can appear would be 'What was the Potsdam declaration?' or 'When was the Manchurian Incident?' Such questions and their model answers can be published in the media without provoking protests. The 'protests' feared most would be extreme right-wing groups paying a visit to the university campus with their sound trucks.

If candidates are learning 'facts' for short answer questions, the problem then becomes which facts to learn. This relates to curriculum, the content of school textbooks and the textbook screening process. In short, there is no list of required components for a Japanese history textbook. Textbooks are screened for 'factual inaccuracies' rather than required to include set topics as part of a national curriculum. The textbook screening system has often been derided as censorship, but on paper at least appears fair and democratic. Textbooks are produced by publishing companies; content is not prescribed but screened for factual accuracy by the Ministry of Education; local boards of education choose a textbook for the schools in their jurisdiction from the textbooks that pass the screening process (in 2001 and 2005 there were eight); and then teachers decide how the book is used in class.

However, the system (notwithstanding the conservative sympathies of many in the Ministry of Education) aids conservatives and nationalists. First, an insistence on 'factual accuracy' allows value judgements to be excised. Words such as 'invasion' can be counted as value judgements in comparison to the more neutral 'advanced into', which was the advice that caused the 1982 crisis (McGregor 1996: 181). Second, by screening out what cannot be said ('factually inaccurate' statements) rather than stating what should be said, the screening process effectively allows conservatives and nationalists to limit the contents of textbooks by continually challenging the 'factual accuracy' of the numbers killed in Nanking or by simply dropping 'masochistic' topics. Progressives, by contrast, have had to go to court to establish Nanking and Unit 731 as 'historical facts' and thereby gain the right to include them in textbooks, or in the case of the 'comfort women' had to wait until acknowledgement of the 'forced transportation' of 'comfort women' became government policy in 1993.

Much of the textbook debate since the 1990s has revolved around the 'comfort women' issue. Despite the government's official acknowledgement of 'forced transportation', many conservatives and nationalists have objected to mentions of the 'comfort women' in textbooks. The appropriateness of teaching children about military prostitution, debates over 'the facts' and criticisms of 'masochistic historical views' have all been raised as reasons. But a further unspoken factor is in play. If the 'comfort women' can be excluded from sufficient textbooks or turned into contested history, it becomes 'unfair' and 'risky' to have questions on the issue in entrance exams. The result is a watered down 'unofficial curriculum by consensus' limited to the least controversial aspects of war history. This helps to account for the predominant focus in textbooks on aspects of victimhood (especially Hiroshima) and dry chronological sections about treaties. These are what can be examined most easily and go first in textbooks as a result. Perpetuating contestation and dropping 'masochistic' topics, therefore, are important tactics for nationalists:

they can make forthright statements in textbooks about atrocities that much more difficult by debating the 'facts', and by just dropping topics they can limit questions in entrance exams (and thereby affect the wider focus of teaching).

In this situation, the fact that nationalist groups keep feeling the need to challenge 'masochistic education' through patriotic textbook campaigns illustrates just how hard progressive teachers and textbook writers, spear-headed by the legendary Ienaga Saburō (Ienaga 2001), have worked to get inclusions of Japanese atrocities into textbooks. Their efforts have meant that the textbooks which are *not* the subject of textbook controversies and which *are* used by the vast majority of Japanese schoolchildren are usually not nearly as controversial (meaning 'nationalistic') as the ones that make the headlines. As Richard McGregor has stated, 'the stereotypical criticism of Japanese school textbooks [is] out of date today . . . most Japanese school students in 1995 learn that Japan did *invade* China, and slaughtered thousands of innocent women and children' (McGregor 1996: 181). Textbooks have steadily introduced more forthright accounts of Japanese atrocities since the 1980s (Cave 2002: 630–1). However, the Tsukurukai's campaigns have precipitated a perceptible overall shift to the right in history textbooks since 2001 and mentions of the 'comfort women' have become less common than in the 1990s: only 20 per cent of children read about the 'comfort women' in their textbooks in 2002–06 (Tawara 2001: 66).

But overall, McGregor's assessment is still valid ten years on. However, as in 2001, not all the latest textbooks (passed for use from April 2006) mention the 'comfort women' by name, and some opt for vaguer mentions of the 'forced transportation' of Asian women (Miura 2005: 166–7). In statements about Nanking, always an ideological litmus test, acceptance of the atrocity is standard, although there are still grounds to argue that statements relating to atrocities like Nanking are brief and vague compared to instances of Japanese victimhood. Tokyo shoseki's textbook reads:

> The Japanese army occupied the capital Nanking at the end of the year. In the process they killed (*satsugai*) a large number of Chinese including women and children (the Nanking Incident) . . . This incident was internationally condemned as the Nanking Massacre (*daigyakusatsu*), but the people were not told about it.

Nihon shoseki shinsha's book states 'it is said 200,000 prisoners and civilians were killed' and mentions rape and pillage too, although it has a qualifying statement that there are various theories about the number killed. These are the more standard versions of what appears in Japanese textbooks. But Fusōsha's book, the one that has gained international notoriety, is evasive:

> At this time, there were many casualties among soldiers and civilians at the hands of the Japanese army (Nanking Incident). However, doubts have been raised concerning the documentary evidence relating to the

number of victims and so on; there are a number of viewpoints and debate
continues to this day.

(ibid.: 161–2)

Nowhere are the biases possible by rearranging 'factually correct' statements
(or at least, statements deemed to be factually correct by Ministry of Education
screeners) clearer than in such examples from Japanese textbooks.

Whereas textbooks are the primary educational materials used by children,
there are also educational materials that do not need to pass the Ministry of
Education's screening process. Many Japanese children attend cram schools
for extra exam preparations. Cram schools and private tutors focus on likely
exam questions, so they are most likely to adhere to the 'unofficial curriculum by consensus' of dates and treaties. Nevertheless, these private schools and
a number of publishing companies issue their own revision aids and exam
practice question books, none of which are subject to government screening.

Publishing companies also issue books appropriate for school libraries, such
as encyclopedias, atlases and educational manga. Educational manga (*gakushū
manga*) are particularly important given the position of manga within Japanese
popular culture: 40 per cent of all books and magazines published in Japan
are manga. Manga are frequently employed by educators to make learning
more enjoyable and educational manga aimed at elementary school children
can be found in virtually every elementary school library.

There are a number of educational manga series about Japanese history
that cover the war years. They follow a standard pattern and the following
discussion is appropriate to three series covering the war years published by
Shōgakukan (Kodama 1983), Kumon shuppan (Kata 1989) and Shūeisha
(Matsuo 1998). The main character is a young boy. This establishes the family
on the home front as the lens through which the war experience is viewed. This
lens acts to promote a victims' view of history: how the war affected innocent
children and their honest, non-jingoistic parents. There are many scenes
that take place overseas, but they predominantly feature characters with
whom little identification is encouraged. Members of the Japanese military,
particularly when they are depicted carrying out atrocities, are nameless and
usually 'faceless' by being drawn from a distance or from behind. Members
of the little boy's family, by contrast, are all referred to by name, their
characters are developed and their faces are drawn in recognizable detail.

Nevertheless, the educational manga do include depictions of Japanese
atrocities. The Shōgakukan manga includes Nanking (52), the 'kill all, burn
all, loot all' policy (58), massacres of Chinese in Singapore (81), the Bataan
Death March (84), the Burma Railroad (93–4), forced labour (106, 111–12)
and the recruitment of 'comfort women' (112). The Shūeisha manga gives a
similar range of atrocities, but mentions human experiments in Unit 731 (101)
instead of the 'comfort women'. The Kumon shuppan manga is the most
explicit: part I includes the infamous '100 heads killing contest' on the road

to Nanking (125; see also p. 196 in this volume) as well as a small but nonetheless actual photograph of a Chinese prisoner being held down and stabbed in the stomach for 'bayonet practice' (126).

This juxtaposition of the photograph and manga in the Kumon series illustrates how much atrocities are sanitized by being drawn in manga rather than illustrated in photographs. However, given that the target age group is six- to eleven-year olds, there are legitimate questions about how graphic the depictions of war violence, human experiments and forced prostitution can be. Beyond the sanitization, the manga do not foster a guilt consciousness because no identification is encouraged with the characters perpetrating the war crimes. Nevertheless, the three educational manga series (particularly the Kumon series) are unequivocal in telling Japanese children that the Japanese army committed many war crimes.

It is difficult to measure precisely how much these manga affect Japanese children in the early stages of their war memory development. The Shōgakukan series is a long-term bestseller with well over forty print runs and half a million copies sold. The Shūeisha series is far more recent and sales are closer to 50,000, but the publishers believe the series has been purchased by most elementary schools in the country for their school libraries. The contents of these manga are consistent with the progressive-leaning nature of most cultural forms aimed specifically at children: museums, television programmes, manga and those textbooks that do not stir international controversy. So, despite international media attention on nationalistic textbooks, the broader picture of the standard war history education received by schoolchildren in Japan reveals it is antiwar in nature, discourages identification with aggressive militarism, and focuses on messages of peace.

The recurrent theme in this chapter has been what history is viewed by whom and for what purpose, and how this relates to ideological interpretations of war history. The content of textbooks has often been equated with what Japanese children learn about the war, but they should be treated as completely separate issues. Ultimately, teachers decide how the textbook is used in the classroom and teachers can easily circumvent 'shortcomings' in the books by using supplementary materials, what Cave calls 'going beyond the textbook' (2005: 319ff.).

In the survey of historical consciousness among 436 university students cited in the last chapter, documentaries, museums, television news, films and non-fiction books were all rated higher than textbooks as influential on their historical consciousnesses. It is highly likely that many of these materials were encountered through school education. Regarding what supplementary materials were used at the students' junior high school (JHS) and senior high school (SHS), the results for the 436 students were as follows:

1   Students who used war-related supplementary materials: at JHS 44 per cent, at SHS 27 per cent. When asked what kinds of materials were used, videos and newspapers were common responses.

2   Students who heard testimony at school from a member of the war generation: at JHS 11 per cent, at SHS 19 per cent.
3   Students who had visited a war museum on a school trip: at JHS 15 per cent, at SHS 46 per cent. Most of these visits were to Hiroshima or Nagasaki.
4   Students whose teachers had expressed their personal opinions about the war: at JHS 12 per cent, at SHS 12 per cent.

Respondents were also asked about a common criticism of Japanese history education, whether the teacher had skipped war history, ostensibly because it was unlikely to be examined (see Cave 2002: 629): 11 and 19 per cent said they had skipped war history at junior and senior high levels respectively.

These results are compatible with other data and research into what Japanese children learn at school. Concerning school trips to museums (discussed in Chapter 8), for example, visiting figures suggest that around a million Japanese children a year visited war museums in the early 2000s, the majority to Hiroshima and Nagasaki. Furthermore, Cave's research based on lesson observations and teacher/student interviews reveals the extent to which education goes 'beyond the textbook'.

> It also seems that teachers may depart from the textbook more than previous research has indicated. Almost all lessons I observed were textbook-based, but two-fifths went significantly beyond the textbook, while a further fifth included short digressions. . . . [In a footnote Cave adds] Here, I define 'going beyond the textbook' as introducing teaching materials, explanations, illustrations, or stories that did not appear in the textbook. . . . In most cases, the extra material was connected to the subject of study and seemed intended to enhance students' understanding and/or arouse their interest. Teachers use the term *dassen* (digression) to describe this apparently common teaching technique.
>
> (Cave 2005: 319ff.)

Finally, evidence of extra-curricular war-related education – such as school plays about war issues, exchange programmes, testimony by the war generation, or even the research of the school history club – can feature in the media, particularly in regional television news programmes. On at least two occasions, research conducted by schoolchildren has even appeared in published books: the research of the Akaho SHS and Hōsei Daini SHS Peace Research Clubs (1991) into the balloon bombs produced by the Noborito Research Institute, and the investigations of Shōwa SHS in Saitama into laboratory rats produced for Unit 731 in their town, despite threats made against them by extreme right wingers (Kasahara *et al.* 1997: 46–61).

These examples of schoolchildren publishing research are atypical, but they are indicative of the overall conclusion: what Japanese children learn at school cannot be equated with the contents of their textbooks. The evidence points to a more complex view of war history education in Japanese schools. Some teachers skip over the topic. Some teachers follow the textbook and limit their teaching to the minimum necessary for exam preparations. Other teachers, however, are proactive in going beyond the textbook. There are many unofficial educational materials aimed at children and for many pupils there are extra-curricular lessons in war history (such as school trips) that may be of even greater significance than textbooks in the creation of historical consciousness among Japanese youth.

Conclusions

Issues of what history features most in Japanese war memories and school history education have been central to the frequent accusations of 'amnesia' made against the Japanese. However, the term 'amnesia' is a blunt term that fails to distinguish the complex variations in interpretation, prioritization of particular issues, methodology and the political uses of history that underpin competing cultural memories of the war. Nationalists do not 'forget' Nanking: they work strenuously to deny it was a war crime. Progressives do not 'forget' the kamikaze, but suicide tactics against military targets are of marginal relevance in making the case for aggressive war and atrocities. Rather than 'amnesia', the term 'selective historical gaze' is useful for highlighting that people are adept at focusing on the events and interpretations of war history that are most compatible with their contemporary identities and political priorities. This applies across the political spectrum in Japan. It may also mean that war history itself is largely ignored if the past–present relationship is considered to be of marginal relevance in people's daily lives. There is, after all, a significant fraction of the Japanese population who 'don't know and don't care' much about war history.

Other important conclusions to be drawn from war history in the publishing industry are that sales of books are not necessarily equivalent to their long-term importance and the contents of textbooks are not necessarily equivalent to what children learn. The evidence from opinion magazines also suggests that nationalists' campaigns play a vital function in preventing wider 'forgetting' of the war by stirring the domestic debate and controversy that keeps the war issue alive. The prominence that nationalists have gained within publishing, whether as prolific writers and consumers of books and magazines or authors of controversial textbooks, is also indicative of nationalists' status as oppositional voices towards the antiwar mainstream. This oppositional role explains the simultaneous success in publishing (where profitability thresholds are attainable) but failure to dominate the wider mass media, in particular the press and television. But as well as non-fiction publishing, nationalists have found fiction an ideal vehicle for disseminating their version of war history, and it is to war stories, particularly in cinema, that the discussion turns in the next chapter.

7 War stories

> Storytelling – narrative – is central to how people communicate their under-standing of the world, and stories are seen as the primary means by which we construct meaning about the world around us. For subscribers to narrative theory, storytelling is at the heart of all human interaction. We tell stories about what has happened to explain events and issues. We tell stories about ourselves and even without an audience we organise in our heads narratives to help interpret and impose some kind of order on the multitude of things we see and hear.
>
> (Williams 2003: 141)

The discussion thus far has focused on non-fictional war stories. Non-fiction can be an 'inconvenient' way of narrating the past: there will always be events and issues that fit uncomfortably into one's historical views and may be ignored or sidelined as a result. Fiction, by contrast, offers no such constraints. The professional and legal requirements for non-fiction to be 'as accurate as possible' do not apply. Major historical inaccuracies or omissions can be attributed simply to 'creative licence'.

Fictional accounts of war have appeared in two main formats: written (literature, novels, short stories and manga) and audio-visual (cinema and television dramas). There is also an oral storytelling tradition in Japan, particularly the *kami shibai* ('paper theatre') raconteurs, who tell stories while showing pictures to the gathered crowd. It is a declining art, but it seems to have a revival each August when groups of children listening to war stories told by *kami shibai* raconteurs are sometimes featured on local television news. This chapter, however, focuses particularly on fictional war stories in cinema, television dramas and simulation fiction (fantasy representations of the war), and how historical consciousness may be based on fictitious history as much as on 'facts'.

War cinema and war memories

By international standards, Japan has a relatively strong cinema industry. Despite a drop in production from a peak of 547 films in 1960 to 249 in 1998, largely due to competition from television and Hollywood imports, the box office share of domestic films in 1993 was 35.8 per cent (at the time an all-time low). Even France with all its industry subsidies and protection managed only 33 per cent (Schilling 1999: 7, 14–15). However, measures of cinematic consumption do not suggest a pivotal role in war memories in recent times. Since the 1970s, Japanese people have averaged just over one trip to the cinema per person per year (Asahi shinbunsha 2005: 246), and in a 1999 survey of people living within a 30 km radius of Tokyo, 70.4 per cent of men and 66.3 per cent of women said they had not watched a Japanese film at the cinema that year. Video rental showed a similar pattern with 65.6 per cent of men and 71.6 per cent of women saying they did not rent any videos in a month (Fujitake 2000: 254, 261). Nevertheless, as demonstrated in Chapter 5, war films can reach extensive audiences when broadcast on television, and the importance of cinema was illustrated in the survey of university students (see Figure. 5.1 on p. 109), who rated war films the fourth most influential cultural form on their historical consciousnesses.

Films are a good place to see some of the narrative conventions within fictional representations of the war. Robert Rosenstone identifies 'six elements that mark the historical practice of mainstream films': films (1) tell a self-contained story and have a moral message; (2) tell the story of the individuals made important by the camera; (3) offer no historical alternatives to what appears on the screen; (4) are 'history as experience' and encourage the audience to respond emotionally to the past; (5) do not separate issues such as gender and economics into separate chapters, as a written history often does, but weave the issues together; and (6) recreate the 'look of the past' (Rosenstone 2000: 29–31). War films tell history as the story of one or more main characters, or heroes. A hero is primarily a *moral* character that the audience is invited to identify with and whose actions set the moral agenda of the film. This narrative convention and the range of ethical judgements concerning Japanese war actions have combined to create three main types of Japanese hero in war cinema: military heroes, the 'good Japanese' and victim-heroes.

Military heroes act morally in a moral military cause. They are by definition conservative or nationalist and appear most regularly in action adventure films. Given the knowledge of Japan's defeat, there can be no truly happy ending. Many conservative–nationalist films stress selfless sacrifice in a losing cause, or the 'survivor's guilt' of those who saw the end of the war. Both these themes are particularly evident in kamikaze films.

Within the category of 'military heroes', distinguishing army heroes from navy and air force heroes is important. Because they were cocooned in ships and planes, seamen and pilots have little of the atrocity-soaked image of Japanese soldiers. In the air and at sea, killing was impersonal. Victory was decided in 'chivalrous' contests of skill, technology and tactics. The Japanese army, by contrast, has an infamous reputation based on its regular use of swords and bayonets in atrocities, which required proximity and dehumanization of the enemy. Furthermore, the navy and air force have less of an image of fighting an 'aggressive war' because they fought primarily against the US, another colonial power, and the fighting was largely in the 'neutral' space of the skies or Pacific Ocean. By contrast, the Japanese army was fighting to colonize Asians, or was fighting against the Allies in occupied Asian/Pacific territories. Consequently, navy and air force films tend to be conservative because they present a moral equivalence between the Japanese and the enemy, while films with army heroes have greater need to affirm the Japanese occupation of Asia or conceal the army's 'aggressive acts', and tend to be more nationalistic as a result.

If the hero casts doubt on the morality of the military's conduct, then the film presents an 'aggressive war' message and the hero typically becomes the second type: a 'good Japanese'. 'Good Japanese' heroes can be civilian or military and behave in an ethical manner inconsistent with wider Japanese misdeeds. 'Good Japanese' heroes often pay for their opposition to Japanese militarism through their own victimization at the hands of the military. In terms of a cinematic device, the 'good Japanese' hero allows progressive film-makers to make self-critical and thought-provoking portrayals of Japanese aggression while simultaneously giving Japanese audiences a moral Japanese hero with whom to associate.

The third type of hero is the victim-hero. The substantial differences between the 'good Japanese' and victim-heroes are the passivity and innocence of victim-heroes. Children, women and A-bomb victims are archetypal victim-heroes, although soldiers sent to die needlessly in remote corners of the Japanese empire may also be victim-heroes. Such films typically present an 'antiwar' message based on the terrible nature of Japanese suffering, although discussion of Japanese war responsibility is usually sidelined.

In short, the three types of heroes signify the film's treatment of Japanese war responsibility: very broadly speaking, military hero films deny or conceal responsibility, 'good Japanese' hero films acknowledge and raise issues of responsibility, and victim-hero films avoid or marginalize issues of responsibility. Consequently, the moral stance taken by the hero is a guide to the political orientation of the film. All three types of film and hero have featured prominently in postwar Japanese cinema.

Japanese war cinema: an overview

The Asia-Pacific War has left a clear mark on Japan's postwar cinematic history. Using the synopses of films listed in *Pia Cinema Club: Japanese film database book 2003–4* (2003, hereafter 'PCC'), I compiled a list of Japanese war films, 1946–2001. War films included those that discuss or depict the war, and/or are set in the war years, 1937–45. According to my calculations, there were at least 235 war films in PCC (about 4 per cent of the listed films, 1946–2001), an average of just over four films per year. However, PCC is not an exhaustive list of Japanese films. It only lists films that have had public screenings in Japan or were available on video during February 2003, and I have discovered a number of war films that are not in PCC. Nevertheless, this sample suggests that the production of war films has mirrored overall levels of production in the Japanese film industry. The greatest number of war films was produced in the 1950s and 1960s, typically four to eight a year. The lower number of war films in the 1980s and 1990s, typically one to four a year, is largely due to the contraction in the overall number of films being produced rather than dwindling interest in the war.

Japanese war films can be categorized by story, genre, mood and topic. By story, the films fall into four categories:

1   *non-fiction* – the more or less accurate story of actual people and events;
2   *fiction* – a fictional story within the context of actual historical events;
3   *fantasy (or 'simulation fiction')* – a dramatic rewriting of history;
4   *documentary* – an educational film featuring real-life witnesses and/or archive footage.

There are a number of genres, principally:

1   *military action-adventure films* – the story is a vehicle for action and battle scenes;
2   *war dramas* – fighting scenes are secondary to the effects of war on the main characters;
3   *wartime dramas* – the war is a background to a largely unrelated plot, such as a wartime romance;
4   *postwar dramas* – the ongoing effects of the conflict in the postwar, or looking back on war experiences.

The films evoke a number of moods:

1   *feel-good films* – action films, or films designed to entertain;
2   *comedies* – humorous films (a surprisingly large genre given the emotionally-charged nature of war debates);
3   *dramas* – serious films with powerful messages;
4   *tragedies* or *weepies* – these films are often antiwar and depict Japanese civilian victimhood.

Finally, in terms of topic the films divided fairly evenly, about 60:40, between films focusing on the military (army, navy, air force, espionage and kamikaze films) and those focusing on the war's effects on the home front (A-bombs, children's films, and wartime dramas focusing on civilians).

Numbers of films and their contents do not reveal the impact these films have on war memories. There are two main criteria by which cinema's impact can be assessed (as opposed to a film's impact by being shown on television): box office earnings and critical acclaim. Box office earnings indicate the number of people who saw the film at the cinema, and critical acclaim indicates films that have probably received greater attention in articles and books penned by film critics. *Postwar Kinema Junpō's Best 10, A Complete History, 1946–2002* (Sekiguchi 2003, hereafter *Kinema*) is an almanac produced by the cinema magazine *Kinema junpō* and gives the top ten films every year (divided into Japanese and imported films) by box office revenues and film critics' choice (calculated by sending a questionnaire to around fifty critics, who choose their top ten films of the year). By cross-referencing the PCC sample with the lists of top ten films in *Kinema*, I calculated that 30 war films have been in the critics' choice top ten, 18 films were in the box office top ten, and 11 films were in both the critics' choice and box office top tens in their release years.

The box office figures in *Kinema* also reveal the influence of a number of foreign films on Japanese war memories. *Bridge on the River Kwai* (1957), *Tora Tora Tora* (1971), *Midway* (1976), *1941* (1980), *The Last Emperor* (1988) and *Pearl Harbor* (2001) have all been among the top ten grossing foreign films in their respective release years. However, given that a study of foreign films turns issues of production and representation into a study of usually American war memories, I will focus on Japanese films, and in particular on the fifty-nine Japanese war films that have enjoyed box office and/or critical success.

Note: The following terminology is used to indicate critical and/or box office success: CC3 (critics' choice) means 'ranked third best of the year by critics in *Kinema*', and BO5 (box office) means 'fifth highest grossing Japanese film of the year'.

War cinema: 1972–2005

The contents of Japanese war films have closely matched the phases of memory over the 'long postwar' outlined in Chapter 2. 'Antiwar films' (*hansen eiga*) proliferated during the 'backlash against the military' phase during and immediately after the occupation. But by the 1950s and with the beginning of cold war conservatism, 'nostalgia films' took centre stage. These 'nostalgia films' dramatically swelled the number of army, navy and air force films in the 1950s and 1960s. They glorified the military, had B-movie quality special effects, and frequently employed the same actors in similar roles. For example, Mifune Toshirō, one of Japan's most internationally recognized actors for his regular appearances in Kurosawa Akira's films, became typecast as a senior naval officer. Many nostalgia films were in formulaic series that were the cash crops of the cinema industry before television became the main producer of drama series. For example, one nine-instalment series, *Soldier Gangster* (*Heitai yakuza*, 1965–8, 1972), was categorized as a 'stress-relieving action series' by PCC and centred on a former gangster continuing his underworld ways in the army in China (PCC 2003: 583). While the length of some of the nostalgia film series indicates they were making profits for their studios, overall, the nostalgia films were notable for their quantity rather than quality. It was antiwar or more progressive films, such as *The Human Condition* (*Ningen no jōken*, Part 1 1959, CC5, BO9) that received critical acclaim.

The early 1970s saw a shake-up in the cinema industry as it came to terms with competition from television. War film production dropped precipitously and the nostalgia boom waned. With formulaic series shifting to television, war film series had largely disappeared by the 1980s. War films became one-off productions and provided diverse representations of the Asia-Pacific War. Furthermore, the path towards greater acknowledgement of Japanese aggression, the third phase of Japanese war memories, was mirrored in the path towards more self-critical war cinema. The major war film of the early 1970s, the three-part epic *War and Humanity* (*Sensō to ningen*, 1970–3, Part I, CC2, BO1[1]), was based on a novel by Gomikawa Junpei (who had also penned *The Human Condition*). It graphically depicted the Japanese military's impact on China: for example, in the opening shots of Part 3 (1973, CC10), the narrator stated that 300,000 people had been massacred in a 'huge hellish incident' (*akuma no yō na daijiken*), while archive footage of the assault on Nanking, and stills of decapitated Chinese and prisoners being bayoneted filled the screen. This film appeared around the same time that Honda Katsuichi's *Journey to China* ignited the Nanking Massacre debate among Japanese historians.

The early 1980s saw a brief nationalist cinema revival, including *The Great Japanese Empire* (*Dainippon teikoku*, 1982, BO3), a jingoistic defence of Japanese imperialism. But overall the 1980s was a rich decade for hard-hitting, thought-provoking Japanese war cinema, and had more domestically and internationally acclaimed war films than any other decade in the postwar. Ōshima Nagisa's *Merry Christmas Mr Lawrence* (*Senjō no merī kurisumasu*, 1983, CC3) was a challenging investigation of both Japanese mistreatment of Allied POWs and victors' justice. Three other Japanese war films won prizes at the Berlin Film Festival, one in 1985 and two in 1987: *The Tokyo Trials* (*Tōkyō saiban*, 1983, CC4), a documentary made using archive footage of the trials; *The Sea and Poison* (*Umi to dokuyaku*, 1986, CC1), about vivisection; and *The Emperor's Naked Army Marches On* (*Yuki yukite shingun*, 1987, CC2), a documentary about a former Japanese soldier's campaigns to force confessions of atrocities out of other ex-soldiers.

The end of the 1980s also saw a wave of A-bomb films, with at least five produced in 1987–89, including *Black Rain* (*Kuroi ame*, 1989, CC1), based on Ibuse Masuji's best-selling novel. However, the most important Japanese war film in terms of domestic box office success was *The Burmese Harp* (*Biruma no tategoto*, 1985, CC8, BO1), which was seen by 3.87 million people at the cinema. At the time, this made *The Burmese Harp* the second-highest grossing Japanese film ever, and by 2002, it was still eleventh on the all-time list of Japanese box office earners (Sekiguchi 2003: 147).

The Burmese Harp was based on the 1948 novel by Takeyama Michio. It tells the story of a group of Japanese soldiers retreating through Burma in 1945 after the disastrous Imphal campaign. They keep their spirits up by singing and are accompanied on the Burmese harp by Mizushima, the key character in the story. The war ends and the unit is put in a British POW camp.

Mizushima volunteers to persuade a group of Japanese soldiers who are still resisting to surrender. Mizushima's attempts fail, so the British launch an artillery assault. Mizushima is wounded, but the British think he is dead and leave him behind. He recovers with the help of a monk before stealing the monk's clothes and returning to the vicinity of the POW camp. But Mizushima does not reveal his identity to his unit: having seen all the bodies of soldiers scattered around the Burmese countryside, he has decided to stay on in Burma to bury the dead.

Meanwhile, his unit debates whether the familiar-looking monk is Mizushima. The soldiers persuade an old Burmese lady to give the monk a parrot taught to say 'Mizushima, let's go back to Japan together'. After hearing this message, Mizushima finally reveals his identity (by playing the harp from outside the POW camp wires). But, he has made the heart-wrenching decision to stay. The final scene is the unit on the boat back to Japan reading a letter from Mizushima explaining why he cannot go back.

Why was *The Burmese Harp* so popular? It is a touching story from one of Japan's leading directors (Ichikawa Kon, who also directed the first screen version in 1956) and the film is beautifully made. The old Burmese lady (who gives the parrot to Mizushima) speaks endearingly patchy Japanese with a Kansai dialect; and the lack of graphic violence and the antiwar stance makes it suitable for family viewing.

On another level, the popularity of *The Burmese Harp* lies in the avoidance of discussions of war responsibility. This distinguishes the film somewhat from Takeyama's novel, in which one of the soldiers talks of the 'terrible trouble' (*meiwaku*) Japan has brought to Burma, and Mizushima criticizes Japan's colonial ambitions as 'wasteful desires' and for 'forgetting the most important things in life' (Takeyama 1948: 61, 190–1). The film is a 'victim-hero' film and avoids any self-critical references to why Japan was fighting in Burma. The soldiers are presented as cultured men and they do not pillage, but ask villagers politely for food. In one scene, the soldiers are in a village enjoying a meal with their Burmese hosts when they realize they are surrounded by the British. Rather than get into a fire-fight, the British and Japanese join together in a rendition of 'Home Sweet Home', which sentimentally portrays soldiers on both sides as men who simply wanted to go home. The film leaves the cinema audience little wiser about war responsibility issues, but neither does it alienate significant sections of Japanese society by taking a clear political stance. *The Burmese Harp* could appeal to a wide audience as a sentimental melodrama, and with its undeniable technical and dramatic qualities it attracted cinemagoers in their millions.

The 1980s were arguably the golden age of Japanese war cinema. In the 1990s, the level of war film production remained about the same as during the 1980s, but the films received less critical acclaim and box office success, despite at least eight films being released in 1995 to coincide with the fiftieth anniversary commemorations. The 1990s saw a 'new wave' of young directors working in independent studios, such as Iwai Shunji, who stole the critical limelight (Schilling 1999: 35). Meanwhile, animated films stormed the box office: *Princess Mononoke* (1997) and Oscar-winning *Spirited Away* (2001) both smashed all previous box office records (Sekiguchi 2003: 147). The pattern of war cinema, however, had largely been set by the late 1980s, with film-makers tackling the war in diverse and often challenging ways.

The 1990s saw a greater focus on Asia, not only in war films but in cinema in general (Schilling 1999: 43–50). This sometimes became a vehicle for critical self-reflection. In a progressive docudrama called *Duet at 15° North* (*Hokui 15° no dyuo*, 1991), a plot about a man and a woman visiting kamikaze sites in the Philippines became a vehicle for letting Filipinos tell the duo how they had suffered under Japanese occupation. And *Three Trips Across the Straits* (*Mitabi no kaikyō*, 1995), about the brutal treatment of Korean forced labourers, had a Korean central character (albeit played by a Japanese actor) who returned to Japan in the 1990s to face his tormentor from fifty years before. It contained many graphic scenes of beatings and torture.

A number of films, including *Three Trips Across the Straits*, were 'postwar films' that juxtaposed a story in the present with flashbacks to the war years. In *War and Youth* (*Sensō to seishun*, 1991), a story in the present about a young girl investigating her family's war memories for a school project is told alongside flashbacks to her father and aunt's experiences of the Tokyo air raids; and in *Summer of the Moonlight Sonata* (*Gekkō no natsu*, 1993), a school's decision to throw out an old piano rekindles a teacher's memories (told in flashbacks) and precipitates an investigation into two kamikaze pilots who had played the piano the day before flying their mission. A variation on the flashbacks device was a time travel device. In *Winds of God* (1995, also an award-winning play – see Imai 1999), two young comedians are transported back to the war years after a traffic accident and become kamikaze pilots. Despite knowing that Japan will lose the war, both men eventually fly their missions. The film presents the message that in war, even when armed with hindsight (or foresight), social pressure can make it very difficult to swim against the tide of events.

Young people are a key target audience for film-makers and the use of flashbacks from a story in the present can be seen as an attempt to make the war more relevant to postwar generations. Other film-makers have used different approaches. One example is *Fly Boys Fly* (*Kimi wo wasurenai*, 1995), a conventional kamikaze film set entirely in the war years that presents the kamikaze in a tragic-heroic light. However, it stars Kimura Takuya, a singer from SMAP (one of Japan's most successful boy bands) and has a high comedy element provided by Matsumura Kunihiro, a rotund comedian who is a regular on Japanese television. The film also has a catchy soundtrack giving it a pop video feel.

Such representations of the war in an entertainment format lend themselves to a more conservative view of war history. After the 'focus on Asia' in the mid-to early-1990s, the end of the 1990s and early 2000s saw another mini-revival in nationalistic films, including *Pride* (discussed below) and *Murudeka* (*Murudeka 17805*, 2001) about Japanese soldiers fighting with Indonesian independence forces against the Dutch colonial forces after 1945. As the sixtieth anniversary approached in 2005, the film gaining all the attention was *Yamato* (*Otokotachi no yamato*, 2005), which was yet another cinematic eulogy to the last suicide mission of the Battleship *Yamato*.

The secrets of success in war cinema

Box office receipts and critical acclaim are the two key measures of success in cinema. In 1991–2001 four war films made the *Kinema* top ten lists: *Rhapsody in August*, *Pride*, *Fireflies* and *Listen to the Voices from the Sea*. These four films indicate that it is difficult to make definitive generalizations about why films are successful. They all had big studio backing, which enabled them to compete visually and technically with Hollywood imports, and to be widely distributed. Beyond that, the reasons for their success were quite different.

Rhapsody in August (*Hachigatsu no kyōshikyoku*, 1991, CC3) was the only critics' top ten choice. Richard Gere plays a second-generation Japanese-American who offers an apology to his aunt for the Nagasaki A-bomb (which killed her husband). Director Kurosawa Akira was attacked by non-Japanese critics for presenting the Japanese simply as victims, and for not detailing Japanese aggression before Nagasaki (McGregor 1996: 174–5). However, the message of the film was familiar and conventional to a Japanese audience with the victim-heroine aunt still suffering from the after-effects of the A-bombs. Its appearance in the critics' top ten was probably largely due to respect for Kurosawa's iconic status in Japan.

By contrast, *Pride* (*Puraido*, 1998, BO5) was a nationalistic box office hit that tells the story of the Tokyo War Crimes Trials and presents wartime Prime Minister Tōjō Hideki as a caring family man who was the victim of a judicial lynching. Another main character in the film is Indian Judge Radhabinod Pal, who gave the sole dissenting judgment at the trials and has become an iconic figure for nationalists as a result. The film presents the 'Asian liberation' theory of the war through its portrayal of Japan's role in the independence of India and support for Subhas Chandra Bose, leader of the Indian National Army. *Pride* had strong endorsement from nationalist magazines, which ensured widespread support for the film among nationalists, and the storm of controversy surrounding the film gave it the sort of publicity that advertising alone cannot achieve.

Fireflies (*Hotaru*, 2001, BO9) is a kamikaze film with a Korean twist. Yamaoka, a kamikaze who survived the war, goes to South Korea with his wife in 1990 to return a trinket belonging to a Korean kamikaze pilot (called Kim) to the surviving relatives in Korea. The trip provides a chance for Koreans to vent their historical frustrations at the central Japanese characters, but also allows for reconciliation. Yamaoka's wife, Tomoko, had been in love with Kim, and reconciliation is achieved through her and Kim's aunt (who had heard about Kim's Japanese sweetheart in letters). However, the Korean kamikaze is eulogized as having the same spirit of sacrifice as Japanese, not necessarily a line that would be well received in South Korea. *Fireflies'* commercial success probably lay in its combination of superb cinematography (including a hauntingly beautiful musical score) and its star power: it had a director and famous leading actor (Takakura Ken) combination that had just had another enormous hit (*Poppoya/Railway Man*, 1999) and also starred one of Japan's top actresses (Tanaka Yūko).

Finally, *Listen to the Voices from the Sea* (*Kike, wadatsumi no koe*, 1995, BO7) was the highest-grossing war film released in 1995. It managed virtually the same box office receipts as *Pride* (10.5 billion yen to *Pride's* 11 billion yen) with little of the accompanying controversy. *Listen* starred a young A-list actor (Oda Yūji) and is part of one of the most recognisable 'brands' in Japanese war discourses: as described in Chapter 2, *Kike wadatsumi no koe* was the best-selling collection of memoirs of student-soldiers who lost their draft exemptions in 1943, and shares its name with two films (1950 and 1995), a subsequent volume of memoirs, a statue (housed in Ritsumeikan University), an activist group (the Wadatsumi Society), and an academic journal (Nihon senbotsu gakusei kinenkai 1995).

The 1995 film contains mixed moral messages. It has some of the most graphic depictions of atrocities in any blockbuster Japanese film, including a scene in which soldiers go to a Filipino village to pillage food (soldiers shoot the villagers in cold blood, set the village alight and strip a young woman who is taken away to be raped) and has a rare depiction of the abuse of 'comfort women'. However, Oda Yūji's character, who starts out as a 'good Japanese' when he opposes the village massacre, ends up as a tragic military hero when he sacrifices his life in a futile suicide charge on American positions. Another student becomes a kamikaze and is eulogized in a way reminiscent of conservative 'nostalgia' films. The film also introduces nurses, who are archetypal victim-heroines. With its differing types of heroes/heroines, *Listen* is a microcosm of the contradictions and tensions within Japanese war memories.

The most striking aspect of these four films is the diverse moral messages they present through their heroes: *Rhapsody in August* has a victim-heroine, the grandmother who experienced the A-bomb; *Pride* has a nationalistic soldier-hero, Tōjō Hideki; *Fireflies* presents conservative pilot-heroes and eulogies to their sacrifice, but it also presents the ongoing historical tension between Japan and South Korea; and in *Listen to the Voices from the Sea* there is a contradictory mixture of a 'good Japanese', conservative military-heroes, and nurse victim-heroines.

This broad range of stances in successful cinema in 1991–2001 suggests that films of any political orientation can achieve success in Japan. However, the sample of fifty-nine films that achieved top ten critical and/or box office success, 1946–2001, suggests that with all other things being equal, 'antiwar films' with victim-heroes such as *The Burmese Harp* are the most likely to achieve both critical and box office success; nationalistic films with military heroes, such as *Pride*, are quite likely to do well at the box office but do not often make the critics' top ten lists; and progressive films, which tackle the difficult questions about Japanese war responsibility and have 'good Japanese' heroes, are more likely to gain critical acclaim beyond their box office success. Overall, political stance is no guarantee of success or failure: the cinematic qualities of a film, famous actors and directors, and a film's ability to reach its target audience (in terms of publicity and distribution at local cinemas) are also vital. Nonetheless, this conclusion explains why on balance, nationalistic and victim-hero films are made in greater numbers than progressive films in Japan: they are safer commercial ventures for profit-conscious studios.

The challenges of progressive film-making

Progressive film-makers face some significant disadvantages in presenting their war stories within what is essentially an entertainment format. This is partly because military heroes and victim-heroes both fit tried and tested formulae for cinematic narrative: a moral hero on a moral mission, and an innocent victim in a melodrama. In more progressive films, however much the audience is invited to associate with the moral behaviour of 'good Japanese' heroes, the painful question of collective responsibility is raised.

Another serious problem facing progressive film-makers is how to represent atrocities in a way that does not sanitize them but, at the same time, keeps them legal and watchable. There is little official censorship of cinematic violence in Japan, and no film classification system except for pornography (although some films now receive an R-certificate for violence, its application is inconsistent). Legally speaking, the atrocities of the Japanese army could be shown in grisly detail without being censored and I am unaware of any war film receiving a restrictive rating. However, while progressive film-makers face few real legal constraints, how to prevent violent scenes from becoming pornographic or voyeuristic is a constant challenge.

One film that managed to find a balance between depicting the horror of atrocity and keeping the film serious and watchable is *The Sea and Poison* (*Umi to dokuyaku*, 1986, CC1). *Poison* is about the vivisections carried out by doctors at Kyushu Imperial University and contains a number of extremely realistic scenes of internal organs being operated on. Such a film could easily degenerate into a 'splatter film', but *Poison* masterfully avoids this, largely because it is filmed in black-and-white. The black-and-white photography provides a sense of watching an historical document. It deglamourizes/ decolourizes the operation-to-the-death on a young American pilot, but does not detract from the film's devastating impact and horrific subject matter.

A number of progressive film-makers have avoided the problem of representing atrocity by using a documentary or docudrama format. Documentaries also have the benefit of being cheaper to make, an important consideration for film-makers embarking on what is usually more of a pet project than a purely profit-making enterprise. In Japanese cinema, two documentaries about the Japanese army stand out.

The Emperor's Naked Army Marches On (Yuki yukite shingun, 1987, CC2) is a fly-on-the-wall documentary that has gained cult status in Japan. It is about the campaigns of former soldier Okuzaki Kenzō, who travels around Japan investigating why two soldiers were executed after the war had ended. Okuzaki is a volatile character who first became famous for shooting pachinko (pinball) balls at the emperor. His investigative methods would make most researchers shudder: he turns up uninvited and bullies confessions out of his interviewees. At first, he merely had an aggressive questioning style but throughout the film things turn more violent. Towards the end, Okuzaki kicks an infirm veteran for admitting he has worshipped at Yasukuni Shrine, an assault which brings the police to the house and requires the veteran to be hospitalized for an X-ray. However, this is not before Okuzaki has harangued the veteran into admitting cannibalism. Outside the hospital, Okuzaki defends his methods using the contradictory logic that violence is justified to get results, namely forcing other people to confess their violence.

This is the last 'interview' in the film. The epilogue describes how Okuzaki's campaign came to include thoughts of murder, and he shot and critically wounded the son of his platoon commander in 1983. Okuzaki was sentenced to twelve years in prison in 1987, after which the film was released. Consequently, the film has a very hard edge. The confessions of cannibalism are real, as is Okuzaki's assault on the veteran and his conviction for attempted murder. The film is a fascinating close-up of soldiers coming to terms with their actions and experiences, not least Okuzaki himself.

Another film that uses a documentary format is *Japanese Devils (Rīben kuizu,* 2000). *Devils* is a straightforward film of the confessions of fourteen soldiers from the China Returnees Association (Chūkiren) who committed serious atrocities in China. The interviews are interspersed by historical commentary to give context to the testimony. One former military policeman confesses to killing 328 and torturing 1,917 Chinese people. Others admit to bayonet practice on live prisoners; vivisection; human experiments in Japan's biological and chemical weapons Unit 731; the gang rape of a woman before dragging her outside by the hair, throwing her into a well along with her young son and throwing in a grenade after them; decapitation 'practice'; and kidnapping for forced labour. The list is sobering and very long (160 minutes).

For the most part, nationalists have not produced similar cinematic documentaries, although many military films contain short sections of archive footage and narration to give historical context and an air of historical authenticity. This relative lack of nationalist cinematic documentaries is probably because narrative conventions within cinema give nationalists a significant advantage over progressives: military heroes are easy to represent within an entertaining action film and the sanitization of war not only gives the military a positive image makeover but also makes a film more watchable to audiences. Progressives, by contrast, face great difficulties in making entertaining, watchable films. A market exists for 'serious, thought-provoking drama' and a number of progressive films have drawn high critical acclaim and box office success, too (such as *War and Humanity*). But the evidence of cinema suggests that progressive film-makers are more at home in the world of non-fiction: documentaries, news and current affairs programmes.

Television dramas

Apart from cinema, television is the other producer of fictional war stories in an audio-visual form. Some television dramas are one-off programmes which share cinema's challenge of telling a self-contained story in 90–180 minutes. Others are series and rely on cliffhangers at the end of episodes to attract return viewers. Plentiful war dramas exist, but unlike the wide variety of stances in cinema, television dramas play firmly to the mainstream: they are almost invariably 'antiwar', most have Japanese victim-heroines, and while there may be firebrand militarists whose actions are not portrayed favourably, there are very few explicit depictions of Japanese atrocities or themes of responsibility.

These issues are typified by one of the key war dramas broadcast on television in August 2005 (see Table. 5.2 on p. 124). On 2 August, Nippon Television broadcast a for-television remake of *Twenty-Four Eyes* (*Ni-jū-shi no hitomi*), based on the bestselling novel by Tsuboi Sakae that had already been made into two films (1954 and 1987, see Orr 2001: 109–16). The story is about a teacher on a small island in the Seto Inland Sea and the war experiences of her twelve pupils. At first, the teacher from the mainland struggled to fit in at the tiny rural school, but with time she won the children's trust. After the war breaks out, tragedy is piled upon tragedy. The teacher's husband is killed in battle and her young daughter dies; her male pupils go to war and are killed or maimed; one of the girls dies of disease and malnutrition, while another is forced by poverty into prostitution. Nevertheless, the bond between teacher and pupils survives, and at the end of the drama there is a nostalgic reunion in which they remember the old times and find hope in the future.

Twenty-Four Eyes epitomizes the standard narrative form of a war drama in Japan. It focuses on 'ordinary people' and stresses the tragedy that war brings. There are idealized central characters: the children embody *kawai rashisa* ('cuteness' or child-like innocence) and the selflessly dedicated teacher pre-empts postwar pacifism by cautioning her boys against volunteering for the war, for which she is reprimanded. The bravery of the characters in the face of adversity accentuates the pity of war. Tear-jerking scenes occur at regular intervals and the final message is antiwar.

An example of a more conservative-feeling drama that nonetheless has an antiwar message is Fuji Television's drama *Battleship Yamato* (*Senkan Yamato*, 1991). It is about the battleship's last voyage on a kamikaze mission in April 1945. The drama has many of the standard conservative themes, such as the 'survivor's guilt' of the officers who beg the captain to be allowed to go down with the ship together. However, the hero is Yoshioka, a kind officer who stands up to the nationalistic firebrands in the crew who pick on radio operator Nakahara for being a Japanese-American. In one key scene, Nakahara reads a letter from his mother in the US who hopes for peace so she can be reunited with her son; and in the final scene, Yoshioka (who survived *Yamato*'s sinking) visits Nakahara's grave with the mother. Despite all the conservative eulogies of the crew's duty and sacrifice, the drama takes an 'antiwar' stance against the militarists in the crew, and presents a message of peace based on the tragic deaths of sailors who just wanted to be reunited with their families.

But most usually, heroes in Japanese dramas are civilian victim-heroines. Nowhere is this clearer than in the key drama institution on Japanese television: NHK's *renzoku terebi shōsetsu*, the morning soap opera, broadcast Monday to Saturday, 8.15–8.30 and repeated 12.45–13.00. Each story runs for six months to a year and is aimed primarily at housewives. It attracts huge viewing figures: an average daily rating for an entire series is typically between 25 and 40 per cent. The most popular drama ever was *Oshin* (Harvey 1995), which averaged 52.6 per cent ratings over its year on air, April 1983 to March 1984 (NHK 2003: 183).

The morning drama was first broadcast in 1961, and in the 43 years to 2003 there were 68 series. The series is an epic biopic of the heroine (almost always a heroine), and the actress who will star in the next series is always unveiled to great media publicity. Of the 68 series, the plots of 28 series included sections during the war years, 1937–45 (ibid.: 180–7). Most of these can only be loosely categorized as wartime dramas (the plots are largely unrelated to the war and only partially take place against the backdrop of war). However, some series were predominantly set during the war years, or were 'war/postwar dramas' that focused on the heroine's war experiences. Nine of the most war-related series since the 1970s are listed in Table 7.1. These dramas constitute hundreds of hours of drama programming set during the war years that have consistently received viewing ratings of over 30 per cent. But these dramas are not necessarily, if ever, asking the difficult questions about Japanese war responsibility. They are social dramas centred on a heroine and her experiences in the war years.

The other flagship dramas on NHK are the *taiga dorama*, which are typically major historical series. *Taiga dorama* usually focus on the samurai era, but there have been two major series penned by best-selling novelist Yamasaki Toyoko. Yamasaki is the queen of the epic war melodrama in Japan, with three novels running to over 1,000 pages each: *Barren Land* (*Fumō chitai*, about Siberian internment), *Two Fatherlands* (*Futatsu no sokoku*, about Japanese-American internment) and *Child of the Continent* (*Daichi no ko*, about war orphans in China). *Sanga moyu*, the television drama based on *Two Fatherlands*, has been credited with igniting Japanese scholarly interest in Japanese-Americans' war experiences in the 1980s (Shimada 2004: i), while *Daichi no ko* was NHK's major war drama in 1995 (*Daichi no ko*, November–December 1995, 11 episodes).

Table 7.1 Nine war-related renzoku terebi shōsetsu broadcast on NHK

Title	Set in	Synopsis	Average ratings	Broadcast dates
Niji (Rainbow)	1943–65	The war/postwar experiences of a university lecturer's wife.	37.9	April 1970–April 1971
Ai yori aoku (Deeper than Indigo)	1943–63	Biopic of a war widow and her postwar struggles to raise her son.	47.3	April 1972–March 1973
Hatako no umi (Hatako's Ocean)	1945–75	The nomadic wanderings of a girl whose war trauma caused amnesia.	47.2	April 1974–April 1975
Watashi wa umi (I am an Ocean)	c.1928–c.1946	A woman who raises war orphans.	35.9	October 1978–March 1979
Mā nēchan (My sister Mariko)	1934–c.1945	The family of the cartoonist who created Sazae-san.	42.8	April 1979–September 1979
Honjitsu mo seiten nari (Today will also be Sunny)	1944–present	A radio presenter's war experiences.	36.6	October 1981–April 1982
Oshin	1908–present	Epic biopic of a woman's life through the twentieth century.	52.6	April 1983–March 1984
Miyako no kaze (Winds of the Capital)	1940–1956	The lives of three sisters in war/postwar Kyoto.	39.3	October 1986–April 1987
Kimi no na wa (What's Your Name?)	1945–1955	Lovers who meet during the great Tokyo air raid.	29.1	April 1991–April 1992

Source: NHK (2003: 56–61; 180–7).

Yamasaki describes *Daichi no ko* as 'fiction based on fact' stemming from her interviews with war-displaced children (Yamasaki 1994: 8). The drama follows the story of a young boy called Katsuo, who is stranded in China when his mother is killed by the advancing Russians in August 1945. Katsuo and his sister Atsuko become separated when two Chinese families take the 'Little Japanese Devils' to be child labourers. Katsuo runs away and eventually finds a loving foster home with a Chinese couple who treat him like the son they never had: Katsuo's foster-father, a school teacher called Liu, is the real star of the drama for his deep compassion and fatherly love.

During the Cultural Revolution, Katsuo is interned in a labour camp for being Japanese, but eventually he is released and marries a nurse he met in the camp. He joins a steel company where his Japanese background means he works in industrial cooperation projects with Japanese companies. Katsuo's work stimulates an interest in his Japanese roots, and, unbeknown to Katsuo, his work has already brought him into direct contact with his biological father.

Katsuo's biological father had been on military duty at the end of the war. Back in Japan after the war, he believes his entire family to be dead. But, along with other Japanese seeking to find out what happened to their children, he makes enquiries from Japan. The enquiries bear fruit: he discovers the whereabouts of Atsuko and travels to China to see her. Coincidentally, Katsuo has found Atsuko too, through his wife's trips to field hospitals. The simultaneous discovery of Atsuko brings father and son together. They immediately recognize each other: they have been working together on the same steelworks project without ever knowing each other's real identity.

Atsuko has had a terrible life of poverty and is on her deathbed when her father and brother reach her. There is only time for the briefest of reunions before she dies. The discovery of his natural father creates a terrible dilemma for Katsuo between his feelings for his Japanese roots and his adoptive parents, wife and child in China. On a business trip to Japan, Katsuo visits his biological father's house to pray at the family shrine, but his absence from the hotel where the Chinese delegation is staying provides an opportunity for a Chinese co-worker to steal documents from Katsuo's luggage and frame him for industrial espionage. The man who framed Katsuo wanted revenge on the Japanese for his family's death during the war. This is the only explicit reference to Japanese aggression in the drama's eleven hours.

After three years in 'exile' at a steelworks deep in China's interior, Katsuo's name is cleared and he meets his biological father again. In the final episode, Katsuo and his father take a river trip together to become properly acquainted. The father raises the possibility of Katsuo returning to Japan, but Katsuo has to tell his biological father that he is a 'child of the continent', and China is his home.

Child of the Continent has numerous tear-jerking scenes as the leading characters experience their roller-coaster lives through war, revolution, bereavement, love, hope and reunion. The drama epitomized the typical treatment of the war in Japanese television dramas. The war is viewed from the point of view of ordinary people who suffer terribly, but the roots of the war are barely treated.

Simulation fiction

Most war fiction relies on a measure of historical accuracy or authenticity to appeal to consumers. Yet even the most conscientious author or film director striving for historical authenticity must inevitably resort to some fabrication. This is particularly so in cinema, where the 'look of the past' must be recreated in sets and costumes. Actors portraying an actual historical figure can never look exactly the same, and unless there is a precise transcript of the person's words, it is impossible (or perhaps undesirable for dramatic purposes) to use the exact words of the historical figure. The historical accuracy of war stories, therefore, exists on a sliding scale from 'as accurate as possible' through 'liberties being taken with the historical record' to outright fantasy and invention.

Fantasy in Japanese war stories has become a particular issue within simulation fiction, a story in which Japan wins the war or the passage of war history takes a dramatically different course. The story usually rests on one of two premises: eminently possible changes in fortune precipitate major differences in the outcome of the war (the fine dividing line between disaster and victory at the Battle of Midway has made it a particular favourite in such counterfactual stories), and a new superweapon turns the war decisively in Japan's favour.

Sales of simulation fiction run to the millions, much of it in pulp fiction novels or manga. There is a significant element of revisionist reverie in much simulation fiction and the conduct of their military heroes is certainly most compatible with nationalist ideology. Simulation fiction has been widely criticized as a result (for example, Hicks 1997: 90–2). However, simulation fiction is not equivalent to apologia. Frederik Schodt's survey of *Combat Comic*, one of the main magazines featuring serialized simulation manga, describes how the president of its publisher, Nippon shuppansha, stressed to him that the publication was not pro-war (Schodt 1996: 119). Schodt found one particularly successful story, *The Pacific War: Reversal!*, to be 'a fairly well-reasoned speculation about what might have happened if the US had lost a series of Pacific Fleet battles and General Patton had run amok and attacked the approaching Soviet Army in Europe' (ibid.: 118). The manga itself (Ueda 1991) contains photographs and historical explanations at the end of each chapter to give the actual history alongside the counterfactual. This is a common feature of any counterfactual history in Japanese or any other language (Schodt 1996: 118; see Cook 1999 for an example in English). Furthermore, counterfactuals are not necessarily in jingoistic, victorious scenarios. Another manga from *Combat Comic*, *The Decisive Pacific War Battle* (Kobayashi 1995) depicts the slaughter that could have occurred if an invasion of the Japanese mainland had taken place and concludes it was better that Japan surrendered when it did (ibid.: 224).

The high level of historical knowledge required to appreciate a counterfactual scenario, in which the changes from real history can be very subtle, is a clue to the target audience for simulation fiction. *Combat Comic*'s readers, for example, are 'almost all male and tend to be *mania*, or hard-core fans of guns, "survival games" and "mecha" (weaponry and hardware)' (Schodt 1996: 116). These interests of the target audience are evident in the narrative styles of simulation novels based on fantastical scenarios. In part one of the six-part novel *The Imperial Fleet* (1992) by Shimoda Kageki, Admiral Yamamoto Isoroku was not killed in 1943 but has been spirited away to a secret island base where he will captain a fleet, including submarine aircraft carriers armed with revolutionary aircraft that greatly outperform any planes the Americans and Soviets have. Japan surrenders in 1945, but the new fleet is launched and starts its devastating counteroffensive against the occupying Americans and the Soviets in conjunction with the Japanese resistance. The story is reminiscent of *20,000 Leagues Under the Sea*, with Yamamoto as a wartime Captain Nemo operating from a secret island base and wreaking havoc in a super-submarine. In *The Imperial Fleet*, the specifications of all the superweapons are given in loving detail, characters are predominantly male, and female characters exist mainly for romantic interest. The 'male military enthusiast' target audience could not be clearer.

But simulation fiction has not just been limited to the male *mania* ('techno-geek') audience. The four-part novel *Lorelei* by Fukui Harutoshi sold 1.8 million copies (compared to *Combat Comic*'s 100,000 copies circulation) and was turned into a hit film in 2005, which suggests much broader appeal. 'Lorelei' is a revolutionary radar system in a German submarine given to the Japanese. It is powered by a psychic, Paula, who developed her special powers after being the victim of Nazi human experiments. In August 1945, the submarine is sent on a mission to prevent a third atomic bomb being dropped on Tokyo. On the surface, *Lorelei* seems like another nationalistic reverie. But the real bad guy in the film is a Japanese militarist who actually wants the bomb dropped to clear out the corruption in Japan. Furthermore, the crew members are humanitarian towards the traumatized Paula, who experiences pain any time people are killed. Rather than destroying the Americans in pursuit of them, the crew decides to disable the American fleet to spare Paula pain. This is simulation fiction with a sensitive touch, a fantasy adventure story more than a story that can be said to present a particular message about war history. Indeed, its popularity may lie in the fact that it did not simply target *mania*.

In sum, while simulation fiction clearly lends itself most to nationalism, many of the general criticisms made about simulation fiction overlook the fact that diversity of message and target audience exist within the genre. But there are two further issues. First, the primary consumers of simulation fiction are typically highly interested in military history. This is not to say that the military heroes in simulation fiction do not play to or nourish existing nationalist historical consciousness, but it does mean the consumers will be *relatively* able to distinguish fiction and non-fiction, even if the actual history is not placed next to the simulation. Second, the fantastical nature of simulation fiction such as *The Imperial Fleet* and *Lorelei* clearly mark them as fantasy, as do the references to real history in many counterfactuals. In short, the lines between fiction and reality can be blurred far more subtly in stories that consciously give the impression of being based on historical fact. These are significant grounds for arguing that historical films in which 'liberties have been taken with the facts' (a major issue from Japanese war cinema through to Hollywood films like *Braveheart* and *U-571*) are much more dangerous than simulation fiction. Here, the historical inaccuracies introduced to strengthen the message or to tell a 'better story' are much harder to spot, and the danger of historical consciousness being influenced by fiction is greater as a result.

Conclusions

The narrative considerations of war fiction mirror the core dilemma faced by contemporary Japanese: when war history is so contentious and the level of suffering across Asia caused by Japanese actions was so great, how can war stories be told in a way that allows positive identification with the actions and experiences of the war generation? Japanese people have developed a number of conceptual frameworks for dealing with this issue and three basic frames – the conservative–nationalist, progressive and Japanese as innocent victims frames – are evident in the military, good Japanese and victim-heroes in Japanese fiction. But the bottom line is that there must be a Japanese central character whose morality gains the empathy and identification of the audience.

Nationalists have many commercial advantages over progressives in cinema because the narrative conventions of mainstream films facilitate heroic renditions of war history. In successful mainstream cinema, however, and particularly in war dramas on television, the dominant fictional representation of the war sends an antiwar message and focuses on victim-heroes. Progressive war stories exist too, although progressive film-makers have often found documentaries a more appropriate form of film for their message. For many people, these fictional representations of war may be of equal if not greater significance than non-fictional accounts in the composure of their historical consciousnesses. This is because message clarity, which is so often complicated by professional codes of accuracy and inclusiveness in non-fictional accounts, can be achieved more easily in fictional accounts.

8   Regional memories

Local memories, local victimhood

Japan is a country of strong regional identities. Reinforced by the annual migrations back to hometowns during the New Year and O-bon (mid-August) holidays, Japanese people typically have a strong sense of where they originally came from, their *furusato* (home village). Strong regional identities coexist with strong local culture: there are many local festivals, regional specialities (virtually every town has a characteristic food, or gift, *omiyage*) and dialects. Strong local media production exists, too. The circulations of some regional newspapers, such as the *Hokkaidō shinbun* and *Nishi nihon shinbun* (1.24 million and 850,000 in 1999 respectively), match some of the English-speaking world's major papers, such as *The New York Times* and *The Times* of London (1.11 million and 721,000 in 2003 respectively) (Asahi shinbunsha 2005: 249; Fujitake 2000: 38–42). Television broadcasting is through regional affiliates of the main networks, and all the terrestrial channels (except NHK-Educational) typically have around two or three hours a day of prefectural level news and programming.

War history also contributes to regional identity. The war affected the regions of Japan in distinct ways. The major cities were bombed, while the rural areas hosted children evacuated from the bombing. Some regions saw influxes of workers or forced labourers to work in vital war industries, while other regions experienced depopulation due to poverty, destruction or migration to Japan's colonies. Local men were enlisted in the same unit, so people from a particular region frequently died en masse in the same place. And, from April to June 1945, Okinawa witnessed some of the bloodiest fighting of the war, the only combat on Japanese soil.

These regional war experiences have spawned a rich variety of local war history and memories. Some of the narratives have transcended the local level to become central to national war history, such as the A-bombs, but others remain unknown to many outside or even inside the region. Nevertheless, local history is a much overlooked aspect of Japanese war memories: Japanese schoolchildren typically visit municipal and prefectural history museums on school trips and study some local history at school, most commemorative events are organized at a local level, and war sites may even become key attractions in the local tourism industry.

But local history has another important function within Japanese war memories. Remembering war history at the national level presents an uncomfortable contrast between what 'Japan' did to others and others did to 'Japan'. The 3.1 million Japanese dead compare uncomfortably with the over 20 million killed by Japanese militarism. Local history offers a much more comfortable comparison: the number of Japanese killed in each prefecture by air raids and in battle can be quantified, but how many deaths the people of that prefecture caused can never be accurately assessed. The unfavourable victim–perpetrator balance is lost at the local level.

In many instances, this has facilitated victim mentality and avoidance of war responsibility issues. In Chapter 2, I described the common 'leaders' responsibility view', in which the blame for Japanese aggression was placed on the militarists while the 'ordinary people of Japan' were largely innocent. Local narratives often constitute a variation on this theme: while the nation aggressed the local people suffered, and identification at the local rather than national level underpins victim mentality. Not all local narratives, however, focus on victimhood, as the prominence of forced labour narratives in Niigata and Hokkaido (described below) illustrates. Nevertheless, the more comfortable levels of collective responsibility that can be assumed by viewing war history through local eyes make local memories an important theme within Japanese war memories.

Local war history has been narrated in a variety of cultural forms – particularly regional newspapers, regional television news and museums – but this chapter focuses on museums. Museums offer another set of economic and political conditions affecting the representation and consumption of war history; the role of local governments in managing museums illustrates how local official narratives can differ substantially from the narrative of the national government; and museums have been key actors in the collection and exhibition of testimonies by the war generation.

War museums in Japan

Museums are powerful sites of memory creation for the vested interests that finance them. They require enormous financial backing to be housed in an often purpose-built building, and to employ full-time staff and curators. Museums typically recoup only a small percentage of their running costs in entrance fees, so the profitability threshold does not work at an economic level but relates to prestige, the promotion of vested interests or 'the public good'. Financial backers are often national and local government, which gives museums an air of official legitimacy. Museums also gain legitimacy through being entrusted by society to preserve and display priceless artefacts of yesteryear, and by being deemed worthy of educational visits by schools.

Japan has many war-related exhibits. *The Peace and War Museum Guidebook* (Rekishi kyōikusha kyōgikai 2000) reviews 111 museums with Asia-Pacific War exhibits. It reveals some of the main trends. Many museums were planned during the 'bubble' era in the 1980s when local authorities had cash to spare. A number of older museums were renovated in this period, too. There is an emphasis on 'peace' rather than 'war' in the naming of museums. Of the 111 museums, 32 have the word 'peace' (*heiwa*) in their names. By contrast, only one uses the word 'war' (*sensō*). Specialist war museums are often called 'documentation centres' (*shiryōkan*) or 'memorials' (*kinenkan*). 'Museum' (*hakubutsukan*) is a legal status in Japan and *hakubutsukan* must fulfil government-set criteria for the preservation of artefacts and research activities. 'Documentation centres' or 'memorials', by contrast, face no specific government restrictions.

In particular, there are four types of institution with war-related displays:

1   National and prefectural history *museums (hakubutsukan)*: generic history museums focusing on artefact display whose exhibits include the war years. War exhibits tend to avoid detail or constitute a small percentage of the total exhibits.

2   Municipal *peace museums* (typically, 'documentation centres' or 'memorials'): specialist war museums presenting local history and narrating primarily social history. The museums present their narrative through photographs, audio-visual or interactive multimedia, testimony, models and panels more than period artefacts. Peace museums frequently double up as a research centre for local history, specialist public library, site for school visits, tourist attraction and multi-purpose convention centre.

3   *Military museums*: museums commemorating the actions of a branch of the military. They use a military memorabilia display style (uniforms, weapons, medals and other memorabilia in display cases). Explanations of war history focus on military strategy and stories of warrior courage.

4   *Sectional interest museums*: museums representing a particular war experience (such as repatriation) or promoting a political message. Many privately funded museums fall within this category.

The politics of war and peace exhibits

The National Museum of Japanese History (NMJH)[1] is in Sakura, about an hour by train east of Tokyo. When I visited NMJH in September 2002, the Asia-Pacific War and Japanese imperialism were conspicuous by their absence from the exhibits. There was only a small collection of five or six nondescript photographs depicting scenes on the home front tagged onto the end of the modern history exhibits, which covered the period to 1923.

According to Ichinose Toshiya, a researcher in the Modern Period Section, ideally, the modern period exhibits should cover the period at least up to the 1960s. An application to the Ministry of Education for funds to develop the

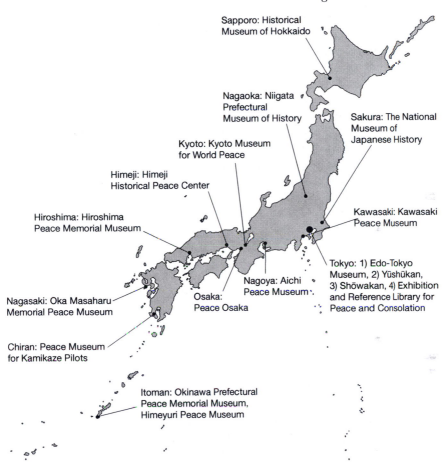

Sapporo: Historical
Museum of Hokkaido

Nagaoka: Niigata
Prefectural
Museum of History

Sakura: The National
Museum of
Japanese History

Kyoto: Kyoto Museum
for World Peace

Himeji: Himeji
Historical Peace Center

Kawasaki: Kawasaki
Peace Museum

Hiroshima: Hiroshima
Peace Memorial Museum

Tokyo: 1) Edo-Tokyo
Museum, 2) Yūshūkan,
3) Shōwakan, 4) Exhibition
and Reference Library for
Peace and Consolation

Nagoya: Aichi
Peace Museum

Osaka:
Peace Osaka

Nagasaki: Oka Masaharu
Memorial Peace Museum

Chiran: Peace Museum
for Kamikaze Pilots

Itoman: Okinawa Prefectural
Peace Memorial Museum,
Himeyuri Peace Museum

Figure 8.1 Locations of museums

modern history exhibits was being processed (September 2002) and the new exhibits will cover the war (although as I write in 2006 there is no visible progress). The war did not feature in the original exhibits because the modern history displays were designed around the time of the 1982 textbook crisis. NMJH is funded by the Ministry of Education, the department at the centre of the crisis. Fearing further controversy, the Modern Period Section did not want to get involved in a war exhibit (Ichinose 2002).

In fairness to the NMJH, its Japanese name includes the word *minzoku*, 'the people', which implies a cultural, anthropological approach to Japanese history rather than a political or military one. Most of the exhibits are archaeological finds or discuss everyday life and culture in Japan over the centuries. A war exhibit would either follow this pattern and risk criticism for ignoring the overseas effect of Japanese militarism, or would be very different in nature from all the other exhibits. Furthermore, NMJH faces the same thankless task as every other national institution in Japan, including the government, NHK and the education system: how can a national history that satisfies everyone be told when the nation is so divided and external scrutiny is so severe? NMJH took the avoidance option, although this draws its own criticism, too.

This dilemma does much to explain why depicting the war in museums is largely left to regional museums and museums representing sectional interests: these museums can present *coherent* regional and sectional narratives of the war. But even operating at a local or sectional level does not prevent museum controversies. Any clear narrative concerning Japanese war actions is a recipe for controversy, especially when large sums of public money are involved in the construction and running of the museum. Two museums that have generated controversy, albeit for very different reasons, are Shōwakan in Tokyo, and Peace Osaka, the municipal peace museum of Japan's third city.

Shōwakan[2] is just down the road from Yasukuni Shrine in central Tokyo. It was meant to be the national 'peace memorial to the war dead' and plans were first unveiled in 1992. It received massive financial support from the government and was meant to represent all victims of war, not only Japanese (Arai 1997: 182). However, by the time of the museum's opening, its character had changed radically. The visitor's pamphlet states, 'Shōwakan was opened on 27 March 1999 and the running of the museum was entrusted to the War Bereaved Association by the Ministry of Health and Welfare'. The exhibits are conservative in a manner consistent with the WBA leadership's conservatism and its close links to the ruling LDP elite. The exhibits focus on Japanese victimhood on the home front and avoid discussion of Japanese responsibility. Protests erupted at public money being used for such a project, but officials merely replied, 'The museum was not intended as an apology to Asian nations' (Arai 1997: 182).

The War Bereaved Association–Yasukuni Shrine–LDP–Shōwakan links have created a conservative–nationalist haven in the Kudan area of Tokyo. Away from Kudan, municipal museums presenting more progressive stances exist. The most progressive is Peace Osaka.[3] In the first exhibit room, a local narrative of victimhood, the Osaka air raids, is presented. The second room gives a forthright exhibition about Japanese aggression, although references to the A-bombs and the Holocaust send the message that Japan was not alone in committing atrocities. In the final exhibition room, cold war conflicts and nuclear proliferation are discussed.

Peace Osaka is much more progressive than most museums and has been vilified by nationalists as a result. A local citizen's group and the nationalistic *Sankei* newspaper launched a campaign against Peace Osaka in 1996–97, claiming that some of the gruesome photographs on display were not what the panels said they were. Peace Osaka changed three photograph exhibits from 1 July 1997, although Peace Osaka did not view the errors as necessitating a change in overall stance. Nonetheless, the controversy reached the local assembly where councillors raised the Peace Osaka exhibits issue (Peace Osaka 1997).

Museums such as Peace Osaka indicate that official *municipal* stances on the war in Japan are not necessarily the same as the official *national* stance. Whereas the conservative LDP has a grip on the national official narrative, local political power can be of a different colour. Local politics is the key to understanding the stance in Peace Osaka and the Kawasaki Peace Museum, another municipal museum which shares Peace Osaka's three-tiered presentation of war issues: a local narrative of victimhood (air raids), Japanese aggression, and postwar conflicts and nuclear issues. Both Osaka and Kawasaki have more industrial, working-class populations who vote for more centre-left mayors and local assemblies. The more progressive war stances of centre-left parties translate into political support for more progressive narratives in municipal peace museums. Furthermore, both cities have large Korean and Chinese communities (Peace Osaka is very close to Osaka's 'Koreatown'). Given that many Koreans and Chinese in Japan are, or are descendants of, people brought to Japan as imperial subjects or forced labourers, this results in added pressure for a progressive stance in local war commemoration (Kikuchi 2002).

In short, while most regional museums are funded by public money, local official narratives can be at odds with each other and the conservative national official narrative. But wherever a clear line on Japanese war actions is presented and large sums of public money are involved, controversy quickly follows.

Consuming museums: museums as sites of education

The real significance of local official positions is that schoolchildren in state schools can only visit officially approved museums as part of their education, although private schools can take pupils to any museum. The attendance figures at Japanese museums reveal that educational visits by schoolchildren are central roles, and by extension, rationales for local authorities building museums in the first place. School trips are a standard part of a Japanese child's education. They can be day trips, or visits that last for up to three or four days. If children visit a peace museum, the standard visit involves the museum sending preparatory materials to the school in advance, around one hour going around the museum, and the students writing a report about the visit for homework. Sometimes, teachers use worksheets provided by the museum, but not all museums produce such materials and many teachers opt to produce their own materials. Which museum the school visits and what type of study the trip involves are at the discretion of the school.[4]

Students on school trips account for a significant percentage of many museums' visitors. In 1995, the peak year of attendance at Peace Osaka, 60.3 per cent of the 115,654 visitors were schoolchildren (under 18). In 2001, overall attendance figures had dropped to 82,191, but schoolchildren accounted for 67.6 per cent of visitors. The Nagasaki Atomic Bomb Museum saw a decline in visitor numbers from 1,070,651 in 1991 to 808,444 in 2001. However, the percentage of visitors who were children remained quite constant in the 41–48 per cent range. The Kawasaki Peace Museum's attendance figures declined from 73,666 in 1992 to 43,628 in 2001, and the percentage of schoolchildren ranged between 20 and 40 per cent.

Declining museum attendance is an across-the-board trend and is partly due to Japan's declining birth rate, which means that fewer schoolchildren visit museums on school trips. But falling attendance figures do not mean that fewer schools are organizing trips to museums. The Edo-Tokyo Museum, for example, is one of Tokyo's top tourist attractions. It attracted 3 million visitors in its opening year (1993) but 1.2 to 1.5 million visitors per year in the late 1990s. The number of schoolchildren visiting declined from 71,600 in 1995 to 65,751 in 2001, but the number of schools organizing trips to the museum over the same period actually rose from 725 to 1,096.

Since the 1990s, the number of schoolchildren visiting the museums mentioned above has exceeded 500,000 per year, even in the years of lowest attendance. Factoring in the dozens of other municipal and regional war museums (particularly Hiroshima), over a million Japanese children visit museums with war exhibits every year, mainly on official school trips. To put this in perspective, the school population in Japan in 2002 was about fifteen million. Consequently, a high percentage of Japanese children visit a war museum at some stage during their school education. This is consistent with the historical consciousness survey I carried out among university students: 15 per cent said they visited a war museum on a junior high school trip, and 46 per cent said they did at senior high school. Museums were also ranked as the second most influential cultural form overall by the 436 university students, which illustrates the powerful impression that such visits can make on schoolchildren.

Museums have different stances and focuses, so children receive different educations depending on which museum they visit. On balance, however, the educational focus of school museum visits is 'peace' rather than 'war', and 'local history' rather than 'national history'. The vast majority of students visit museums with strong narratives of Japanese victimhood (particularly the A-bomb museums in Hiroshima and Nagasaki) or municipal museums with a significant focus on air raids. But while many of these museums place comparatively little focus on Japanese aggression, they typically present progressive-leaning 'both victim and perpetrator' stances. Controversial conservative–nationalist museums receive relatively few schoolchildren visitors: in the 1990s, schoolchildren only made up 4–8 per cent of the 140,000–170,000 visitors a year to Yūshūkan (in the grounds of Yasukuni Shrine), and in 2001, only 17,675 of Shōwakan's 220,000 visitors (8 per cent) were schoolchildren.

Japanese pacifisms

In Chapter 1 I argued that 'victim mentality', despite its ubiquity, cannot be considered a unified phenomenon within Japanese war memories. The rhetoric of 'peace' is also ubiquitous and no less open to interpretation by groups across the political spectrum. This is evident in the museums that call themselves 'peace' museums. The following eight 'peace museums' represent almost the entire progressive–nationalist spectrum.

1 *Condemning Japanese Aggression* The Oka Masaharu Memorial Peace Museum (OMMPM)[5] in Nagasaki is a small, private museum near Nagasaki Station and is the most progressive of any museum I have visited. Oka Masaharu was a peace activist who campaigned for Korean victims of the Nagasaki A-bomb. OMMPM is a private museum established in 1995 in his memory. The display style is rudimentary, reflecting the museum's shoestring budget. Some of the oral testimony Oka collected is displayed on panels and in books in the lobby. On the stairs up to the second floor, and on the second floor itself, Japanese aggression in Asia is brutally exhibited in a sickening collection of war photographs. Interspersed among the photos are chronologies and commentaries. Books relating to various topics, including the Nanking Massacre and slave labour, are laid out on tables for people to leaf through. There are documentary videos and equipment provided for visitors to watch them. OMMPM makes a hard-hitting call for peace by condemning the horrors of war, and the suffering of Asians at the hands of the Japanese.

2 *Condemning Aggression* The Kyoto Museum for World Peace (KMWP)[6] is a private museum on the campus of Ritsumeikan University, ten minutes walk from Kyoto's famous Golden Pavilion. Rather than simply condemning Japanese war crimes, KMWP looks in more general terms at aggression and imperialism. In the first half of the museum, KMWP describes Japanese aggression and war crimes in forthright terms and concludes with a discussion of 'unresolved war responsibilities'. But the second half looks at Western colonialism in Asia, American involvement in Vietnam and nuclear prolifera-tion. The condemnation of Japanese imperialism is directed at other nations, particularly at American involvement in Vietnam. KMWP's call for peace is based on a broad criticism of aggression, including Japan's.

3 *Nuclear Victimhood* The Hiroshima Peace Memorial Museum (A-bomb museum, HPMM)[7] is Japan's best known and most visited specialist war museum, by both Japanese and non-Japanese alike (1.08 million visitors in 2000, 93,000 of them non-Japanese). Hiroshima's place in history as the target of the world's first nuclear attack makes HPMM a place of not only local, but national and global significance. HPMM can feel as if it is the 'national shrine of Japanese victimhood'. However, when the museum reopened after its renovation in 1994, the new exhibits mentioned Japanese aggression, including that 'Chinese were being slaughtered' in Nanking in 1937. From the museum's point of view, these mentions of Japanese aggression do not

delegitimize Hiroshima's peace message. They demonstrate that HPMM has recognized the need for Japanese aggression to be acknowledged for the Hiroshima narrative to maintain its global currency.

Once the acknowledgement of Japanese crimes has been made, the atomic crime perpetrated in Hiroshima is presented. The Allied 'lives saved' theory is rebutted: the bomb was dropped 'to limit Soviet influence in East Asia after the war' and resembled a scientific experiment: 'conventional bombing in these cities [selected as potential targets – Hiroshima, Kyoto, Kokura and Niigata] was forbidden to allow more accurate measurement of the A-bomb's power' (Hiroshima Peace Memorial Museum 1999: 24–5). Exhibits about American medical teams examining but not treating A-bomb victims and censorship of reports about the bombing by the occupation force (Hiroshima Peace Memorial Museum online), reinforce the impression that the A-bombs were war crimes of debatable military necessity. Horrific pictures of burns and keloids (burns scars that balloon up), and other exhibits such as bottles melted together, graphically illustrate the destructive power of nuclear weapons. HPMM's call for peace, embodied in the 'spirit of Hiroshima', stems from the warning of apocalypse in the nuclear age, a warning that can be given from first-hand experience.

4 *Local Victimhood (Air Raids)* While Hiroshima's narrative of regional suffering has been transformed into a national narrative, there are many regional narratives that have remained as purely local narratives. These local narratives are often of air raids. The Kyoto Museum for World Peace's guidebook (1997) lists ninety-three Japanese cities that suffered major air raids (including the A-bombs) in which a total of over 600,000 people died (ibid.: 113). A number of cities have founded municipal 'peace' museums to commemorate the raids, such as Himeji which has built the Himeji Historical Peace Center. This museum will be analysed in the section on air raid narratives below.

5 *Sectional Narratives of Victimhood* The Exhibition and Reference Library for Peace and Consolation (ERLPC)[8] is located on the thirty-first floor of the Sumitomo building in Shinjuku, Tokyo's skyscraper district. It presents three sectional narratives of victimhood: soldiers who did not serve long enough to receive pensions, repatriates from Japanese colonies after the war, and Siberian internees. These groups' sufferings are depicted in exhibits such as a reconstruction of the cramped inside of a Siberian labour camp hut, and a jacket without any sleeves (which the Japanese owner had cut off to exchange for food). The ERLPC conceals Japanese aggression by giving only minimal context as to why these groups experienced what they did. For instance, the museum does not refer to the actions of the Japanese soldiers in China prior to them being interned. Based on three decontextualized sectional narratives of Japanese suffering, the ERLPC, in its pamphlet, calls on visitors to appreciate 'the sufferings of those who were in the war so as to convey to later generations the inestimable value of peace'.

6 *Sectional Narrative of Military Suffering* The Peace Museum for Kamikaze Pilots (PMKP)[9] in Chiran, Kyushu, 'has now become the principal site where "the brave young warriors who disappeared beyond the far horizon" are commemorated' (PMKP pamphlet). PMKP is conservative and the museum's stance is that it was the pilots who were the real victims:

> Today, with the diversification of values, interpretation is up to individuals and one can hear voices glorifying the kamikaze and militarism. . . . What we hope visitors will understand, even if just a little, is that the real situation was that just before the end of the war, this kind of tragic tactic was used.
>
> (Peace Museum for Kamikaze Pilots 2002)

The exhibits also present the message that the kamikaze pilots were the real victims. Apart from some planes and panels outlining the operations, the exhibits are dominated by the pictures of all the pilots who flew from Chiran and dozens of heart-wrenching final letters to their mothers from men who knew they would die. The characterization that the real tragedy belongs to the kamikaze is achieved by omitting the victimhood of the Americans killed aboard ships attacked by the kamikaze, and the military motivations for employing suicide tactics: to decisively turn the war in Japan's favour. Had the kamikaze succeeded, they would have been heroes and martyrs, as they are for nationalists now. However, with the kamikaze portrayed as the victims, their tragedy becomes the basis for a call for peace.

7 *Local Narrative of Military Suffering* Aichi Peace Museum (APM)[10] is located just to the west of Aichi prefecture's Gokoku ('Nation Protecting') Shrine in Nagoya, Japan's fourth city. The location is significant because Gokoku shrines are the prefectural branch shrines of Yasukuni Shrine and enshrine local soldiers. The museum itself is run by the local WBA and commemorates local units from Aichi Prefecture. APM only has one small exhibition room but houses an impressive collection of military memorabilia: uniforms, models, maps, photographs of handsome young soldiers and military equipment. Rather than panels outlining the museum's stance, the exhibits are left to speak for themselves and focus attention on the sacrifice of the Japanese military. There is only brief mention of who the military was fighting against, and no presentation of how others might have been affected by the Japanese military's actions. The APM makes its call for peace by highlighting the bereavement of Japanese families, and a desire that future generations do not have to go through what the bereaved families have suffered.

8 *Integrated Peace Message* The Kawasaki Peace Museum (KPM)[11] is the final type of peace museum and employs a mixture of peace messages: a local air raid narrative, condemnation of Japanese aggression and exhibits about modern conflicts. The museum contains a few artefacts but provides primarily an audio-visual experience. In every section of the museum, television screens are the main display medium. The Kawasaki air raid of 15 April 1945 is

depicted in a video, which includes interviews with survivors, and a photographic comparison of Kawasaki in 1945 and 1998. In the section 'Japan and the War', videos talk about forced labour, the Nanking Massacre, human experiments in Unit 731 and Koreans being forced to learn Japanese. The ongoing work (in the 1990s) to clear chemical weapons left by the Japanese army in China is also discussed in the section on weapons of mass destruction.

These museums have disparate rationales for calling themselves 'peace museums', and certainly not all of them could be called 'pacifist': the kamikaze and Aichi museums are archetypal military museums, albeit sombre rather than jingoistic. But the museums all share a pattern of moral reasoning. They represent the sufferings of one or more victim groups, encourage visitors to identify with that group's suffering, and base their call for peace on how the suffering of the group must not be repeated. Japanese pacifisms, therefore, are closely linked to Japanese victim mentalities and ultimately return to issues of judgemental memory. Defining and identifying with a victim group relies on a judgement about the guilt of the perpetrator 'other', although such responsibilities are often kept in the vague territory of 'the inevitable suffering caused by defeat' or 'the horrors of war'.

The prominence of the rhetoric of 'peace' within Japanese museum exhibits is indicative of a general lack of jingoistic nationalism – with the exception of military museums such as Yūshūkan[12] and the Nasu War Museum[13]. It is also indicative of the importance within Japanese war memories of local or sectional narratives: these are the levels at which coherent messages about peace based on Japanese victimhood can be made without needing to refer back to the always problematic statistic that Japanese militarism killed at least six times more people in Asian countries than Japanese people died in the war. These narratives of victimhood most commonly co-exist with limited (but, in museums like Peace Osaka, extensive) acknowledgement of Japanese aggression, which makes the stance of the majority of municipal peace museums 'progressive-leaning'.

Air raids: from distinctive local memories to generic narrative

As with all narratives, local narratives must compete with other war narratives for attention and prominence within cultural memory. Narratives about air raid narratives, a common local war experience, reveal the distinctive nature of local memories. They also illuminate the processes by which local memories are incorporated into dominant sectional narratives of a specific war experience (others include evacuation, military training and so on) and wider cultural memory. I have chosen to compare air raid narratives in Himeji, Nagaoka, Tokyo and Sapporo. These were selected for the somewhat unscientific reason that they are the four Japanese cities I have lived in (or near), but getting to know the local area provided an opportunity to sense how wider local history and the characteristics of the local people have informed patterns of remembering.

Himeji is a city of 500,000 people just west of Kobe. It is most famous for its magnificent 'White Egret' Castle. Many Japanese castles were pulled down following the collapse of the feudal system in 1868. Of those that survived, many were destroyed in air raids. Most castles today are concrete reconstructions, but Himeji Castle is Japan's finest original castle and a UNESCO World Heritage Site. It is also the centrepiece of Himeji's air raid narrative.

Himeji experienced two major air raids, on 22 June and 3–4 July 1945, in which 519 people were killed. The 22 June raid targeted a Kawanishi aircraft factory, but the raids of 3–4 July were aimed at the city centre and reduced Himeji to ashes. Protected by its location on a hill and surrounded by a moat, Himeji Castle survived the raids unscathed. The imagery of Himeji Castle surviving while the city burned around it is similar to the image of St Paul's Cathedral surviving the London Blitz. This image dominates the exhibition in the Himeji Historical Peace Center[14], whose five sections are: 'Himeji, the beautiful castle town' (pre-war history), 'Himeji Castle among the flames' (the air raids), 'Concealing Himeji Castle' (the castle was camouflaged with netting to protect it), 'The revival of Himeji Castle' (postwar reconstruction) and 'Praying for peace'.

The people of Himeji had always wondered if the Americans deliberately spared the castle in the same way that they spared Kyoto's cultural treasures. The answers came on 1 July 1995 when some of the surviving B-29 fliers who took part in the 3–4 July 1945 raid visited Himeji for a fiftieth anniversary meeting of peace and reconciliation (a meeting I attended with some local friends). At the meeting, a pilot admitted that there were no orders to spare the castle. It was cloudy that night so the targeting was done by radar, which could only distinguish land, sea and mountains. The castle's survival had been a miracle (Himeji sengo chizu wo tsukurukai 2001: 319–21).

While the story of the Himeji air raid is also a story of civilian suffering, the local air raid narrative centres on the castle rather than the human cost. The castle is the centre of a municipal narrative of resilience and survival in which the castle is a metaphor for the people of Himeji, standing firm in the face of adversity.

Nagaoka is a city of 200,000 in Niigata Prefecture. It is famous for rice, *sake* (rice wine) and its annual fireworks display. Straddling the Shinano River for the 70 km from Nagaoka to Niigata on the coast is one of the most expansive agricultural plains in Japan. Nagaoka is also in 'snow country' (*yukiguni*). In winter, cold winds from Siberia collect moisture as they pass over the Japan Sea and dump metres of snow on Nagaoka as the moist air rises to pass over the Japan Alps.

Nagaoka's harsh winters and separation from Edo (Tokyo) by the Japan Alps had long made it a geographical backwater. But Nagaoka was also a political backwater following the fateful decision of Nagaoka *han* (fiefdom) to remain loyal to the Tokugawa clan during the Boshin War, 1868–69. Forces urging the restoration of the emperor ousted the Tokugawas and the Meiji Restoration ended 270 years of feudal rule under the Tokugawas. Nagaoka had backed the wrong side and was neglected by subsequent governments during Japan's rapid modernization of the late nineteenth century. Nagaoka was a provincial city of 75,000 when it was destroyed by the Nagaoka air raid on 1 August 1945.

The rumour in Nagaoka is that the city was destroyed primarily in revenge for Pearl Harbor: Admiral Yamamoto Isoroku, the mastermind of the Pearl Harbor attack, was from Nagaoka (and is commemorated in the Yamamoto Isoroku Memorial Museum).[15] Otherwise, Nagaoka was a target of little or no strategic value. It had some war industries but sufficiently few for some of Nagaoka's school children drafted as labourers to be sent to Nagoya to work (Minowa 1987: 37). However, the war exhibits in the Niigata Prefectural Museum of History[16] in Nagaoka show that the town did have war industries. The war exhibit divides into three sections: POW forced labour, Manchurian settlers and the Nagaoka air raid. The POW panel describes the harsh experiences of the nearly 3,000 Allied POWs working as forced labourers in Niigata prefecture in 1945, 300 of whom were in two camps in Nagaoka. The air raid exhibit includes incendiary bomb casings, photos of the destruction in Nagaoka and a list of names of the approximately 1,500 people who died in the raid.

The main municipal commemorations have centred on the Nagaoka Festival held on 1–3 August every year. On 1 August and early on the morning of 2 August, prayers are said at shrines and memorials around the city to those who died in the air raid. Then, the *musha gyōretsu*, warrior's parade, is held on the afternoon of 2 August. Dressed in period costumes from the Boshin War, people march from the outlying villages and congregate on the main Ōte-dōri avenue, where a peace message is read. The nationally famous fireworks festival is held on the evenings of 2 and 3 August. The fireworks symbolize reconstruction and revival after the devastation.

The festival commemorates Nagaoka's double victimhood, in 1868 and 1945. By the time Nagaoka castle had finally fallen in September 1868 after months of fighting, much of Nagaoka was in ashes. War in 1868 brought defeat and years of neglect. War in 1945 killed 2 per cent of the population in one night. The air raid narrative is half of the Nagaoka narrative of how war destroyed a provincial city twice in eighty years.

As Japan's capital and core industrial hub, Tokyo bore the brunt of American air raids. The Tokyo experience of air raids is depicted in a corner of the Edo-Tokyo Museum,[17] a visually sumptuous museum tracing the history of Tokyo since the seventeenth century.

Tokyo's first air raid was the Doolittle Raid on 18 April 1942 when sixteen carrier-borne bombers took part in a morale-boosting raid on Japan's major cities. However, it was not until November 1944 following the capture of Saipan that the US could effectively use its land-based B-29 bombers against Japan. Initially, the raids concentrated on military and industrial targets but by March 1945, area incendiary bombing was the strategy employed.

In a clear acknowledgement that Japan also used indiscriminate bombing, the museum's panels state: 'That incendiary bombs caused widespread damage to cities packed with wooden houses was already proven by the Japanese army when it bombed the Chinese city of Zhonquing.' But the US Air Force had refined the technique by building a replica of a Japanese city and testing various combinations of high explosives and incendiaries. The most devastating effects of the incendiary campaign were on the night of 9–10 March 1945, the great Tokyo air raid. The raid targeted the densely populated downtown area of Tokyo and 'some 100,000 people perished in a single night'. The museum gives the force of the attack, the density of the wooden constructions, the strong wind that night which fanned the inferno, and the Air Defence Law which forbade people to evacuate without official permission as the primary reasons for the massive loss of life. The exhibits include bomb casings, steel girders twisted by the heat and pictures of charred bodies.

The person who has done more than perhaps anyone else to shape the Tokyo air raid narrative is novelist Saotome Katsumoto. In his long-time bestseller on the Tokyo air raid, Saotome describes a meeting on 20 June 1970 at which Ienaga Saburō was speaking of his textbook trials. Saotome asked Ienaga why a raid that killed 80,000 in a mere two hours and twenty-two minutes did not merit the same treatment as the A-bombs in textbooks (Saotome 1971: 215–6). Saotome's narrative is that the Tokyo air raid ranks alongside Hiroshima and Nagasaki as the three instances where indiscriminate bombing killed tens of thousands of civilians in a matter of hours. Saotome has worked with the Edo-Tokyo Museum and contributed an essay to the guidebook for the museum's fiftieth anniversary special exhibition in 1995. Saotome's narrative is also the museum's: the permanent air raid exhibit concludes: 'The extent of the damage to Tokyo rivalled that inflicted on Hiroshima or Nagasaki.'

Sapporo is Hokkaido's largest city and the fifth largest in Japan with a population of 1.85 million. Construction of the city started in 1869 after the settlement of Hokkaido became government policy following the Meiji Restoration. Pioneers from all over Japan converged on the vast expanses of land sparsely inhabited by the Ainu people. Ainu culture was forced into decline by the settlers and Hokkaido became associated with a 'pioneer spirit'. The port cities of Otaru and Hakodate played a larger role in Hokkaido's early development, but since the war, and particularly since the 1972 Winter Olympics, Sapporo has become Japan's modern capital of the north.

In 1945, Sapporo's population was around 200,000. It was a relatively insignificant target for American air raids. More importantly, it was out of the range of B-29s based in Saipan. Attacks on Hokkaido's key military installations were carried out by carrier-borne aircraft on 14 and 15 July 1945. Rather than area bombing with incendiaries, fighters strafed and bombed. The main targets for air raids in Hokkaido were the major port cities with military facilities (Nemuro, Kushiro and Hakodate) and shipping. The steelworks and munitions factories in Muroran were also shelled by the American fleet. These attacks accounted for 80 per cent of the 1,925 people killed across Hokkaido by air raids and naval bombardment. Sapporo itself suffered only one fatality (Hokkaidō shinbunsha 2005: 236).

The Sapporo air raid, therefore, is a footnote in local history and memory. This is reflected in the exhibits in the Historical Museum of Hokkaido (HMH).[18] The exhibits about the war era, 'From Recession to World War II', include a video titled 'Two days when war came to Hokkaido – a record of the Hokkaido air raids' that focuses on Nemuro and Kushiro. The video uses footage taken by American pilots (Historical Museum of Hokkaido 2000: 47–8). Sapporo's experiences are absent.

Overall, air raids form a relatively small part of HMH's war period exhibits. In the guidebook, for example, forced labour in Hokkaido occupies approximately twice the space of the air raid narratives (ibid.: 42, 45). Forced labour is a key issue in Hokkaido because around 160,000 forced labourers toiled in Hokkaido's mines, or 20 per cent of all Korean and 42 per cent of all Chinese forced labourers in Japan (Hokkaidō shinbunsha 2005: 222). This helps explain the museum's use of progressive rhetoric in panels of general war history, such as '15-year war' (the name preferred by progressives) and Japanese 'aggression' (*shinryaku*). In Hokkaido's case, a significant narrative of local aggression – and perhaps the effects of the 'pioneer spirit' in reducing conservatism or a feeling of separateness from the 'mainland' and conservative Tokyo elites – acts as a counterbalance to regional narratives of suffering. Nevertheless, Hokkaido memories also focus on the heavy death toll of people from Hokkaido in the Battle for Okinawa (10,085, more than from any prefecture other than Okinawa – Historical Museum of Hokkaido 2000: 47); the experiences of settlers who went to Manchuria; and the invasion of the four northern islands just off the eastern coast of Hokkaido and expulsion of their Japanese residents by the Soviets after Japan's surrender.

These four narratives are distinct not only in nature but also in the extent they have been incorporated into regional and national war narratives. The Sapporo air raid barely registers within Hokkaido memories. The Himeji raid is significant at a municipal level, but not so at a prefectural level. A total of ten cities were bombed in Hyogo, of which three suffered more casualties than Himeji. Prefectural narratives (in the *Kobe shinbun*, for example) focus more on the bombing of Kobe, the prefectural capital, where 6,235 people died compared to Himeji's 519. In rural Niigata prefecture, by contrast, the Nagaoka air raid is the key air raid narrative. Niigata is the prefectural capital, but despite the strategic importance of its port (which was a gateway to Manchuria) it was spared bombing to be 'preserved' as a potential A-bomb

Table 8.1 Casualties in air raids on four Japanese cities

	Himeji	Nagaoka	Tokyo	Sapporo
Population in 1945	104,000	74,508	6,578,000	*c.* 200,000
Number of raids	2	1	120	1
People killed	519	1,457	*c.* 115,000	1
(in %)	*(0.49)*	*(1.96)*	*(1.75)*	*(trace)*
Buildings destroyed (%)	71.6	65.5	50.8	Negligible

Sources: Okuzumi (1988: 37, 166–8, 220); Minowa (1987: 116); Edo-Tokyo Museum Exhibits; Okumura (1971: 175–6); Kyoto Museum for World Peace (1997: 113); Hokkaidō shinbunsha (2005: 236).

target. The Tokyo air raids have assumed a place within national narratives, not only because Tokyo is Japan's capital but because of the high number of raids and casualties.

In short, these four municipal narratives have assumed different powers within cultural memory. They have evolved into forgotten (Sapporo), municipal (Himeji), prefectural (Nagaoka) and national (Tokyo) narratives. The basic explanation for this is the level and nature of victimhood, which is shown in Table 8.1. The archetypal air raid in educational materials or documentaries includes B-29s dropping incendiaries, women with children strapped to their backs fleeing the flames, charred bodies lying in the streets, and survivors roaming the 'burnt wastelands' (*yakinohara*). The Nagaoka and Tokyo narratives accentuate the human cost and closely fit the archetypal air raid experience. In Himeji's case, competing regional narratives, the prominence of a distinctive municipal symbol (the castle) in the narrative, and the comparatively low casualty rate illustrate why Himeji's experience has been incorporated less into wider regional and national narratives. Sapporo barely fits the archetypal air raid pattern and is all but forgotten. Japanese air raid narratives, therefore, illustrate how distinct regional narratives can result from a broadly similar war experience and the processes through which narratives assume different levels of power within a wider cultural memory.

Okinawa: unique and personalized memories

Whereas some aspects of local history – such as air raids, forced labour and evacuation – have commonly had their regional variations flattened out in the composure of generic narratives within Japanese cultural memory, some narratives can never escape their regional origins. In particular, the A-bombs and the Battle for Okinawa were events that are both unique to a particular region and also occupy a central position in national memories.

Okinawan memories are particularly interesting given Okinawa's broader position within Japanese history outlined briefly in Chapter 2: a distinct history and culture, 'annexation' in 1879, seeing the only fighting on Japanese soil during which one third of the population was killed, and occupation by the

US until 1972. These memories underpin a distinct regional (one might even argue 'ethnic minority') opposition towards the ruling elite in Tokyo and their conservative war narrative. Opinion poll data from 1993 to 1995 indicated that only 6–7 per cent of Okinawans agreed that the Battle for Okinawa was 'an unavoidable battle necessary for the defense of the fatherland', while 81–87 per cent agreed the battle was 'a reckless battle which sacrificed countless Okinawan lives'. 'These polls', argues Okinawan oral historian Ishihara Masaie, 'demonstrate that the vast majority of Okinawans totally reject the position of the ABF [Association of Bereaved Families, Izokukai, in other words a conservative position]' (Ishihara 2001: 88).

Okinawan museums, therefore, have little incentive to present conservative narratives of the war. The exhibits at Okinawa's two principal museums, the Okinawa Prefectural Peace Memorial Museum (OPPMM)[19] and the Himeyuri Peace Museum[20] (commemorating the schoolgirl nursing corps), present strong narratives of victimhood but are simultaneously critical of Japanese militarism. In OPPMM, this message is movingly captured in the disturbing photograph of an entire family who had cut their own throats rather than be captured by the Americans, a tragedy largely due to Japanese propaganda.

The two museums are also notable for the highly personalized nature of their exhibits, and in particular for the use of testimony. 'The Cornerstone of Peace' in the grounds of OPPMM lists every person known to have died in the Battle for Okinawa regardless of nationality; room four of the museum's permanent exhibits has books of testimony laid out on reading stands for people to leaf through; and in the Himeyuri Peace Museum there are also books of testimonies, along with photographs of over 200 schoolgirls that died. This is social history and war commemoration taken to the most personal level.

What are the origins of this personalized form of commemoration, and particularly the use of testimony as a museum exhibit? As a prefectural peace museum, the OPPMM decided to tell primarily Okinawan people's stories. Feeling that video footage, artefacts and official documents did not bring home the extreme experiences that civilians had in the 'war zone hell', it was decided there was 'no better way' to represent Okinawans' experiences than through testimony. Testimony was chosen on the basis of its impact, and with a view to allowing an overall picture of the Battle for Okinawa to emerge. Debates ensued over the extent to which testimony was appropriate as a museum exhibit. Concerns were also raised about whether testimony was a valid historical 'document' because it could be infused with inaccuracies and biases (Arakaki 2002). Nonetheless, testimony became a dominant feature of the exhibits and tells a disturbing tale of how Okinawans suffered. Whereas OPPMM is exceptional for the extent to which it has collected and exhibited testimony, it is not exceptional in terms of the rationale for the use of testimony.

Conclusions

The Okinawa Prefectural Peace Memorial Museum case study neatly summarizes many key themes in the chapter, particularly concerning peace museums: local funding means local narratives; museums present the message of the vested interest groups that fund them; these messages can be sharply at odds with the position of central government although they are themselves the object of local contestation; the local level generally allows a coherent narrative of victimhood to contrast with a national narrative of aggression; visitor identification is encouraged at the local rather than national level; the sufferings of the group identified with become the basis for an appeal for peace; and museums function as sites of local memory creation, but also as destinations for school visits and tourists.

Privately funded museums, by contrast, can afford to ignore wider public opinion and appeal to a specific constituency, as long as they have sufficient funds. Private museums presenting both strong progressive (for example, the Kyoto Museum for World Peace) and nationalistic stances (for example, Yasukuni Shrine's Yūshūkan) exist. But publicly funded museums face different challenges. While publicly funded museums mostly represent local narratives, their high profiles and roles as official narrators of history mean that they cannot simply appeal to a local, or even national, audience. Herein lies the need for the Hiroshima museum, for example, to acknowledge Japanese aggression to appeal to its foreign visitors. And as Tanaka Kazunori of Niigata Prefectural Museum of History told me, the museum realized that it could not gain 'international understanding' if aspects of Japanese aggression were not presented, hence the decision to represent Allied POWs' experiences as well as those of air raid victims and Manchurian settlers (Tanaka, K. 2002).

So, while many regional narratives in Japan are based on strong narratives of victimhood, this does not mean narratives of aggression are avoided in Japanese museum exhibits or that local victimhood cannot underpin regional antipathy towards the Japanese government's war conservatism. Some history museums avoid war exhibits because of the political controversy they can generate, and other peace museums avoid discussing Japanese aggression within a conservative narrative that accentuates only Japanese suffering. But the trend in official municipal and regional museum displays since the 1980s, as it has been in overall Japanese historical consciousness, has been towards a progressive-leaning stance: a balance, although usually not an even one, between presenting narratives of 'Japanese as victims' and 'Japanese as aggressors'.

9 War and the family

Thus far, Japanese war memories have been discussed at various levels in a broadly 'macro to micro' order: from long-term and international overviews, to the national government and media, then sectional and regional narratives, and finally to the levels in this chapter, the individual and the family. But Japanese people's historical consciousnesses typically evolve from the micro to the macro. For Japanese children, parents are the key role models who instil moral values from an early age, along with relatives and teachers. Knowledge of war history often starts from a family story: a grandfather saying 'When I was your age . . .' or an explanation of how grandma's sister died during the war. At school, children start formal history education, but the focus may be regional as much as national: schools typically use some local history materials produced by a local board of education or conduct trips to local museums. As children become consumers of the media, they start picking up the ideological, sectional and regional narratives it presents alongside a heightened awareness of national identity. Unless the child has significant overseas experience or contact with non-Japanese, an international perspective of war issues is unlikely until adulthood, if at all.

In short, Japanese and non-Japanese typically approach the issue of Japanese cultural memory from opposite directions. For non-Japanese, the orthodox view concerning what Japanese war memories 'should' be is an 'acceptable' official narrative acknowledging Japanese guilt, backed up by the endorsement of Japanese public opinion; for Japanese people the main priority is a cultural memory that vindicates and affirms their own views and the memories or experiences of family members. This book has followed the 'macro to micro' approach because it allows the most widely known aspects for an international audience to be treated first. But given this book's main aim – to account for the nature of Japanese war memories – this final chapter about testimony and war in the family possibly should have been Chapter 1. It surveys testimony of personal experiences (the 'raw materials' of Japanese cultural memory), how testimony has affected Japanese families in the postwar and how Japanese individuals have turned memories into activism as participants in war discourses.

Testimony: the voice of the individual

Given the extent to which many international observers criticize the 'amnesia' of Japanese people, it is easy to assume that Japanese testimony is comparatively rare. This, however, is not the case: the charge of Japanese 'amnesia' is typically overstated. On the contrary, the large volume of published testimony is a conspicuous feature of war discourses in Japan. Published testimony appears in a variety of formats:

1 *senki* ('war memoirs') – the memoirs of those who served in the armed forces that were written up and published after the war;
2 *jibunshi* ('self-history') and autobiographies – histories that place one's own experiences in the context of the wider course of history;
3 *nikki* ('diaries') – published diaries chronicling the day-to-day experiences of the war generation;
4 letters home – letters from soldiers to their families during the war that tell of their experiences;
5 letters to the editor – letters written by Japanese people about their war experiences and published on the letters pages of newspapers; and
6 oral history – recorded interviews of witness testimony.

The format of the testimony has implications for its nature. Within testimony intended for public consumption, published memoirs and autobiographies always contain a carefully constructed portrayal of the testifier. This carefully constructed portrayal may not be so easy in the spontaneous atmosphere of an interview. Oral testimony also relinquishes editorial power to the interviewer, who decides which excerpts of testimony are included in any publication stemming from the interview. Private testimony is intended only for the particular public that the testifier is addressing, although not all testimony that was intended to be private remains so. For example, a soldier's diary or letters to relatives might be published posthumously by relatives. In this case, the publication of the testimony reveals much about the relatives' agendas, as well as the soldier's. Finally, editors at newspapers and publishing companies play roles in determining which testimony is published in newspapers' letters pages or published testimony collections.

Tens of thousands of Japanese people have testified to their war experiences in published materials. Petra Buchholz states that 'the popular or private level of writing and publication of memories is especially lively in Japan, and this phenomenon becomes even more remarkable if it is compared to the corresponding situation in Germany' (Buchholz 1998). Just one illustration of the Japanese public's continued interest in testifying and reading testimony is the letters pages of newspapers. For example, Frank Gibney (1995) presents a selection from the 1,100 letters about wartime experiences published in the *Asahi* newspaper between July 1986 and August 1987. The *Asahi* asked for readers' letters about their war experiences and 'the response was extraordinary. *Asahi* had succeeded in capturing the attention of its readers far beyond the original hopes of the op-ed page editors.' A further 2,900 letters were sent in that could not be published (ibid.: vii).

This interest in testimony raises two questions: what makes Japanese people *voluntarily* talk about the war in such numbers, and what are they saying?

Ultimately, talking about war experiences is an individual decision for which all people have their own reasons. In Japan, there are many reasons for staying silent, such as guilty secrets about war actions, the fear of being embroiled in controversy, or even the fear of threats against personal safety if people become ideological participants in war debates. But the volume of testimony in Japan could not exist unless there were also powerful reasons for people to speak out.

On a cultural and literary level, there is a strong tradition of auto-biographical writing in Japan, whether in 'I-novels' (often semi-fictional stories based on actual personal experiences), *senki* (war memoirs) or in *jibunshi*, 'self-history'. Gerald Figal estimates the number of ordinary people involved in adult 'self-history' writing courses at community centres 'probably runs in the thousands' (Figal 1996: 909). As a percentage of the total population, thousands of 'self-history' writers are not high numbers, but participants in 'self-history' classes are a significant subset of people who manage to have their writings published. There are numerous competitions and auto-biographical publications on war experiences frequently emanate from these 'self-history' writing classes.

There are other reasons why Japanese people might want to speak out about their war experiences stemming from the processes of war memory-making in a society where war memories are contested. First, the inability to settle on a dominant narrative means that the struggle to shape a dominant narrative is ongoing. This has made many Japanese eager to have their say in how war history is thought through:

> Yet among some authors of *jibunshi* ['self-histories'] there is a serious sense of leaving one's take on the Shōwa period [1926–89] to future generations because of inadequacies in standard histories, whether written from the right, left, or center. In such *jibunshi* one does find a degree of critical historical consciousness, often couched in terms of moral duty if not political purpose.
>
> (ibid.: 930–1)

Second, given the wide range of ethical judgements about Japanese war actions, ideologues of all shades enthusiastically endorse testimony that substantiates their views. Such public affirmation of testimony (and often financial reward too in the form of speaking engagements or book royalties) facilitates, or even motivates, some people to speak out.

Finally, there might be psychological needs to testify. All Japanese in the war generation face issues of personal and collective responsibility, and testifying can be a way of clarifying to others (or perhaps even oneself) personal responsibility, or lack of it. The number of people breaking their silences in old age also indicates that many Japanese have felt the need to 'get things off their chests', or 'lay the past to rest' as they consider their own mortality and look back on their lives.

But what about the nature of Japanese testimony? Oral historians Haruko Taya Cook and Theodore Cook (1992) give four insights into Japanese memories based on their interviews. First, 'there is no well-established narrative form for telling the tale of the defeated'. Japanese memories can have 'a structureless quality in which the individual wanders through endless dreamlike scenes of degradation, horror, and death, a shapeless nightmare of plotless slaughter'. Second, 'war responsibility is not clearly established in the minds of many'. The memories are extremely personal in nature and '[l]arger questions of causality and responsibility were either passed along to the small group of convicted military leaders, politicians, industrialists, and bureaucrats singled out by the Allies, or deferred to the Occupation forces'. Third, many interviewees mentioned the idea of a 'good defeat', or the personal journey to find some good meaning from their war experiences. Finally, hatred for the enemy does not infuse recollections, which makes the war seem like an enemy-less conflict (ibid.: 14–17).

The result of my own investigations into Japanese testimony[1] is that the majority of published testimony is civilian testimony, and/or testimony of victimhood. Chino Kaori has identified a similar trend and characterized it as the feminization of war memories, a shift away from 'masculine' memories of military exploits towards 'feminine' or 'women and children's' memories of suffering on the home front (Chino 2000: 126–7). On numerical grounds, the predominance of civilian testimony is partially understandable given that six-sevenths of Japanese saw the war from the home front. The prevalence of testimony of victimhood, both military and civilian, can be traced to Japan's defeat, high levels of hardship and widespread death, but it also indicates the relative ease of portraying oneself as a victim compared to giving confessional testimony of wrongdoing (although the difficulty of testifying to having been raped is an important exception and helps explain the long postwar silence of many 'comfort women').

Also important are the priorities of groups collecting testimony and the financial and political support they enjoy. As described in Chapter 8, local museums like those in Okinawa commonly have major testimony collection functions and receive significant backing from local governments. Or, in the case of groups such as Siberian internees and A-bomb victims, the victims are sufficiently numerous (in the hundreds of thousands) for their representatives to receive broad political and financial backing. In such cases, huge testimony collections can be created. For example, the Japan Confederation of A- and H- Bomb Sufferers collected testimony from over 13,000 surviving *hibakusha* in 1985–86, which resulted in a large volume containing around 850 people's testimony (Hidankyō 1994). By contrast, the collection of confessional testimony by Japanese soldiers or non-Japanese victim testimony tends to be undertaken by conscientious researchers or progressive activist groups. Here there is no broad-based political backing. Issues of profitability – whether financial, political or the altruistic 'public good' – affect testimony just like all other cultural forms and there is certainly no level playing field in terms of the ability for individual voices to reach the public arena.

In summary, the volume of testimony in Japan cannot be explained by arguments such as 'the Japanese do not like talking about the war'. For some, the natures of their war experiences and the contested nature of Japanese memories offer incentives or moral imperatives to speak out, while for others they provide reasons to remain silent. No clear-cut generalization is possible. But in all cases, a branch of the media – whether a book, documentary or museum panel – is required to turn private thoughts into a recorded part of public discourse. As the following case studies indicate, individual circumstances, particularly the precise rationale for speaking out and the format in which testimony is made public, are vital for understanding the voices of Japanese individuals. But rather than focus on the war generation's testimony, I have chosen to concentrate on the testimony of the postwar generation and how they have reacted to learning of their relatives' war actions and experiences. Rather than solely a narration of a war experience, this testimony offers insights into the dilemmas that the war generation has faced concerning testifying and the impact of testimony on family members.

War and the family: when love and historical consciousness collide

When cultural memory is contested, any publicly expressed memories or opinions risk provoking the disapproval of people with whom there are important relationships. At worst, the consequence may be painful rifts among family members and other immediate social groupings. I have witnessed the risks of discussing the war in the family first hand. I was having dinner with some Japanese friends and the conversation turned to my research. The grandfather expressed some quite nationalistic views, which I challenged but avoided getting into a heated debate over. The dinner ended very amicably, but at a later stage his daughter thanked me for asking her father questions she had never felt able to ask him herself. She also told me her school-age son was not sure how to reconcile his grandfather's views with those of his history teacher at school. Despite being a close-knit family, I sensed some deep philosophical divisions concerning the war. Over dinner I had played the role of a go-between: my presence enabled the war to be raised without the need for direct confrontation among the family members.

Philosophical and ethical divisions among family members on issues such as war, religion and politics are a normal part of any society. How the family deals with the divisions – open feud, avoidance, agreeing to disagree – depends on the personalities, situation and family dynamics involved. But in Japan any war-related expressions must run the gauntlet of family opinion. This is an issue I have developed elsewhere in an oral history project about the investigations of a weapons scientist's niece into her uncle's wartime activities and her discovery that her investigations are not welcomed by all her relatives (Seaton 2006a: 59). In this case, as in others, the dilemmas become particularly acute when war memories must directly confront issues of the personal responsibility or guilt of family members.

War guilt: inherited traumas in Japanese families

The NHK documentary *A Soldier's Diary: learning about grandfather's war* (*Hitoheishi no jūgun nikki: sofu no sensō wo shiru*, NHK-E, 25 December 2000) is about the reactions of the children and grandchildren of Yamamoto Takeshi to reading his war memoirs. Yamamoto was a farmer from Fukui prefecture (north of Kyoto facing the Japan Sea) and first went to China as a soldier in September 1937. He participated in various operations, including the drive to Nanking, and kept a diary of his experiences. After the war, he returned to life as a farmer in Fukui. Thirty years later, Yamamoto started writing up his memoirs based on the diaries. The memoirs reached 800 handwritten pages and had a devastating impact on his family after he died in 1986 aged seventy.

The memoirs include frank descriptions of the war crimes the Japanese army committed in China. Yamamoto describes how hatred of the Chinese built up with every friend he lost in action. Gradually, the hatred facilitated atrocity, but Yamamoto remained aware of how the war was dehumanizing him. In his diary entry for 11 December 1937, Yamamoto describes how he took part in the executions of Chinese prisoners who had attacked one of their units. He reflected on how he had 'never even killed a frog or a snake' before coming to China, but now, killing human beings 'made his dinner taste better'. 'War turns people into devils,' Yamamoto wrote.

Yamamoto's most traumatic experience came on 20 May 1938. his unit moved into a Chinese village with orders to destroy it. They massacred fifty to sixty women and children in cold blood. One of the soldiers bayoneted a baby, but in stabbing the baby, it got stuck on the end of the rifle. With the baby still screaming, the soldier waved his rifle around in the air trying to dislodge the baby. After witnessing this scene, Yamamoto wrote simply, 'War is terrible.' In the most gripping scene of the documentary, this episode is recounted by Yamamoto's son, Toshio. There is a pained expression on his face as he mimics the rifle being waved around with the baby impaled on the end.

There are a number of other scenes in the documentary where Yamamoto's children and grandchildren recount their memories of him in the light of what they now know. Granddaughter Yūko describes asking her grandfather how he got his scars when she was in the bath with him as a little girl.[2] Yamamoto would reply how he was hit by shrapnel or bullets. When Yūko asked if he killed anyone he simply answered, 'I will tell you when you are older.'

He never did. Yūko never believed that her loving grandfather could have killed people until she read the memoirs.

Yamamoto's sons also express shock and disbelief at how their kind and loving father could have committed such acts during the war. As a family, they made the decision to publish the diaries because, as eldest son Fujio explained, the 'right understanding' of the war and the past can only be achieved when such memories are made public. The family seems to have been helped considerably in this decision by the lack of any obvious disagreement over publishing the diaries. The family could have ensured that the diaries never became public, but their sense of duty stemming from both Yamamoto's intentions and their own historical consciousnesses/consciences prevailed.

Another revealing case study of a family's struggles with a relative's war actions is Kurahashi Ayako's *What My Military Policeman Father Left Me* (2002). Just before Kurahashi's father died in 1986, he handed her a piece of paper with the instructions, 'please write this on my gravestone'. Her father had written the places in China where he served as a military policeman and the message 'I participated in the war of aggression, am sorry for the acts I committed against the people of China and apologize unreservedly' (ibid.: 11–12).

Kurahashi describes her struggle to carry out her father's last wishes. There were worries about how such a gravestone would affect the family's standing where they lived, and her older brother objected: he asked why their father should apologize when Japan's wartime leaders had more responsibility. Kurahashi's uncle (her father's older brother) made a different argument: the apology was probably taking responsibility for the actions of subordinates (ibid.: 15, 27). Between her brother's and uncle's positions, we can see how many Japanese people deal with the issue of their relatives' personal responsibility by shifting the responsibility elsewhere.

Kurahashi felt she had to find out exactly why her father was apologizing. She realized she could and should have investigated her father's actions much earlier and saw herself fitting a common pattern in Japan: although people have silent knowledge of Japanese aggression, it is a taboo to talk about it. It was also extremely difficult for her to think of her father as a war criminal. While her two older brothers had difficult relationships with their authoritarian, perfectionist father, she was the apple of his eye. However, through her investigations of her father's past in military archives and contact with people who served with him, Kurahashi came to feel that the postwar generation in Japan has been 'tricked' into not talking about the war and lacks the resolution to break the silence. Furthermore, blaming the war solely on Japan's leaders is not a satisfactory conclusion (ibid.: 43–4).

Kurahashi's story was featured in an NHK documentary in January 1998.[3] The publicity invited negative comments from a number of neighbours and friends. This shocked her, but crystallized her feeling that she had been compromising on her father's request all along. She found new resolution and gained the support of the wider family to erect a memorial stone. Feeling that it was wrong to go against her father's wishes, and that apologies can be beneficial, her father's apology was put by his grave in 1998, twelve years after his death (ibid.: 47, 51–8).

Kurahashi then describes how she worked through the traumas that her family had suffered, which included her brother committing suicide and her mother's own 'suicide-like' death. Kurahashi underwent counselling, attended 'feminist therapy' and 'self-history' writing classes, and became active in local progressive activist groups. She published a number of fictional stories in the early 1990s in which she worked through her own relationship to her father's war actions (these were the catalyst for the production of the documentary). She eventually came to see most of the traumas as inherited from her father's trauma. With this in mind, she wonders how many other families in Japan endure their own unending postwars (ibid.: 87).

Finally, Kurahashi recounts her trips to China to visit war sites such as the Nanking Massacre museum and the village where her father was stationed. During these trips, she told her father's story and conveyed not only his but her own apologies to Chinese people. She attempts to find out precisely what her father did by asking local people, but is unsuccessful. What is worse, nobody seems to remember him, so she fears that people are being 'kind' by not revealing what they know. Nevertheless, through her activism and fulfilling her father's wishes for his gravestone, Kurahashi feels she has come to terms with her father's war crimes (ibid.: 166, 176).

Her activism has also earned her much gratitude in China. In the afterword to her semi-autobiographical novel *Eternal Shadows* (2005), Kurahashi describes how she was invited to be a guest at the sixtieth anniversary commemorations in August and September 2005 by the Tianjin provincial government. During her ten-day trip she was repeatedly told how Chinese pain would be eased if more Japanese apologized unreservedly like her father (Kurahashi 2005: 350). She ends both books with messages about the healing effects of apology, and with passionate appeals for the Japanese government to do more to apologize to and compensate the victims of Japanese aggression.

The experiences of the Yamamoto and Kurahashi families illustrate the pain of acknowledging the war crimes of a family member. In addition, many Japanese soldiers returned from the war utterly traumatized by what they had done or seen, what is now recognized as post-traumatic stress disorder (PTSD). These are ongoing aspects of the Japanese war experience for which there is generally little coverage or sympathy, the key exception in Japanese being the work of social psychologist Noda Masaaki (1998, especially Chapter 3). Internationally, there is little sympathy for Japanese people who 'deservedly suffer for their crimes', or whose suffering 'does not even compare with the horrors inflicted by the Japanese on others'. From within Japan there are conservatives and nationalists critical of those expressing moral conscience for 'giving Japan a bad name', 'inviting international criticism' or for being 'masochistic'. Directly facing the actions of relatives requires great courage and ongoing resolution. The guilty conscience of knowing what a loved one has done and/or struggles to cope with the PTSD of a family member have meant that being the relative of a perpetrator has been a form of victimhood in its own right for many Japanese families in the postwar.

In these circumstances, many have taken what they consider the least painful options: silence, denial or composing their historical consciousnesses in ways that maximize the morality of their relatives' war actions and thereby minimize the issues of guilt. For example, some relatives of convicted war criminals continue to protest their innocence. Mukai Chieko is the daughter of Mukai Toshiaki, one of the two lieutenants executed for taking part in the '100 heads killing contest' reported in the Japanese press in 1937. Mukai (2000) describes how there were whisperings about her as the daughter of a war criminal when she was a child, but how she was gradually able to move on and have a normal life. Then, Honda Katsuichi's descriptions of the killing contest in *Journey to China* (1972) put her back in the spotlight, as did Iris Chang's *The Rape of Nanking* (1997). Mukai is resentful of Honda's naming and shaming of her father and repeats her father's claims that one day the world will see his side of the story. She draws on the research of leading Nanking Massacre deniers and her father's diary to proclaim her father's innocence: the contest was media hype and never really happened. The families of the two lieutenants filed a suit for libel in 2003 against the *Tōkyō nichinichi* newspaper (forerunner of the *Mainichi*), the *Asahi* and Honda Katsuichi (www.japantimes.co.jp 8 July 2003). The case was rejected in August 2005.

Other descendants of executed war criminals have written about their plights, too, often presenting themselves as victims of social stigma for the actions of their relatives. Saeki Yūko, the granddaughter of Doihara Kenji (executed as a class A war criminal for being the POW camps' supervisor and Kwantung Army chief) describes how her father was devastated by his father's death and turned to alcohol. Saeki also tells how the family had to accept the verdict in silence and bear the ostracism and animosity from society (Saeki and Hosaka 1997). And Tōjō Yūko (2000), granddaughter of Tōjō Hideki, has broken the family dictum of 'don't say a word' with a book of the same title about her postwar experiences. Particularly since the release of the film *Pride* in 1998 (see Chapter 7), she has become a regular contributor to right-wing magazines and vocal supporter of Yasukuni Shrine worship.

So, while members of the postwar generation in Japan have reacted quite differently to revelations concerning relatives' war guilt, one common thread is clear: family bonds make it extremely painful for Japanese people to make critical judgements of their relatives. Herein lies the reason for the strong political pressure placed on the government by the War Bereaved Association to resist categorization of the entire war as 'aggressive': it criminalizes all Japan's war dead and injects the painful issue of individual guilt into the commemorative process. Despite this, many examples exist of moral consciences about Japanese aggression, allowing painful condemnations of the actions of relatives. The most important group is the National Association of the War Bereaved Families for Peace (NAWBFP), which broke away from the main WBA in protest at Nakasone's 1985 Yasukuni Shrine visit and the WBA's conservative stance. The NAWBFP has published a book of testimonies by bereaved relatives cataloguing their struggles to reconcile the loss of their loved ones with their beliefs that it was an aggressive war. The book contains essays with titles such as 'It is hard to acknowledge my brother as an invader, but. . .' (Heiwa izokukai zenkoku renrakukai 1999).

More usually, in the absence of proof of what a relative has done, it is comfortable for people to assume that their kind relatives could not have been directly responsible for Japanese atrocities. This does not mean that Japanese people are unaware of Japanese aggression or that they cannot criticize it in general terms. What it does mean is that evaluating the individual responsibility of loved ones is extremely painful. The topic is often avoided, or the responsibility gets passed to those up or down the chain of command.

Patriotism: commemorating sacrifice

When family members are implicated in war crimes, it tends to polarize relatives into progressive acknowledgement or nationalistic denial. However, many in the Japanese military are untainted by war crimes. As was described in Chapter 7, navy and air force men tend to be associated with tragic heroism. Others were on troop ships torpedoed before they ever reached a battle zone, died of disease and malnutrition, or even earned the gratitude of local people (particularly in isolated island outposts) for their engineering and technical contributions to the local community.[4] In these situations, memories of relatives' war actions can be separated from the wider discussion of Japanese war responsibility. Regardless of the rights and wrongs of Japan's wars, people can remember their relatives for serving honourably and fulfilling their duty when their country called upon them.

The highest profile figure in this category is Admiral Yamamoto Isoroku. Yamamoto was the architect of the Pearl Harbor attack but has earned a generally positive reputation among military historians on both sides of the Pacific. He is widely credited as the father of carrier tactics, was prescient in his assessment of Japan's chances against the industrial might of America, and died in battle in 1943 (which spared him any associations with the Tokyo War Crimes Trials). Yamamoto is Japan's equivalent of Erwin Rommel, the military man whose conduct, genius and conflicts with Japan's most aggressive militarist elements have separated his personal reputation from that of the regime he served. Yamamoto has become a popular military hero in magazines, manga and novels; and Yamamoto's son, Yoshimasa, has written a book (2001) and articles eulogizing his father and portraying him as a loving father as well as a dignified navy man.

Issues of patriotism and the desire to remember relatives who died but are untainted by war crimes are the key to explaining why support for official Yasukuni Shrine worship (opinion polls since 2001 typically indicate 45–50 per cent) overlaps with opinions that it was an aggressive war (typically 60–70 per cent). The prime minister is seen to be commemorating the individual sacrifice of family members rather than affirming an aggressive war (Seaton 2005: 303–4).

The war and day-to-day family relationships

The desire to positively remember family members who died during or after the war is strong, but when members of the war generation are still alive their moral interpretations of the war carry even more weight. Nakajō Takanori's *Grandpa, Tell Me About the War* (1998) is a dialogue between a member of the war generation and his granddaughter. It gives rich insights into how family bonds impact on war memories. Nakajō's granddaughter Keiko was at school in America and had to write a project about the historical experiences of someone she knew. Nakajō answered her questions about the war, which she then turned into a top class project and he turned into a bestseller.

Nakajō had not seen action himself but was in military training when the war ended. While the first 100 pages are an autobiographical account of his training, the period after the defeat and his postwar career in the beer industry, the second half is a familiar general history of the war. Nakajō gives a conservative defence of Japanese actions and says he worships at Yasukuni Shrine every day on his morning walk (ibid.: 143). In the epilogue, Keiko gives her reactions to what her grandfather has taught her. She says that having read her grandfather's long replies to her questions, she likes him even more than before and that she empathizes with his opinions (ibid.: 242). She also expresses reservations concerning the contents of American textbooks, such as the way Hiroshima is represented.

The grandfather–granddaughter partnership was a hit with conservatives. This is probably because since the eruption of the 'comfort women' controversy in the early 1990s, Japanese conservatives had alienated many Japanese women with their defences of the 'comfort station' system. While avoiding the 'comfort women' issue completely, *Grandpa* used an appealing format for many conservatives: distinguished male member of the war generation presents a conservative historical view to a cosmopolitan young woman, who develops an even stronger bond with her grandfather as a result. This affirmation of a conservative view by someone from a demographic group typically unsympathetic to conservatism in the wake of the 'comfort women' issue gave the book something different from the dozens of other books by older Japanese men giving their emotional defences of Japanese actions. The book's stance was also given greater legitimacy by a glowing review of Keiko's project by her American teacher. Overseas endorsements of Japanese conservatism, whether intentional or unintentional, are usually leapt upon by Japanese conservatives as vindications of their views.

The book illustrates how interpretations of relatives' actions and experiences are heavily dependent on the ways in which the members of the war generation pass down their memories to the postwar generation. It would have been painful for Keiko to respond to her grandfather's views by saying she felt that Japan should apologize for its crimes. Such a confrontation could have deeply damaged her relationship with her grandfather. As a result, her response (saying how she liked her grandfather even more than before) cannot be thought of only in terms of her being conservative on the war issue: her answer was the answer that best maintained a loving family relationship.

Not all families, however, are harmonious. In his nationalistic manga *Sensōron* (1998), Kobayashi Yoshinori gives a fascinating insight into how strained family relationships and childhood experiences can impact on historical memory.

Kobayashi paints an unflattering picture of his parents. His father had communist sympathies and continually argued with his religious mother. Kobayashi also depicts being hit 'mercilessly' by his father. These family experiences left him with a deep antipathy towards Marxism and individualism (ibid.: 65–6). Instead, Kobayashi idolized his grandfather, who had served in the Japanese army. Kobayashi's grandfather performed in a soldiers' theatre troupe whose mission was to improve morale in Papua New Guinea. The performances of samurai tales in the middle of the jungle, and in particular the emotional reaction of units from Japan's snowy Tōhoku district to seeing *Snow Falling in a Southern Island*, became the subject of a book by the theatre troupe's director Katō Daisuke and two films (1961 and 1995). Kobayashi depicts himself listening intently to his grandfather recounting these stories and describes how he cannot bear the thought of his grandfather or other soldiers being characterized as evil for having served in the Japanese army (ibid.: 59–64).

Kobayashi's antipathy towards his parents and idolization of his soldier grandfather are significant factors in understanding the roots of his nationalism. A further factor is that as a boy, Kobayashi got into numerous fights, often suffering beatings at the hands of bigger boys. He idolized kamikaze pilots because they were people who did not shy away from a fight just because they knew it would result in their deaths. The kamikaze went to their deaths knowing that they were dying for something larger than their own lives, namely their families and country. Kobayashi had his pride to protect, which was more important than avoiding a beating. Before a fight he would resolutely say, 'Let's go and lose, I am a kamikaze', and describes how his inspiration came from the war memoirs in manga magazines (ibid.: 73).

These autobiographical sections of Kobayashi's controversial bestseller have typically featured less in the extensive literature discussing *Sensōron* than his arguments affirming the war, but they illustrate how family dynamics, even on issues not directly related to the war, can contribute to the construction of moral frameworks used in historical consciousness. Kobayashi is one of

Japan's best-known nationalists, but his war views did not originate from a political awakening about his national identity or national consciousness: they originated from his antipathy towards his parents and their world views, his strong identification with his soldier grandfather, and the inspiration the kamikaze gave him during childhood playground scraps.

Activism: the personal is political

There are multitudes of situations in Japan that have all required different approaches to narrating the war within the family. However, the common theme is that as far as is possible the war must be narrated in a way that does not generate *unacceptable* levels of conflict between family bonds and historical consciousness. Silence is most probable in close-knit families with incompatible historical consciousnesses among relatives, but high levels of disagreement over the war may be no barrier to speaking out if relationships are distant. The different conditions within each family and levels of war interest among individuals have led to a wide range of participation in war discourses, from silence and avoidance through to activism or discussion of the war as a full-time occupation.

So, whereas the family in Japan has often acted as a brake or restraining influence on the expression of views about the war, this has not stopped millions of people from becoming involved in war-related activism. The largest special interest groups can have huge memberships. The War Bereaved Association[5] and the Eirei ni kotaeru kai (Society for the Commemoration of Fallen Soldiers)[6] both have over a million members. Comprised mainly of the families of the 2.46 million military dead enshrined at Yasukuni, they press for official remembrance of their relatives through Yasukuni Shrine worship by Japanese prime ministers and the emperor. Whereas the WBA has existed since the war, the Eirei ni kotaeru kai was established in 1976 after the 'private vs official' distinction became an issue in worship at Yasukuni Shrine following Prime Minister Miki's 'private' worship in 1975.

In a different vein, the lay Buddhist association Soka Gakkai[7] takes pride in the way that its founder Makiguchi Tsunesaburō stood up to Japanese militarism and died in prison in 1944 as a 'thought criminal'. Kōmeito (the 'clean government party') was established in 1964 by parliamentarians endorsed by Soka Gakkai, although the constitutional separation of religion and the state prevents official links between the two. Kōmeito has been the LDP's coalition partner in government since 1999, but opposes both Prime Minister Koizumi's Yasukuni Shrine worship and attempts to amend the war-renouncing clause of the constitution (Article Nine). Soka Gakkai has been highly active in peace activism. In the 1970s and 1980s, it published fifty-six volumes of war testimonies focusing on Japanese suffering but with some confessional testimony of atrocities, too (Yoshida 1995: 157; for selections in English, see Soka Gakkai Youth Division 1978). Soka Gakkai has more than ten million members in Japan.

There are many other groups too. The Japan Confederation of A- and H-Bomb Sufferers[8] represents *hibakusha*; feminist activist groups (particularly VAWW-NET Japan[9]) have emerged in the wake of the 'comfort women' issue; the Center for Research and Documentation on Japan's War Responsibility[10] was set up in 1993 by progressive scholars and they also issue their own academic journal (*Kikan sensō sekinin kenkyū*); the Chinese Returnees Association (Chūkiren)[11] represents soldiers who have confessed to atrocities in China; the Tsukurukai[12] has campaigned for more patriotic textbooks and has been opposed by the progressive group Children and Textbooks Japan Network 21[13]; there are countless other groups, including veterans' associations, right-wing (*uyoku*) groups, lawyers assisting Asian plaintiffs in their battles for justice against the Japanese government (Rose 2005: 75–7), local discussion groups organizing meetings, school history clubs and university circles. The combined membership of these groups, who represent positions across the spectrum of opinion, runs into the millions.

Beyond the volunteers and association members who devote what time they can in between family, work and other social commitments, there is a significant number of people for whom war history impinges on work. Bureaucrats – particularly in the Ministry of Education, local boards of education and the Ministry of Foreign Affairs – have day-to-day responsibility for history education and the international fallout from the 'history issue'. Thousands of other people work behind the scenes in the war representations business. Editors at publishing companies, the lighting crews and actors on the sets of war-related films and television dramas, attendants in peace museums, the designers of Pacific War flight simulators and plastic model kits of Japanese battleships: all these jobs involve extensive contact with war issues at work.

Then there are the full-time professionals whose jobs involve narrating the past: school history teachers, museum curators, academics, writers and journalists. The inherently political nature of war debates has meant that neutral postures are extremely difficult to maintain in any of these jobs. Particularly for researchers, the lines between research and activism are very blurred in Japan. Most prominent researcher-activists within the public arena of debate are not exclusively interested in war issues but combine war-related research with other research in the fields of philosophy, history, politics, education, literature, media studies and women's studies. The three main types – university lecturers, journalists and freelance pundits – each face different challenges in sustaining a career as a war history specialist.

University lecturers face the problems of a dearth of modern history posts and potentially being vetoed for jobs if their research is overly political or sensitive. However, a research background in war history is not necessarily a barrier to receiving scholarships, jobs or research grants: academic record and patronage (academic mentors work hard to find jobs for their student protégés) are more important. Furthermore, the tenure system offers a way to circumvent any systemic discrimination against war history researchers. Tenure is achieved in a 'less controversial' or even unrelated field, after which research on sensitive topics can be conducted without fear of dismissal. Many prominent researcher-activists working in war history started out in different fields: Takahashi Tetsuya (French philosophy), Fujioka Nobukatsu (education), Nishio Kanji (German literature) and Watanabe Shōichi (linguistics) to name but a few. The tenure system is not without its problems (such as allowing some academics to effectively 'retire' from serious research after being tenured), but it does ensure academic freedom of speech by making politically motivated dismissal extremely difficult. The status and publishing opportunities afforded by a university lectureship and the length of university holidays make an academic career ideal for war activism, and for many academics, media punditry is a lucrative side job.

Journalists follow a different route. As company employees they must work their way up the ranks and cannot specialize in a particular area until they are quite senior. Investigative journalists such as Honda Katsuichi who manage to carve out an individual reputation within the press are the exception. Punditry is usually the preserve of senior journalists within the editorial divisions of their newspapers or magazines. The relationships between newspapers and television stations mean that many regular commentators on programmes have backgrounds in the station's related newspaper. In the media conglomerates, success and promotion depends heavily on the individual's ability to toe the corporate line. 'Defections', however, are possible. Inagaki Takeshi, who has the regular 'media watching' column in *Seiron*, successfully 'defected' from the *Asahi* newspaper to conservative punditry, and his scathing criticisms of the *Asahi* based on insider knowledge have undoubtedly fuelled his popularity in right-wing publications.

Whereas academics and journalists draw a salary from their university and newspaper/magazine employers, freelance researchers must publish to earn a living. The more marketable their books and articles, the more viable freelancing is as a career. This means that freelancers tend to be sensationalist or conservative–nationalist because these offer the greatest potential for trade press publications and royalties (see Chapter 6). Other freelancers rely on a high profile gained in academe or journalism prior to going freelance: Sakurai Yoshiko was a popular newscaster before becoming a conservative pundit, while many nationalist books are written by emeritus professors who have reached retirement age but continue teaching part-time and publishing. The most successful even become brands in themselves: Kobayashi Yoshinori and Tahara Sōichirō are both so prominent that they have been given editorial control over their own magazines (*Washism*, 'Me-ism', and *Ofureko*, 'Off the Record', respectively).

But the ultimate activists are politicians. Politicians are not limited to the few hundred MPs in Nagatachō. There are thousands of local mayors and councillors around the country whose jobs touch on war history: the financing of local peace museums, organization of local commemorative events (such as the Nagaoka fireworks or Hiroshima ceremony) and municipal peace declarations. Japan's national politicians, however, epitomize how the personal is political and can always be related back to the family. Politics is a hereditary business in Japan: in 2000, a quarter of all MPs had inherited their seats from parents or other close relatives. A number of prominent politicians are direct descendants of the wartime elite. One cabinet minister with a wartime past is Aso Tarō, whose family firm (of which he was president in the 1970s) used over 12,000 mainly Korean but also POW slave labourers (Reed 2006). Another is Abe Shinzō, who succeeded Koizumi as prime minister in September 2006. Abe is the grandson of Kishi Nobusuke, the class A war criminal suspect released from prison in 1948 who became prime minister in 1957. Both Aso and Abe are well known for their hawkish views on war history. Their views probably owe much to their family histories: being progressive would mean denouncing the families who made their careers possible. The war in the family, therefore, relates not only to the struggles of individuals to narrate opinions and experiences within a private setting, but also affects all levels of discourse right up to the political views of Japan's leaders, who are responsible for the official narrative.

Conclusions

The family is one of the most important yet overlooked loci of war-related discussion in studies of Japanese war memories. The private nature of the family setting makes it difficult to record what is happening across Japan, but those Japanese people who have made their private situations public have collectively demonstrated the diversity of situations and responses to the knowledge of relatives' experiences. Given the difficulties, conflicts and rifts that can stem from discussing war responsibility in the family, narratives couched in the language of family suffering predominate: air raids, repatriation, hunger, soldiers dying of disease and malnutrition in distant outposts, and bereavement. This is not to say that people do not also have views about individual and collective responsibility. These are simply more risky to narrate. Nevertheless, the levels of published testimony, activism and professional involvement in war history issues reveal that millions of Japanese have taken public stands on war issues. These public stands have been taken despite the risks, or in many cases have enabled like-minded family members to forge stronger ties through a common purpose.

There are perhaps only a few thousand people earning a living exclusively from war history, but for millions of people, work involves war issues or they choose to be involved in war-related activism. These people's experiences shed a different light on 'the war in the family': the war may be discussed simply through the question 'How was your day?' Realistically, however, the war constitutes only a tiny fraction of discussion within most Japanese families compared to all the other things that must be discussed, from children's homework to the main news story of the day.

Ultimately, historical memory composure for any individual is a cumulative process that starts closest to home. People acquire more knowledge over time as an inevitable result of their consumption of the media and interactions within society. War memories are also composed and reworked over time so that they become acceptable to those with whom there is most identification: this usually means the family and other day-to-day social groupings, but it may equally mean a different role model, such as a favourite teacher or author. These privately composed memories are the raw materials of cultural memory and affect every level of discourse from private conversations up to the statements of the prime minister. The complexity of dealing with war issues in the family, where the remembrance of loved ones becomes entangled with painful issues of collective guilt and responsibility, works its way up to all levels of public discourse in Japan. Japan's contested war memories exist because there is no single obvious way to reconcile Japanese war actions with the strongest of human emotions: love for family and home, senses of moral right and wrong, and visions for the world in which Japanese people want their children to grow up.

Epilogue

Beyond the sixtieth anniversary

The most important family occasion in Japan is New Year. There is no more typical way to see in the New Year than for the family to sit around the *kotatsu* (a low heated table), eat, drink and watch *Kōhaku*, 'The Red and White Song Contest'. On 31 December 2005, the last day of *sengo 60-nen* ('postwar 60'), my family and I, along with 42.9 per cent of Japanese households (according to viewing figures), shared this Japanese institution. These days, in twenty-four-hours-a-day, seven-days-a-week media-saturated Japan, this is as close to a truly shared national experience as one gets, matched only by World Cup, Olympic or World Baseball Classic fever.

In an idle moment I channel-hopped to see what else was on: a rival song contest, a variety show, K-1 (kickboxing), a documentary about the Battle of Okinawa . . . . I checked the newspaper: NHK-Educational had an evening of war documentaries, but determined to have a break from research on this family evening, I turned back to NHK-G.

However, at 9.10 p.m. I reached for my pen. In a break from the song contest, Yoshinaga Sayuri, an actress well known for her recitations of *hibakusha* poetry, read A-bomb testimony to an organ accompaniment in the Philia Museum, Yamanashi Prefecture. It was followed by a song for Hiroshima. A little later, the haunting ballad *Satōkibi batake* ('The Sugar Cane Field') was performed. This has become an unofficial anthem for the victims of the Battle of Okinawa and was the theme song for a popular drama *Satōkibi batake no uta* ('Song of the Sugar Cane Fields', 4 August 2004, TBS, 15.9 per cent viewing figures). Next, there was a retrospective about popular songs in the sixty years of the postwar, including *The Apple Song* (*Ringo no uta*), whose release on 11 October 1945 was for many the 'moment when hope dawned' after the bleakness of defeat (Dower 1999: 172). At 11.00 p.m., pop star Matsutoya Yumi joined singers from Korea and China in a live broadcast from Shanghai. Images of the fall of the Berlin Wall accompanied the song, *Smile Again*, which presented a message of breaking down barriers with Asia. The final song of the evening was from boy band SMAP, and the five members each stood on an individual podium inscribed with one of the letters P, E, A, C, E. As the curtain fell on the evening, presenter Minō Monta announced the end of the fifty-sixth Red and White Song Contest and the end of 'postwar 60'.

We raised our glasses to the New Year, the sixty-first of Japan's 'long postwar'. NHK continued its programming with a relay around the country showing how the New Year had been welcomed in. At 12.10 a.m., in between the familiar scenes of street parties and bells being rung at shrines, there were pictures from a mass at the Hiroshima World Peace Memorial Cathedral. NHK's newscaster commented with customary precision that 'last year was the sixtieth anniversary of the A-bomb'. I wondered if any other New Year celebrations around the world had been so infused with a sombre mood of World War II remembrance, or if any other channels worldwide (other than specialist history channels) had dedicated New Year's Eve 2005 to war documentaries. I concluded most likely not.

It has been over twelve years since my first conversation about the Asia-Pacific War with a Japanese person at the practice for the school sports day in 1994. As I look back over the years, I realize I spent my first few years in Japan believing the orthodox English-language media interpretation of Japanese war memories. The state-centric orthodoxy is neat, self-affirming, beneficial, morally comfortable, and has enough truth in it to stand up to *moderate* scrutiny. This is why the charges of Japanese 'ignorance', 'amnesia', 'denial' and 'failure to address the past' can be recycled in English-language discourses with very little challenge. The problem is that the orthodoxy's survival relies on ignoring the vast majority of what the Japanese say about the war. One simple illustration of this is to search for discussion of war-related television in the Japanese war memories literature. I have yet to see more than a few pages in any given English-language book or article about Japanese war memories that discuss war-related television, even though television's importance today as an information source needs no explanation. Why? The methodological problems of television surveys are an issue, but perhaps the greater issue is that the orthodox modes of discourse in English are so comfortable and entrenched that there is little desire to challenge them, despite such obvious flaws.

The Red and White Song Contest is a prime example of how war-related information reaches Japanese people through their daily lives. People did not watch the programme intending to learn about the war, but nevertheless, perhaps forty or fifty million Japanese people had some contact with war issues that night. Admittedly, many viewers were en route to inebriation, talking to an aunt, or had even changed channels to the kickboxing during the war-related sections, but the fact that the New Year's Eve institution on Japanese television was so infused with the memories and legacies of a conflict sixty years ago is significant in itself. It is not the act of a nation suffering from 'amnesia', but rather a sign of a nation unable to break free from the past and let the war become 'history'. The focus was overwhelmingly on Japanese victimhood, as befits war representations playing to virtually the largest television audience of the year, but the song from Shanghai epitomized Igarashi Yoshikuni's important notion of an 'absent presence of the country's war memories'. It was tacit acknowledgement of Japan's strained relations with its neighbours and rich in undertones of a desire for reconciliation. Nothing about the war was stated explicitly, but the primary source of friction in East Asia and the need to break down barriers did not need an explicit explanation: it had been on the front pages of newspapers throughout 2005.

A cultural studies approach to Japanese war memories is about identifying such implicitly understood cultural meanings and how they relate to the privatized senses of the past among millions of individuals who are united in the need to deal with the complicated legacy of Japanese war actions but divided in how they respond to that legacy. Such a cultural studies approach is not a culturally determinist approach (which treats Japanese war memories as explicable in the context of unique Japanese characteristics). Neither is it polemical. I am offering no firm message about whether Japanese remembering overall is 'adequate' or not: I leave this to the individual judgement of the reader. However, given the range of opinions and experiences in Japan, regardless of one's own views of World War II history, there are probably Japanese people with whom one can find extensive common ground and other Japanese people with whom one will vehemently disagree.

The common representation of 'Japan vs the rest of the world' in war history issues is a stereotypical myth that needs to be dispelled. The hegemonic international media view condemns the Japanese military's aggression throughout Asia and the Pacific and is critical of popular and official Japanese responses to war responsibility issues. At the same time, the Japanese government's compensation stance is supported in Washington, DC, there is gratitude in Jakarta for Japan's help in the war against the Dutch, and former Malaysian President Mahathir (a vocal proponent of Asian pride and values) has said Japan should acknowledge past wrongs but 'should not be burdened by a permanent sense of guilt over actions committed more than half a century ago' (Kyodo online 3 November 2003). In terms of popular remembering, a majority of Japanese are closer to the hegemonic international interpretation of the war than a nationalistic interpretation, many Americans see the A-bombs as cruel and unnecessary like almost all Japanese do, and there are some Taiwanese (often with axes to grind with China) who remember the colonial era with fondness.

In other words, whereas the Asia-Pacific War involved multiple savage conflicts between nations, and whereas the historical issues that the Japanese and others must address are still largely framed in national terms, there is no monopoly of *national identity* as the lens through which war history is viewed. Trans- and sub-national identities are also employed, and understanding *contested* memories *within* nations is impossible unless these other identities are recognized.

This is why I have proposed the notion of memory rifts, the 'Japanese war memories as seismic activity' metaphor and a media/cultural studies approach as a challenge to the state-centric orthodoxy. My critiques of the orthodoxy are in no way a challenge to the evidence of Japanese aggression and atrocities in World War II, and neither is it intended to undermine the efforts of those still seeking justice: indeed, I would argue the greater the understanding of the dynamics, nature and processes of Japanese war memories and official policy, the greater the likelihood of campaigns for justice being successful. My challenge to the orthodoxy is based mainly on an academic concern for the ubiquity of debatable representations of Japanese war memories (see Appendix), and a belief that the Japanese case study has much to offer the growing theoretical literature of war memory studies if only it can be analysed dispassionately from many angles rather than descending into polemic and political agendas.

The acid test of the Japanese case study's broader relevance for international war memory theory is whether the lessons from it can apply in other situations. The evolution of Japan's contested war memories fits a pattern that has been broadly mirrored by three other cases: Germany in World War II, the US in Vietnam, and the US and UK in Iraq, 2003. Other cases exhibiting selected similarities might include the Suez Crisis, the Soviet invasion of Afghanistan, Serbia during the Balkan Wars and wars of colonial liberation since 1945 from Algeria to Kenya.

1 *Invasion* The nation, acting alone or with allies, wages a war of invasion overseas. The war is waged in the face of international criticism, while any domestic opposition is suppressed or ignored

2 *The 'just' cause* Due to fear, ideology, self-interest or lack of a better alternative, some people in the invaded country collaborate. This lends a measure of plausibility to the invader's claims of a war fought for the benefit, freedom or liberation of others, but the war is widely condemned internationally as aggression.

3 *Resistance* Despite initial military victories, resistance to the occupiers grows. The war becomes bogged down and casualties mount, particularly among civilians in the occupied country.

4 *Defeat* The war ends in defeat or an inability to achieve a clear victory. The invader is forced to withdraw and may be occupied as a result. Defeat is a catalyst for reassessing the wisdom of the decision to go to war.

5 *'Aggressive acts'* Either during or after the war, there are revelations about atrocities committed by the invaders and widespread civilian casualties suffered by the invaded countries. These revelations undermine continued assertions that the war was just.

6 *'Justice'* There are calls for those who planned and executed the war to be held to account. However, 'justice' depends on a victorious power or international body with sufficient power to oversee trials and postwar treaties. The 'justice' handed down on those soldiers and politicians tried by their own people is at best limited or lenient, and at worst non-existent.

7 *Memory rifts* The war's legacy is of contestation and national division as popular opinion becomes divided between those who defend the war in retrospect and those who condemn it. A dominant cultural memory cannot

emerge. The intensity of contestation depends on many variables, such as the extents of clearly morally indefensible acts (for example, genocide), pockets of international apologia or support, and the war's direct effects on non-combatants as well as the military.

8 *The official narrative in the postwar* War leaders and their political descendants are mindful of their places in history and/or potential legal consequences, so they only reluctantly admit responsibility or issue apologies. They may not even do so in the absence of decisive domestic/international pressure. Apologies for aggressive war are typically less explicit than for particular war actions. Apologies for isolated war crimes carry fewer implications for national guilt or collective legal liability.

9 *Commemoration and mourning* These are complicated by the ambiguous roles of soldiers as aggressors or victims. Official commemorations tend to be sombre rather than jingoistic. Where the invader has also suffered large-scale civilian casualties, their victimhood becomes far easier to commemorate than the actions of the military. Victimhood also spawns pacifism, but pacifism is typically based more on the suffering brought to the nation and its people than the suffering inflicted on others. Nevertheless, the suffering of others is widely represented in the media and becomes common knowledge among the population.

10 *Privatized senses of the past* As the public field of representations fails to offer a clear national narrative for how the war can be remembered, levels of identity other than national identity – such as gender, ideology and family bonds – assume greater importance in the composure of war memories. Remembering and narrating the past must deal with uncomfortable issues of responsibility and guilt, but these issues can be avoided by employing identities other than national identity and casting perpetrator compatriots as the 'other'.

11 *The end of the 'postwar'* The war remains the primary referential frame through which other wars are viewed until the passing of the war generation or a subsequent war can displace it in the nation's historical consciousness.

It goes without saying that the circumstances of every war are different. However, the warning from history is clear: wars judged over time to be aggressive or mistaken by significant sections of society leave a legacy of national division that may burden postwar generations for decades. This is not the only form of contested memories: a national debacle or collaboration with the enemy (as in France) may also create memory rifts. But the combination of aggression, defeat and widespread suffering is a volatile cocktail and can cause bitter recriminations long after the war has ended.

By contrast, the key to the creation of a truly dominant narrative (although it will never be completely uncontested) is unity in judgemental memory: an overwhelming and long-term popular majority belief that the war and its conduct were just, which becomes the unifying theme woven through all the disparate war experiences of the people. There are two particular instances in which this can occur: first, a victorious war, particularly against an enemy easily portrayed as an atrocity-soaked aggressor, in which any excesses can be subsumed by the belief it was a just war (such as the British and American dominant memories of World War II); or second, a war to expel an invader (such as Chinese and Russian accounts of the wars against Japan and Germany respectively).

In all of these types of national remembering, the ethical dimension is paramount. War memories cannot be studied without considering people's retrospective moral judgements of the war. The combination of factors in Japan's case, particularly debate over the war's (im)morality, has made a dominant cultural memory impossible. The result is probably the most *contested* memories of any of the major World War II combatant nations. This is not necessarily equivalent to memories being the most prominently *remembered*: contestation brings incentives to avoid the issue, and the strong national identity that can be forged in nations with truly dominant cultural memories makes it expedient to place great political, educational and cultural focus on war history. Nevertheless, the ongoing relevance of World War II history in Japan is significant given that the conflict ended over sixty years ago.

But what about the future of Japanese war memories beyond the sixtieth anniversary? Contestation looks likely to continue for the foreseeable future, particularly since Prime Minister Koizumi's potential successors seem determined to continue Yasukuni Shrine worship. Japanese conservatives' moves to change the constitution and take a more proactive military role will also ensure the lessons of the Asia-Pacific War remain a key issue. But by the time of the next major anniversary cycle, the seventieth (perhaps the seventy-fifth), the generational shift to entirely second-hand memories will be in its final stages. After the postwar generations have taken full control of the nation's war narrative, it is conceivable that much of the heat will be taken out of the issue as the war's personal relevance to Japanese people is diluted by time. Alternatively, a new conflict (perhaps involving North Korea) may reset the 'postwar clock' to zero and give the term 'Japanese war memories' an entirely new meaning. Whatever the future holds, the course of Japan's Asia-Pacific War memories ultimately depends on the uses that war history can be put to in the context of the unpredictable challenges that the Japanese nation will face.

Appendix
Critiques of orthodox arguments

This appendix provides critiques of representative 'orthodox' statements in some of the Japanese war memory literature. Many of the authors/works cited have powerful voices within the English-language media/academy. It is not my intention to suggest that these texts do not also provide extremely valuable insights into Japanese war memories. However, the appendix shows specific examples of statements that are inconsistent with the arguments presented in this book.

The criticisms come under seven main categories:

1 culturally determinist or state-centred arguments that over-generalize what 'the Japanese' think;
2 statements inconsistent with the available evidence (such as opinion poll data);
3 ambiguous/misleading representations;
4 debatable comparisons with German memory and responsibility;
5 over-focus on conservatives/nationalists and under-representation of progressives, or the characterization that conservatives/nationalists are 'typically Japanese' while progressives are 'un-Japanese';
6 orientalist arguments or thinly veiled cultural superiority complexes that condescend Japanese views and/or encourage the Japanese to share/ adopt 'our' views;
7 'prescriptive not descriptive' accounts that leave a stronger impression of the author's views than Japanese views.

Japan (Insight Guides)

Guidebooks are frequently of great importance in shaping the impressions of first-time visitors to a country. For a book aimed at people considering a visit to Japan (and therefore presumably interested in things Japanese), the *Insight Guide* is surprisingly hostile. It also gives archetypal culturally determinist arguments about the conformity and homogeneity of the people, and routinely uses the phrase 'the Japanese' in broad generalizations. Here are two examples related to war memory:

Collectively, the Japanese seem unable to recall 50 years of Japanese aggression capped by a Pacific War killing 20 million people. But Japan's neighbours – Korea, the Philippines and China – do. Recently, the Imperial Army's own documents confirming the brutality have been surfacing, and aging veterans have publicly purged their nightmares. But schools still minimise Japan's aggressive past, if it is mentioned at all, and conservative politicians still rewrite history. In 1994, the Minister of Justice declared that the 1937 Rape of Nanking – when 150,000 to 300,000 Chinese were slaughtered by an out-of-control Japanese army – was an unsubstantiated myth.

Notable both for the linguistic hedging and for the insight into Japanese thinking is the difference of how Japan and the rest of Asia, if not the world, remember World War II. Recent prime ministers have made efforts to address the past despite the vociferous views of right-wing politicians, nationalists, and university scholars to the contrary. Yet the linguistic nuances, when properly translated and understood, reveal not the expected apology as it first seems to be when translated from Japanese, but rather a promise of 'reflection' or 'remorse concerning unfortunate events', hardly an admission of wrong action or a sincere apology.

(Rutherford 2003: 43, 69–70)

Despite hinting that some people in Japan might be attempting to address the past, the two citations clearly make the case that 'Japan' does not. Some of the arguments are simply misleading. For example, the conservative politician implied to be rewriting history, Nagano Shigeto, had to resign because of his outburst: calling the Nanking Massacre a 'myth' is not official policy, although the *Insight Guide* implies it is. And the assertion that the Japanese education system 'minimises mentions of Japanese aggression' and that university scholars try to prevent prime ministerial moves to address the past are at best only half-truths. They overlook the facts that many Japanese educators at all levels have liberal tendencies and many educational materials are progressive-leaning.

Learning to Bow, Bruce Feiler

Learning to Bow is an engaging book about Bruce Feiler's year spent teaching in Japan. It comes within the large 'my time in Japan' genre that is popular within the trade press. I read many of these books in my first few years in Japan and *Learning to Bow* was a particular favourite.

However, the brief section about Japanese war memories is pure orthodoxy.

But in recent years an international controversy has sprung up over how Japanese textbooks depict the behavior of the Japanese during the Second

World War. The Japanese have tried to present themselves as victims of the West. They point out that the Greater East Asian Co-Prosperity Sphere and its promise to 'throw off the yolk of Imperialism' appealed to the peoples of Asia who had suffered under European colonial rule.

(Feiler 1991: 142)

Feiler's account focuses on the inadequacy of teaching about the war in Japanese schools, a key component of the orthodoxy. There is an all-encompassing use of 'the Japanese' for a fairly right-wing viewpoint, which is by no means shared by all Japanese people.

Feiler then discusses how little the war was treated in the textbook in use at his school and the overwhelming emphasis on Japanese victimhood, particularly the A-bombs. Feiler's two-page section draws to a close with a quotation from a friend who teaches history at the University of Tokyo: 'The Japanese have a collective historical amnesia. . . . Most students are not taught the history of Japan's invasion into China and other nations' (ibid.: 143). The combination of personal experience narrated by an engaging writer and implied expert opinion (the friend's status and expertise are not mentioned) is persuasive, but the representation of Japanese war memories as a mixture of nationalistic denial, historical amnesia and victim mentality is pure orthodoxy.

Long Shadows: truth, lies and history, **Erna Paris**

I found *Long Shadows* in the bestsellers section at Waterstones in Piccadilly, one of London's largest bookshops. It covers struggles with war history in Germany, France, Japan, America, South Africa and Yugoslavia. The chapter on Japan, 'Erasing history: pretense and oblivion in Japan', starts with the clichéd proverb 'If the nail sticks out, hammer it down'. It sets the tone for the chapter, which is a clear example of the problematic culturally determinist 'denying is typically Japanese' and 'free thinking is un-Japanese' thesis.

> Tradition is *wa*, the stifler of memory and debate; tradition is the ongoing, hierarchical organization of society where ideas and orders emanate from the top; tradition is hammering down any nail that dares to stick out; tradition is a culture that says no one is to blame because 'it can't be helped.' What he [then Nagasaki Mayor Motojima Hitoshi] embraces is the openness of Western democracies, the diversity of populations, the freedom to speak one's mind and the search for undoctored fact. What he rejects is conformity.

(Paris 2000: 151)

This line of argument is orientalist and presents the self-satisfied argument that Japanese war memory will be acceptable when 'they' discover 'our' values of Western openness.

Furthermore, there is a major contradiction in her conclusion. In her introduction, Paris stated that 'Japan [has] managed its history of defeat [by] denial' (ibid.: 5), but in the conclusion she states:

> In the end, the decades-long denial will be rejected by the young as they gradually come to know what was done in their country's name. . . . Already, in a poll taken back in 1994, a massive 4 to 1 majority of Japanese said they disbelieved their government on war crimes and desired an official apology, including paying adequate reparations.
>
> (ibid.: 163)

Rather than denial, Paris's poll result indicates significant levels of *acknowledgement*, opposition to authority, and knowledge of Japanese aggression sufficient to insist that the Japanese government should apologize more and pay more compensation. Conspicuously lacking is an explanation of how or why all these 'sticking up nails' are not being 'hammered down', and what the processes are that allow such levels of knowledge and opposition to the government.

The Rape of Nanking, Iris Chang

Iris Chang's 1997 book, *The Rape of Nanking*, is probably the biggest-selling book that has discussed Japanese war memories. As well as selling over half a million copies, it gained enormous media attention. Chang's book is also important because it established the Chinese-American voice on Japanese war responsibility issues, and gave prominence to the Global Alliance for Preserving the History of World War II in Asia,[1] which is now perhaps the key group within contemporary American activism working on the issue of Japanese war responsibility. Whereas Chang and the Global Alliance have done much to raise awareness of Japanese war actions, publications by Global Alliance members sometimes make indiscriminate and poorly substantiated generalizations about Japanese war memories (see p. 219, *Japanese War Crimes*).

Chang's Chapter 10, 'The forgotten holocaust: a second rape', gives many examples of Japanese nationalistic denial. While they are all important aspects of Japanese memories, the analysis is one-sided and portrays nationalism as representative of Japanese war memories. One disingenuous tactic was to list nationalistic opinions uttered by Japanese cabinet ministers rather than explaining the actual official position. Chang then casually referred to these as 'official denials' (Chang 1997: 204) when they were no such thing: they frequently resulted in resignations precisely because they were not the official line and had caused a diplomatic row. Chang presented progressives as either barely existing or as minnows crushed by the force of nationalists. She titled one section 'The academic cover-up' and stated 'serious research on the Rape of Nanking has largely been left up to the efforts of those operating outside of traditional academic communities' (ibid.: 209). She also made the serious over-generalization that '[t]he entire Japanese education system suffers from collective amnesia' (ibid.: 205). This is a 'cover-up' of the extent of progressive educators in Japan.

The similarities between Chang's arguments and the *Insight Guide*'s stance make it seem reasonable to assume that Chang's book was the primary source for the *Insight Guide*'s text, which would be further evidence for the reach of Chang's arguments.

'The problem of memory', Nicholas Kristof

Kristof is a Pulitzer Prize-winning journalist who reported regularly on war issues for the *New York Times* in the 1990s. As a leading columnist in one of the English-speaking world's most influential newspapers, he has had one of the most powerful platforms available to influence Western views on Japanese war memory.

His arguments are distilled in the 1998 *Foreign Affairs* article, 'The problem of memory'. The tone is unashamedly polemical (it contains the word 'should' numerous times) and he assumes the tone of a preacher speaking to sinners. For example, he cites the way that the war is not properly taught in Japanese schools as the reason why 'most Japanese know very little of their country's dark past, and thus may be genuinely ignorant of what there is to repent' (Kristof 1998: 41).

However, this reasoning makes two assumptions. First, he ignores the possibility that the Japanese media and popular culture could be Japanese people's most important source of war information rather than school education. The reality, as I have extensively documented, is that the Japanese media covers war issues prominently and the war remains a current affairs issue. Kristof's argument that little education at school means little knowledge among the population is a surprising non-sequitur for a journalist.

The second assumption concerns the word 'ignorant' itself. 'Ignorant' contains many undertones, but basically it has a polemical meaning: 'they do not know what I think they should know'. There is a further problem: is the ignorance absolute or relative? If the ignorance is absolute, then the belittling of the role of the media severely damages the argument. If the ignorance is relative to American knowledge about World War II, then the case can be made that Japanese people are relatively knowledgeable. A poll in June 2004 concerning the D-Day sixtieth anniversary commemorations found that:

> A little more than a third of Americans don't know specific details about D-Day, including the country against whom the Allies were fighting or the geographic location of the D-Day landing. Younger Americans (aged 18 to 29) are least likely to be able to recall these specifics.
>
> (Gallup 2004)

Ignorance about World War II history is a worldwide phenomenon, particularly among young people with their own era to live in, but none of the opinion poll data I have found about Japan suggests ignorance at the level of one third cannot recall who the enemy was.

'Don't mention the war . . .', Philip Brasor

One of my primary criticisms of the Japanese war memories literature is that it rarely addresses war-related television. One of the few articles I have found on the subject is Philip Brasor's column in *The Japan Times*, 'It's the black comedy of Japan: "don't mention the war . . .".'

> A point that tends to be overlooked in the debate over textbooks that whitewash Japan's actions during World War II is that Japanese junior high school history classes rarely make it past the Meiji Restoration. Whether or not 'comfort women' or the Rape of Nanking is mentioned in textbooks becomes an academic issue if children don't learn anything about the Pacific War in the first place.
>
> Japanese people are more likely to learn about the war from the media, especially this time of year when there are TV specials commemorating the anniversaries of the battle of Okinawa, the two atomic bombings, and the surrender itself. It's the end of the war that merits remembrance because the incredible losses that Japan suffered in the final months can be used to mask the incredible losses that Japan inflicted throughout Asia.
>
> This being the 60th anniversary, there are even more specials scheduled, and the more dramatic ones exclusively address the sacrifice and suffering of the Japanese people – without any mention of the nation's cruel empire-building escapades. However, one drama special, which was broadcast last Monday night on TV Tokyo, stands apart. In fact, considering how little publicity it received, maybe it stands too far apart.
>
> (www.japantimes.com 24 July 2005)

The first paragraph contains a familiar (and debatable, see Chapter 6) dismissal of Japanese education. But Brasor's article is most interesting for its *preconceptions* about television: the sixtieth anniversary programmes were largely dismissed as inadequate before they were ever broadcast. Brasor's prediction of '[no] mention of the nation's cruel empire building' turned out to be simply mistaken (particularly regarding NHK's marathon studio debate on 15 August), as could have been predicted by looking back over war-related programming since the early 1990s. And while Japanese television does have a heavy focus on victimhood, the charge that Japanese victimhood can be 'used to mask' Asian suffering is cynical. The predominant pattern is that once the A-bomb anniversaries have passed, Japanese war responsibility issues are treated more in the lead up to 15 August.

In short, Brasor uses a classic trick by which progressives or media texts worthy of some praise are discussed but ultimately marginalized to maintain the overall critical tone vis-à-vis Japan: he sets up the programme (*Seidan*, about the emperor's role in the decision to surrender) as 'the exception that proves the rule' about inadequate Japanese remembering. Treating isolated media texts in this way means that however many 'adequate' texts are analysed, the orthodoxy about inadequate remembering need not be challenged.

The BBC

The BBC is one of the most respected news organizations in the world, but as I have argued elsewhere (Seaton 2005), the reporting on Japanese war issues on the BBC's website is a key example of the orthodoxy. Part of the Japan profile reads as follows:

> Japan has the world's second-biggest economy, but it remains a traditional society with strong social and employment hierarchies – Japanese men have always tended to work for the same employer for the whole of their life.
>
> But this and other traditions are under pressure as a young generation more in tune with Western culture and ideas grows up.
>
> Japan's relations with its neighbours are still heavily influenced by the legacy of Japanese actions before and during World War II. Japan has found it difficult to accept and atone for its treatment of the citizens of countries it occupied.
>
> A Japanese court caused outrage by overturning a compensation order for Korean women forced to work as sex slaves. South Korea and China have also protested that Japanese school history books gloss over atrocities committed by the Japanese military.
>
> (www.bbc.co.uk 11 July 2006)

This profile highlights Japanese tradition and contains the orientalist overtones that modernization is synonymous with Westernization. The statement that 'Japan has found it difficult to accept and atone' is an archetypal state-centric generalization; it is also a polemical expectation for Japan to conform to the British view of World War II. This is followed by two specific criticisms of Japan's failure to address the past, which are both related to government policy (and thereby state-centric) and greatly under-represent the complexities of the issues. In particular, the BBC fails to distinguish between individual nationalistic textbooks that provoke most international protests and the wider state of Japanese history education.

Compare this to the sympathetic war-related section of the Germany profile:

The pain of Germany's Nazi-era history remains a sensitive element in the country's collective modern-day psyche. Out of the devastation of World War II grew European awareness of the need to guard against any such catastrophe recurring on the continent.

(www.bbc.co.uk 16 May 2006)

This could equally have been said about Japan, where war history is sensitive and the rhetoric of pacifism is widespread. The BBC avoids any direct criticism of Germany through ambiguous language: the agents of 'pain', 'devastation' and 'catastrophe' are not stated and the wording allows for the interpretation that Germans themselves were victims of the Nazis.

The BBC's country profiles are emblematic of the way in which Germany has been largely forgiven for its war actions, but Japan has not. Or perhaps the BBC feels uncomfortable about antagonizing Germans but feels little compunction about criticizing Japanese. Overall, the attitude towards Japan that is evident in the country profile illustrates why I consider the BBC a key proponent of the orthodoxy.

George Hicks, *Japan's War Memories: Amnesia or concealment?* And regarding the 'comfort women' issue

Extraordinarily, George Hicks's *Japan's War Memories* is one of the only book-length overviews of Japanese war memories available in English that comes reasonably up to date. Hicks uses a chronological approach and describes many of the key developments over the postwar era. Hicks also raises the important point of distinguishing between popular and official 'amnesia' on the war:

Debate on the war only became prominent, particularly on the international scene, after the decline of the Cold War order. Until then, as Japan had been the only clearly viable Asian ally of the Western camp in the confrontation with Communism, the Second World War tended to be treated as a dead issue. . . . This made it possible for Japanese official and business circles to avoid reference to the war to an extent that, to foreign observers especially, seemed to amount to a kind of 'national amnesia'. . . . [H]owever, [the amount of published memoir type material, sometimes semi-fictionalized] has been so voluminous as to cast some doubt on how far such apparent official 'amnesia' affects the population as a whole.

(Hicks 1997: vi–ix)

Despite initially casting doubt on the level of popular amnesia, as the title suggests, Hicks' position is ultimately critical. The book demonstrates many orthodox tendencies. For example, it focuses on conservatives and official 'amnesia' rather than the less clear realm of popular 'amnesia'. This makes the book predominantly state-centred. In addition, the 'amnesia' thesis is ultimately polemical: it is the by now familiar line of 'why do the Japanese not say what I think they should say?' This polemical stance is evident in the final sentences of the book: 'Japan must accept more responsibility for its future. Ienaga Saburo and his associates as the conscience of Japan will be watching and waiting' (ibid.: 135).

By isolating one group of progressives as the 'conscience of Japan', Hicks casts them as 'un-Japanese'. So while there are frequent references made to progressives other than Ienaga, ultimately they are marginalized. This is epitomized by a serious oversight in Hicks' book: the lack of a single reference to Japanese feminists and their campaigns on behalf of former 'comfort women' in the chapter on the 1990s. This omission is also repeated in a later essay (1999, adapted from Hicks 1995) when, under the misleading sub-heading 'Public opinion against reparations' (Hicks 1999: 119–22), Hicks ignored any Japanese support for the 'comfort women' and focused entirely on right-wing opposition in the *Sankei* newspaper (the most right-wing and smallest in terms of circulation of the national dailies) and by Uesaka Fuyuko (*sic* Kamisaka Fuyuko, who is a prominent conservative commentator but not representative of particularly female public opinion in Japan regarding the 'comfort women' – see Seaton 2006b: 108).

In reality, public opinion poll data consistently shows that a small majority of the Japanese public is in favour of compensation and 'proper apologies' to groups like the 'comfort women'. A 1993 poll in the wake of Hosokawa's 'aggressive war' comments (and just a month after the government's 4 August 1993 apology to the 'comfort women') revealed that 55 per cent said additional financial compensation was 'necessary' or 'necessary to some extent' to Asian victims, while 29 per cent said it was 'not necessary' or 'not particularly necessary' (Yoshida 1995: 3). And in a 1997 opinion poll specifically about the 'comfort women' issue, 50.7 per cent said '[politicians have] made many thoughtless remarks and should apologize properly to Asian countries and the victims'. 'Japan has apologized too much', the response closest to the image of Japanese public opinion that Hicks paints, accounted for 27.4 per cent of responses (Yoshimi 2000: 27). These figures are emblematic of contested public opinion, not 'public opinion against reparations'.

Japanese War Crimes: the search for justice, Peter Li (ed.)

Orthodox interpretations of Japanese war memory are not limited to journalists. One example of a scholarly polemical account is *Japanese War Crimes: the search for justice*. Editor Peter Li's introduction begins:

> There comes a point in time when it is no longer necessary to try to understand why Japan cannot apologize . . . This book expresses in the simplest and clearest terms possible the reasons why Japan should take

up the responsibility for its war crimes, apologize to the victims of its wartime atrocities, and pay appropriate reparations to the victims. This book is a call to action. There is no need for complicated arguments and sophisticated analysis.

(Li 2003: ix)

The book is primarily about Japan's unresolved war responsibility issues, but a number of essays in it also tackle memory and present archetypal orthodox approach arguments. For example, Maria Hsia Chang and Robert P. Barker write in 'Victor's justice and Japan's amnesia':

Given the attitude of its government leaders, it is not surprising that the Japanese people, with the exception of certain intellectuals and war veterans, remain at once ignorant and in denial of their country's war atrocities. As an example, notwithstanding the Imperial Japanese Army's brutalities against the Allied POWs and the inhumane experiments of Unit 731, Tokyo University professor Fujioka Nobukatsu argued that Japan was fundamentally different from Nazi Germany in that although Japan might have fought 'a slightly high-handed patriotic war,' it did not commit 'crimes against humanity.' In 1999, Fujioka and a colleague published a book declaiming Iris Chang's *The Rape of Nanking* for its 'untruths' and 'disinformation.' That October, a Japanese civic group canceled its plan to show a film about the massacre after receiving dozens of phone calls warning of possible interference. On January 23, 2000, a seminar claiming the Nanjing massacre never happened was held in a 'peace museum' in Osaka. The fact that the museum was founded by the Osaka prefectural and municipal governments seemed to confer official imprimatur and approval on the seminar. According to Shizuoka University lecturer Koike Yoshiyuki, many Japanese simply refuse 'to accept that the Massacre ever took place.'

(Chang and Barker 2003: 35)

This paragraph contains numerous misrepresentations. First, saying that Japanese people (baring a few exceptions) are unaware of their country's atrocities because their government does not tell them implies a rigid state-centred approach, ignores the role of the media, and disregards opinion poll data, which consistently shows that over 50 per cent of Japanese people support more compensation and apologies.

Second, nationalist-academic Fujioka's views are portrayed as representative of Japanese denial, but he was a prominent member of the Japanese Society for History Textbook Reform (Tsukurukai) and opinion poll data from 2001 showed that more Japanese people opposed than supported Fujioka's brand of nationalism: 28 per cent supported the Tsukurukai while 44 per cent opposed it (with 28 per cent 'don't knows') (Kondō 2001: 3).

Third, the activities of nationalists are prioritized over the actions of progressives in the description of the cancelled screening of the film about Nanking. Dozens of phone calls (which conceivably could have been the work of one or two individuals) is deemed more important than the fact that a citizens, group wanted to raise awareness of the massacre by screening a film.

Fourth, sensing something strange in a Nanking Massacre denial seminar in what is one of Japan's most progressive museums, I asked staff at Peace Osaka for an explanation. They told me (at the museum on 29 November 2003) that nationalists had demanded that as taxpayers their views should also be allowed in Peace Osaka, which is a publicly funded museum. A one-off seminar in Peace Osaka's facilities was the concession given to nationalists when the museum refused to tone down its progressive war exhibits. Peace Osaka only '*seemed* to confer official imprimatur and approval on the seminar': the seminar had no official endorsement and was actually a result of Peace Osaka's resolution not to include nationalists' arguments in the exhibits.

Finally, rounding off the paragraph with the statement about 'many people' believing the massacre did not occur is disingenuous because it is not contextualized. How many is 'many'?

War and Memory in the Twentieth Century, **Martin Evans and Ken Lunn (eds)**

The following is a description of events surrounding the Hiroshima anniversary in the introduction of the scholarly edited volume *War and Memory in the Twentieth Century*:

> The further the commemorative cycle went the more memory became fraught with tension, and nowhere was this more obvious than with the anniversary of the dropping of the atomic bomb on Hiroshima. Calls from within Japan, demanding that the Allies should apologize, led to fury among Far East veterans in America, Britain and several other former dominions. For many of the latter, the atomic bomb was justified because it shortened the war and thus saved lives. And anyway, they went on, does not undue focus upon Hiroshima risk forgetting the terrible atrocities carried out by Japanese militarism? . . . [List of Japanese atrocities: 'comfort women', POWs, Nanking] . . . Surely the Japanese government should be willing to acknowledge these aspects of the war as well. The Hiroshima controversy was symptomatic of a general problem facing each anniversary, namely *what* was the purpose of remembering? . . . Furthermore, the Hiroshima anniversary underlined the significance of the national perspective, namely how any one person's memory of the Pacific conflict is heavily dependent on whether you are American, British, Australian or Japanese.

(Evans and Lunn 1997: xv–xvi)

This paragraph illustrates much about the nature of the orthodoxy in the Allied nations. The angry rejection of the 'calls from within Japan' demanding an apology illustrates the resistance towards narratives of Japanese victimhood: only Japanese acknowledgement of guilt is acceptable. These views are being handed down within the Allied nations and are politically and emotionally difficult to challenge because they originate from what is frequently called 'the greatest generation'.

Furthermore, the extract blurs official policy and unofficial views in Japan. The extract cites 'calls from within Japan' for an apology. However, the Japanese government has stated that it has no official policy of asking for an A-bomb apology (*Yomiuri shinbun* 2 December 1991). It sees no benefit in antagonizing the US when it knows an American apology will not be forthcoming (see Chapter 3) and official calls for a Hiroshima apology would only strengthen international calls for Japanese apologies. So the sentence 'Surely the Japanese government should be willing to acknowledge these aspects of the war as well', allows two misunderstandings. First, it could be interpreted as if it is really the Japanese government calling for apologies, when that is not the case. Second, it makes it sound as if the Japanese government has not apologized for Japanese atrocities when in fact the Japanese government has issued numerous apologies (see Table. 4.1, p. 88).

The 'calls for apology' were most probably coming from survivors' associations and possibly local officials in Hiroshima. As I have discussed, Japanese peace activism in Hiroshima is far more based in liberal/progressive groups (that acknowledge Japanese guilt) than in conservative groups; furthermore, the Mayor of Hiroshima issued an apology at the Hiroshima commemorations on 6 August 1995, the anniversary in question (see Chapter 2).

The blurring of the official position and unofficial positions is completed by the final sentence which stresses the 'national perspective' and inclines the overall tone of the passage to criticism of 'Japan'.

The Emptiness of Japanese Affluence, Gavan McCormack

Gavan McCormack is a professor of Japanese history at the Australian National University and his *The Emptiness of Japanese Affluence* is a key orthodox text by an academic Japan specialist. *Emptiness*, as its title suggests, is a polemical book, which is epitomized by the final sentences of the chapter 'Remembering and Forgetting the War': Japan has an 'obligation to be scrupulous in facing the reality of its past militarism and in addressing the wounds caused by it' (McCormack 1996: 277). In a section titled 'Memory' and a chapter about 'remembering and forgetting', the final comments are about what the Japanese should do to address war responsibility. This exemplifies two common aspects of orthodox texts: the oscillation between memory and responsibility issues and a polemical conclusion that reveals the author's views more than those of the Japanese.

The chapter contains a number of problematic arguments, mainly relating to the Germany–Japan comparison. Concerning the level of debate in Japan, McCormack cites Lee Kwan Yew in saying that 'there has not been an open debate within Japan on its role in the war as there has been in Germany' (ibid.: 276). This is debatable given the evidence presented in this book. The following passage also fails to distinguish clearly between official policy and popular remembering:

> The consistent Japanese focus on its war experience as victim (Hiroshima and Nagasaki), rather than as aggressor (Nanking, Singapore, and countless other cities), contrasts with Germany's public penitent stance. The continuing efforts to sanitize the history that is taught to the country's youth, and especially to deny the massacre at Nanking and the atrocities of Unit 731 at Harbin and elsewhere, and the countless atrocities against women, evoke distrust and suspicion on the part of Japan's neighbors. Financial compensation, it is understood, would be hollow without honest confrontation with the historical record in Tokyo and the assumption of a moral responsibility by the contemporary Japanese state for the innocent victims of the crimes of their fathers.
>
> (McCormack 1996: 245)

The passage slips between official and unofficial war views and agency is left fuzzy. The 'Japanese focus on its experience as victim', for example, seems more applicable to public remembering, yet this is compared with German government policy. 'The continuing efforts to sanitize' may relate to textbook screening, but denial of the massacre at Nanking is not official policy: Nanking appears in government-approved textbooks, although some politicians (Nagano Shigeto in particular) have denied Nanking. Overall, such vagueness concerning agency, while very difficult to call 'inaccurate', obscures divisions of opinion within Japan and leads the reader towards a state-centric critical appraisal of 'Japan'.

McCormack also tends to marginalize progressives. For example, referring to the German *Historikerstreit* ('historians' debate') in the 1980s in which conservative German historians attempted to historicize and relativize the Nazi past, McCormack writes:

> One commentator remarked on the comparison between the two countries, *with only mild exaggeration*, that Japan was full of conservative nationalists like Stürmer, but had no radical voices like Habermas at all.
>
> (ibid.: 234, emphasis added)

But later, McCormack states 'by late 1993, nearly 60 percent [of Japanese people] agreed it had been an aggressive war, and well over 50 percent that some form of compensation should be paid' (ibid.: 271). Given that 'an aggressive war' and the need for more compensation are the most basic progressive positions, McCormack's statement that '[Japan] had no radical voices' is 'only mild exaggeration' stretches plausibility. Japanese progressives clearly exist, have widely supported voices and cannot simply be portrayed as unrepresentative or un-Japanese.

But perhaps the most troubling aspect of the chapter is McCormack's decision to cite Ben Hills of the *Sydney Morning Herald* comparing Germany with Japan:

> But imagine a country equally responsible for a war in which upwards of 20 million people were killed, whose armies committed atrocities of the nature of Hitler's 'final solution,' – and yet 50 years on is still living in a fantasy world of denial and disbelief. Imagine a country where Adolf Hitler never died, but lived on to a ripe old age, stripped of his power but still worshipped by his people. Imagine a country where schoolchildren still line up each morning to salute the swastika, and sing the anthem of the Hitler Youth. Imagine a country where Government ministers regularly pronounce that Auschwitz never happened, and the invasion of Poland, Czechoslovakia, Holland and France was really aimed at 'liberating' those countries.
>
> (ibid.: 230)

Such emotive, tabloid rhetoric does not bear much resemblance to the reality in Japan. Its inclusion, without challenge or qualification, is emblematic of the problematic Germany–Japan comparision throughout McCormack's chapter.

Summary

When one compares the arguments above to the evidence presented throughout this book, the gulf between the English-language orthodoxy and the thesis of 'Japan's contested war memories' becomes clear. As progressive scholar Yoshimi Yoshiaki has written (with a perceptible hint of frustration at the frequent marginalization of progressives), 'The impression some in Europe and America have that Japanese people who demand an apology and compensation are isolated and threatened in Japanese society is clearly mistaken' (Yoshimi 2000: 28).

The English-language orthodoxy concerning Japanese war memories is in need of revision. This is not a call for international observers to relax their scrutiny of how the Japanese address war issues or war responsibility. It is a call for greater precision in discussion of the following issues:

1   agency: defining exactly whose opinions are being discussed;
2   context: assessing how representative particular views are and the wider social processes that have accompanied the development of those views;

3 official vs unofficial views: clarifying what authority people have to speak on behalf of a group or the nation;
4 memories vs responsibility: recognizing that public remembering and government policy are quite separate issues;
5 distinctiveness vs universalism: isolating which aspects of Japanese war memories are peculiar to the Japanese and which are common aspects of war memories in any country;
6 international complicity: acknowledging that international views and government policies impact on Japanese responses to war issues, and re-evaluating the effects of our own countries' war memories, media representations of others, and policies on war, justice and human rights.

Notes

Introduction

1 There are a variety of names used to describe Japan's participation in World War II. I am using the term 'Asia-Pacific War' and focusing on memories of the period 1937–45, from the start of full-scale hostilities with China to Japan's surrender in 1945. Many scholars in Japan use the term 'Fifteen-Year War' to describe the period from the Manchurian Incident (1931) to 1945. I am not focusing on the earlier stages of the conflict (1931–36) or Japanese colonialism following the Meiji Restoration of 1868, even though they are inextricably linked to memories of the Asia-Pacific War. However, I make references to this period when necessary.

2 Similar attitudes frequently emanate from Asia and non-English-speaking Western countries such as France. It may well be appropriate to term the orthodoxy in the English-speaking world the 'international orthodoxy' concerning Japanese war memories. However, I have limited the discussion to English-language texts.

3 'Orthodox' is also a term used by Said in relation to dominant Western media representations of the Muslim world (Said 1997: lviii).

1 Historical consciousness in contemporary Japan

1 The term 'comfort women' is a direct translation of the Japanese *ianfu*. I use the term 'comfort women' in inverted commas to indicate its euphemistic nature. Many former 'comfort women' prefer to call themselves 'survivors', but I avoid this term to prevent confusion with other survivors.

2 It has been suggested to me that 'war guilt' might be a more appropriate translation for *sensō sekinin*. In *Sengo sekininron*, Takahashi Tetsuya translates *sekinin* as responsibility and deconstructs responsibility as the 'ability to respond' (Takahashi 1999: 23). Takahashi's analysis has informed my own. Furthermore, 'responsibility' is more consistent with the thesis that war history is contested: people have the ability to respond in different ways. 'Guilt', by contrast, is a rigid term. It indicates a firm judgement that a crime has been committed and immediately assumes a moral and political position.

3 I am grateful to Takahashi Tetsuya for this point and example.

4 The hypothesis has been derived from opinion poll data. See Seaton (2004: 73–82) for a detailed justification. Saaler (2005) and Dower (2002) also draw compatible conclusions. Opinion poll data supportive of this hypothesis can be found in Yoshida (1995) and Hicks (1997).

2 The 'long postwar'

1 The Northern Territories – the islands of Etorofu, Kunashiri, Shikotan and Habomai – are claimed by Japan but were occupied by the Soviets after the war and have never been returned despite repeated Japanese demands.
2 In 2002 the fact that Japanese had been abducted by North Korean agents was confirmed with the return of five Japanese. The Kim Jong-il government claimed other abductees had died in North Korea, but DNA tests on the repatriated remains confirmed they did not belong to any of the abductees. The issue has generated significant resentment towards North Korea in Japan, which makes any moves to sign a peace treaty while the abduction issue remains unresolved extremely unlikely.
3 In the period 1973–2004, a total of 6,246 Japanese stranded in China at the end of the war (mainly orphans) had returned to Japan, while 547 had opted to stay in China (Asahi shinbunsha 2005: 90).
4 In Japanese folklore, folding 1,000 origami cranes is supposed to make a wish come true. Young *hibakusha* Sasaki Sadako had folded 1,300 cranes in the hope she would recover from her radiation sickness. Chains of 1,000 origami cranes are left by visitors to the Peace Memorial Park as a wish for peace.
5 The Japanese omits the subject and *ayamachi* can be singular or plural, so what the 'mistake(s)' is/are and who made it/them are unclear.

3 'Addressing the past'

1 *Kakō no kokufuku*, associated with Richard von Weizsäcker' famous 1985 speech that attracted much attention in Japan (Buruma 1995: 228).
2 See Sands (2005: 33) for discussion of this distinction in the context of the Pinochet case in 1998–99.
3 Hata Ikuhiko classifies the German and Japanese 'comfort systems' as similar in both nature and size (approximately 400 Japanese and 500 German 'comfort stations'). The German and Japanese systems contrasted with the 'free dating' (non-military brothel) system of the Americans and British, and the 'rape system' of the Soviets, in which no sexual provision was made and soldiers committed widespread rape (Hata 1999: 145–50). Yoshimi Yoshiaki, citing the same German sources as Hata, writes: 'In France and Holland, German military personnel used existing brothels. Many of the women who were drafted in the eastern occupied territories were forced to choose between doing forced labor and working in a brothel reserved for soldiers' (Yoshimi 2000: 189).

4 The war as a current affairs issue

1 The data in this section has been compiled from the website of the Japan Newspaper Publishers and Editors Association www.pressnet.or.jp/english/index.htm; the websites of the *Nikkei* newspaper www.nikkei.co.jp/ad/info/jpmarket/paperinjp.html and *Yomiuri* newspapers www.adv.yomiuri.co.jp/m-data/english/index.html; and Fujitake (2000: 27-92).
2 See Tanaka (2002: 249) for a list of over forty court rulings. The *nenpyō* mentioned eight of these plus two after Tanaka's book was published: Fukuoka 7 April 2004 and Osaka 30 September 2005.
3 These dynamics are also illustrated in Yayama Tarō's study of the 'mad rhapsody' the Japanese media conducted over the 1982 textbook crisis, when the sharing of erroneous information within a press club about textbook screeners' advice precipitated months of media coverage and diplomatic wrangling (Yayama 1983).
4 For example: www.comfort-women.org; the Asian Women's Fund's official page, www.awf.or.jp/english/; and the Korean Council for the Women Drafted for Military Sexual Slavery by Japan, www.womenandwar.net/english/menu_014.php.

5 August commemorations

1 The Broadcast Library: www.bpcj.or.jp/; NHK Archives: www.nhk.or.jp/nhk-archives/.
2 Newspaper listings were chosen in preference to a monthly television guide because they contain more information about programme content and accommodate short-notice changes in scheduling. The listings were for the Tokyo area and taken from the *Mainichi* newspaper.
3 According to Japan's 2001 census, Japan's adult (twenty years old plus) population was about 100 million. From this I am assuming a viewing rate of 1 per cent equates to one million viewers.
4 Video Research Ltd: www.videor.co.jp/data/ratedata/r_index.htm.

7 War stories

1 This is based on estimated revenue. Industry mergers mean that exact box office data is unavailable for 1970–73. Parts II and III of *Sensō to ningen* also featured in the lists of highest estimated box office.

8 Regional memories

1 Kokuritsu rekishi minzoku hakubutsukan: www.rekihaku.ac.jp/index_ne.html.
2 Shōwakan: www.showakan.go.jp.
3 Pīsu Ōsaka: www.mic.e-osaka.ne.jp/peace/.
4 This is a summary based on the explanations provided by officials at museums in Hiroshima, Osaka and Kawasaki: October 2003.
5 Oka Masaharu kinen Nagasaki heiwa shiryōkan: www.d3.dion.ne.jp/~okakinen/English/indexE.htm.
6 Ritsumeikan daigaku kokusai heiwa myūjiamu: www.ritsumei.ac.jp/mng/er/wp-museum/e/eng.html.
7 Hiroshima heiwa kinen shiryōkan: www.pcf.city.hiroshima.jp/.
8 Heiwa kinen tenji shiryōkan: www.heiwa.go.jp/tenji/.
9 Chiran tokkō heiwa kaikan: www.town.chiran.kagoshima.jp/cgi-bin/hpView Contents.cgi?pID=20041215091804.
10 Aichi heiwa kinenkan: www.asahi-net.or.jp/~ku3n-kym/heiki2/oukakai/heiwa.html.
11 Kawasaki-shi heiwakan: www.city.kawasaki.jp/25/25heiwa/home/heiwa.htm.
12 Yūshūkan: www.yasukuni.or.jp/english/index.html.
13 Nasu sensō hakubutsukan: www.homepage3.nifty.com/tompei/WarMuseum Nasu.htm.
14 Himeji heiwa shiryōkan: www.city.himeji.hyogo.jp/heiwasiryo/.
15 Yamamoto Isoroku kinenkan: see www.city.nagaoka.niigata.jp/dpage/kankou/kankou/spot/subwin32.html.
16 Niigata kenritsu rekishi hakubutsukan: www.nbz.or.jp/index.html.
17 Edo Tōkyō hakubutsukan: www.edo-tokyo-museum.or.jp.
18 Hokkaidō kaitaku kinenkan: www.hmh.pref.hokkaido.jp/.
19 Okinawa kenritsu heiwa kinen shiryōkan: www.peace-museum.pref.okinawa.jp/en_index.htm.
20 Himeyuri heiwa kinen shiryōkan www.himeyuri.or.jp/index2.html.

9 War and the family

1 After the 2001 Texts of Testimony Conference held at Liverpool John Moores University I was asked by conference organisers Timothy Ashplant and Elspeth

Graham to compile a Japanese testimony database (submitted August 2003, unpublished).
2 Fathers and grandfathers taking an evening bath together with their young (grand)children is a common custom in Japanese families.
3 NHK (1998) *Bunka seishin igakusha – Noda Masaaki, senjo no chichi no tsumi wo meguru taiwa* (Social Psychologist Noda Masaaki: conversations about fathers' war crimes), 20 January.
4 For example, *Sekai ururun taizaiki* (Nippon television, 8 August 2004) featured grateful villagers in Papua New Guinea describing how Japanese soldiers had taught them new agricultural and fishing skills.
5 www.nippon-izokukai.jp/index2.html.
6 www.eireinikotaerukai.net/.
7 www.sokagakkai.info/.
8 www.ne.jp/asahi/hidankyo/nihon/.
9 www.www1.jca.apc.org/vaww-net-japan/.
10 www.jca.apc.org/JWRC/index-j.html.
11 www.ne.jp/asahi/tyuukiren/web-site/.
12 www.tsukurukai.com/.
13 www.ne.jp/asahi/kyokasho/net21/.

Appendix

1 The Global Alliance's website, www.global-alliance.net/related.html, is a good starting point for seeing the generally hostile representation of Japanese remembering within the American media.

Bibliography

Online news resources

Access to all webpages was confirmed on 5 August 2006. Links to online sources (where still available, or their updated versions) are at the online appendix for this book: www.philipseaton.net/jcwm.html.

www.asahi.com (*Asahi shinbun* online) 'Editorial: emperor and Yasukuni', 22 July 2006.

www.bbc.co.uk (BBC News online), 'Government will not support PoWs' campaign', 29 April 1998.

—— 'Vietnam says no apologies needed', 16 December 1998.

—— 'Judge dismisses sex slave suit against Japan', 5 October 2001.

—— 'Japan court rejects germ warfare case', 27 August 2002.

—— 'US questions Japan's pacifism', 13 August 2004.

—— 'Country profile: Germany' 16 May 2006. Note: the country profiles get updated regularly. 16 May was the 'last updated' date when accessed on 4 August 2006.

—— 'Country profile: Japan', 11 July 2006. Note: the country profiles get updated regularly. 11 July was the 'last updated' date when accessed on 4 August 2006.

—— 'Japanese "oppose PM shrine trips"', 24 July 2006.

www.iht.com (*International Herald Tribune* Online), 'US walks fine line in shrine fight', 20 October 2005.

www.japantimes.co.jp (*The Japan Times* online), 'Wartime killing contest trial starts', 8 July 2003.

—— 'Japan to pay victims of mustard gas leak in China 100 million yen', 3 September 2003.

—— 'Probe ties WWII poison gas to 138 sites', 29 November 2003.

—— 'It's the black comedy of Japan: "don't mention the war . . ."', 24 July 2005.

—— 'NHK censorship story had "uncertain" info: Asahi', 1 October 2005.

—— 'War-displaced man visits home', 3 July 2006.

www.korea.net (Korean Overseas Information Service), 'Government says Japan legally responsible for atrocities', 27 August 2005.

Kyodo online (2003) 'Mahathir leaves lasting legacy to Malaysia-Japan ties', 3 November. (Available at http://www.findarticles.com/p/articles/mi_m0WDQ/is_2003_Nov_3/ai_109563574)

Newspaper/magazine articles

Asahi shinbun, 'Danyaku mo minami betonamu e' (Munitions also sent to South Vietnam), 22 May 1972.
—— 'Shin-san ni hibaku techō' (Hibakusha treatment card for Mr Shin), 26 July 1974.
—— 'Yōnin dekinai' (We cannot approve), 1 November 1975.
—— '21-nen mae kara ryōkai zumi' (An understanding for the last 21 years), 18 May 1981.
—— 'Chihō gikai no funkyū hirogaru' (Confusion in local assemblies widens), 30 September 1988.
—— 'Hibakusha kikin wo sōsetsu' (Hibakusha fund created), 17 May 1990.
—— 'Ianjo, gun kanryo shimesu shiryō' (Comfort stations, documents show army's involvement), 11 January 1992.
—— 'Chūgoku ni shimeshita atarashii tennōzō' (New imperial image shown to China), 28 October 1992.
—— 'Hosokawa san, kata no chikara wo nukō' (Mr Hosokawa, take it easy), 11 August 1993.
—— 'Sengo hoshō, 10-nen de 1,000-oku en' (Postwar compensation, 100 billion yen over 10 years), 13 August 1994a.
—— '"Nihon wa shinryaku sensō shiyō to omotte tatakatta no de wa nai"' ('Japan did not fight with the intention of aggressive war'), 13 August 1994b.
—— 'Kieta kinen kitte no kyōkun' (The lesson of the cancelled stamps), 10 December 1994.
—— 'Watashitachi to aushuvittsu' (Auschwitz and us), 1 February 1995.
—— 'Doro wo mamirareta kokkai ketsugi' (The sullied parliamentary resolution), 11 June 1995.
—— 'Iyashigatai kizuato nokoshita' (It left painful scars), 9 September 2001.
—— 'Saikinsen no sonzai nintei' (Biological warfare acknowledged), 28 August 2002.
—— 'Me wo somukete sumu no ka' (Is it OK to avert our eyes from this?), 29 August 2002.
—— 'Rekishi to mukiau: dai 1-bu, tōkyō saiban 60-nen' (Facing history: part one, the sixtieth anniversary of the Tokyo Trials), 1 May 2006.
Da Capo, 'Kokki/kokka wo megutte Sankei, Asahi ga shasetsu de ōshū. Korya, kōsō boppatsu ka?' (An exchange between the Sankei and Asahi over the flag and anthem. So, is this the start of hostilities?), 16 June 2004.
Daily Yomiuri, 'US top court rejects appeals over slave labor', 8 October 2003.
Los Angeles Times, 'Japan falls short on war apology', 9 September 2001.
Mainichi shinbun, '"O-kotoba" wo yūkō no zenshin no kiten ni' (His majesty's words as a starting point for progress in friendly relations), 24 October 1992.
—— '"Hachi-tōha gōi" ni maibotsu suru na' (Don't get buried by an 'eight-party consensus'), 11 August 1993a.
—— 'Sensō sekinin, ippo fumikomu' (War responsibility, a step taken), 11 August 1993b.
—— '"Nankin daigyakusatsu detchiage"' (Nanking Massacre a fabrication), 4 May 1994.
—— 'Bungei shunjū wa dō shita no ka' (What has Bungei shunjū done?), 1 February 1995.
—— 'Konna shūtai wa mappira da' (No way to this shameful behaviour), 11 June 1995.
—— 'Saikinsen no sonzai nintei' (Biological warfare acknowledged), 28 August 2002.

The New York Times, 'Pointless provocation in Tokyo', 18 October 2005.
Nikkei (*Nihon keizai shinbun*), ' "O-kotoba", nicchū ryōkoku ni hairyo' (His majesty's words, consideration for both Japan and China), 24 October 1992.

—— 'Hosokawa enzetsu ni kanjiru atarashii jidai no tōrai' (The new era one can feel coming in Hosokawa's speech), 24 August 1993.

—— 'Doro mamire "heiwa no chikai" ' (Sullied 'peace pledge'), 10 June 1995.

—— 'Saikinsen no sonzai hatsunintei' (Biological warfare acknowledged for the first time), 28 August 2002.

Sankei shinbun, ' "Zure" wa kakudai shite inai ka' (Isn't the gap widening?), 28 October 1992.

—— 'Fukami kaku shushō no sensō ninshiki' (The PM's deeply lacking war views), 12 August 1993.

—— 'Go-jū-nen ketsugi no kyōryō taru fūkei' (The bleak landscape of the fiftieth anniversary resolution), 11 June 1995.

—— 'Chūgokujin izoku no seikyū kikyaku' (Chinese families' claims rejected), 28 August 2002.

The Times, 'Hiroshima apologises for Japan's wartime atrocities', 7 August 1995.

Yomiuri shinbun, 'Kako no jiken yori shōrai no kōchiku jūyō' (Building the future is more important than past events), 2 December 1991.

—— 'Watashitachi no kokoro wo tsutaeta "o-kotoba" ' (His majesty's words that conveyed our feelings), 24 October 1992.

—— 'Iyoku wa wakatta, ato wa jikkō da' (We've seen your will, next is action), 24 August 1993.

—— 'Fuhatsu ni owatta bei "genbakuten" ' (The non-starter American 'A-bomb exhibit'), 2 February 1995.

—— 'Seiryaku ni mamireta "50-nen kokkai ketsugi" ' ('Fiftieth anniversary parliamentary resolution' mired in politics), 11 June 1995.

—— '731-butai saikinsen wo hatsunintei' (Unit 731's biological warfare acknowledged for the first time), 28 August 2002.

Films

Synopses and full production details are available (Japanese only) at the online film database www.movie.goo.ne.jp/.

Asian Blue: ukishima maru saikon (Horikawa, H. 1995: Cinema Work).

Biruma no tategoto / The Burmese Harp (Ichikawa, K. 1985: Fujiterebi *et al.*)

Dainippon teikoku / The Great Japanese Empire (Masuda, T. 1982: Tōei).

Gekkō no natsu / Summer of the Moonlight Sonata (Kamiyama, S. 1993: Herald Ace).

Hachigatsu no kyōshikyoku / Rhapsody in August (Kurosawa, A. 1991: Kurosawa puro).

Heitai yakuza / Soldier Gangster (Nine films, various directors 1965–68, 1972: Daiei).

Himeyuri no tō / Monument to the Himeyuri (Imai, T. 1953: Tōei).

Hokui 15° no dyuo / Duet at 15° North (Nemoto, M. 1991: N & N puromōshon).

Hotaru / Fireflies (Furuhata, Y. 2001: Hotaru seisaku iinkai).

Kike, wadatsumi no koe / Listen to the Voices from the Sea (Deme, M. 1995: Tōei).

Kimi wo wasurenai / Fly Boys Fly (Watanabe, T. 1995: Nippon herarudo eiga).

Kuroi ame / Black Rain (Imamura, S. 1989: Imamura puro/Hayashibara gurūpu).

Lorelei (Higuchi, S. 2005: Tōhō).

Mitabi no kaikyō / Three Trips Across the Straits (Kōyama, S. 1995: Mitabi no kaikyō seisaku iinkai).

Murudeka 17805 / Independence (Fuji, Y. 2001: Tōkyō eizō).

Ningen no jōken / The Human Condition (Kobayashi, M. 1959/1959/1961: Ninjin kurabu *et al.*).

Otokotachi no yamato / Yamato (Satō, J. 2005: Tōei).

Puraido / Pride (Itō, T. 1998: Tōei).

Rīben kuizu / Japanese Devils (Matsui, M. 2000: Rīben kuizu seisaku iinkai).

Senjō no merī kurisumasu / Merry Christmas Mr. Lawrence (Ōshima, N. 1983: Ōshima Nagisa puro / Asahi hōsō).

Senkan yamato / Battleship Yamato (Ichikawa K. 1991: Fuji Television).

Sensō to ningen / War and Humanity (Yamamoto, S. 1970/1971/1973: Nikkatsu).

Sensō to seishun / War and Youth (Imai, T. 1991: Kobushi purodakushon *et al.*).

Taiheiyō no washi / Eagles of the Pacific (Honda, I. 1953: Tōhō).

Tōkyō saiban / The Tokyo Trials (Kobayashi, M. 1983: Kōdansha).

Umi to dokuyaku / The Sea and Poison (Kumai K. 1986: Umi to dokuyaku seisaku iinkai).

Winds of God (Narahashi, Y. 1995: Shōchiku daiichi kōgyō / KSS).

Yuki yukite shingun / The Emperor's Naked Army Marches On (Hara K. 1987: Shissō puro).

Books and journal articles

Akaho SHS and Hōsei Daini SHS Peace Research Clubs (1991) *Kōkōsei ga ou rikugun noborito kenkyūjo* (Senior High School Students Investigate the Army's Noborito Research Institute), Tokyo: Kyōiku shiryō shuppankai.

Arai, S. (1997) 'Sensō, heiwa hakubutsukan setsuritsu no ayumi' ('Trends in the Establishment of War and Peace Museums'), in S. Arai and K. Saotome (eds) *Sekai no 'sensō to heiwa' hakubutsukan: shashin kaiga shūsei, vol. 6, nihon* (The World's War and Peace Museums: a photographic and pictorial collection, vol. 6, Japan), Tokyo: Nihon tosho sentā.

Arakaki, A. (2002) Personal correspondence, 9 October 2002.

Asahi shinbunsha (eds) (2002) *Japan Almanac 2003*, Tokyo: Asahi shinbunsha.

—— (eds) (2005) *Japan Almanac 2006*, Tokyo: Asahi shinbunsha.

Ashplant, T.G., Dawson, G. and Roper, M. (eds) (2000) *The Politics of War Memory and Commemoration*, London: Routledge.

Aspinall, R.W. (2001) *Teachers' Unions and the Politics of Education in Japan*, New York: State University of New York Press.

Atarashii rekishi kyōkasho wo tsukurukai (2001) *Atarashii rekishi kyōkasho* (New History Textbook), Tokyo: Fusōsha.

Awaya, K., Tanaka, H., Hirowatari, S., Mishima, K., Mochida, Y. and Yamaguchi, Y. (1994) *Sensō sekinin, sengo sekinin: nihon to doitsu wa dō chigau ka* (War and Postwar Responsibility: how are Japan and Germany different?), Tokyo: Asahi shinbunsha.

Bernstein, B.J. (1996) 'Understanding the atomic bomb and the Japanese surrender: missed opportunities, little-known near disasters, and modern memory', in M.J. Hogan (ed.) *Hiroshima in History and Memory*, Cambridge: Cambridge University Press.

Brook, T. and Wakabayashi, B.T. (eds) (2000) *Opium Regimes: China, Britain, and Japan, 1839–1952*, Berkeley, CA: University of California Press.

Buchholz, P. (1998) 'Tales of war: autobiographies and private memories in Japan and Germany'. Online, available at www.unu.edu/unupress/m-war.html#tales.

Buruma, I. (1995 edn) *Wages of Guilt: memories of war in Germany and Japan*, London: Vintage.

Cave, P. (2002) 'Teaching the history of empire in Japan and England', *International Journal of Educational Research*, 37: 623–41.

—— (2005) 'Learning to live with the imperial past?: history teaching, empire, and war in Japan and England', in E. Vickers and A. Jones (eds) *History Education and National Identity in East Asia*, New York: Routledge.

Chang, I. (1997) *The Rape of Nanking: the forgotten holocaust of World War II*, New York: Basic Books.

Chang, M.H. and Barker, R.P. (2003) 'Victor's justice and Japan's amnesia: the Tokyo war crimes trial reconsidered', in P. Li (ed.) *Japanese War Crimes: the search for justice*, New Brunswick, NJ: Transaction Publishers.

Chino, K. (2000) 'Sensō to shokuminchi no tenji: myūjiamu no naka no "nihon"' ('Exhibitions of war and colonialism: "Japan" in museums'), in A. Kurihara, Y. Komori, M. Satō and S. Yoshimi (eds) *Ekkyō suru chi 1: shintai, yomigaeru* (Knowledge Which Crosses Boundaries 1: the body, revival), Tokyo: Tōkyō daigaku shuppankai.

Chūkiren (2004) 'Chūgoku kikansha renrakukai kanren bunkenshū' (Bibliography of publications related to the Chinese Returnees Association). Online, available at www.ne.jp/asahi/tyuukiren/web-site/bunken.htm.

Cohen, R. (1994) *Frontiers of Identity: the British and the others*, Harlow: Longman.

Cook, H.T. and Cook, T.F. (1992) *Japan at War: an oral history*, New York: The New Press.

Cook, T.F. (1999; 2001 edn) 'Our Midway disaster: Japan springs a trap, June 4, 1942', in R. Cowley (ed.) *What If?: military historians imagine what might have been*, London: Pan Books.

Curtis, M. (2004) *Unpeople: Britain's secret human rights abuses*, London: Vintage.

de Lange, W. (1998) *A History of Japanese Journalism: Japan's press club as the last obstacle to a mature press*, Richmond, Surrey: Curzon Press.

Dobson, H. (2002) 'Japanese postage stamps: propaganda and decision making', *Japan Forum*, 14, 1: 21–39.

Dower, J.W. (1986) *War Without Mercy: race and power in the Pacific War*, New York: Pantheon Books.

—— (1996) 'The bombed: Hiroshimas and Nagasakis in Japanese memory', in M.J. Hogan (ed.) *Hiroshima in History and Memory*, Cambridge: Cambridge University Press.

—— (1999) *Embracing Defeat: Japan in the wake of World War II*, New York: W.W. Norton.

—— (2002) '"An aptitude for being unloved": war and memory in Japan', in O. Bartov, A. Grossmann and M. Nolan (eds) *Crimes of War: guilt and denial in the twentieth century*, New York: The New Press.

du Gay, P., Hall, S., Janes, L., Mackay, H. and Negus, K. (1997) *Doing Cultural Studies: the story of the Sony Walkman*, London: Sage Publications.

Endō, J. (1958; 1971 edn) *Umi to dokuyaku* (The Sea and Poison), Tokyo: Kōdansha bunko.

Evans, M. and Lunn, K. (eds) (1997) *War and Memory in the Twentieth Century*, Oxford: Berg.

Feiler, B. (1991) *Learning to Bow: inside the heart of Japan*, New York: Ticknor and Fields.

Field, N. (1991; 1993 edn) *In the Realm of a Dying Emperor: Japan at century's end*, New York: Vintage.

Figal, G. (1996) 'How to *jibunshi*: making and marketing self-histories of Shōwa among the masses in postwar Japan', *The Journal of Asian Studies*, 55, 4: 902–33.

Fiske, J. and Hartley, J. (1978; 2003 edn) *Reading Television*, London: Routledge.

Fogel, J.A. (ed.) (2000) *The Nanjing Massacre in History and Historiography*, Berkeley, CA: University of California Press.

Fujihara, Y. (1996) *Shichōritsu '96* (Viewing Figures '96), Tokyo: Ōzorasha.

Fujioka, N. (1997) *Jiyūshugi shikan to wa nani ka: kyōkasho ga oshienai rekishi no mikata* (What is the Liberalist View of History?: ways of looking at the history not taught in textbooks), Tokyo: PHP bunko.

—— (2000) *'Jigyaku shikan' no byōri* (An Analysis of Masochistic Historical Views in Japan), Tokyo: Bunshun bunko.

Fujitake, A. (2000) *Nihon no masumedia* (The Japanese Mass Media), Tokyo: NHK bukkusu.

Fujiwara, K. (2001) *Sensō wo kioku suru: Hiroshima, horokōsuto to genzai* (Remembering War: Hiroshima, the Holocaust and the present), Tokyo: Kōdansha gendai shinsho.

Fulbrook, M. (1999) *German National Identity after the Holocaust*, Cambridge: Polity Press.

Gallup (2004) 'Almost all Americans consider World War II a "just" war', 3 June. Online. Available at www.galluppoll.com/content/?ci=11881&pg=1.

Gamble, A. and Watanabe, T. (2004) *A Public Betrayed: an inside look at Japanese media atrocities and their warnings to the west*, Washington, DC: Regnery Publishing.

Gerow, A. (2000) 'Consuming Asia, consuming Japan: the new neonationalist revisionism in Japan', in L.E. Hein and M. Selden (eds) *Censoring History: citizenship and memory in Japan, Germany and the United States*, New York: M.E. Sharpe.

Gibney, F. (ed.) (1995) *Sensō: the Japanese remember the Pacific War*, trans. B. Cary, New York: M.E. Sharpe.

—— (1999) 'Editor's introduction', in K. Honda *The Nanjing Massacre: a Japanese journalist confronts Japan's national shame*, Armonk, NY: M.E. Sharpe.

Glasgow University Media Group (1985) *War and Peace News*, Milton Keynes: Open University Press.

Gluck, C. (1991) 'The "long postwar": Japan and Germany in common and in contrast', in E. Schlant and J.T. Rimer (eds) *Legacies and Ambiguities: postwar fiction and culture in West Germany and Japan*, Washington, DC: The Woodrow Wilson Center Press.

—— (1993) 'The past in the present', in A. Gordon (ed.) *Postwar Japan as History*, Berkeley, CA: University of California Press.

Habermas, J. (1996) 'On how postwar Germany has faced its recent past', *Common Knowledge*, 5, 2: 1–13.

Hall, S. (ed.) (1997) *Representation: cultural representations and signifying practices*, London: Sage Publications.

Hamada, Y. (1995) *Nihon eiga to sensō to heiwa: eiga hyakunen, sengo gojūnen* (Japanese Films, War and Peace: 100 years of cinema, postwar 50), Tokyo: Issuisha.

Hardacre, H. (1989) *Shintō and the State, 1868–1988*, Princeton, NJ: Princeton University Press.

Harris, S.H. (1994) *Factories of Death: Japanese biological warfare, 1932–45, and the American cover-up*, London: Routledge.

Harvey, P.A.S. (1995) 'Interpreting *Oshin* – war, history and women in modern Japan', in L. Skov and B. Moeran (eds) *Women, Media and Consumption in Japan*, Honolulu: University of Hawai'i Press.

Hata, I. (1999) *Ianfu to senjo no sei* (The 'Comfort Women' and Sex in War Zones), Tokyo: Shichō sensho.

—— (2001) *Gendaishi no sōten* (The Issues on Japan's Modern History [*sic*]), Tokyo: Bunshun bunko.

—— (2006) *Yugamerareru nihon gendaishi* (Collection of Essays Opposing the Many Arguments that Wrongfully Interpret Modern Japanese History [*sic*]), Tokyo: PHP.

Hein, L.E. and Selden, M. (eds) (2000) *Censoring History: citizenship and memory in Japan, Germany and the United States*, New York: M.E. Sharpe.

Heiwa izokukai zenkoku renrakukai (National Association of the War Bereaved Families for Peace) (eds) (1999) *Nihon no shimin kara sekai no hitobito e: sensō izoku no shōgen* (Our Messages, From Japanese Citizens to the People of the World: testimonies of the war bereaved), Tokyo: Nashinokisha.

Herf, J. (1997) *Divided Memory: the Nazi past in the two Germanys*, Cambridge, MA: Harvard University Press.

Herman, E.S. and Chomsky, N. (1994) *Manufacturing Consent: the political economy of the mass media*, London: Vintage.

Hicks, G. (1995) *The Comfort Women: sex slaves of Japan's imperial forces*, Tokyo: Yenbooks.

—— (1997) *Japan's War Memories: amnesia or concealment?*, Aldershot: Ashgate Publishing.

—— (1999) 'The comfort women redress movement', in R.L. Brooks (ed.) *When Sorry Isn't Enough: the controversy over apologies and reparations for human injustice*, New York: New York University Press.

Hidankyō (The Japan Confederation of A- and H- Bomb Sufferers) (1994) *Hiroshima, Nagasaki shi to sei no shōgen: genbaku higaisha chōsa* (Hiroshima and Nagasaki, Testimony of Life and Death: a survey of A-bomb victims), Tokyo: Shin nihon shuppansha.

Higashinakano, S. and Fujioka, N. (1999) *'Za rēpu obu nankin' no kenkyū: chūgoku ni okeru 'jōhōsen' no teguchi to senryaku* (Research about *The Rape of Nanking*: the methods and strategies of the 'information war' in China), Tokyo: Shōdensha.

Hijiya-Kirschnereit, I. (1991) 'Post-World War II literature: the intellectual climate in Japan, 1945–1985', in E. Schlant and J.T. Rimer (eds) *Legacies and Ambiguities: postwar fiction and culture in West Germany and Japan*, Washington, DC: The Woodrow Wilson Center Press.

Himeji sengo chizu wo tsukurukai (Himeji Postwar Map-Making Association) (ed.) (2001) *Kikikaki: himeji no sengoshi II* (Himeji's Postwar History II), Himeji: SSP shuppan.

Hirano, K. (1996) 'Depiction of the atomic bombings in Japanese cinema during the US occupation period', in M. Broderick (ed.) *Hibakusha Cinema*, London: Kegan Paul International.

Hiraoka, T. and Motojima, H. (1995) 'Hibaku 50-nen wo mukaete' (Towards the fiftieth anniversary of the A-bombs), *Sekai*, February: 96–112.

Hiroshima Peace Memorial Museum (1999) *The Spirit of Hiroshima: an introduction to the A-bomb tragedy*, Hiroshima: HPMM Guidebook.

Hiroshima Peace Memorial Museum online 'Survey activities under the occupation'. Available at www.pcf.city.hiroshima.jp/virtual/VirtualMuseum_e/exhibit_e/exh 0307_e/exh03076_e.html.

Historical Museum of Hokkaido (2000) *Fukyō kara sensō e: jōsetsu tenji kaisetsusho 6* (From Recession to World War II: a guide to the permanent exhibits, vol. 6), Sapporo: Hokkaidō kaitaku kinenkan.

Hokkaidō shinbunsha (eds) (2005) *Senka no kioku: sengo 60-nen, 100-nin no shōgen* (Memories of the Devastation of War: 100 people's testimony in postwar-60), Sapporo: Hokkaidō shinbunsha.

Honda, K. (1972) *Chūgoku no tabi* (Journey to China), Tokyo: Asahi shinbunsha.

—— (1999) *The Nanjing Massacre: a Japanese journalist confronts Japan's national shame*, New York: M.E. Sharpe.

Horie, N. (2001) *Shiberia yokuryū: ima towareru mono* (Siberian Internment: an issue for today), Tokyo: Tōyō shoten Eurasia Booklet.

Hosaka, M. (2002) *'Kike wadatsumi no koe' no sengoshi* (The Postwar History of 'Listen to the Voices from the Sea'), Tokyo: Bunshun bunko.

Hoshi, T. (2002) *Watashitachi ga chūgoku de shita koto: chūgoku kikansha renrakukai no hitobito* (What We Did in China: members of the Chinese Returnees Association), Tokyo: Ryokufū shuppan.

Ichinose, T. (2002) Interview at the National Museum of Japanese History, 20 September.

Ienaga, S. (2001) *Japan's Past, Japan's Future: one historian's odyssey*, trans. R.H. Minear, Lanham: Rowman & Littlefield.

Igarashi, J., Kaneko, M., Kitagawa, K., Kobayashi, H., Makihara, N. and Yamada, A. (eds) (1999) *Nippon 20-seiki kan* (The 20th Century of Japan), Tokyo: Shōgakukan.

Igarashi, Y. (2000) *Bodies of Memory: narratives of war in postwar Japanese culture, 1945–1970*, Princeton, NJ: Princeton University Press.

Imai, M. (1999) *'Kamikaze' kōenki in NY: the winds of god* ('Kamikaze' Play in New York Diary), Tokyo: Iwanami shoten.

International Society for Educational Information (1994) *Japan in Modern History: junior high school*, Tokyo: ISEI.

Ishihara, M. (2001) 'Memories of war and Okinawa', trans. D. Dreistadt, in T. Fujitani, G.M. White and L. Yoneyama (eds) *Perilous Memories: the Asia-Pacific War(s)*, Durham, NC: Duke University Press.

Ishihara, S. (1989; 1991 edn) *The Japan That Can Say No: why Japan will be first among equals*, New York: Simon & Schuster.

Ishizawa, Y. (2004) 'Koizumi wa "shizumiyuku fune" no senchō da: "nihon tataki" kara "nihon mushi" e' (Koizumi is the captain of a "sinking ship": from "Japan bashing" to "ignoring Japan"', in Y. Ishizawa (ed.) *Nihon wa dō hōjirarete iru ka* (How is Japan Reported?), Tokyo: Shinchō shinsho.

Iwanami henshūbu (Iwanami Co. Editorial Division) (2001) *Kindai nihon sōgō nenpyō: dai-4 ban* (General Chronology of Modern Japan: 4th edn), Tokyo: Iwanami.

Kanda, F. and Kobayashi, H. (2005) *Sengoshi nenpyō* (Chronology of Postwar Era, 1945–2005 [*sic*]), Tokyo: Shōgakukan.

Kasahara, T., Matsumura, T., Yoshimi, Y., Takashima, N. and Watanabe, H. (eds) (1997) *Rekishi no jijitsu wo dō nintei shi ō oshieru ka* (How Are We to Understand and Teach the Facts of History?), Tokyo: Kyōiku shiryō shuppankai.

Kata, K. (1989) *Shōwa no rekishi: jō/chū* (Shōwa History, parts I and II), Tokyo: Kumon shuppan.

Katō, T., Seno, S., Toriumi, Y. and Maruyama, Y. (2001) *Nihonshi sōgō nenpyō* (General Chronology of Japanese History), Tokyo: Yoshikawa kōbunkan.

Kawasaki, Y., Harada, T., Naramoto, T. and Konishi, S. (2003) *Nihonshi: yomeru nenpyō* (Japanese History: a readable chronology: 8th edn), Tokyo: Jiyū kokuminsha.

Kikuchi, T. (2002) Interview at Kawasaki Peace Museum, 27 September.

Kim, P.J. (2001) 'Global civil society remakes history: "the Women's International War Crimes Tribunal 2000"', *Positions*, 9, 3: 611–20.

Kim, S.K. (2001) 'Korea's "Vietnam question": war atrocities, national identity, and reconciliation in Asia', *Positions*, 9, 3: 621–35.

Kimijima, K. (2000) 'The continuing legacy of Japanese colonialism: the Japan–South Korea joint study group on history textbooks', in L.E. Hein and M. Selden (eds) *Censoring History: citizenship and memory in Japan, Germany and the United States*, New York: M.E. Sharpe.

Kisa, Y. (2001) '*Sensō sekinin' to wa nani ka: seisan sarenakatta doitsu no kako* (What is 'War Responsibility'?: Germany's unresolved past), Tokyo: Chūkō shinsho.

Kobayashi, M. (1995) *Nichibei taiheiyō senso* (The Japanese–American Pacific War), Tokyo: Nihon shuppansha.

Kobayashi, Y. (1997) *Shin gōmanizumu sengen 3* (A New Declaration of Arrogantism 3), Tokyo: Shōgakukan.

—— (1998) *Sensōron* (On War), Tokyo: Gentōsha.

—— (2005) *Yasukuniron* (On Yasukuni), Tokyo: Gentōsha.

—— Takeuchi, Y. and Nihon no sensō enzai kenkyū sentā (Centre for Research into the False Accusations Made Against Japan) (1999) *Jigyakushi de yansu* (Masochistic History), Tokyo: Gentōsha bunko.

Kodama, K. (1983; 1998 edn) *Shōnen shōjo nihon no rekishi 20: ajia to taiheiyō no tatakai* (Japanese History for Young Boys and Girls, vol. 20: the war in Asia and the Pacific), Tokyo: Shōgakukan.

Kojima, I. (1997) *Hōsō, tsūshin: gyōkai saihen chizu* (Broadcasting and Communications: a map of the industry), Tokyo: Paru shuppan.

Kondō, T. (2001) *Rekishi kyōiku to kyōkasho: doitsu, ōsutoria, soshite nihon* (History Education and Textbooks: Germany, Austria and Japan), Tokyo: Iwanami Booklet.

Kōno, K., Moriguchi, H., Tomomune, Y., Hara, Y., Saitō, K., Hattori, H. and Itani, Y. (1996) 'Sekai no terebi wa sengo 50-shūnen wo dō tsutaeta ka' (Worldwide TV coverage of the 50th anniversary of the end of World War II), *NHK hōsō bunka chōsa kenkyū nenpō*, 41: 1–110, 270–3.

Krauss, E.S., Rohlen, T.P. and Steinhoff, P.G. (eds) (1984) *Conflict in Japan*, Honolulu: University of Hawai'i Press.

Kristof, N.D. (1998) 'The Problem of Memory', *Foreign Affairs*, 77, 6: 37–49.

Ku, D.Y. (1985) *Korea Under Colonialism: the March First Movement and Anglo-Japanese relations*, Seoul: Seoul Computer Press.

Kurahashi, A. (2002) *Kempei datta chichi no nokoshita mono* (What My Military Policeman Father Left Me), Tokyo: Kōbunken.

—— (2005) *Nagai kage* (Eternal Shadows), Tokyo: Hon no izumi.

Kyoto Museum for World Peace (1997) *Jōsetsu tenji shōsai kaisetsu* (Detailed Guide to the Permanent Exhibits), Kyoto: Ritsumeikan University.

Lakoff, G. and Johnson, M. (1980; 2003 edn) *Metaphors We Live By*, Chicago, IL: The University of Chicago Press.

Lewis, J. and Steele, B. (2001) *Hell in the Pacific: from Pearl Harbor to Hiroshima and beyond*, London: Channel 4 Books.

Li, P. (ed.) (2003) *Japanese War Crimes: the search for justice*, New Brunswick, NJ: Transaction Publishers.

Lie, J. (1993) *The Impoverished Spirit in Contemporary Japan: selected essays of Honda Katsuichi*, New York: Monthly Review Press.

Lifton, R.J. and Mitchell, G. (1995) *Hiroshima in America: a half century of denial*, New York: Avon Books.

Lonely Planet (2003; 8th edn) *Japan*, Melbourne: Lonely Planet Publications.

McCormack, G. (1996) *The Emptiness of Japanese Affluence*, New York: M.E. Sharpe.

—— (2000) 'The Japanese movement to "correct" history', in L.E. Hein and M. Selden (eds) *Censoring History: citizenship and memory in Japan, Germany and the United States*, New York: M.E. Sharpe.

—— (2005) 'War and Japan's memory wars: the media and the globalization of consciousness', *Japan Focus*. Online, available at www.japanfocus.org/products/details/2123.

McDougall, G.J. (1998) 'Contemporary forms of slavery: systematic rape, sexual slavery and slavery-like practices during armed conflict'. Online, available at www.unhchr.ch/Huridocda/Huridoca.nsf/0/3d25270b5fa3ea998025665f0032f220?Opendocument.

McGregor, R. (1996) *Japan Swings: politics, culture and sex in the new Japan*, St. Leonards, NSW: Allen & Unwin.

McNaught, A. (2002) 'Correspondent: Unit 731' (BBC, broadcast 3 February). Online, available at www.news.bbc.co.uk/hi/english/static/audio_video/programmes/correspondent/transcripts/1796044_2.txt.

Maier, C.S. (1988; 1997 edn) *The Unmasterable Past: history, holocaust, and German national identity*, Cambridge, MA: Harvard University Press.

Matsuda, H. (2005) *NHK: towareru kōkyō hōsō* (NHK: public broadcasting under scrutiny), Tokyo: Iwanami shinsho.

Matsui, Y. (2003) 'Women's International War Crimes Tribunal on Japan's Military Sexual Slavery: memory, identity, and society', in P. Li (ed.) *Japanese War Crimes: the search for justice*, New Brunswick, NJ: Transaction Publishers.

—— and Shoji, R. (2001) 'An open letter and inquiry concerning "The question of wartime sexual violence" (aired on January 30), part 2 of the ETV 2001 series, "How is war to be judged?"', 6 February. Online, available at www.www1.jca.apc.org/vaww-net-japan/english/backlash/openletter_to_nhk.html.

Matsuo, T. (1998) *Nihon no rekishi 18: ajia taiheiyō sensō* (Japanese History, vol. 18: the Asia-Pacific War), Tokyo: Shūeisha.

Midori, Y. (2004) *Igirisu hatsu nihonjin ga shiranai nippon* (Japan in the UK: stereotyped, misrepresented, misunderstood), Tokyo: Iwanami active shinsho.

Ministry of Education (1947; 2001 edn) *Atarashii kenpō no hanashi* (About the New Constitution), Tokyo: Dowaya.

Ministry of Foreign Affairs (2005) '60 years: the path of a nation striving for global peace'. Online, available at www.mofa.go.jp/policy/postwar/pamph60.pdf.

Minowa, K. (ed.) (1987) *Nagaoka no kūshū* (The Nagaoka Air Raid), Nagaoka: Nagaoka City Hall.

Miura, S. (2005) *Zen 'rekishi kyōkasho' wo tettei kenshō suru* (A Thorough Examination of All History Textbooks), Tokyo: Shōgakukan.

Miyake, A. (2003) *'Kokoro no nōto' wo kangaeru* (Thinking About 'Kokoro no nōto'), Tokyo: Iwanami Booklet No. 595.

Mizuma, M. (2003) *Chikushi Tetsuya wo kiru: mohaya chūgoku, kita chōsen no daibensha ka* (Cutting Down Chikushi Tetsuya: is he no longer China and North Korea's spokesman?), Tokyo: Nisshin hōdō.

Mochida, Y. (1994) '"Sensō sekinin, sengo sekinin" mondai no suiiki' (The waters of the 'war and postwar responsibility' issues), in K. Awaya, H. Tanaka, S. Hirowatari, K. Mishima, Y. Mochida and Y. Yamaguchi, *Sensō sekinin, sengo sekinin: nihon to doitsu wa dō chigau ka* (War and Postwar Responsibility: how are Japan and Germany different?), Tokyo: Asahi shinbunsha.

Morimura, S. (1981; 2000 edn) *Akuma no hōshoku* (The Devil's Gluttony), Tokyo: Kakugawa bunko.

Morris-Suzuki, T. (2005) 'Free speech, silenced voices: the Japanese media, the comfort women tribunal, and the NHK affair', ZNet. Online, available at www.zmag.org/content/showarticle.cfm?ItemID=8514.

Mukai, C. (2000) '"Mujitsu da!": chichi no sakebi ga kikoeru' (I can hear my father crying 'I'm innocent'), *Seiron*, March: 60–71.

Munakata, K. (1996) *Senki ga kataru nihon rikugun* (What Memoirs Say About the Japanese Army), Tokyo: Ginga shuppan.

Nagel, T. (1974) 'War and massacre', in M. Cohen, T. Nagel and T. Scanlon (eds) *War and Moral Responsibility*, Princeton, NJ: Princeton University Press.

Nakajō, T. (1998) *Ojīsan, sensō no koto wo oshiete* (Grandpa, Tell Me About the War), Tokyo: Tōchi shuppansha.

Nakamura, A. (1997) 'NHK uocchingu' (NHK Watching), *Seiron*, November: 184–9.

Nakamura, M. (ed.) (2004) *Nenpyō shōwashi 1926–2003, zōhoban* (Chronology of the Showa Era, 1926–2003: supplementary edition), Tokyo: Iwanami Booklet.

Napier, S.J. (2000) *Anime from Akira to Princess Mononoke: experiencing contemporary Japanese animation*, New York: Palgrave.

Natsume, F. (1997) *Manga to 'sensō'* (Manga and War), Tokyo: Kōdansha gendai shinsho.

Nelson, J. (2003) 'Social memory as ritual practice: commemorating spirits of the military dead at Yasukuni Shinto shrine', *Journal of Asian Studies*, 62, 2: 443–67.

Neumann, K. (2000) *Shifting Memories: the Nazi past in the new Germany*, Ann Arbor, MI: University of Michigan Press.

NHK (2003) *Terebi 50-nen* (Television's 50 Years), Tokyo: NHK Service Centre.

NHK hōsō bunka kenkyūjo (NHK Broadcasting Culture Research Institute) (2003) *Terebi shichō no 50-nen* (Fifty Years of Television Viewing), Tokyo: NHK shuppan.

Nihon senbotsu gakusei kinenkai (Japan Memorial Society for the Students Killed in the War – Wadatsumi Society) (eds) (1995 edn) *Kike wadatsumi no koe*; trans. M. Yamanouchi and J.L. Quinn (2000) *Listen to the Voices from the Sea*, Scranton, PA: University of Scranton Press.

Niven, B. (2002) *Facing the Nazi Past: united Germany and the legacy of the Third Reich*, London: Routledge.

Noda, M. (1998) *Sensō to zaiseki* (War and Guilt), Tokyo: Iwanami shoten.

Nozaki, Y. and Inokuchi, H. (2000) 'Japanese education, nationalism, and Ienaga Saburō's textbook lawsuits', in L.E. Hein and M. Selden (eds) *Censoring History: citizenship and memory in Japan, Germany and the United States*, New York: M.E. Sharpe.

O'Brien, S. (2000) 'Translator's introduction', in Y. Yoshimi, *Comfort Women: sexual slavery in the Japanese military during World War II*, New York: Columbia University Press.

Okada, S. (1983) *Henkō NHK e no kōkai shitsumonjō* (Questions for Biased NHK), Tokyo: Sankō.

Okumura, Y. (1971) *Nihon kūshū: kiroku shashinshū* (Japan's Air Raids: a pictorial record), Tokyo: Mainichi shinbunsha.

Okuzumi, Y. (1988) *Chūshō toshi kūshū* (Air Raids on Small and Medium Cities), Tokyo: Sanseido sensho.

Onoda, H. and Nakajō, T. (2006) *Dakara nipponjin yo, yasukuni e ikō* (So, Japanese People, Let's Go to Yasukuni), Tokyo: WAC.

Orr, J.J. (2001) *The Victim as Hero: ideologies of peace and national identity in postwar Japan*, Honolulu: University of Hawai'i Press.

Ōta, M. (1996) *Okinawa: sensō to heiwa* (Okinawa: war and peace), Tokyo: Asahi bunko.

Paris, E. (2000) *Long Shadows: truth, lies and history*, New York: Bloomsbury.

Peace Museum for Kamikaze Pilots (2002) Personal correspondence, 17 September.

Peace Osaka (1997) 'Tenji shiryō no ichibu minaoshi' (Revising part of the exhibits), Peace Osaka Newsletter, 30 August.

Penn, W. (2003) *The Couch Potato's Guide to Japan: inside the world of Japanese TV*, Sapporo: Forest River Press.

Pharr, S.J. (1996) 'Media as trickster in Japan: a comparative perspective', in S.J. Pharr and E.S. Krauss (eds) *Media and Politics in Japan*, Honolulu: University of Hawai'i Press.

Pia Cinema Club (2003) *Pia shinema kurabu: nihon eiga hen, 2003–2004* (Pia Cinema Club: Japanese film database book 2003–4 [*sic*]), Tokyo: Pia.

Popular Memory Group (1998) 'Popular memory: theory, politics, method', in R. Perks and A. Thomson (eds) *The Oral History Reader*, London: Routledge.

Reed, C. (2006) 'Family skeletons: Japan's foreign minister and forced labour by Koreans and Allied POWs', *Japan Focus*. Online, available at www.japanfocus.org/products/details/1627.

Rekishi kyōikusha kyōgikai (Association of History Educators) (eds) (2000) *Heiwa hakubutsukan, sensō shiryōkan gaidobukku* (Peace and War Museum Guidebook), Tokyo: Aoki shoten.

—— (2002) *Yasukuni jinja: Q&A motto shiritai* (Yasukuni Shrine: Q&A, I want to know more), Tokyo: Ōtsuki shoten.

Rose, C. (1998) *Interpreting History in Sino-Japanese Relations: a case study in political decision making*, London: Routledge.

—— (2005) *Sino-Japanese Relations: facing the past, looking to the future?*, London: Routledge-Curzon.

—— (2006) 'The battle for hearts and minds: patriotic education in Japan in the 1990s and beyond', in N. Shimazu (ed.) *Nationalisms in Japan*, London: Routledge.

Rosenstone, R.A. (2000) 'Oliver Stone as historian', in R.B. Toplin (ed.) *Oliver Stone's USA: film, history, and controversy*, Kansas: University of Kansas Press.

Ruoff, K.J. (2001) *The People's Emperor: democracy and the Japanese monarchy, 1945–1995*, Cambridge, MA: Harvard University Asia Center.

Rutherford, S. (ed.) (2003) *Insight Guides: Japan*, Singapore: Apa Publications.

Saaler, S. (2005) *Politics, Memory and Public Opinion: the history textbook controversy and Japanese society*, Munich: iudicium.

Saeki, Y. and Hosaka, M. (1997) 'Waga sofu wa "A-kyū senpan" Doihara Kenji' ('My grandfather was "class A war criminal" Doihara Kenji'), *Shokun!*, April: 124–31.

Said, E.W. (1997) *Covering Islam: how the media and the experts determine how we see the rest of the world*, London: Vintage.

Sands, P. (2005; 2006 edn) *Lawless World: the whistle-blowing account of how Bush and Blair are taking the law into their own hands*, London: Penguin.

Sankei shinbun ronsetsu iinshitsu (Sankei Editorial Board) (eds) (2002) *Shasetsu no daikenkyū: shinbun wa konna ni chigau!* (A Study of Editorials: newspapers are this different!), Tokyo: Sankei shinbunsha.

Saotome, K. (1971) *Tōkyō daikūshū: shōwa 20-nen 3-gatsu tōka no kiroku* (The Great Tokyo Air Raid: a record of 10 March 1945), Tokyo: Iwanami shinsho.

Sasaki, T., Tsurumi, S., Tominaga, K., Nakamura, M., Masamura, K. and Murakami, Y. (2005) *Sengoshi daijiten* (Encyclopedia of Postwar Japan, 1945–2004), Tokyo: Sanseidō.

Satō, T. (2005) *Hachigatsu jūgonichi no shinwa: shūsen kinenbi no mediagaku* (The Myth of 15 August: media analysis of the war end commemorations), Tokyo: Chikuma shinsho.

Schilling, M. (1999) *Contemporary Japanese Film*, New York: Weatherhill.

Schodt, F.L. (1996) *Dreamland Japan: writings on modern manga*, Berkeley, CA: Stone Bridge Press.

Seaton, P.A. (2004) 'Japanese memory of the Asia-Pacific War: the struggle to reconcile defeat, aggression and suffering, 1991–2001', unpublished Ph.D. thesis, University of Sussex.

—— (2005) 'Reporting the 2001 textbook and Yasukuni Shrine controversies: Japanese war memory and commemoration in the British media', *Japan Forum*, 17, 3: 287–309.

—— (2006a) ' "Do you really want to know what your uncle did?": coming to terms with relatives' war actions in Japan', *Oral History*, 34, 1: 53–60.

—— (2006b) 'Reporting the "comfort women" issue, 1991–1992: Japan's contested war memories in the national press', *Japanese Studies*, 26, 1: 99–112.

Sekiguchi, Y. (ed.) (2003) *Sengo kinema junpō besuto ten zenshi 1946–2002* (Postwar Kinema Junpō's Best Ten, A Complete History 1946–2002), Tokyo: Kinema junpōsha.

Shimada, N. (2004) *Sensō to imin no shakaishi: hawai nikkei amerikajin no taiheiyō sensō* (A Social History of War and Immigration: Hawaiian Japanese-Americans and the Pacific War), Tokyo: Gendai shiryō shuppan.

Shimano, I. (2000) *Hōsō: hikaku nihon no kaisha* (Broadcasting: comparing Japan's companies), Tokyo: Jitsumu kyōiku shuppan.

Shimizu, K. (1998) *Shinryaku no sekaishi: kono 500-nen, hakujin wa sekai de nani wo shite kita ka* (A World History of Aggression: what have white people done these 500 years?), Tokyo: Shōdensha.

Shimoda, K. (1992) *Teikoku no kantai* (The Imperial Fleet), Tokyo: Jitsugyō no nihonsha (Joy Novels).

Smith, A.D. (1991) *National Identity*, London: Penguin Books.

Smith, P. (1997) *Japan: a reinterpretation*, New York: Pantheon Books.

Soka Gakkai Youth Division (1978) *Cries for Peace*, Tokyo: The Japan Times.

Soysal, Y.N. (2000) 'Identity and transnationalization in German school textbooks', in L.E. Hein and M. Selden (eds) *Censoring History: citizenship and memory in Japan, Germany and the United States*, New York: M.E. Sharpe.

Tachibana, S. (1996) 'The quest for a peace culture: the A-bomb survivors' long struggle and the new movement for redressing foreign victims of Japan's war', in M.J. Hogan (ed.) *Hiroshima in History and Memory*, Cambridge: Cambridge University Press.

Takahashi, T. (1999) *Sengo sekininron* (A Theory of Postwar Responsibility), Tokyo: Kōdansha.

—— (2003a) *'Kokoro' to sensō* (War and the 'Heart'), Tokyo: Shōbunsha.

—— (2003b) 'Nation and sacrifice', *University of Tokyo Center for Philosophy Bulletin*, 1: 33–44.

—— (2005) *Yasukuni mondai* (The Yasukuni Issue), Tokyo: Chikuma shinsho.

Takeda, T. (2001) 'ETV "Sensō wo dō sabaku ka": NHK no rekishi ninshiki wo tadasu' ('ETV's "How should war be tried?": correcting NHK's historical consciousness'), *Shokun!*, April: 94–104.

Takeyama, M. (1948) *Biruma no tategoto* (The Burmese Harp), Tokyo: Shinchō bunko.

Tanaka, H. (1994) 'Nihon no sengo hoshō to rekishi ninshiki' (Japan's postwar reparations and historical consciousness), in K. Awaya, H. Tanaka, S. Hirowatari, K. Mishima, Y. Mochida and Y. Yamaguchi, *Sensō sekinin, sengo sekinin: nihon to doitsu wa dō chigau ka* (War and Postwar Responsibility: how are Japan and Germany different?), Tokyo: Asahi shinbunsha.

Tanaka, K. (2002) Personal correspondence, 11 October.

Tanaka, N. (2002) *Yasukuni no sengoshi* (A Postwar History of Yasukuni), Tokyo: Iwanami shinsho.

—— Tanaka, H. and Hata, N. (1995) *Izoku to sengo* (The War Bereaved and the Postwar), Tokyo: Iwanami shinsho.

Tawara, Y. (2001) ' "Tsukurukai" kyōkasho no fusaitaku undō to kongo no kadai' ('The anti-Tsukurukai textbook movement and future issues'), *Sensō sekinin kenkyū*, 34: 59–73.

—— (2006) ' "Atarashii rekishi kyōkasho wo tsukurukai": naibu kōsō no shinsō' ('The Tsukurukai: the depth of internal strife'), *Ronza*, June: 228–35.

Tezuka, O. (1997) *Boku no manga jinsei* (My Life in Manga), Tokyo: Iwanami shinsho.

Thomson, A. (1994) *ANZAC Memories: living with the legend*, Melbourne: Oxford University Press.

Tōjō, Y. (2000) *Sofu Tōjō Hideki: 'issetsu kataru nakare'* (My Grandfather Tōjō Hideki: 'don't say a word'), Tokyo: Bunshun bunko.

Trefalt, B. (2003) *Japanese Army Stragglers and Memories of the War in Japan, 1950–1975*, London: Routledge Curzon.

Ueda, S. (1991) *Gyakuten!! Taiheiyō sensō* (The Pacific War: Reversal!), Tokyo: Nihon shuppansha.

Ueno, C. (1998) *Nashonarizumu to jendā* (Engendering Nationalism), Tokyo: Seidosha.

Underwood, W. (2006) 'Mitsubishi, historical revisionism and Japanese corporate resistance to Chinese forced labor redress', *Japan Focus*. Online, available at www.japanfocus.org/products/details/1823.

Utsumi, A. (2002) *Sengo hoshō kara kangaeru nihon to ajia* (Japan and Asia from the Perspective of Postwar Reparations), Tokyo: Yamakawa shuppansha.

van Wolferen, K. (1990) *The Enigma of Japanese Power*, New York: Vintage.

van Zoonen, L. (1994) *Feminist Media Studies*, London: Sage Publications.

Wakamiya, Y. (1999) *The Postwar Conservative View of Asia: how the political right has delayed Japan's coming to terms with its history of aggression in Asia*, Tokyo: LTCB International Library Foundation.

Wakō, T. (2000) '"Shimin" to iu mayakashi' (The fraud of 'the people'), *Seiron*, January: 282–8.

Walzer, M. (1977; 3rd edn 2000) *Just and Unjust Wars: a moral argument with historical illustrations*, New York: Basic Books.

Watanabe, T. and Wakamiya. Y. (2006) *Yasukuni to Koizumi shushō* (Yasukuni and Prime Minister Koizumi), Tokyo: Asahi shinbunsha.

Weiner, T. (1994) 'CIA spent millions to support Japanese right in 50's and 60's', *The New York Times*, 9 October.

Williams, K. (2003) *Understanding Media Theory*, London: Arnold.

Winter, J.M. and Sivan E. (eds) (1999) *War and Remembrance in the Twentieth Century*, Cambridge: Cambridge University Press.

Yamamoto, Y. (2001) *Chichi Yamamoto Isoroku* (My Father Yamamoto Isoroku), Tokyo: Kobunsha.

Yamasaki, T. (1994) *Daichi no ko: ichi* (Child of the Continent: vol. 1), Tokyo: Bunshun bunko.

Yamazaki, J.W. (2006) *Japanese Apologies for World War II: a rhetorical study*, London: Routledge.

Yayama, T. (1983) 'The newspapers conduct a mad rhapsody over the textbook issue', trans. J. and T. Roehl, *Journal of Japanese Studies*, 9, 2: 301–16.

Yomiuri shinbun geinōbu (Yomiuri Newspaper Arts Division) (1994) *Terebi bangumi no 40-nen* (40 Years of Television Programmes), Tokyo: NHK shuppan.

Yomiuri shinbun ronsetsu iinkai (Yomiuri Editorial Board) (eds) (2001) *Yomiuri vs Asahi: shasetsu taiketsu 50-nen* (Yomiuri vs Asahi: 50 years of editorial confrontation), Tokyo: Chūkō shinsho (La Clef).

Yomota, I. (2000) *Nihon eigashi 100-nen* (100 Years of Japanese Film History), Tokyo: Shūeisha shincho.

Yoshida, S. (1983) *Watashi no sensō hanzai: chōsenjin kyōsei renkō* (My War Crimes: the forced transportation of Koreans), Tokyo: Sanichi shobō.

Yoshida, Y. (1995) *Nihonjin no sensōkan: sengoshi no naka no henyō* (Japanese Views on the War: postwar transformations), Tokyo: Iwanami shoten.

Yoshimi, S. (1998) 'Zasshi media to nashonarizumu no shōhi' (Magazines and the consumption of nationalism), in Y. Komori and T. Takahashi (eds) *Nashonaru hisutorī wo koete* (Beyond the National History [*sic*]), Tokyo: Tōkyō daigaku shuppankai.

—— (2001) '"Hōtei" to nashonaru media no chinmoku' ('The trial' and the reticence of the national media), in R. Nishino and P.J. Kim (eds) *Sabakareta senji seibōryoku* (Sexual Violence in Wartime on Trial), Tokyo: Hakutakusha.

Yoshimi, Y. (2000) *Comfort Women: sexual slavery in the Japanese military during World War II*, trans. S. O'Brien, New York: Columbia University Press.

Index

Numbers in *italic* indicate tables and those in ***bold italic*** indicate figures.

of war conduct 39; cultural forms 34–6, 45; defined 3, 8, 16, *21*, **22**, 21–3, 24–6, 131, 137, *138–9*, 150; Germany–Japan comparison 78; magazines *133*, 135–6, 140; marginalization of 6, 74, 211, 214–19, 223–4; museums 174–5, 177–8, 184, 187; portrayed as 'un-Japanese' 4, 25; support for Asian plaintiffs 60; television 116, 122–3; *see also* feminism, Ienaga Saburō
propaganda: propaganda model 32–3
public narratives 11–14, 18
public opinion 62, 68, 74, 137, 188, 198; changes in opinion 30; relationship to cultural forms 34; *see also* opinion polls
public–private relationship 11–12, 16–18, 22; in testimony 189–92
publishing 110; industry 32, 132, *133*, 134–7, 140, 145, 150, 202; during occupation 39; profitability threshold 34–5, 120; published testimony 189–92, 194–5

radio 63
Reagan, Ronald 71
realism 142
regional narratives/memories 188; incorporation into national memory 180–5; links to victim mentality 80, 170–1; museums 49, 170–87; official 15, 175, 187; television 112, 124–5
regret/remorse: criticized as inadequate 212; imperial statements 54, 96; Korean 82; prime ministerial statements 58, *88–91*
regulation 29
Reischauer, Edwin 54
religion 77–8, 199; a Christian worshipping at Yasukuni Shrine 78, 88; religious freedom 93; *see also* Shintō, Soka Gakkai
remains, repatriation of 46
reparations 44, 66, 67–70
repatriation 1, 38, 46, 138, 178
representation 29, 55; public field of representations 63
resistance to occupation 208
responsibility *see* war responsibility
reverse course 41, 54, 61
revisionism 142, 167–8; *see also* nationalism
Rhapsody in August 159
Rommel, Erwin 20, 197
Ronza 133, 134, 136
Rose, Caroline 4
Russia 44, 46, 210; *see also* Northern Territories, Soviet Union

sacrifice: in cinema 160, 164; importance in conservative views 8, 24, 59, 137, *138–9*, 152; literary tradition of *hōganbiiki* 25; in museums 179; of relatives 197–8; Yasukuni worship 71; *see also* patriotism

Saeki Yūko 196
Saipan 97, 183
Sakurai Shin 95
Sakurai Yoshiko 114, 121, 202
San Francisco Peace Treaty 44, 52, 66, 68, 72–3
Sanichi shobō *133*
sanitization 148, 161–3
Sankei newspaper 85, *111*, 119–20, 174, 219; 'comfort women' 99; compensation 99; emperor 97; 50th anniversary statement 94–5; Hosokawa's apology 92; orphans 105; sales 85; textbooks 102; Unit 731 100; Yasukuni Shrine 93–4; *see also* Fuji–Sankei group
Saotome Katsumoto 183
Sapio 132
Sapporo 123, 183–5, *185*
Satō Takumi 107
SCAP (Supreme Command for the Allied Powers) 40–4
Schodt, Frederik 167
schools 76–7, 212; elementary 147; junior high 1, 40, 59, 144, 148–9; senior high 144, 148–9; trips to museums 149, 170, 175–6, 187; *see also* education, textbooks
Sea and Poison, The 45, 156, 161–2
sectional narratives 14, 16, 188; in museums 172, 178–80
Seiron 111, 118, *133*, 134–5, 202
Sekai 39, *133*, 134–5, 140
Self Defense Forces (SDF) 62, 71, 128–9
self-history (*jibunshi*) 189–91, 195
Senda, Kakō 49
sensationalism 137, 202
Shiba Ryōtarō 136
Shimoda Kageki 168
Shinchō 45 133
shinsho see cheap paperbacks
Shintō 93; Shintō Directive 42–3; state Shintō 58; *see also* religion
Shōgakukan 132, *133*, 147–8
Shoji Rutsuko 118
Shokun! 118, *133*, 134–5
Shōwa era 53–4, 190
Shōwa Senior High School 149
Shōwakan **173**, 174, 176
Shūeisha *133*, 147–8
Siberia *see* internment
silence (on war issues) 190–1, 194, 196, 200; *see also* avoidance
simulation fiction 55, 154, 167–9
Singapore 147
slave labour/sexual slavery *see* forced labour, 'comfort women'
SMAP 158, 205
Smithsonian *Enola Gay* exhibit 57, 103–4, 114
Snow Falling in a Southern Island 199

CPSIA information can be obtained at www.ICGtesting.com
Printed in the USA
BVOW042034221012

303667BV00002B/6/P